CRITICAL ISSUES IN LAW ENFORCE- MENT

CRITICAL ISSUES
IN
LAW ENFORCEMENT

FOURTH EDITION

Edited by

HARRY W. MORE, JR., Ph.D.

GOLDEN GATE UNIVERSITY

AND

SAN JOSE STATE UNIVERSITY

Criminal Justice Studies
Anderson Publishing Co., Cincinnati, Ohio

CRITICAL ISSUES IN LAW ENFORCEMENT, FOURTH EDITION
© 1972, 1975 by The W.H. Anderson Company
© 1981, 1985 by Anderson Publishing Co.

Third Printing—February, 1987

Library of Congress Cataloging in Publication Data

Critical issues in law enforcement.

  (Criminal justice studies)
  Includes index.
  1. Police—United States—Addresses, essays, lectures.
  2. Law enforcement—United States—Addresses, essays, lectures.
I. More, Harry W. II. Series.
HV8141.C68 1984   363.2'3'0973   83-24385
ISBN: 0-87084-583-7

Contents

Preface

The police are the part of the criminal justice system that is in direct daily contact both with crime and the public. The entire system—courts and corrections as well as the police—is charged with enforcing the law and maintaining order. What is distinctive about the responsibility of the police is that they are charged with performing these functions where all eyes are upon them and where the going is roughest, on the street. Since this is a time of increasing crime, increasing social unrest and increasing public sensitivity to both, it is a time when police work is peculiarly important, complicated, conspicuous, and delicate.

Because the police have the responsibility for dealing with crime daily—where, when and as it occurs—the public and often the police themselves have a tendency to think of crime control almost exclusively as police work.

The fact is, of course, that even under the most favorable circumstances the ability of the police to act against crime is limited. The police did not create and cannot resolve the social conditions that stimulate crime. They did not start and cannot stop the convulsive social changes that are taking place in America. They do not enact the laws that they are required to enforce, nor do they dispose of the criminals they arrest. The police are only one part of the criminal justice system; the criminal justice system is only one part of the government; and the government is only one part of society.

The police are confronted with a broad spectrum of critical issues such as the police role in a democracy, the use of deadly force, police unionization, and police professionalization. Other vital areas of concern are stress, organized crime, terrorism, and police discretion.

These topics were selected for inclusion in the text because they represent what might best be defined as potentially perennial problems. Students of criminal justice must give serious consideration to these problems if law enforcement is to be relevant in today's society.

I wish to express my appreciation to the authors and publishers who so graciously granted permission to reprint their work. In addition, I would like to dedicate this book to my wife, Ginger, for her assistance and encouragement.

Harry W. More, Jr.
Santa Cruz, CA.
1984

Contributing Authors

(Reprinted with permission of the author and/or publisher)

Richard M. Ayres, "Police Strikes: Are We Treating the Symptoms Rather Than the Problem?", *The Police Chief*, Vol. XLIV, March 1977.

Albert A. Bedrosian, "An Occupational Hazard—The Subculture of Police," *Journal of California Law Enforcement*, Vol. 15, No. 3, Spring 1981, pp. 95-101.

Daniel J. Bell, "Collective Bargaining: Perspective for the 1980's," *Journal of Police Science and Administration*, Vol. 9, No. 3, 1981, pp. 296-304.

Peter J. Donnelly, "Investigation of the Use of Deadly Force," *Police Chief*, Vol. XLV, No. 5, May 1978, pp. 24-26.

John D. Elliot, "Contemporary Terrorism and the Police Responses," *The Police Chief*, Vol. XLV, No. 2, February 1978.

William A. Geller and Kevin J. Karales, *Split-Second Decisions: Shootings of and by Police* (Chicago: Chicago Law Enforcement Study Group, © 1981 by William A. Geller), pp. 1-3, pp. 8-9, and pp. 13-14.

Herman Goldstein, "Police Policy Formulation: A Proposal for Improving Police Performance," *Michigan Law Review*, Vol. 65, No. 6, April 1967 pp. 1123-1146.

Mary Jan Hageman, Robert B. Kennedy, and Norman Price, "Coping With Stress," *The Police Chief*, Vol. XLVI, February 1979.

George L. Kelling, "Police Field Services and Crime: The Presumed Effects of a Capacity," *Crime and Delinquency*, Vol. 24, April 1978, pp. 173-184.

Carl F. Lutz, "Overcoming Obstacles to Professionalism," *The Police Chief*, Vol. XXXV, No. 9, September 1968, pp. 42-52.

Kenneth R. McCreedy and James L. Hague, "Administrative and Legal Aspects of a Policy to Limit the Use of Firearms by Police Officers," *The Police Chief*, Vol. XLII, January 1975.

Richard V. Mecum, "Police Professionalism—A New Look at an Old Topic," *The Police Chief*, Vol. XLVI, August 1979.

Richard S. Michelson, "Terrorism: Does it Affect the Street Cop?", *Law and Order*, February 1983, pp. 42-45.

Catherine H. Milton, Jeanne Wohl Halleck, James Lardner and Gary L. Albrecht, *Police Use of Deadly Force* (Washington, D.C.: Police Foundation), 1977, pp. 38-64.

Harry W. More, Jr., "The Delphi Analysis of Police Corruption," *Journal of Police Science and Administration*, Vol. 8, No. 1, 1980, pp. 107-115.

W. Ronald Olin and David G. Born, "A Behavioral Approach to Hostage Situations," *FBI Law Enforcement Bulletin*, January 1983, pp. 19-24.

C. E. Pratt, "Discretion: The Essence of Professionalism," *Law and Order*, October 1981, pp. 46-50.

Barbara Raffel Price, "Integrated Professionalism: A Model for Controlling Police Practices," *Journal of Police Science and Administration*, Vol. 7, No. 1, 1979, pp. 93-97.

James T. Reese, "Life in the High-Speed Lane: Managing Police Burnout," *The Police Chief*, Vol. XLIX, No. 6, June 1982, pp. 49-53.

Earl W. Robitaille, "Terrorism and the Role of the Police," *Law and Order*, September ·1981.

James M. Sands, "Counter Terrorism Target Assessment Form," *The Police Chief*, Vol. XLV, No. 12, December 1978, p. 83.

Charles B. Saunders, Jr., *Upgrading the American Police* (Washington: The Brookings Institution, 1970, pp. 13-34).

James D. Sewell, "The Development of a Critical Life Events Scale for Law Enforcement," *Journal of Police Science and Administration*, Vol. II, No. 1, 1983, pp. 109-116.

Joseph D. Smith, "Police Unions: An Historical Perspective of Causes and Organizations," *The Police Chief*, Vol. XLII, No. 11, November 1975.

Richard J. Terrill, "Complaint Procedures: Variations on the Theme of Civilian Participation," *Journal of Police Science and Administration*, Vol. 10, No. 4, 1982, pp. 398-406.

Leonard Territo and Robert L. Smith, "The Internal Affairs Unit: The Policeman's Friend or Foe." *The Police Chief*, Vol. XLIII, July 1976.

Leonard Territo and Harold J. Vetter, "Stress and Police Personnel," *Journal of Police Science and Administration*, Vol. 9, No. 2, 1981, pp. 195-207.

John B. Wolf, "Anti-Terrorism: Operations and Controls in a Free Society," *Police Studies*, Vol. 1, No. 3, September 1978, pp. 35-41.

Reports

The Pennsylvania Crime Commission, *Report on Police Corruption and the Quality of Law Enforcement in Philadelphia* (Pennsylvania: Pennsylvania Crime Commission, 1974), pp. 5-26.

Chapter 1
POLICE IN A FREE SOCIETY

Introduction

There are no greater immediate needs in this free society than the control and reduction of crime. The accomplishment of these objectives is of the utmost concern to all Americans. In recent years, the tasks performed by criminal justice agencies have become increasingly complex, especially those of local law enforcement agencies. Evaluating the goals of police departments has never been more important or necessary than it is today. Time has wrought many changes in our society. In the decades ahead, societal transformations will require law enforcement administrators to evaluate their programs and prepare their agencies to meet new challenges.

Law enforcement officials must make a serious and realistic attempt to outline a police role that will be accepted by all segments of society; above all, that role must be made fully understandable to the public. Some authorities feel that the police must not reflect an attitude of moral self-righteousness, an attitude that gives the public the impression that the sole purpose of law enforcement is to "enforce the laws." An analysis of actual police performance clearly shows that enforcing the laws is only one facet of police work.

Sir Robert Peel, founder of the British police system enunciated nine principles of law enforcement that are just as applicable today as they were in 1822:

1. Prevention of crime is the basic mission of the police.
2. Police must have the full respect of the citizenry.
3. A citizen's respect for law develops his respect for the police.
4. Cooperation of the public decreases as the use of force increases.
5. Police must render impartial enforcement of the law.
6. Physical force is used only as a last resort.
7. The police are the public and the public are the police.

1

8. Police represent the law.

9. The absence of crime and disorder is the test of police efficiency.[1]

A review of the literature reveals four strikingly similar definitions of traditional police duties. The customary police role is generally defined by the following objectives:

1. Protection of life and property.
2. Maintenance of the peace and public order.
3. Control and prevention of crime and vice.
4. Traffic control.
5. Regulatory responsibilities.[2]

O.W. Wilson, a leading police administrator, has written that police duties may be classified according to their more immediate objectives:

1. The prevention of the development of criminal and anti-social tendencies in individuals.
2. The repression of criminal activities.
3. The arrest of criminals, the recovery of stolen property, and the preparation of cases for presentation in court.
4. The regulation of people in their non-criminal activities and the performance of non-regulatory services.[3]

Another authority, John P. Kenney, has stressed that, "It is well accepted that under our form of government, the general purpose of the police is to protect life and property and to preserve peace. In light of present trends, an additional end may be sighted—rendering special services to the public." The basic police functions, according to Kenney, are:

1. Control of crime.
2. Crime prevention.
3. Control of conduct.
4. Provision of services.[4]

Finally, J. Edgar Hoover defined the basic responsibilities of the police as being:

1. The protection of life and property.
2. The preservation of the peace.
3. The prevention of crime.
4. The detection and arrest of violators of law.
5. The enforcement of laws and ordinances.

---

1. Edward M. Davis, "Professional Police Principles," *Federal Probation*, Vol. 1, XXV, March 1977, pp. 29-34.

2. V.A. Leonard and H.W. More, *Police Organization and Management*, 4th ed. (Brooklyn: The Foundation Press, 1974), p. 14.

3. O.W. Wilson and R.C. McLaren, *Police Administration*, 3rd ed. (New York: McGraw-Hill Book Company, Inc., 1972), p. 22.

4. John Kenney, *Police Management Planning* (Los Angeles: Jack Kenney, 1956), p. 70.

6. The safeguarding of individual rights.[5]

The authorities cited above reflect a consensus as to the *fundamental* tasks police are expected to fulfill. And this consensus reflects the general expectations of the public at large: very simply and on the broadest terms, the public expects the police to preserve the peace and protect society from crime through the enforcement of laws.

The American Bar Association, however, in its 1972 study, suggested that local committees should recognize that most police agencies are also given responsibility by design and default. This study provides a list of responsibilities that clearly extends the police task beyond the "basics" as presented in the preceding lists. According to the Bar's study, the police are expected to:

1. Identify criminal offenders and criminal activity and, where appropriate, to apprehend offenders and participate in subsequent court proceedings.

2. Reduce the opportunities for the commission of some crimes through preventative patrol and other measures.

3. Aid individuals who are in danger of physical harm.

4. Protect constitutional guarantees.

5. Facilitate the movement of people and vehicles.

6. Assist those who cannot care for themselves.

7. Resolve conflict.

8. Identify problems that are potentially serious law enforcement or governmental problems.

9. Create and maintain a feeling of security in the community.

10. Promote and preserve civil order.

11. *Provide other services on an emergency basis.*[6] [Emphasis added.]

A careful analysis of this list indicates that the police in our cities are expected to spend a considerable portion of their time involved in activities that are completely unrelated to criminal activities. This list also reveals the fact that the police perform many duties which they have assumed by default of other governmental agencies or by virtue of their being the only primary municipal agency available at all times. Through the years, then, the police have been required to provide such services as animal protection, ambulance attendance, tax collection, and licensing. Police administrators are in general agreement that these duties should be performed by other units of government.

Additional problems are inherent in the present classification of police duties. In terms of actual performance, the police objective of crime

---

5. J. Edgar Hoover, *Should You Go Into Law Enforcement?* (New York: New York Life Insurance Company, 1961), p. 7.

6. Advisory Committee on the Police Function, *The Urban Police Function* (New York: American Bar Association, 1972), p. 53.

prevention defies definition. Is it the same as "the control of crime" or "the repression of criminal activities," or is it something that is unique and distinct? Is it something peculiar to the police function or do other components of the criminal justice system have primary, secondary, or even tertiary responsibility in this area?

Another area of current dispute is the parameters involved in "maintaining the peace." On the one hand, there is an increasing cry for "law and order"; and on the other hand, some still espouse a policy of "absolute permissiveness" in the cause of democratic freedom. The police have always suffered from the tension caused by this dichotomy. It is imperative, then, in setting standards for this aspect of policing that standards also be established that will protect us from anarchy while allowing for reasonable dissent.

There are two conflicting approaches that must be resolved before the policeman's role can be clearly defined. It is believed by some that law enforcement must consider societal inequities that place many individuals and groups at a disadvantage and, consequently, in conflict with the law. At the same time, many feel that there should be a structured standard by which all must abide, regardless of their position or station in life.

Reconciliation and convergence of these dissenting views is essential. Experience tells us that double standards cannot be tolerated and that the perpetuation of such divergent beliefs has led and will continue to lead to chaos. A deep discontentment exists because of the perpetuation of a police role that has frequently permitted differential treatment of violators because of race, political pressure, influence, or graft. There is, of course, a genuine need for police discretion in enforcement of the law, but it must be based upon a clear-cut policy reflecting a dynamic and viable police role. But the police, while fully aware of their wide discretionary powers, have never given serious attention to this issue and its relationship to responsible law enforcement. In short, the police must be responsible to both the community and to political leadership in local governmental units, but a mode of control must be established that places police administration above "partisan politics." Law enforcement officers need positive public and political support which will allow them to render services that are both equitable *and* effective.

One leading expert, Herman Goldstein, points out that:

> The competition between objectives also becomes apparent. It may surface at the administrative level in the form of a policy question about the distribution of limited police manpower, the priority to be given to calls for police assistance, or the use to be made of the limited time available for training programs. Or it may arise at the operating level in the context of a given incident calling for a quick judgment. For example, what is the primary objective of the police in handling a tense situation on a city street stemming from a speaker

attempting to address a hostile audience? Is it to protect the speaker's constitutional right to speak, or to avoid violence, or to resolve the conflict, or to facilitate the movement of disrupted traffic? Often, much to the dismay of the parties involved, it has been the concern for traffic that has dictated police operating procedures.[7]

Many factors will influence the analysis and eventual definition of the functions to be performed by the police of tomorrow. These include such constituents as urbanization, the population explosion, technological advancement, a larger youth population, a changing morality, and a more educated populace. Each must be carefully assessed and evaluated in light of the evolving needs of society. For example, the potential influence of these factors is best illustrated by the fact that in a short time this nation will be close to being megalopolized. By the end of this decade, slightly more than three-fourths of our population will be living in metropolitan areas, and at that time, 56 percent of the population will be under twenty-five years of age. During the same period of time, the number of people over age sixty-five will increase by 21 percent. This growth and change will certainly create social problems that one can hardly envision; the prediction of human behavior will continue to defy an immediate or simple solution. The role of the police will, then, of necessity, have to be flexible, and at the same time cognizant of the "cross-functional ripple effect."[8]

The changing morality of this nation presents an additional dilemma. Support for many of the sumptuary laws is no longer evident. In the past, it was far easier to obtain community consensus for the control and regulation of behavior based on moral grounds. If it is clear to the police that a law is not appropriate to the "times," it is imperative that they work toward changing the law. To be effective, a law must be accepted by the majority of the people. The police are the implementors of the law and are therefore in an advantageous position to measure and interpret popular morality.

In our nation the fabric of our society is essentially legalistic. Without law, we could not function as we do today. Fundamental to our democracy is the concept of liberty under law. Each and every citizen has the inalienable right to demand equal protection under the law.

The enforcement of laws that maintain a reasonable balance between the collective need and individual rights *must* be guided by a single and pervasive mission—"justice."

The most illustrious and inspiring definition of "justice" was included

---

7. Herman Goldstein, *Policing A Free Society* (Cambridge: Ballinger Publishing Company, 1977), p. 36.

8. The solution of one problem usually creates or modifies another. For example, censorship will control pornography and at the same time infringe on the freedom of the press.

in the Justinian Code by Roman lawyers: "justice is the constant and perpetual will or rendering to each his right. . . ."[9]

The concept of justice has long been the subject of discussion by scholars, philosophers and theologians. Although it is a universal concept and an ideal, there are a multiplicity of definitions and interpretations. What is of concern is the implementation of the concept; it should not be lost in repetitive rhetoric.

A contemporary philosopher defines justice in three parts, according to the three theories of justice: "justice is. . . conformity to law; doing what is useful for the social good; and rendering to each what is his own or due by right."[10]

This combined definition encompasses the positive law, social, and natural right theories of justice. It is a definition that meets the needs of a dynamic and changing society.

Justice as a mission of our justice system should be the philosophical foundation and the pervasive guide for every decision. Each officer should direct total action toward the attainment of absolute justice. In each conflict with the law, justice must be tempered in terms of equity. Each human action or reaction resulting in an infraction of the law must be analyzed and legal sanctions applied in the interest of justice.[11]

The police alone do not bear the responsibility for preserving a peaceful society; that responsibility is shared by every element of society—each person, institution, and area of government within that society. However, because crime is an immediate threat to the order of all communities, the police exist foremost to overcome that threat and to reduce the fear of it.

The degree to which society achieves public order through police action depends on the price that its members are willing to pay. That price is measured, literally, in tax levies and the surrender of certain liberties. For example, if the people are willing to live in a totalitarian state where the police had unlimited resources and power, they might find their parks always safe to walk in, but impossible to enjoy. That balance must be determined by the people if a productive relationship with their police is to be achieved.[12]

Unfortunately, it is clear that there is no single or simple answer to what the role of the police should be in a free society. The studies that

---

9. Otto A. Bird, *The Idea of Justice* (New York: Frederick A. Praeger, Publishers, 1967), p. 122.

10. *Op.Cit.*, p. 164.

11. Harry W. More, Jr., (Ed.), *Contemporary Criminal Justice*, 2nd Edition (San Jose: Justice Systems Development, Inc., 1977), p. 24.

12. National Advisory Commission on Criminal Justice Standards and Goals, *Police* (Washington: U.S. Government Printing Office, 1973), p. 13.

follow present some of the problems inherent in defining the police role, examine the factors involved, and present proposals for role definition of a democratic police force.

POLICE FIELD SERVICES AND CRIME*

During the past fifteen years, policing has been recognized by the public and its leaders as a major social institution—one in need of great political and financial support. While some have perhaps overstated the importance of the police in problems occurring during the last two decades (e.g., Godfrey Hodgson has asserted that the police were largely responsible for most of the riots in the sixties), it is fair to say that the police contribute significantly to both the solution and the exacerbation of social problems.

This period will also be noted in the history of policing as the time when the remarkable insularity of the police ended. The police began to collaborate—at first begrudgingly but finally with enthusiasm—with other major institutions such as universities, foundations, and research institutes.

Other changes occurred as well. Salaries for police increased greatly. The size of police departments doubled and tripled. Major investments were made in technology. Women and minorities were slowly admitted into police service. University programs developed to educate the police, and officers entered these programs on both a preservice and a postservice basis. Entrance requirements were modified in light of this emphasis on education. Many police benevolent associations became powerful unions, forcing police managers to adjust to a new force in police policy making. Finally, the police and police services were probably more thoroughly scrutinized and evaluated than almost any other part of the criminal justice system.

It is not hard for many of us to remember those days when police agencies were almost totally inaccessible to researchers. Police business was considered to be just that—police business. However, during the past twenty-year period, researchers and police have developed interorganizational and interprofessional strategies and techniques which allow for successful collaboration. The police have learned that they can become successfully involved in research and that research can contribute significantly to the improvement of public service.

*   George L. Kelling, "Police Field Services and Crime: The Presumed Effects of a Capacity," *Crime and Delinquency*, Vol. 24, April, 1978, pp. 173-184. Reprinted with permission of the National Council on Crime and Delinquency.

The purpose of this paper is to review research related to the changing police role to determine what this suggests about the future of police tactics. On the surface, much of the research seems contradictory and confusing, but I believe that consistent themes do emerge. These themes provide the basis for continued research, development, and innovation.

The Police as a Public Service Agency

The myth of the police as primarily a crime-fighting, deterring, and investigating agency is deeply ingrained in our society. This view is reinforced each day by the media, which portray the police as going from critical event to critical event, constantly dealing with crime, and often resorting to weapons. The effect of this is considerable. Young persons are drawn toward policing as a career because of the excitement of such activities. The police themselves cite crises in their attempt to get public, financial, and moral support. Even today, some police chiefs go beyond the title "law enforcement officers" and describe themselves as "crime fighters enforcing the law."

However, considerable research done since 1950 has shown this image to be inaccurate.[1] The police have been found to spend a relatively low percentage of their time on crime-related matters (less than 20 percent); most of their time is spent in activities related to public service—settling family fights, handling drunks, dealing with teenagers, maintaining order, and so on.

The importance of this knowledge is clearly consequential. If it is true—and every bit of evidence suggests it is—almost every aspect of present police organization is affected. As Herman Goldstein has pointed out, this awareness of the multiple functions of the police has significant implications for recruitment, training, and organization.[2] Thus, if service activities do dominate over crime-fighting activities, the police will have to recruit different kinds of people than those presently attracted to the stereotyped crime-fighting functions. Training will have to focus less on legal and crime-related matters and more on conflict management and social relations. Less organizational emphasis need be placed on command, control, and on technological systems to get police to the scenes of crime quickly. More can be placed on developing quality relations with

---

1. W. A. Westley, *Violence and the Police* (Cambridge, Mass.: MIT Press, 1970); E. Cumming, I. Cumming, and L. Edell, "Policeman as Philosopher, Guide and Friend," *Social Problems*, Winter 1965; James Q. Wilson, *Varieties of Police Behavior* (Cambridge, Mass.: Harvard University Press, 1968); A. J. Reiss, Jr., *The Police and the Public* (New Haven, Conn.: Yale University Press, 1971); American Bar Association, *The Urban Police Function* (Chicago: American Bar Association Project on Standards for Criminal Justice, 1971).

2. Herman Goldstein, *Policing a Free Society* (Cambridge, Mass.: Ballinger, 1977).

citizens. Further, people tend to concentrate on performing well in those activities for which they receive rewards—both financial reimbursement and promotions. Unless organizations reward non-crime-related activities, successful performance in these functions will remain less crucial.

But the most important consequence of this mistaken conception of the police function is its impact on patrol. By defining themselves as crime fighters the police have developed crime-prevention strategies that emphasize patrol; allocation for patrol, in turn, is almost entirely based on police functions that relate directly to crime. We are only now beginning to understand that this strategy has been at the expense of other important activities.

Preventive Patrol as the Primary Means of Police Service Delivery[3]

O. W. Wilson has best described—and best justified—the concept of preventive patrol, as we know it today.[4] According to Wilson, the automobile was first used to increase the patrol range of foot beat officers by enabling them to move quickly from one beat to another.[5] While cars could be used to pursue offenders, their primary function was to increase the number of beats officers could handle. The theory of preventive patrol developed only after cars had been used for some time transporting officers between stations and between beats. Wilson theorized that, by moving police vehicles rapidly through beats and unpredictably past likely crime targets, police could create the feeling of police omnipresence. The benefits of this omnipresence were to be decreased crime, increased apprehensions, reduced citizen fear, and increased citizen satisfaction. Coupled with rapid response to calls for service, this police omnipresence would dramatically and effectively reduce crime.

With some variations, this attempt to affect crime through preventive patrol became the dominant mode of delivering police service. Beats were structured to facilitate this proposed impact. As allocation models became more complex, it became apparent that, although the police had multiple functions, patrol came to be organized around the presumed effects of police on crime. Some persons called for "getting rid of" the non-crime-related functions;[6] others developed models for "interception patrol,"[7] a

---

3. For a wider discussion of this and the following section, see George L. Kelling and David Fogel, "The Future of Policing," in *Sage Criminal Justice Annuals*, vol. 9, Alvin W. Cohn, ed. (Beverly Hills, Calif.: Sage Publications, Spring 1978).

4. O. W. Wilson and Roy Clinton McLaren, *Police Administration*, 3d ed. (New York: McGraw-Hill, 1963).

5. Ibid.

6. William J. Bayer, "Service-Oriented Functional Management in Patrol," *The Police Chief*, April 1975, pp. 42-45.

7. J. F. Elliot, *Interception Patrol* (Springfield, Ill.: Charles C. Thomas, 1973).

form of rapid patrol with the goal of intercepting crimes in action. Still others advocated covert patrol,[8] a form of inconspicuous patrol in which the police force would "blend into" a community.

As practice and theory developed, the use of the car substantially changed. Whether intentional or not, that change in the use of the car brought a substantial skew in the activities of the police. Wilson continued to advocate police-citizen interaction,[9] but the trend was away from this personal contact. Modeling theorists such as J. Elliot and Richard Larson provided a justification for police officers' remaining in their police vehicles rather than using them as a means of getting from place to place.[10] Police came to describe themselves as being "in-service" when they were cruising in their cars—attempting to create the effect of police omnipresence—and "out-of-service" when outside their vehicles actually dealing with citizens. To be patrolling was to be "in the action"—or at least apparently available for "action." The goal of police action was to "bust criminals." Obviously, contact with citizens diminished in importance.

This rationale behind the creation of police omnipresence was logical. In many respects, it made sense. But were the effects as predicted?

The theory of preventive patrol was first challenged in the early 1960s. Albert Reiss found that the time spent in preventive patrol was remarkably unproductive, contradicting the idea that the self-initiated, proactive (interception) activities of the police would increase apprehensions.[11] James Press found mixed effects of markedly increasing manpower.[12] The Institute for Defense Analysis reported that interviews with prison inmates suggested fear of police was not a significant deterrent.[13] Donald Fisk studied the Indianapolis Fleet Car Plan, an effort to simulate police presence by having police officers use their police vehicles off duty, and essentially found no positive effects.[14] In the Kansas City Preventive Patrol Experiment, preventive patrol once again failed to demonstrate its proposed effect.[15]

---

8. James D. Bannon, "Foot Patrol: The Litany of Law Enforcement," *The Police Chief*, April 1972, pp. 44-45.

9. O. W. Wilson, "Put the Cop Back on the Beat," *Public Management*, June 1953.

10. Elliot, *Interception Patrol;* and Richard C. Larson, *Urban Police Patrol Analysis* (Cambridge, Mass.: MIT Press, 1972).

11. Reiss, *The Police and the Public.*

12. J. S. Press, Some Effects of an Increase in Police Manpower in the 20th Precinct of New York City, Report R704-NYC (New York: New York City Rand Institute, October 1971).

13. "Part III: Analysis of Response to Police Deterrence," unpublished study cited with permission (Washington, D.C.: Institute for Defense Analysis, 1966).

14. D. Fisk, *The Indianapolis Police Fleet Plan* (Washington, D.C.: Urban Institute, October 1970).

15. George L. Kelling, et al., *The Kansas City Preventive Patrol Experiment* (Washington, D.C.: Police Foundation, 1974).

Other, nonempirical challenges to preventive patrol can be inferred from the report by the President's Commission of 1967 on Law Enforcement and Administration of Justice[16] and from researchers studying the problem of police-citizen alienation.[17] The commission report, while backing preventive patrol because of its assumed crime-preventive effectiveness, conceded that the strategy may create serious community relations problems. Others have suggested that the tactic of preventive patrol has contributed to police officers' image as an alien force that is remote from the community. In minority communities, police vehicles have grown to symbolize the establishment's repression and occupation. The result has been a mutual withdrawal—the police from the citizens, and the citizens from the police. Proposals for community relations programs and public service officers can now be seen as attempts to make up for some of the problems created by preventive patrol. However, since preventive patrol has failed to demonstrate its effectiveness, it becomes clear that such proposals were misplaced attempts to change image rather than improve service.

If police critics are correct, the strategy of preventive patrol has not only failed to demonstrate its effectiveness but has also created the worst possible situation: an ineffectiveness that alienates citizens.

Response Time

As preventive patrol strategy developed it was linked with a second and, in many respects, complementary tactic—rapid response to calls for service. If police could reduce the time between commission of a crime and the arrival of the police on the scene, increased apprehension of offenders, deterrence, increased citizen satisfaction, and decreased fear should result. The goal of most police departments became a response time of three minutes. Evaluators became so convinced that there would be a causal link between response time and police effectiveness (apprehensions, deterrence, etc.) that response time itself became an outcome variable, an indicator of police effectiveness.

Two recently published studies measured the effects of response time. Studying data from the Kansas City Police Department, Deborah Bertram and Alexander Vargo found that response time had no effect on apprehensions for the crime of robbery.[18] They also learned that citizens who have experienced serious crimes allow considerable periods of time to

---

16. President's Commission on Law Enforcement and Administration of Justice, *Task Force Report: The Police* (Washington, D.C.: U.S. Govt. Printing Office, 1967).

17. Irving Piliavin, "Police-Community Alienation: Its Structural Roots and a Proposed Remedy" (Andover, Mass.: Warner Modular Publications, Module 14, 1973), pp. 1-25.

18. D. K. Bertram and A. Vargo, "Response Time Analysis Study: Preliminary Finding on Robbery in Kansas City," *The Police Chief*, May 1976, pp. 74-77.

elapse before contacting the police. Pate, et al. correlated response time with levels of citizen satisfaction and found that response time was not the critical variable in determining citizen satisfaction.[19] What was important was the expectation of how long it would take the police to arrive. If police response time exceeded the citizen's expectation, he tended to be dissatisfied; if, however, response time was shorter than anticipated, the citizen was generally satisfied. The authors suggest that dispatchers could play an important role in controlling citizens' expectations about the police arrival.

As in the case of effects of preventive patrol, it appears logical that police response time should make a difference in effectiveness. But this strategy lacks empirical support. It was assumed that citizens called the police immediately. In fact, citizens called someone else first and considerable time elapsed.

Here we have a police strategy that is expensive to develop and maintain. To reduce response time, multimillion-dollar automatic vehicle locator systems have been developed. Yet evaluations of the strategy have bypassed the question of whether it affected apprehensions, only measuring the extent to which it reduced response time.[20] But it has been a tremendous expense in terms of its effect on police allocation plans, in the way it confines police in their automobiles, and in its impact on police supervision and organization.

Team Policing

One of the most promising developments in the past several decades has been the concept of team policing. There is much about it that seems "right": Team policing encourages close interactions between citizens and police; it emphasizes a decentralized decision making by police officers and supervisors actually working in the prescribed area; it acknowledges the multipurpose functions of the police and often provides general and special training for police; and it encourages police officer familiarity with community agencies and other resources.

Yet the implementation of this promising form of policing has been an elusive goal. Team policing has been tried in Detroit, New York, Dallas, Cincinnati, and many other cities, but no large city has been able to implement or maintain it on a city-wide basis.

A recent evaluation of team policing in Cincinnati may best illustrate this point.[21] Team policing was begun on an experimental basis with great

19. Pate, et al., *Police Response Time: Its Determinants and Effects* (Washington, D.C.: Police Foundation, 1976).

20. Richard C. Larson, Kent W. Colton, and Gilbert C. Larson, "Evaluating a Police-Implemented AVM System: The St. Louis Experience," Phase I (unpublished paper).

21. Alfred I. Schwartz and Sumner N. Clarren, *Evaluation of Team Policing in Cincinnati (after 30 months of Experimentation)* (Washington, D.C.: Police Foundation, 1978).

enthusiasm. After the first year, citizen satisfaction had increased, crime had decreased, and officers remained enthusiastic about the project. The program appeared to be a truly amazing success. However, at the end of year two, citizen satisfaction had returned to levels comparable with other areas of the city, crime had returned to comparable levels, and officer satisfaction had diminished. Team policing simply expired. Police officers went back to "business as usual," and authority was recentralized.

Two interpretations are possible. The first is that an "innovator effect" was operating during the first year; in other words, programs tend to start with flourish and promise because of factors such as participants' enthusiasm and publicity. This might well explain Cincinnati's initial success.

However, there is a second interpretation which I find more plausible since the Cincinnati experience followed the pattern of almost every other team policing effort. Team policing can start with enthusiasm, commitment, and great promise and then either remain confined to one or two districts or, as in Cincinnati, simply be terminated.

Two factors seem to operate. First, team policing represents a real threat to police departments' formal and informal power distribution. While officers can mobilize considerable enthusiasm for such attempts, organizational decentralization threatens established and entrenched interest groups that have considerable power inside the organization, often control employee organizations, and, in the case of detectives, often have important ties with the press and politicians.[22]

The second factor is that the present police orientation around rapid response to service calls is essentially incompatible not only with team policing but also with almost every other approach which emphasizes planning of "out-of-service" activities. Meetings with citizens' groups and with individual citizens involve considerable out-of-service time. Regardless of what a sergeant or team leader may plan for police officers during any tour of duty, as long as the primary goal of the police department revolves around rapid response to calls for service, that will have priority over almost every other activity.

The conflict between supervisory and dispatch goals may well have contributed to the failure of innovations such as team policing. Yet the role of supervision has received little attention. So far as I know, there is not one good study examining the impact of the sergeant on the police force. Jonathan Rubinstein suggests both sergeants and dispatchers may significantly control police activities,[23] but we have little understanding of how this operates.

---

22. A forthcoming evaluation of the attempt in Dallas to decentralize operations and develop generalist/specialist police officers will describe this resistance in detailed and stark terms.

23. Jonathan Rubinstein, *City Police* (New York: Farrar, Straus and Giroux, 1973), pp. 73-87.

Information

At least five studies suggest that, to the extent that police can affect crime, availability of information and the management of that information seem to be of critical importance. These findings, though still tentative, run counter to the present police concern with interception of crimes or rapid response to calls for service. The Rochester program, which studied case management to identify factors contributing to the solution of a crime,[24] the Rand study of investigative effectiveness,[25] the Police Foundation's evaluation of the Criminal Information Center in Kansas City,[26] the San Diego program of field interrogations,[27] and the San Diego community profile program[28] are exploratory studies, but they suggest that continued research and program development in the gathering and managing of information may be useful.

These findings lead to the following questions. How can we improve the quality and quantity of police-citizen contacts so that citizens report more crime, give police information—both formally and informally—about crime patterns, and discuss their community concerns? How can we improve the ability of the individual police officer and the organization to gather that information, store it, and bring it to bear on appropriate events and issues? How can we improve the police officer's and the police organization's ability to understand their community so that they can better interpret the information they receive? How can we modify the reward structures of police organizations so that sharing, not retaining, information is properly encouraged and rewarded? These questions combine issues of police organization, police strategy, and police technology.

Organizational issues pertinent to effectively obtaining information include supervision, training, and incentives for gathering and sharing useful information. Strategy issues include how to maximize police-citizen contacts so that they can be most productive of relevant information. The technological issue is how to properly arrange for the easy storage and retrieval of information.

---

24. Peter B. Bloch and James Bell, *Managing Investigation: The Rochester System* (Washington, D.C.: Police Foundation, 1976).

25. Peter W. Greenwood, et al., *The Criminal Investigation Process*, 3 vols. (Santa Monica, Calif.: Rand Corporation, 1976).

26. Tony Pate, Robert A. Bowers, and Ron Parks, *Three Approaches to Criminal Apprehension in Kansas City: An Evaluation Report* (Washington, D.C.: Police Foundation, 1976).

27. John E. Boydstun, *San Diego Field Interrogation: Final Report* (Washington, D.C.: Police Foundation, 1975).

28. John E. Boydstun and Michael E. Sherry, *San Diego Community Profile: Final Report* (Washington, D.C.: Police Foundation, 1975).

Investigations

The myths about investigative work are perhaps best summarized by Goldstein:

> Part of the mystique of detective operations is the impression that a detective has difficult-to-come-by qualifications and skills; that investigating crime is a real science; that a detective does much more important work than other police officers; that all detective work is exciting; and that a good detective can solve any crime. It borders on heresy to point out that, in fact, much of what detectives do consists of very routine and rather elementary chores, including much paper processing; that a good deal of their work is not only not exciting, it is downright boring; that the situations they confront are often less challenging and less demanding than those handled by patrolling police officers; that it is arguable whether special skills and knowledge are required for detective work; that a considerable amount of detective work is actually undertaken on a hit-or-miss basis; and that the capacity of detectives to solve crimes is greatly exaggerated.[29]

Both the Rand study and the Rochester study underline this issue. The Rand study, which has been the subject of much controversy, suggests that the role played by investigators in crime solution has been overrated. The study is exploratory, but the authors' findings and recommendations are highly plausible. The Rochester study demonstrated that one problem in investigations is case management. Thus, investigators found that their time could be spent more efficiently if they concentrated on those cases which had a high probability of success. Further, it was found that patrol officers could provide the necessary information for that screening process by identifying "solvability factors."

Clearly, much research is still needed. Only preliminary studies of the relationship between patrol and investigation are available. However, the combined findings of the Rand study and the Rochester study identify significant problems in investigation and suggest means of using patrol officers to improve investigative effectiveness.

Technology

There have always been high hopes that technology would greatly enhance police effectiveness or would at least give officers an "edge" over the criminals. In 1929, when the radio was first installed in police vehicles, some predicted that radios would enable police to eliminate city crime altogether.[30] While we may not be as enthusiastic today, we continue to invest heavily in devices such as helicopters, computers, new

---

29. Goldstein, *Policing A Free Society.*
30. Rubinstein, *City Police.*

weapon systems, and surveillance systems, with the expectation that new technology will significantly improve police functioning.

Certainly, innovations such as the personal radios have great utility for police agencies. Radios—especially personal radios—can be used to both protect the officer and increase his effectiveness. Yet one might argue that they are more important as management devices than as crime-fighting instruments, for there is little evidence that radios have given police any "edge" over criminal offenders. Recent lightweight bullet protection devices are useful and should be available; however, they are warm, uncomfortable, and restrictive. It is unlikely that more than a few officers are willing to wear them routinely.

With these possible exceptions, there is no evidence that any technological devices have significantly improved the effectiveness of police service. Helicopters may have been useful as ambulances, but their effectiveness in patrol remains hypothetical. And the cost of use has not been analyzed.

Computer-aided dispatch and automatic vehicle locator systems have failed to demonstrate that they can reduce response time.[31] Besides, there is no evidence that reduced response time achieves anything. This is not meant to imply that computers and other instruments cannot be used effectively in police departments. I have no doubt that they have great potential in efficient management. But their impact on the multiple police services remains to be seen.

Critics of technological innovation generally see new devices as being, at worst, expensive, useless "toys." But this criticism does not go far enough. The "worst" is not the wasting of money but the deterioration in the quality of service. The radio, for example, has been used to decrease police response time. The beneficial effect of rapid response to calls for service was presumed, not proved. Nevertheless, the radio created a priority, spawning other hardware such as computer-aided dispatch and automatic vehicle locator systems. All this came as a result of a capacity to achieve a *presumed effect.*

Technology does not, "at worst," create wasteful expensive toys; technology used in organizations can lead to goal displacement, the dominance of one function over another because of presumed effects, and a substantial change not only in how services are delivered but also in what those services are.

In discussing technology and the military, Joseph Lewis has suggested that when people have money and are facing difficult problems, they are easily diverted to the technology which seems to be related to those problems (capacity for presumed effect).[32] It is much more fun to play with

---

31. Joseph H. Lewis, "Evaluation of Systems Effectiveness," unpublished paper (Washington, D.C.: Police Foundation, 1964).

32. Ibid.

computers (be scientific) than to solve hard problems. You can prove that you are "doing something about the problem" by spending large sums of money in dignified, scientifically respectable, socially acceptable ways.

The problem can also be stated quite briefly in this way. What we have been saying is that there is not a firm bridge in the area of command and control between scientific and technical capabilities and operational utility. In most areas of application of science and technology, it is easy to see the connection between the scientific or technical ability to do something and the use that can be made of doing that something. That is not true here. There is technology lying around in heaps that we have not the remotest idea how to employ usefully. There is technology lying around in heaps that we know something about employing but have no valid way to establish what it is worth, or how much we should pay for it.[33]

The question in policing is, technology for what purpose? That question simply has not been answered.

Conclusion

The police have developed strategies oriented around just one of their many functions. These strategies have not only failed to obtain their desired results but have also led the police to ignore other important functions and have alienated citizens, whose support is vital in effective police performance.

Except for the period between World War I and World War II, our cities and countryside have probably never been safer. Those who respond hysterically to our present crime problems and claim that we are experiencing a complete breakdown in law and order should read about crime in the past.[34] Cities have always been unsafe places. And, not long ago, those leaving the city to travel in the countryside were hardly better off. Unless they hired protection, travelers were lucky to arrive at their destination with their horse (if they had a horse) and their boots. Even with protection, it was essential that they reach their destination—or stop in a city or at an inn—before nightfall. Today, one can travel throughout the countryside with little fear of crime. Campers can sleep outside with little risk of losing their equipment. A person can safely walk in most city neighborhoods during the day with relatively little fear. If one is reasonably prudent, the probability of becoming a victim is really quite low.

I do not mean to suggest that crime is not a serious problem. It is. But our fear far exceeds the danger and is seriously affecting our lives in the cities.

---

33. Douglas Hay, et al., *Albion's Fatal Tree* (New York: Pantheon, 1975).
34. See, for example, Christopher Hibbert, *London: The Biography of a City* (London: Longmans, Green and Co., 1969).

At this time, it appears that the police officer's impact on crime must remain relatively limited. This is not only because of the kind of open society in which we live but also because of the nature of particular kinds of crime. Most assaults and murders are hard to control because they involve friends, neighbors, relatives, or lovers. Subtract these from the total number of murders and assaults and the number of potentially suppressible crimes is greatly reduced. Subtract those crimes committed indoors or in places inaccessible to police, and those committed by professionals, and the number decreases further.

Consider armed robbery, a threatening, potentially violent crime. If the Vera Institute study is correct, fully one-third of all armed robberies are committed by people who are known by their victims.[35] Here too, if one subtracts those robberies committed in inaccessible places and those committed by professionals, the number that actually may be suppressible is reduced to an extremely low level.

Consider child molestation, most of which occurs in the home. How do the police mobilize to deal with this?

Certainly there are murders, assaults, armed robberies, and child molestations that are potentially suppressible. However, it is likely that a "floor effect" is operating—that the remaining cases are at such a low level that massively mobilizing the police to deal with those problems can have only a very marginal effect and at enormous cost. And that cost probably includes undesirable police-citizen relations.

Acute problems or a threatening series of crimes may demand mobilization, but as a routine policy this seems to have a limited effect and be enforced at enormous financial cost and at the expense of other functions.

What does this mean for the development of future plans, styles of policing, strategies, and research innovation? Briefly, the critical need is to improve the quality and quantity of police-citizen interaction. This must be a central task, not for the purpose of improving the police image but rather to encourage the normal social control exercised by a healthy community. The police must be seen as only an aid to the community, as the community itself deals with social problems. The police certainly are essential, but policing is too important to be left to the police alone.

Police methods must reflect the entire police task. We must examine how information is handled and how officers are rewarded for sharing it. The focus on rapid response time must be modified in part by changing citizens' expectations about police service. Police must see reduction of fear as an important part of their purpose. Citizens must be encouraged to use streets prudently but comfortably. We have never tested the hypothesis that it is the extent to which the police provide the full range of police services—in a civil and helpful way—that determines the degree to

35. Vera Institute, "Felony Arrests: Their Prosecution and Disposition in New York City's Courts," monograph published by Vera Institute of Justice, 1977.

which *citizens* fully exploit and mobilize the police to deal with crime. The time has come when we should test that hypothesis. As Lewis has suggested with the military,[36] we should declare a ten-year moratorium on technology and concentrate hard on learning just what it is that the police should—and can—do.

---

36. Joseph H. Lewis, "Evaluation of Systems Effectiveness" (lecture sponsored by the University of California, 1964); shortened version published in *Operational Research and the Social Sciences*, J. K. Lawrence, ed. (London: Tavistock, 1966), p. 46.

UPGRADING THE AMERICAN POLICE*

The view of police work as undemanding is an anachronism dating from the early development of metropolitan forces in the mid-1800's as a number of political appointees paid to serve as watchmen. An early student of police administration wrote:

> It is certainly not necessary and some have even maintained that it is not desirable that police patrolmen be men of large intellectual ability.... [It is] extremely unlikely that, for the present at least, any considerable number of men who have enjoyed even a secondary education will turn to the police business.... The most important asset of the ideal policeman is unquestionably his physical constitution and condition.[1]

But this view of the police was obsolete by the time it appeared in print. In the same year, August Vollmer, chief of police in Berkeley, California, was applying new principles of organization and professionalism that made him a pioneer of scientific criminal investigation and police administration.

A decade later, the first scholarly assessment of American police emphasized that:

> The heart of police work is the contact of the individual policeman with the citizen.... The action that is first taken by the policeman of lower rank, operating independently, must, in each case, remain the foundation of the department's action ... the quality of a department's work depends on the observation, knowledge, discretion, courage and judgment of the men, acting as individuals.... Only as the training of the policeman is deliberate and thorough, with emphasis on the social implications and human aspects of his task, can real success in police work be achieved.[2]

A concurrent judgment was expressed by Chief Vollmer, then beginning a single-handed campaign within the police profession to raise personnel standards. In 1916 he founded the first school of criminology at the University of California and advertised in the college newspaper for

---

* Charles B. Saunders, Jr., *Upgrading the American Police* (Washington: The Brooking Institution, 1970), pp. 13-34. Reprinted by permission.

1. Leonhard Felix Fuld, *Police Administration* (G.P. Putnam's Sons, 1909), pp. 90-91.

2. Fosdick, *American Police Systems*, p. 306.

bright young men to enter law enforcement as a career. Vollmer argued that:

> The police service has been completely revolutionized in the last few years, and an entirely different type of individual is needed. In addition to higher personal qualifications, there must also be added the professional training in order that the service may not be hampered and police candidates may be educationally equipped to perform the duties that are now assignable to policemen.[3]

Informed observers outside the law enforcement field agreed. An early specialist in public administration called attention to the growth of heterogeneous urban populations and the attendant problems which "this country has barely begun to approach . . . rationally." The police department, as the direct crime prevention agency, "is concerned with a social problem that is interrelated with all the social and economic conditions in the community. . . . Obviously, the task of combatting crime calls for superior abilities together with training and education."[4] Since effective law enforcement may require the exercise of more power than is actually conferred by law, the authority of police to use personal discretion "should be increased and the character of personnel improved so that this discretion will be wisely exercised."[5]

The International City Management Association told its membership in 1931 that "because of the enormity of the task of policing a community it is necessary to emphasize the fact that the best human material in the country is none too good for police service."[6] A joint study by the Los Angeles Police Department and the California State Department of Education in the early 1930s found that a competent patrolman should possess knowledge of one hundred fifty-eight different fields.[7]

Bruce Smith, the foremost scholar of police administration, emphasized the human factor in the law enforcement equation in his landmark study which appeared in 1940:

> The policeman's art, then, consists in applying and enforcing a multitude of laws and ordinances in such degree or proportion and in such manner that the greatest degree of social protection will be secured. The degree of enforcement and the method of application will vary with each neighborhood and community. There are no set

---

3. Letter (1932) quoted in Donald E. Clark and Samuel G. Chapman, *A Forward Step; Educational Backgrounds for Police* (Springfield, Ill.: Charles C. Thomas, 1966), p. 22.

4. Lent D. Upson, *Practice of Municipal Administration* (The Century Co., 1926), pp. 324-25.

5. Ibid., p. 321.

6. *City Managers' Yearbook, 1931* (International City Managers' Association, Chicago), p. 143.

7. U.S. Department of the Interior, Office of Education, *Training for the Police Service,* Vocational Division Bulletin No. 197, Trade and Industrial Series No. 56 (1938).

rules, nor even general guides to policy, in this regard. Each policeman must, in a sense, determine the standard which is to be set in the area for which he is responsible. Immediate superiors may be able to impress upon him some of the lessons of experience, but for the most part such experience must be his own.... Thus he is a policy-forming police administrator in miniature, who operates beyond the scope of the usual devices for popular control....

Hence the task of raising the level of police performance does not hinge upon the use of mechanical aids, as so many suppose. It depends upon sound organization and efficient procedures which are applied to—and by—alert and intelligent servants of police organization. Since the human factor proves the most difficult to control and may actively resist all change, the process of raising the general level of police service sometimes proves to be a lengthy one.... [8]

In the last three decades the human factor has assumed ever greater importance as police agencies have had to cope with the tensions and dislocations resulting from population growth, increasing urbanization, developing technology, the civil rights revolution, changing social norms, and a breakdown of traditional values. Such factors have enormously complicated the law enforcement task, making more critical the need for the "truly exceptional men" Vollmer sought in the 1930s. [9]

Today's local patrolman must be aware of these factors and understand their psychological and sociological implications for his community. He must deal with all of its citizens—rich and poor, young and old, of whatever cultural and ethnic backgrounds—in ways which will maintain their support and confidence. He must be able to provide a variety of services while serving as protector of life, property, and personal liberty. He must be a law enforcement generalist with a working knowledge of federal, state, county, and municipal law, traffic law, and criminal procedures.

The Police Patrolman: A Job Description

The complex demands of the patrolman's job and the attributes required for successful performance have recently been analyzed by a university research team whose findings, reported as a list of essential behavioral requirements, serve as scientific validation of the point Vollmer made three decades earlier. On the basis of extensive field observation, the scholars concluded that a patrolman must:

8. Smith, *Police Systems in the United States* (New York: Harper & Bros., 1940), pp. 21-22. The continuing validity of this point is indicated by the use of the identical passage two decades later in the second revised edition (Harper & Row, 1960), pp. 19-20.

9. August Vollmer, *The Police and Modern Society* (University of California Press, 1936), p. 223.

1. endure long periods of monotony in routine patrol yet react quickly (almost instantaneously) and effectively to problem situations observed on the street or to orders issued by the radio dispatcher (in much the same way that a combat pilot must react to interception or a target opportunity).

2. gain knowledge of his patrol area, not only of its physical characteristics but also of its normal routine of events and the usual behavior patterns of its residents.

3. exhibit initiative, problem-solving capacity, effective judgment, and imagination in coping with the numerous complex situations he is called upon to face, e.g., a family disturbance, a potential suicide, a robbery in progress, an accident, or a disaster. Police officers themselves clearly recognize this requirement and refer to it as "showing street sense."

4. make prompt and effective decisions, sometimes in life and death situations, and be able to size up a situation quickly and take appropriate action.

5. demonstrate mature judgment, as in deciding whether an arrest is warranted by the circumstances or a warning is sufficient, or in facing a situation where the use of force may be needed.

6. demonstrate critical awareness in discerning signs of out-of-the-ordinary conditions or circumstances which indicate trouble or a crime in progress.

7. exhibit a number of complex psychomotor skills, such as driving a vehicle in normal and emergency situations, firing a weapon accurately under extremely varied conditions, maintaining agility, endurance, and strength, and showing facility in self-defense and apprehension, as in taking a person into custody with a minimum of force.

8. adequately perform the communication and record-keeping functions of the job, including oral reports, preparation of formal case reports, and completion of departmental and court forms.

9. have the facility to act effectively in extremely divergent interpersonal situations. A police officer constantly handles persons who are acting in violation of the law, ranging from curfew violators to felons. The officer continually works with people who are in trouble or who are victims of crimes. Besides dealings with criminals, there is contact with para-criminals, informers, and people on the border of criminal behavior. (He must also be "alley-wise.") At the same time, he must relate to the people on his beat—businessmen, residents, school officials, visitors, etc. His interpersonal relations must range up and down a continuum defined by friendliness and persuasion on one end and by firmness and force at the other.

10. endure verbal and physical abuse from citizens and offenders (as when placing a person under arrest or facing day-in and day-out race

prejudice) while using only necessary force in the performance of his function.

11. exhibit a professional, self-assured presence and a self-confident manner in his conduct when dealing with offenders, the public, and the courts.

12. be capable of restoring equilibrium to social groups, e.g., restoring order in a family fight, in a disagreement between neighbors, or in a clash between rival youth groups.

13. be skillful in questioning suspected offenders, victims, and witnesses of crimes.

14. take charge of situations, e.g., a crime or accident scene, yet not unduly alienate participants or bystanders.

15. be flexible enough to work under loose supervision in most of his day-to-day patrol activities (either alone or as part of a two-man team) and also under the direct supervision of superiors in situations where large numbers of officers are required.

16. tolerate stress in a multitude of forms, such as meeting the violent behavior of a mob, arousing people in a burning building, coping with the pressures of a high-speed chase or a weapon being fired, or dealing with a woman bearing a child.

17. exhibit personal courage in the face of dangerous situations which may result in serious injury or death.

18. maintain objectivity while dealing with a host of "special interest" groups, ranging from relatives of offenders to members of the press.

19. maintain a balanced perspective in the face of constant exposure to the worst side of human nature.

20. exhibit a high level of personal integrity and ethical conduct, e.g., refrain from accepting bribes or "favors," provide impartial law enforcement, etc.[10]

These behavioral requirements are basic to the job of an officer regardless of the size and nature of the community. If competent performance of the law enforcement task is expected, these attributes should characterize every member of the force, from the newest recruit to the oldest veteran. They should be standard equipment for anyone in uniform, whether patroling a sleepy rural street, a congested business district, or a ghetto alley.

Numerous proposals have been made for restructuring the officer's job by eliminating routine tasks such as checking parking meters, directing traffic, delivering summonses, or performing social services. None of these

---

10. Melany E. Baehr, John E. Furcon, and Ernest C. Froemel, *Psychological Assessment of Patrolman Qualifications in Relation to Field Performance*, Preliminary Report to Office of Law Enforcement Assistance, Department of Justice (processed, 1968), pp. II-3 to II-5. The project was conducted by the Industrial Relations Center of the University of Chicago under a grant to the Chicago Police Department.

proposals would alter the behavioral requirements outlined above. However this job may be restructured, the officer will continue to be the first to respond in any community when citizens call to report a serious traffic accident, a noisy crowd of teenagers on the street, trouble in a bar, a domestic quarrel, a mental patient on the loose, a man unconscious on the sidewalk, prowlers in a building, or a neighbor burning trash. The abilities, skills, and intelligence of those answering such calls are of vital concern to every member of the community.

The Peacekeeping Function

One fundamental but generally neglected aspect of the police role is that of peacekeeping. The enforcement function, which occupies only a small part of the officer's time, is carefully recorded by reporting procedures. The peacekeeping function, which consumes most of the officer's time and includes all occupational routines not directly related to making arrests, is largely unaccounted for. Police departments literally do not know and cannot explain how individual officers spend most of their time. When asked how they discharge the peacekeeping function, officers say they merely use common sense, although they admit that experience is valuable. Police textbooks and manuals give little attention to peacekeeping, except to suggest that it takes personal wisdom, integrity, and altruism. To the public, this phase of the officer's duties is a constant cause of misunderstanding:

> . . . the citizen will observe that when the officer is not handling the citizen's momentary emergency, he is standing on a street corner, walking along the sidewalk, or driving a patrol car—apparently "doing nothing." What the officer *is* doing, of course, is waiting to be called to cope with someone else's emergency, and if he were not "doing nothing" he would not be immediately available. The citizen, forgetting this, is likely to wonder why he isn't out "looking for the man who stole my car," or whatever.[11]

The importance of the peacekeeping function, and its relevance to the question of preparation and training, is emphasized in a psychiatrist's recent study dealing with the treatment of skid row derelicts by the police. He concludes that peacekeeping requires very real practical skills but that the police themselves are not aware of it:

> Quite to the contrary, the ability to discharge the duties associated with keeping the peace is viewed as a reflection of an innate talent of "getting along with people." Thus, the same demands are made of barely initiated officers as are made of skilled practitioners. Correspondingly, beginners tend to think that they can do as well as

---

11. James Q. Wilson, *Varieties of Police Behavior: The Management of Law and Order in Eight Communities* (Boston: Harvard University Press, 1968), p. 26.

their more knowledgeable peers.... The license of discretionary freedom and the expectation of success under conditions of autonomy, without any indication that the work of the successful craftsman is based on an acquired preparedness for the task, is ready-made for failure and malpractice. Moreover, it leads to slip-shod practices of patrol that also infect the standards of the careful craftsman.

The uniformed patrol, and especially the foot patrol, has a low preferential value in the division of labor of police work. This is in part, at least, due to the belief that "anyone could do it." In fact, this belief is thoroughly mistaken. At present, however, the recognition that the practice requires preparation, and the process of obtaining the preparation itself, is left entirely to the practitioner.[12]

This conclusion is highly significant for several reasons. It exposes the inadequacies of any view of the police task which undervalues the peacekeeping function. It points up a major aspect of police performance that is seriously neglected in training. It identifies a need for further research to determine with greater precision the requirements for effective police patrol. And it emphasizes that even routine police work requires a high order of abilities and preparation. The general failure to understand this last point (by the police as well as the public) has surely contributed to our society's unwillingness to accord the police status "either in the European sense . . . as representatives of the State or in the more typically American sense of prestige based on a claim of occupational competence."[13]

---

12. Egon Bittner, "The Police on Skid-Row: A Study of Peace Keeping," *American Sociological Review*, vol. 32 (October 1967), p. 715.

13. David J. Bordua and Albert J. Reiss, Jr., "Environment and Organization: A Perspective on the Police," in *The Police: Six Sociological Essays*, ed. David J. Bordua (New York: John Wiley & Sons, 1967), p. 51.

AN OCCUPATIONAL HAZARD—
THE SUBCULTURE OF POLICE*

The Young Police Aspirant

The public image of the police officer has undergone a major shift over the past two decades. The tall heavy-set machismo cop that was all brawn and short on brains has given way to an image quite diverse. The modern-day police officer, unlike his earlier counterpart, must subject himself to rigorous character and personality evaluations which would place him beyond reproach should (he)[1] be selected for the job. The individual today who entertains aspirations of becoming a police officer in most metropolitan departments will, by necessity, be more intelligent, more emotionally stable, and more compassionate than his predecessors. These stringent requirements are not wholly attributable to the altruistic nature of contemporary police departments who desire them, but to the public-at-large who demands them.

One of the biggest problems facing a young police aspirant in today's society is that of being able to distinguish the reality from the myth. The individual who steadfastly prepares himself for a police career based solely on the images and stereotypes made popular on television and the movies will realize a grave disappointment should the eventuality occur that he is hired. This is not to say that all movie and television portrayals of the police should be eliminated; it is only to say that an individual who bases his aspirations solely on the entertainment media without tempering this with information from other more reliable sources will be committing a grave injustice to himself, and to the police profession should he be hired.

It is quite evident that the quality of recruits in any police agency will be no better than those that apply to join its ranks. With this fact in mind current police administrators have gradually come to realize that in order to attain a higher degree of police professionalism it will be necessary to

---

*   Albert A. Bedrosian, "An Occupational Hazard—The Subculture of Police," *Journal of California Law Enforcement*, Vol. 15, No. 3, Spring 1981, pp. 95-101. Reprinted by permission of the publisher.

1. For purposes of convenience the masculine gender will be utilized to avoid such cumbersome devices as "he/she" or the constant use of the word "person."

attract a higher caliber of candidates to the job. As simple as this may sound it has long been the philosophy of many police officials that the selection process of police candidates was not nearly as important as was the training they received subsequent to their being hired. Clearly, it has been demonstrated within relatively recent times that this philosophy is slowly giving way to one which is tending to place a greater emphasis on the selection process of all aspiring police candidates — at least in the more progressive departments.

Unlike many occupations which strive to attract better educated and more highly qualified personnel, the police occupation is faced with somewhat of a dilemma. It has been suggested by one writer that although the college-trained applicant is apt to be more qualified educationally and possess a "cleaner" past, he has likewise been more socially immune from the day-to-day trials of competing "in the streets." As a consequence, it is almost virtually impossible to predict his behavior when he becomes faced with the "pressure and strain inherent in police life."[2] This should not be construed as being an indictment against the majority of college-educated police candidates, but more as a realistic grounds for assessing the potentialities of prospective police recruits. Ideally, an individual's educational attainments must necessarily be tempered by an emotional fitness and social sense which would make him more amenable to dealing with police problems.

With reference to the psychological qualifications of police applicants one source stated that of those persons who choose the career of police work there was a manifest display of paranoid ideation, more emphasis on male virility, and more of a "tendency to act out than in the nonpolice population."[3]

It is certainly more evident today that police recruitment and hiring practices are undergoing more careful scrutiny than was the case in past decades. Unlike his counterpart a couple of decades ago, the modern police aspirant is subjected to a battery of tests and examinations which run the gamut from intelligence to medical and psychiatric evaluations. It is also not uncommon in most larger departments to have the applicants submit to a thorough polygraph examination by a competent examiner. Such an examination would make it possible for hiring boards to further weed out those individuals who successfully "cheated" on one or more of the initial tests by use of devious methods, or more importantly, those who were able to successfully con the medical or psychiatric evaluator.

The ultimate success or failure of any police department can be attributed to many factors and variables which affect its daily operations. In that these operations involve direct contact with citizens under a

---

2. Arthur Niederhoffer, *Behind the Shield*, p. 38.

3. "American Journal of Psychiatry," 124, 11 (May 1968), pp. 1575-80.

myriad of circumstances, no one thing can affect this function, or have a more lasting influence, than the cop on the street. The delicacy and significance of such a relationship was perhaps best stated by August Vollmer in a book written about forty years ago: "To the poor, the ignorant, and the immigrant, he is not merely a government representative: he is the government, or as expressed in some states he is 'the law.' "[4]

Transition: Citizen to Police Officer

Preparing an individual for police work is usually a relatively long, tedious and sometimes arduous task. The recruiting and hiring of prospective officers is done with the utmost care, especially in most modern, public-conscious departments. The individuals who successfully meet the requirements of the job, pass the numerous testing and evaluation hurdles, and successfully convince the members of the oral board of their legitimate desire to serve the public are, if they are fortunate, sworn in.

As in the case in most police agencies new recruits are generally sworn in, given their badges or shields, and welcomed aboard as new fledgling police officers. Unfortunately the transition process from applicant to police officer involves a great deal more time than the simple bestowing of a title. If the young, newly ordained officer does not realize it then, he most certainly will in the days ahead.

The transition from citizen to police officer is one which takes varying lengths of time depending on the individuals involved and the training that is provided. For some alert, quick-minded, self-motivated individuals this transition period can be relatively short. For the less mature and unmotivated individuals the transition may be retarded or, in fact, never occur. This is not to imply that "ordinary individuals" would not make successful police officers, only that those who do aspire to being successful are necessarily going to need to develop talents and instincts not normally associated with common day-to-day behavior. Along with these acquired skills the new recruit must begin to acclimate himself to a way of life which is inherently more dangerous than that of most other occupations. Coupled with this the new recruit will slowly become increasingly aware of the wide latitude of discretion permitted him in the performance of his duties, not to mention the responsibility incurred from such decisions. Lastly, as the recruit gains the confidence of his fellow officers he will slowly become aware of the unwritten code of secrecy which is shared among his peers, a code so strong that to violate it would mean certain censure from his coworkers.

The following will be devoted to a discussion of these three important aspects of a police officer's career — namely, danger, discretion and

---

4. August Vollmer, *The Police and Modern Society*, p. 216.

secrecy, and how each affect and promote that which is known as the police occupational subculture.

Danger. The aspects of danger in the life of any police officer is a real factor which must be dealt with every day — workdays and off days alike. The police officer who conscientiously performs his duties by arresting known law violators is constantly subject to reprisals from those arrested whether he be recognized in or out of uniform, on or off-duty.

Many people will argue that the police risk is not all that great. This is generally supported by citing examples of other professions which incur a much higher rate of injuries and deaths, such as acrobats and race car drivers. However, such lines of work involve no interpersonal quality that is evident in the social interaction between the police and their assailants. It is this interpersonal quality that accounts for the gruesome statistics published annually by the F.B.I. showing the number of officers killed while in the line of duty.[5]

The aspects of danger and how the officer perceives it accounts considerably toward how the officer will respond to any given situation. Should the officer believe himself to be in a dangerous situation he will most likely utilize certain expedients in handling an arrest, a search, or any other matter of routine procedure. In doing this the officer may circumvent certain legal mandates to expedite the course of events to a stage in which he no longer feels threatened or endangered.[6]

The most salient feature of the danger aspect for the police officer is that he tends to isolate himself from not only criminals but the public in general. Since everyone with whom he comes into contact is potentially a "customer," the police officer will tend to exaggerate the anxieties by treating individual contacts as potential threats to his welfare and safety. This anxiety level becomes thoroughly reinforced among the police collectively every time an officer is killed anywhere.

Discretion. In viewing the powers given to law enforcement officers by the various sources of government there is probably no greater power than that of simple discretion. As the typical police officer wades through his daily activities he may encounter a host of situations which call for discretionary choices on his part. These choices may run the gamut from whether or not to issue a speeding violation to the ultimate choice of whether to take a life.

Unfortunately, the exercise of discretionary powers is not something that can be easily imbued to a candidate as he matriculates through the police academy, but is something which he hopefully acquires through a

---

5. Ronald K. Tauber, *Danger and the Police*, in *The Sociology of Punishment and Correction*. Norman Johnston, et al. (eds.), p. 96.

6. Jerome Skolnick, *Justice Without Trial*, taken from Ronald K. Tauber, *Danger and the Police*, p. 95.

process of mature and intelligent judgment. It is simply for this reason that most progressive police agencies realize the need to recruit members that possess a degree of maturity that would enable them to distinguish between logical and illogical choices, between responsible and irresponsible decisions.

As one author points out, the issue of discretion can be broken down into two types of policy — one policy advocating "full enforcement" while the latter would advocate "discretion."

As its name would imply, "full enforcement" would mandate that all violations of law — large or small — be strictly enforced. This type of enforcement policy would leave little room for the humanistic officer who would be required to arrest any and all violators who came to his attention. As unrealistic and unmanageable as this may seem there are those around who would strongly support such a policy.

More realisitic, and by its nature more easily manageable, would be a system whereby discretion could be employed. A system such as this would attribute to people a necessary sense of understanding and compassion whereby certain mitigating factors could impinge upon the decision by the officers to make or not make the arrest. Such a system would further lend credence to the ability of the police to act as reasonable individuals capable of making rational judgments as opposed to functioning as automatons.

The choice between the type of law enforcement the public wants, whether it tends toward full or discretionary enforcement, will be a decision which they alone will have to make. Should this choice tend toward the latter, as the trend now appears, the public should realize the responsibility that it is investing in the hands of a relatively small segment of its members. Along with this realization the public must recognize the limitations inherent in such an administration of justice and be prepared to deal with the associated problems when and as they occur.

Secrecy. One of the strongest codes adhered to within any policy agency is that of secrecy. It is this code which every officer tacitly agrees to uphold in order to claim solidarity rights to the unit or agency of which he belongs. By ignoring the basic tenents of this code the individual police officer risks chastisement, ostracism and worse, by his fellow officers. In 1930, August Vollmer wrote:

"Eradication of disgruntled agitators, incompetent policeman, police crooks, and grafters takes much time since it is next to impossible to induce police officers to inform on each other. It is an unwritten law in police departments that police officers must never testify against their brother officer."[7]

---

7. August Vollmer; in Buckner, *The Police: The Culture of a Social Control Agency*, p. 256.

The phenomenon of secrecy in social groups is nothing new to researchers of social behavior. By exercising a code of secrecy among its members the police are able to protect themselves from unwanted public scrutiny that might undermine their methods. Analogous to this would be the type of secrecy customarily employed in other occupations and professions (e.g. medicine, law, etc.) where such scrutiny would cast a very negative light over certain "professional" revelations.

The most salient feature of a secrecy code among any group is the solidarity it creates within the group. Within the police ranks specifically, secrecy is of the utmost importance as witnessed by the numerous illegal and semi-legal decisions made by police officers from time to time.[8] Should this code be violated by any one officer the consequences for departmental relations might be severely impaired — while the consequences for the offending officer would be certain retaliation by his peers.

In one questionnaire submitted to about fifteen police officers concerning the norm of secrecy, it was shown that only one of the respondents "stated he would both report and testify against his partner." The particular respondent in question, not suprisingly, was a rookie.

As is pointed out by Westley, the primary threat to the secrecy code is the novice officer whose ties with the "outer world" are not yet completely severed. It is for this reason Westley states that the oncoming rookie must be carefully assessed while being made constantly aware of the code. So strong is the need for secrecy, affirms Westley, "that policemen will break the law to support it."[9]

The Police Personality Formation

Due to the type and nature of the work carried out by the police it has long been believed by many behavioralists that the occupation itself is conducive to a type of personality formation. Jerome Skolnick referred to this specifically as a "working personality."[10]

The personality developed by the police, according to Skolnick, is not unique to that occupation, but evidenced in many other occupations and professions. The degree to which it differs is primarily due to the specific occupation under study. Perhaps what sets apart the "working personality" of the police is the degree and extent to which it circumscribes its members. In that the entire civilian world is potentially an audience for the police, it would stand to reason that the effects of such a personality would be far-reaching.[11]

---

8. William A. Westley, *Secrecy and the Police*, in *The Sociology of Punishment and Correction*. Norman Johnston, et al. (eds.), p. 82.

9. *Ibid*, p. 83.

10. Jerome Skolnick, *The Policeman's "Working Personality,"* in *The Sociology of Punishment and Correction*. Norman Johnston, et al. (eds.), p. 3.

11. *Ibid*, p. 5.

The factors that heavily contribute to the formation of the "police personality" are those that tend to isolate him from the general public. Skolnick states that, "the element of danger seems to make the policeman especially attentive to signs indicating a potential for violence or lawbreaking" that affords him a highly suspicious nature. This nature, although highly regarded by most police administrators, affords the individual officer little benefit among his social peers, as it tends to implicate them in his work. [12]

The "police personality" itself is not limited in scope to the individual officers but is much more pervasive throughout the entire collectivity of police, perhaps more so than in any other occupational field. The teamwork and colleagueship apparent among the police, especially in situations of extreme danger where an officer's life is in jeopardy, is probably unparalleled, with the possible exception of the military. This overriding sense of empathy and cooperation displayed in the "police personality" is not solely restricted to highly volatile situations, but is sometimes carried over to simple courtesies extended to off-duty officers. It is a rare situation when one officer will issue another (off-duty) officer a traffic citation.

It has long been a supported notion that police officers generally tend to be of a conservative bent and support the status quo. According to Skolnick, this is derived from the fact that the people engaged in enforcing a given set of laws also become somewhat implicated in affirming them. [13] If this were not the case, the ordinary police officer would be continually faced with the dilemma of carrying out a mandate that ran counter to his beliefs — a condition of certain psychological consequence.

Akin to the above psychological manifestations of the policeman's "working personality" are other traits that have evidenced themselves among police officers in the performance of their roles. Two such traits are anomie and cynicism.

Niederhoffer discusses the term "anomie" as a process whereby "the old values of a social system are supplanted by a new code," thus creating in the mind of the police officer a degree of uncertainty and lack of purpose. In a condition where anomie exists the individual officer becomes, as Niederhoffer describes, frustrated in his attempt to attain for himself a sense of true belonging to the group of which he is a member. [14] Should this feeling of estrangement become too intense for the individual the end result can be, and often is, self-destruction.

As an adaptation to such intense feelings of anomie, many individuals will develop an attitude of cynicism. This attitude is especially notable among the police, who through their numerous contacts with unsavory

---

12. *Ibid*, p. 4.

13. *Ibid*, p. 15.

14. Niederhoffer, *op. cit*, p. 91.

elements of society, find it easier than most to become cynical. The cynical police officer is one whose personality complex consists of "diffuse feelings of hate and envy, impotent hostility. . .,"[15] in other words, an attitude that there is no hope for society or the people in it. As Niederhoffer points out, this form of cynicism is "endemic" to all police personnel regardless of rank or professional status. The latter form, a cynicism toward the police system itself, is common among the lower ranks, and by virtue of its definition, "excluded from the ideology of the professional policeman."[16]

The fact that police officers demonstrate a high level of isolation and solidarity as a group is not novel. Many behavioralists may argue amongst themselves what accounts for such a phenomenon but few will argue the fact that it does exist. Countless studies have demonstrated that of most occupational fields the police display one of the highest levels of cohesiveness among their members.

The very nature of present-day law enforcement involving constant risk, public apathy, and laws that appear to favor the criminal, makes the police officer somewhat unsure of his role and consequently unsure of himself. Reinforcing such feelings of uncertainty, the police officer is often hampered by bureaucratic restrictions that further limit his ability to socialize and expand his own self-awareness by virtue of residency requirements, political freedoms and the ever present disciplinary procedures. Coupled with this the officer is contantly faced with numerous discretionary decisions that can oftentimes incur severe hardships on those whom he is entrusted to protect. The final reconciliation of these factors in the minds of the individual officers often do not get satisfactorily resolved and thereby tend to precipitate further social withdrawal and increased adversity to the public.

The social cohesiveness or solidarity exhibited among police officers is probably second to none. The only other example which might be drawn as a likely comparison would be soldiers on a battlefield — and this would be mostly of a transitory nature. Police solidarity is much more than a mere point of sociological interest as its existence is contingent upon the very essence of survival. For the cop on the street the knowledge that he is not alone, but supported by every other man who wears a badge, is usually enough to instill in all but the most cowardly the courage required to perform the job.[17] Were it not for this feeling of genuine camaraderie it is unlikely that the job would have much appeal.

It is not an uncommon trait among people of similar occupational groups to share a certain degree of cohesiveness and sense of belonging.

15. *Ibid*, p. 93.

16. *Ibid*, p. 95.

17. Tauber, *op cit.*, p. 98.

This has been abundantly demonstrated among individuals who perform the same work and share similar salary problems. However, the degree and intensity which this solidarity is exhibited by the police is vastly set apart from the conventional worker. The solidarity shared by police officers overrides the normal conventional problems of simple working conditions and salary disputes; the solidarity evidenced by the police is for the very essence of survival itself.

Conclusion

Perhaps the strongest point which can be drawn from the foregoing in respect to the existence of a police subculture is the simple fact that the police function in our society is somewhat vague and poorly defined. Along with this ambiguity of purpose, the police are given tremendous latitudes of discretion in performing their tasks, however nebulous they may be.

The overall uncertainty of the police purpose is further weakened by the general expectations of a public which mandates "enforcement of the law and the preservation of peace." Through such a mandate the public and government alike have tacitly condoned the exercise of extra-legal and illegal controls by the police. In effect, cumbersome legal mandates are circumvented in lieu of the more practical, and generally more successful, police expedients.

Confronted with the demands of the public, the expectations of the administrators, and the pressures from their peers, the police become uniquely caught up in a web of insecurity and confusion. Being generally unsuccessful in resolving these personal dilemmas within themselves the police then resort to group support by reaffirming their interpersonal ties with each other. As a consequence, the police become more occupationally cohesive among themselves as their bonds with the public grow weaker. Thus, as the two groups become more polarized, the relationship between them often turns from one of support to one of adversity.

The police operate and will continue to operate in our society as a body of individuals designed to perform a specific social function. How effectively this task is performed will vary with the times and prevailing social conditions. Perhaps, stated best by one writer, the police task, however simple or complex, is accomplished by "ordinary men whose unfortunate distinction is that they must regularly function in the face of extraordinary human stress, and sometimes in the face of indescribable human tragedy."[18]

---

18. Quote taken from George Kirkham, *Signal Zero*.

Chapter 2
POLICE DISCRETION

Introduction

Enforcement of the law in a dynamic and complex society poses numerous problems to all elements of the criminal justice system, the focal point being the police, especially the officer on the beat. The behavioral, political, and social implications of individual police actions during an arrest are so broad that they defy clear-cut definition and analysis.

The human dynamics involved in an arrest introduce into the criminal justice process a multitude of variables that directly and indirectly affects the stated objectives or roles of law enforcement agencies. Taking an individual suspected of criminal behavior into custody generally occurs in an emotionally charged atmosphere. Because the psychological set of the suspect, victim, witnesses, relatives, observers, and the police officer interjects such a great number of variables, police administrators have allowed officers to establish their individual enforcement standards based upon experience. And as anyone who is familiar with police bureaucracy knows, there has been and continues to be a substantial margin for interpretation of the law in particular situations. The obvious consequence, in the judgment of some, has been selective justice without established standards.

Some police officials have suggested that the courts, in their attempt to minimize discretionary decision making by police, have actually "handcuffed" the police. Their general attitude has been that law enforcers need greater discretionary power; this can only be construed as an encouragement for individual officers to enforce the law according to their personal standards. Police administrators who suggest that discretionary decisions made during arrests are indispensable (considering the complexity of the situations) are endorsing the concept of selective justice. This stance affects not only all police line and staff activities, but has a patent effect on individuals suspected of criminal behavior. The person who is in conflict with the law and is aware of the broad discretionary judgments available to police officers is in a more manipulative position than if he were confronted with enforcement standards that provided no leeway in the police response.

It has been suggested that a requisite to begin a reversal of police discretionary justice is the formation of a new ambience requiring a modern rhetoric essentially directed to changing attitudes toward discretion, its application, its control, and its significance to the criminal justice system.

A major reason for the perpetuation of this unresolved issue is that the majority of police administrators has expressed a common ideological response that all laws are enforced.

> Continued adherence to the myth of full enforcement of the law results in the police exercising wide discretion without acknowledging that it occurs and without attempting to explain and re-evaluate systematically the criteria by which the discretion is exercised.[1]

Still another failure of public understanding is the widely held fiction that a patrolman's job is not discretionary but is simply the enforcement of the law by catching criminals. This combines several mistaken views: that the crime problem is solely the concern of the police, that their task is mainly one of law enforcement, and that this function requires so little intelligence or imagination that anyone can do it.

Until this frame of reference is altered, police administrators will not support studies that result in empirical knowledge about police procedures. This traditional reluctance will continue unless there is considerable pressure from judicial, legislative, or administrative levels of government.[2]

Numerous police chiefs become arbiters of the conflicting tasks of promoting aggressive police action while fulfilling legal requirements. In fact, the police become "actors" of what they perceive as the spirit of the law rather than the letter of the law. The development of definite policies would of course require the administrators to acknowledge that some of the police procedures do not conform to legalistic standards. By adopting a "do-nothing" approach, the chief of police avoids a direct confrontation with the issue and supports existing procedures.[3] It should also be kept in

---

1. Wayne R. LaFave, *Arrest: the Decision to Take a Suspect into Custody* (Boston: Little, Brown and Company, 1965), p. 391.

2. For extended discussions of this problem see Herman Goldstein, "Police Discretion: The Ideal Versus the Real," *Public Administration Review*, Vol. 23, No. 3, September 1963, pp. 140-148 and Frank J. Remington, "The Role of Police in a Democratic Society," *The Journal of Criminal Law, Criminology and Police Science*, Vol. 56, September 1965, pp. 361-365.

3. The President's Commission on Law Enforcement and Administration of Justice, *Task Force Report: The Police* (Washington: U.S. Government Printing Office, 1967), p. 17.

mind that many of the extra-legal sanctions practiced by the police have the support of the public. This is particularly true of enforcement of sumptuary laws, although the continuation of such practices raises many civil rights issues.[4]

Charles B. Saunders puts forth the following notion:

This fiction has long been cherished by some apologists for the police who hold that they are "only doing their duty" as well as by civil libertarian critics who maintain that police do not have the capacity to exercise discretion and therefore should not be allowed to do so. But as the skid row study cited above illustrates, discretion is the better part of peacekeeping, which in turn is the bigger part of policing. To deny officers the use of discretion is to misconceive their basic function. The only realistic recourse is to insist that their qualifications and training be sufficient to assure that they exercise discretion well.

No matter how well or how poorly qualified to exercise discretion, the police are forced to do so for a variety of reasons. Many of the laws under which they operate are highly ambiguous, either by intent to permit greater flexibility in enforcement or by accident as a result of the limitations of language or of failure to foresee the day-to-day operating problems encountered in enforcement. In addition, some statutes were never intended to be enforced to the letter, and others are simply obsolete. Limitations on manpower and other resources, and the pressures of community standards, also force the exercise of discretion. Whatever the reason, the policeman must often determine the forms of conduct that are to be subject to the criminal process.

If the extent to which police must exercise discretion is underestimated, this is partly because police themselves usually prefer to project an image of impartial, full enforcement without fear or favor. To admit that they ignore the laws under certain conditions might contribute to a breakdown of respect for all laws, raise the possibility of corruption, and imply that other criteria for enforcement exist which are difficult to spell out and communicate to members of the force as well as the general public.

No code of conduct could possibly cover all circumstances in which policemen must make instantaneous and irrevocable decisions affecting human life and safety, property rights, and personal liberty. Such awesome responsibility for decision making, indeed, sets the police apart from any other profession—after all, the physician may change the diagnosis, and the lawyer the pleading. Decisions affecting human life cannot be made more wisely by reducing them to

---

4. See Paul G. Chevigny, "The Right to Resist an Unlawful Arrest," *The Yale Law Journal*, Vol. 78, No. 7, June 1969, pp. 1128-1150 and Charles A. Reich, "Police Questioning of Law Abiding Citizens," *The Yale Law Journal*, Vol. 75, No. 7, June 1966, pp. 1161-1172.

rote and removing police discretion entirely. Ironically, some proponents of this course describe it as "taking the handcuffs off the police." But without discretion, the police are handcuffed to the limited role of unthinking enforcers, powerless to perform the peacekeeping function which is the most challenging and time-consuming part of their job.[5]

The disinclination of police executives to deal explicitly with critical enforcement policies is reflected in the prevalent attitude toward "tolerance limits" in the traffic field. The reluctance to publicize "tolerance limits" can be traced to:

1. a concern that the administrative action which they reflect would be criticized as a perversion of legislative intent—a concern which gives rise to the basic issue of the propriety of police policymaking;

2. a fear that publication would lead to a public debate as to what constitutes an appropriate tolerance and would lead to arguments between the officer and the offender in a given case—a concern which relates to the willingness of police to be held publicly accountable for the policy decisions which they make;

3. a concern that the existence of such a document might be used as a basis for litigation in those situations in which an officer chooses to enforce the law and be free to deviate from their own policy in an individual case without having to justify such deviation;

4. a fear that widespread awareness of the existence of such tolerances would result in drivers adjusting their behavior, utilizing the established tolerances rather than the posted and published laws as their guides.[6]

While there are some areas where discretion is limited (such as the handling of juveniles), the majority of law enforcement functions remains outside the purview of carefully defined policies.

One leading authority identified the following situation that illustrates the application of police discretion:

A 19-year-old standing in a street fired three shots at a woman standing in a doorway of her home but missed. The police apprehended him and knew that neighbors witnessed the shooting. But they released him when the woman asked them to. They explained that they do not ordinarily arrest when a victim is able to sign a complaint but does not do so.

We asked more than a hundred officers at various levels what they would do in the preceding case, and about two-thirds of them said

5. Charles B. Saunders, Jr., *Upgrading the American Police* (Washington: The Brookings Institute, 1970), pp. 75-76.

6. The President's Commission on Law Enforcement and Administration of Justice.

they would release. One patrolman volunteered that he had witnessed an armed robbery but that he released the robber because the victim so requested.[7]

There is an increasing demand for greater conformity in the application of criminal law at the arrest stage. If the police are to maintain their proper position in the criminal justice system, they must assume a position of leadership in this administrative, policy-making function. Should the police not assume this position, they will certainly become unequal partners within the system. During the last decade there has been a noticeable extension of judicial review through numerous court decisions such as *Mapp* and *Miranda*.[8] A similar extension in the 1980s will certainly restrict, if not eliminate, the police as potential policy makers.

Kenneth Culp Davis is a proponent of administrative rule-making for the police who expresses the opinion that they are one of the most important policy-making agencies in government. The procedures to be followed would be those advocated by the Federal Administrative Procedures Act, 5 U.S.C. §553. Such a program would be implemented by law enforcement agencies publishing proposed rules and requesting written opinions from interested parties. The agency staff then evaluates the proposals and develops a written policy. In the opinion of Davis, this procedure would help to eliminate unnecessary discretionary power and insure equal justice.[9]

An outstanding example of possible accomplishments in the area of policy-making for the police can be seen in the guidelines regarding the "stop and frisk" law, adopted by the New York State Combined Council of Law Enforcement Officials.

Under the "stop and frisk" law the policy statement listed the following factors to be considered in determining whether or not there is "reasonable suspicion" to stop someone:

1. The demeanor of the suspect.
2. The gait and manner of the suspect.
3. Any knowledge the officer may have of the suspect's background or character.
4. Whether the suspect is carrying anything, and what he is carrying.
5. The manner in which the suspect is dressed, including bulges in

---

7. Kenneth Culp Davis, *Police Discretion* (St. Paul, Minn.: West Publishing Company, 1975), pp. 3-7.

8. For early indications of this trend see Richard C. Donnelly, "Police Authority and Practices," *The Annals*, Vol. 339, January 1962, pp. 90-110 and Sanford H. Kadish, "Legal Norms and Discretion in the Police and Sentencing Process," *Harvard Law Review*, Vol. 75, No. 5, March 1962, pp. 904-931.

9. Kenneth C. Davis, *Discretionary Justice* (Baton Rouge: Louisiana State University Press, 1969), pp. 80-96.

clothing—when considered in light of all of the other factors.

6. The time of the day or night the suspect is observed.

7. Any overheard conversation of the suspect.

8. The particular streets and areas involved.

9. Any information received from third persons, whether they are known or unknown.

10. Whether the suspect is consorting with others whose conduct is "reasonably suspect."

(This listing is not meant to be all-inclusive).[10]

Policy statements of this nature serve as guidelines for line officers and clearly limit police discretionary powers, while at the same time they allow the policeman a necessary degree of freedom when enforcing the law.

Consistent with the policies of local government, the police chief should develop policy to guide employees. Where the chief is silent and there is no policy established by higher authority, the next lower person in the hierarchy (the field policeman) may develop his policy. Thus it may not be consistent with that desired by the governing body or police chief executive.

Many chiefs have intentionally avoided establishing written policy in such sensitive areas as the use of force, particularly the use of weapons, because they fear criticism of the policy and other repercussions that could follow employee actions within the scope of the policy. However, employee actions are less apt to have adverse consequences if employees are guided by sound written policy.

With reference to the establishment of policy, the National Advisory Commission on Criminal Justice Standards and Goals suggested that every chief of police should immediately establish written policies in those areas of operations in which guidance is needed to direct agency employees toward the attainment of agency goals and objectives. The chief should promulgate a policy that provides clear direction without necessarily limiting the employee's exercise of discretion, and special emphasis should be given to sensitive areas such as use of force, and the use of lethal and nonlethal weapons.[11]

The establishment of clear-cut policies that are reviewed periodically presents a challenge to law enforcement administrators which must be met if the police are to adequately serve the public, and protect life and property.

The following articles discuss the nature of police discretion, the problems of controlling discretion, and means of implementing guidelines.

---

10. The President's Commission on Law Enforcement and Administration of Justice, p. 39.

11. National Advisory Commission on Criminal Justice Standards and Goals: *Police* (Washington: U.S. Government Printing Office, January 23, 1973), pp. 53-55.

POLICE POLICY FORMULATION: A PROPOSAL FOR IMPROVING POLICE PERFORMANCE*

The police function in this country is much more varied and much more complex than is generally recognized. This is particularly true today in the congested areas of large urban centers where the demand for police services is especially great and where the police are confronted with an increasing variety of difficult situations, many of which stem from dissatisfaction with the economic and social conditions existing in such areas. As law enforcement has become more difficult, it has, for the same reasons, taken on new importance as a function of local government.

Contributing to the major current concern regarding law enforcement is the growing awareness of the fact that the police are simply not equipped to respond adequately to the increasing demands being made upon them. This should not come as a surprise to anyone. Law enforcement agencies, over the years, have never been provided with the kind of resources, personnel, education, and leadership which their responsibilities have required.[1]

Substantial progress has been made in recent years, especially when compared with the rate of improvement in the past, but such progress has occurred in an uneven manner and its effect has frequently been diminished by backsliding. Within this period, standards and goals have been significantly increased, but they remain modest when related to the magnitude and complexity of existing problems.

Recent improvements have centered upon providing the police with better equipment, more personnel, higher compensation, increased training, and improved management techniques. All of these measures are

* Herman Goldstein, "Police Policy Formulation: A Proposal for Improving Police Performance," *Michigan Law Review*, Vol. 65, No. 6, April 1967, pp. 1123-1146. Reprinted by permission.

1. Among the most significant works spanning the past half century that document the absence of adequate resources in law enforcement are: Fosdick, *American Police Systems* (1920); Fuld, *Police Administration* (1910); National Commission on Law Observance and Enforcement, *Report on Police*, No. 14 (1931); Smith, *Police Systems in the United States*, 2d ed. (1960).

badly needed and each contributes to raising police efficiency. But it is becoming increasingly apparent that operating efficiency alone is not enough.

Future progress toward fulfilling the law enforcement function is likely to depend primarily upon the degree to which the police and others effectively respond to the numerous problems involved in employing our legal system to deal with the infinite variety of behavioral situations which confront the police. Many of these situations are obviously beyond the control of the police. Their improvement depends upon the correction of existing social and economic conditions, increased effort on the part of community welfare agencies, and changes in the law, in court procedures, and in the functioning and orientation of correctional agencies. Nevertheless, there remain many problems that are within the capacity of the police themselves to resolve.

The issues that are involved in these aspects of the law enforcement problem with which the police themselves can deal are much more difficult to resolve than those that are raised in the attempt to increase operating efficiency. They relate, for the most part, to the highly sensitive and delicate function of exercising police authority. Their solution, difficult as it may be, is essential if the police are to achieve a system of law enforcement that is not only efficient, but also fair and effective. The degree to which the police succeed in meeting these latter objectives will determine, in the long run, the strength of the law enforcement function in our democratic society.

The Nature of the Police Function

The most acute problems confronting the police do not receive the kind of attention that they deserve from persons outside police agencies because of a common lack of understanding of the true nature of the police task. Police officers are daily engaged in handling a wide variety of complex situations, but the nature of such situations is rarely communicated to those outside the police establishment. If the police were to analyze their workload in a systematic manner and to make public the results of their findings, it is likely that several of the most widespread notions regarding the police function would be dispelled.

One common assumption is that the police are primarily engaged in activities relating to the prevention of serious crime and the apprehension and prosecution of criminals. Actually, only a small percentage of the time which an average police officer spends on duty is directly related to the handling of serious offenses. This is especially true in small jurisdictions where few crimes occur. But it is equally true in the most congested areas of our large cities where high crime rates are experienced; for, even in such areas, a police officer, during a typical tour of duty, is occupied with a variety of tasks that are unrelated to the crime problem: assisting the aged and the mentally ill; locating missing persons; providing emergency medical services; mediating disputes between husbands and wives, landlords and tenants, or merchants and their customers; caring for neglected children; providing information about various governmental services and processes; regulating traffic; investigating accidents; and protecting the rights of individuals to live where they want to live and say what they want to say.[2]

Another popular misconception is that the police are a ministerial agency, having no discretion in the exercise of their authority. While this view is occasionally reinforced by a court decision,[3] there is a growing body of literature that cites the degree to which the police are, in fact, required to exercise discretion—such as in deciding which laws to enforce, in selecting from among available techniques for investigating crime, in deciding whom to arrest, and in determining how to process a criminal offender.[4] Broad and oftentimes ambiguous statutes defining their power and the limited resources made available to them are the major factors among several that require the police to assume such a discretionary role.

A third widespread notion regarding the police function is that the primary authority available to and used by the police is that of invoking the criminal process—that is, arresting a person for the purpose of prosecuting for having committed a crime. However, for every time that a police officer arrests a person, disposition of scores of incidents has been accomplished by employing a lesser form of authority, such as ordering people to "move on," turning children over to their parents, or separating combatants. Furthermore, when an officer does decide to make an arrest, it is not always with the intention of prosecuting the individual; rather it may be for the much more limited purpose of safeguarding the arrestee or

---

2. While it is rare for police agencies to articulate this range of functions, it is even rarer for them to respond directly to such functions in a structured manner. For an interesting example of the latter, see Winston-Salem, N.C. Police Department, *A New Approach to Crime Prevention and Community Service* (mimeo., 1966).

3. See, for example, *Bargain City, U.S.A., Inc. v. Dilworth*, 407 Pa. 129, 179 A.2d 439 (1960); *State v. Lombardi*, 8 Wis. 2d 421, 99 N.W.2d 829 (1959).

4. See, for example, Banton, *The Policeman in the Community*, pp.131-46 (1964); LaFave, *Arrest*, pp. 61-161, 490-527 (1965); Skolnick, *Justice Without Trial*, pp. 71-88 (1966); Abernathy, "Police Discretion and Equal Protection," 14 *S.C.L.O.* 472 (1962); Breitel, "Controls in Criminal Law Enforcement," 27 *U. Chi. L. Rev.* 427 (1960); H. Goldstein, "Police Discretion: The Ideal Versus the Real," 23 *Pub. Admin. Rev.* 140 (1963); J. Goldstein, "Police Discretion Not To Invoke the Criminal Process: Low Visibility Decisions in the Administration of Justice," 69 *Yale L. J.* 543 (1960); Kadish, "Legal Norm and Discretion in the Police and Sentencing Processes," 75 *Harv. L. Rev.* 904 (1962); LaFave, "The Police and Nonenforcement of the Law" (pts. 1-2), 1962 *Wis. L. Rev.* 104, 179; Remington, "The Role of Police in a Democratic Society," 56 *J. Crim. L.C. & P.S.* 361 (1965); Remington & Rosenblum, "The Criminal Law and the Legislative Process," 1960 *U. Ill. L.F.* 481.

controlling a given type of criminal activity, such as prostitution or gambling.[5]

Finally, it is widely believed that, in the investigation of criminal activity and especially in the identification of offenders, police officers depend primarily upon physical evidence that is subject to scientific analysis. Admittedly, collection and analysis of physical evidence does constitute an important facet of police work; in some cases, it holds the key to identification and is the factor upon which the value of all other evidence depends. But, in the vast majority of cases, the analysis of physical evidence, to the extent that there is any, is merely supportive of evidence acquired through some other means. Despite the major and often fascinating advances that have been made in the scientific detection of crime, primary dependence is still placed upon the work of detectives who, once a crime has been committed, set out in search of motives and bits and pieces of information from victims, witnesses, and various other persons who might have some knowledge that will contribute to the identification of the perpetrator of the crime. It is often a rather tedious and undramatic process that depends, for its success, upon the resourcefulness and perseverance of the investigating officers. Involved in the typical investigative effort are such important practices as the questioning of individuals, the search of private premises, the use of informants, and, in some cases, the employment of a variety of "undercover" techniques to acquire firsthand knowledge of criminal activity.

Absence of Adequate Guidelines

One of the consequences of recognizing the true nature of police activities is that one realizes there are vast areas of the police function which, in the absence of adequate legislative guidelines, are left to the discretion of individual officers. Moreover, even when existing laws are clearly applicable, the police are often required to select from among the various alternative forms of action which exist within the outer limits of the authority prescribed by such laws.

There have been some isolated efforts on the part of the police to fill this gap by providing more detailed guidance for the day-to-day work of their personnel. Such efforts have related primarily to traffic enforcement techniques and the handling of juvenile offenders.[6] The overall picture,

---

5. LaFave, "Arrest," pp. 437-89.

6. In the area of traffic enforcement, a number of jurisdictions have developed "tolerance policies" which establish the point above the speed limit at which officers are to warn a motorist or issue a summons to him. Some also provide criteria for making similar decisions with regard to other types of motor vehicle violations. Such policies are most frequently promulgated by state police organizations, and they demonstrate that a need is felt for providing guidelines for the isolated officer who cannot frequently consult with his supervisor or fellow officers. They also reflect a desire on the part of administrators to achieve uniformity in the overall operations of the agency.

however, reflects a reluctance on the part of police administrators to establish policies to fill the existing void. This reluctance is in sharp contrast to the strong tradition within police agencies for promulgating a variety of standard operating procedures to govern the internal management of the police force. The difference in attitude appears to be attributable largely to the real doubts possessed by the police as to the propriety of their assuming a policy-making role that so closely parallels the legislative function.[7]

Confronted each day by frequently recurring situations for which no guidance is provided, each officer either develops their own informal criteria for disposing of matters which come to his attention—a kind of pattern of improvisation—or employs informal criteria which have, over a period of years, developed within the agency of which he is a part. While such criteria are neither articulated nor officially recognized, they tend to take on some of the characteristics of officially promulgated policies. Functioning in this manner and employing their own imagination and resourcefulness, individual police officers often succeed to an amazing degree in muddling their way through: disputes are resolved; dangerous persons are disarmed; people not in control of their capacities are protected; and many individuals are spared what, under some circumstances, would appear to be the undue harshness of the criminal process. Unfortunately, the results are often less satisfactory, primarily because the criteria that are employed emerge largely in response to a variety of pressures to which the police are exposed and are therefore not carefully developed. For example, the high volume of work which an officer must handle dictates a desire to take shortcuts in the processing of minor incidents. The personal conveniences of an officer—in making a court appearance, completing reports, or working beyond a scheduled tour of duty—become important determinants of how a case is handled. The desire to solve crime becomes a dominant consideration.[8] And such indefensible criteria as the status or characteristics of the complainant, the victim, or the offender may often be among the most seriously weighed factors, since an officer, left to function alone, understandably tends to respond to a given situation on the basis of personal norms regarding individual or group behavior.

Continuation of current practices, which can perhaps best be characterized as a process of "drift," is clearly not in the interest of effective law enforcement. The potential for arbitrariness inherent in an uncontrolled exercise of discretion is clearly inconsistent with the objective of fairness that constitutes so basic an element in the exercise of any form

---

7. For a more detailed discussion of this point, see President's Commission on Law Enforcement and Administration of Justice, *Task Force Report: The Police*, Ch. 2 (1967).

8. This factor is explored in some detail in Skolnick, *Justice Without Trial*, pp. 164-81 (1966).

of governmental power. Nor are current practices desirable from the police standpoint; in the absence of guidelines, police officials are continually vulnerable to criticism for the manner in which an officer chooses to exercise discretion. They are "damned if they do and damned if they don't." Police administrators, moreover, are without an effective means for controlling the behavior of individual officers. Thus, since effective restraints are lacking, incidents tend to arise that prompt legislatures and courts to step in and take actions which often have repercussions—in the form of curtailment of police powers—far beyond the specific situation that initially served to arouse their interests.

There is an obvious need for some procedure by which an individual police officer can be provided with more detailed guidance to help decide upon the action to be taken in dealing with the wide range of situations met and in exercising the broad authority received. Viewed in somewhat different terms, the challenge is to devise procedures which will result in police officers employing norms acceptable to society, rather than their personal norms, in their exercise of discretion.

Alternative Solutions

There is no single way in which the existing policy vacuum can be filled, nor is it likely or desirable that it can be filled in its entirety.[9] But the width of the existing gap—especially as one views the functioning of the police in our large urban centers—affords ample opportunity for reducing its size.

The police are accustomed to looking toward the legislature and the courts for their guidance. There has, in recent years, been a special focus upon the latter since the appellate courts have undertaken to establish, with increasing specificity, the rules of constitutional, procedural due process.[10] Such judicial activity, especially that of the Supreme Court, has been viewed by one commentator as an action of "desperation," taken because of default on the part of others to fill the existing vacuum.[11] It has been argued that the Court, in taking on this rule-making function, has assumed an uncomfortable role which it is not equipped to fulfill and which constitutes, at best, an awkward and somewhat ineffective process for hammering out detailed rules of criminal procedure.[12] Among the ma-

---

9. Banton observes that the only long-term solution to the problem of police discretion is for the police and the public to share the same norms of propriety. Banton, *The Police and the Community*, p. 146 (1966).

10. The most specific rules are found in *Miranda v. Arizona*, 384 U.S. 436 (1966).

11. Packer, "Policing the Police: Nine Men Are Not Enough," *New Republic*, September 4, 1965, p. 19.

12. Ibid., p. 18. See also Friendly, "The Bill of Rights as a Code of Criminal Procedure," 53 *Calif. L. Rev.* 929 (1965); Packer, "Who Can Police the Police?" *The N.Y. Rev. of Books*, September 8, 1966, p. 10.

jor liabilities which are cited with respect to this approach are the breadth and especially the rigidity of the Court's holdings. In addition, in evaluating the courts as a source of guidance, it must be recognized that many of the most important and perplexing problems encountered by the police never become the subject of court proceedings.

Traditionally, both federal and state legislatures have restricted themselves to providing the police with a minimum set of broadly stated guidelines covering the major elements in criminal procedure.[13] They are often cited as the logical branch of government to remedy the need for additional guidelines since they have the capacity to explore problems on their own initiative, to gather facts, to elicit public opinion, and to act in a manner which is subject to later adjustment.[14] The proposal of the American Law Institute, embodied in its Model Code of Pre-Arraignment Procedure, represented an effort to move in this direction, incorporating, as it did, detailed legislative guidelines for police activity during the period from investigation and arrest to the time the suspect is presentenced in court.[15] In at least one major area covered by the Model Code, however, the opportunity for careful legislative consideration has since been significantly restricted by the Supreme Court's action in *Miranda v. Arizona*.

Even if legislatures become active in spelling out guidelines for the police, it must be recognized that there are now, and presumably always will be, many areas—particularly as one gets closer to the day-to-day problems encountered by the police—in which it is neither feasible nor desirable for the legislature to prescribe specific police practices. Variations in the size of police jurisdictions within a state, changing social conditions, and variations in the nature of the police function, among other factors, require that there be room for administrative flexibility. It seems apparent that the infinite variety of complex situations which confront the police today makes it essential that the most detailed and specific policies for handling them be formulated at the level closest to that at which they arise.

In light of the above considerations, it seems reasonable that, within legislative boundaries that may in some areas be more detailed than those which now exist, the police themselves be given the responsibility for formulating policies which will serve as guidelines in their effort to achieve effectiveness and fairness in their day-to-day operations, and that there be an explicit recognition by the legislatures of the necessity and desirability

---

13. See LaFave, "Improving Police Performance Through the Exclusionary Rule—Part II: Defining the Norms and Training the Police," 30 *Mo. L. Rev.* 566, 568-79 (1965); Remington & Rosenblum, "The Criminal Law and the Legislative Process," 1960 *U. Ill. L.F.* 481.

14. See Packer, "Policing the Police," pp. 20-21.

15. Ali, "A Model Code of Pre-Arraignment Procedure," (Tent. Draft No. 1, 1966).

of the police operating as an administrative policy-making agency of government. Obviously, such police-made policies would be subject to challenge if they were not consistent with the general legislative purpose or with such legislative criteria as are provided to guide and control the exercise of administrative discretion. Subject to appropriate review and control, the exercise of administrative discretion in this manner is likely to be more protective of basic rights than the routine, uncritical application by police of laws which are often necessarily vague or overgeneralized in their language.

Police participation in the development of policies to fill the existing vacuum and to cope with rapidly changing social and behavioral conditions would be a valuable contribution to the operation of police agencies, to the professionalization of the police, and to the overall functioning of the criminal justice system. Some of the specific advantages are set forth in detail below.

The Maintenance of Administrative Flexibility

The police have always had a great deal of flexibility in their operations, but this has been primarily as a result of legislative default rather than of deliberate, overt legislative choice. The traditional legislative response with respect to difficult issues like the control of gambling activities or the stopping and questioning of suspects has been either to deal with them by means of an overly generalized statute, as is true with respect to gambling activities, or not to deal with them at all, which has been true, at least until recently, with respect to stopping and questioning suspects. The practical consequence has been to leave police with broad flexibility, but the delegation of responsibility has been implicit at best and police have not taken it as a mandate to develop and articulate proper enforcement policies. The action of appellate courts in setting down increasingly specific rules to govern police conduct is partly a result of this failure. This trend toward judge-made rules is inspired in large part by a prevalent assumption that police are unwilling or unable to develop proper policies and to conform their practices to such policies. The police, by assuming responsibility for the development of appropriate administrative policies, will have the opportunity to reverse the trend and, as a consequence, to preserve the flexibility which they need if they are to meet adequately the wide range of problems which they confront under constantly changing conditions.

A Sound Basis for the Exercise of Discretion

The formulation of administrative policies affords the police an opportunity to establish sound grounds for the exercise of their discretion. Careful analysis of existing practices, which is a necessary step in the formulation of policies, should result in the exposure and rejection of those considerations which, according to standards of fairness and effectiveness, are inappropriate. Development of defensible criteria would, in addition, afford an opportunity to incorporate into police decision-making considerations that are based upon existing knowledge regarding the various forms of behavior with which the police are concerned. In the long run, the exercise of discretion in accordance with defensible criteria would create greater confidence in the police establishment. More immediately, it would lead to a reduction in the number of arbitrary actions taken by individual officers, thereby substantially reducing the tensions which such actions often create—particularly in areas in which minority groups are affected.

Acknowledgment of the "Risk Factor" Involved in Policing

Numerous factors contribute to the defensive posture commonly assumed by the police. Among them is an awareness on their part that members of the public will often question their exercise of discretion in a case in which subsequent developments focus attention upon an officer's decision. For example, a police officer may locate one under-age youth in a group of young people engaged in a drinking party. The fact that the youth is only one month under age may prompt the officer to release him with a warning. However, if the youth subsequently becomes involved in a serious accident, the fact that he was released earlier in the evening will often result in the officer's being castigated by a superior, because the officer has no publicly-acknowledged right to exercise discretion although all agree that it is both necessary and desirable.

Given the wide range of responsibilities that the police have, they cannot be held to a system of decision-making which involves no risk-taking—any more than could psychiatrists in deciding whether to release a person who has attempted suicide or parole board members in voting upon the release of an inmate. The formulation of policy and its articulation to the public would, over a period of time, begin to educate the public to recognize that the police must not only exercise discretion, but must also assume a risk in doing so. Prior statements of policy which "put the community on notice" with regard to police functioning in various areas would afford some relief from the current dilemma in which, in the absence of such policy formulations, the police are subject to both ridicule for not exercising discretion and condemnation for making discretionary judgments when they do not work out.

A Means for Utilizing Police Expertise

Many actions that the police officer takes are based upon the knowledge and experience accumulated in years of service. In concluding that a crime is being committed, an officer may reach a judgment quite different from that which would be reached by an inexperienced layman or even an experienced trial judge, since the officer may have, for example, the ability to recognize the smell of narcotics or the sound of a press used in printing illegal numbers or policy tickets. There has, however, been little effort made to capitalize upon police experience. In order to do so, the police would necessarily have to attempt to assess its reliability; they would have to distinguish accurate inferences (such as, the sound is that of a gambler's printing press) from inaccurate or improper ones (such as, Negroes are immoral). It would also be necessary for the police to systemize their experience so that it can be effectively communicated to new officers through training programs and to others, like judges, when the propriety of police actions is challenged. To the extent that operating criteria reflect police experience, the police are afforded a vehicle in the policy-making process for articulating their expertise.

More Effective Administrative Control Over Police Behavior

While the actions of an individual officer may appear on the surface to be improper, there is often no basis on which a superior can take disciplinary action against him, since the conduct violated neither the law nor any existing departmental policies. In such a situation, the police administrator is caught in a conflict between his desire to be responsive to a citizen who has reason to complain about a policeman's behavior and the fear concerning the reaction of the force to seemingly arbitrary discipline where there is no clear breach of a pre-announced standard of proper conduct.

The reluctance to characterize an officer's conduct as unwise is increased when the administrator feels that to do so will result in either the officer or the municipality being sued for damages. Consideration of this possibility may force the administrator into the position of defending a given action as legal, and thus seemingly "proper," even though it reflected poor judgment on the part of the officer. To minimize the likelihood of similar situations arising in the future, the administrator may urge subordinates to use "common sense," but such a request is of little value unless what is meant by "common sense" can be spelled out precisely.

The promulgation of policies to which police officers are required by regulation to adhere would provide a basis for disciplining those who violate such policies. But, more important, it would serve in a positive way to inform members of a force what is expected of them. Progress in elevating the quality of law enforcement is much more likely to be realized if one views clear and defensible standards as a basis for eliciting a proper response from police officers, rather than considering such standards primarily as the basis for the taking of disciplinary actions against police officers.

The Improvement of Recruit and In-Service Training Programs

Recruit training in police agencies is frequently inadequate because the instruction bears little relationship to what is expected of the officer when working in the field. In the absence of guidelines that relate to an analysis of police experience, the instructor usually is left with only the formal definition of police authority to communicate to the trainee, and this is often transmitted to the student merely by the reading of statutory definitions. Students are taught that all laws are to be fully enforced. The exercise of police authority is similarly taught in doctrinaire fashion. With this kind of formal training, the new officer finds, upon assignment to the field, the necessity of acquiring from the more experienced officers a knowledge of all the patterns of accommodations and modifications. As an awareness emerges of the impracticality and lack of realism of much of what was learned as a student, the recruit unfortunately begins to question the validity of all aspects of formal training.

Obviously, there is a need for training more directly related to the important problems which the officer will face in the field—training which will not only show the limits of his formal authority, but also express the department's judgment as to what is the most desirable administrative practice to follow in exercising authority. Carefully developed administrative policies would serve this important function.

A Basis for the Professionalization of the Police

It is now commonplace to refer to practically any effort that is aimed at improving law enforcement as a contribution to the professionalization of the police. Thus, improved training, application of the computer to police work, adoption of a code of ethics, and increased salaries have all, at one time or another, been cited as contributing to police professionalization.

Certainly, there is much that police do today that would not, under any definition of the term, be viewed as constituting professional work. Directing traffic at a street intersection or enforcing parking restrictions requires stamina, but little knowledge. In sharp contrast to these functions, however, are the responsibilities of a patrolman assigned to police a congested area in which numerous crimes occur; being called upon to make highly sophisticated judgments having a major impact upon the lives of the individuals involved. Such judgments are not mechanical in nature, but rather are every bit as complicated and difficult to make as are the decisions made by any of the behavioral scientists, and in many instances they are more difficult because they must be made under the pressure of the immediate circumstances.

Development of criteria for dealing with such complex social and behavioral problems will require extensive research, the systematizing of experience and knowledge, and continual testing of the validity of the assumptions and findings upon which the criteria are based. The formulation of such criteria will also require adherence to values relating to the role of the police and law enforcement in a democratic society that are more basic than those values which are involved in a consideration of technical operating efficiency. The making of judgments based upon criteria that are formulated pursuant to extensive experience, research, and experimentation together with a commitment to values that reflect a sense of responsibility to society constitute important elements in the development of a true profession.

A Method for Involving the Police in the Improvement of the System of which They are a Part

Decisions relating to the enforcement function have traditionally been made for the police by persons outside the police establishment. The police have typically not even been consulted when changes have been contemplated in the substantive or procedural criminal law, despite the fact they clearly have more experience than anyone else in dealing with some of the basic issues. Failure to involve the police in most revision projects is probably due to the fact that police personnel are not considered qualified to deal with the complicated questions involved. But, if it is true that police lack the necessary skill to participate in such efforts, this lack of ability is in large measure attributable to the fact that in the past they have not been involved in the making of important decisions.

There is, today, a strong commitment to the involvement of disadvantaged groups, like the poor and the young, in decisions about their roles in society. This commitment is based on the belief that they will respond most affirmatively if they have a feeling of participation in such decisions. The same need is apparent with respect to the police, for, in this sense at least, they also are a disadvantaged group. Law enforcement personnel are more likely to want to conform and are more likely to develop an ability to conform if they are made a part of the process for making important decisions affecting their function.

Practically every aspect of police functioning gives rise to important and sensitive issues of a kind which can and should be dealt with through the careful and systematic development of policies by a law enforcement agency. The following are merely illustrative of the types of functions that are in need of attention, the difficult issues to which they give rise, and the importance of facing up to them.

The Decision Whether to Invoke the Criminal Process

Whether a criminal prosecution is initiated against an individual depends, in most instances, upon police judgment. Theoretically, this judgment is based upon the statutory definition of the crime, although it is abundantly clear that there are many situations in which a violation has in fact occurred and is known to the police, but in which there is no effort by the police to make an arrest. Among the factors accounting for this discretionary decision not to invoke the criminal process are the volume of violations of a similar nature, the limited resources of the police, the overgeneralization of legislative enactments defining criminal conduct, and the various local pressures reflecting community values and attitudes.

The social gambling situation affords a good example of the dilemma which the police face. In most jurisdictions, all forms of gambling are illegal. Yet it is apparent that legislatures neither intend nor expect that such statutes be fully enforced. The consequence is that local police are left with the responsibility for developing an enforcement policy for their particular community. The policy of a department may, for example, be clear, albeit unwritten, that games of chance at church carnivals will be permitted because of their charitable nature.[16] However, in the same community, the police response to gambling in a private home may vary with the circumstances of the individual case. Whether the police take enforcement action may depend on the answers they obtain to several key questions: Is there a complainant and, if so, is he adversely affected by the gambling activity; is the gambling the prime purpose for the group's getting together or is it incidental to some other activity or pastime; is the activity organized; do the participants know each other; were they steered to the location for purposes of engaging in gambling or is the assemblage a get-together of old friends; what is the amount of money involved; and is there a profit separate from winnings being realized by the individual hosting the activity or by any of the individuals present? The existence of any one of these factors will not necessarily result in an arrest, but the police usually will take action when there is an insistent complainant or when a combination of factors suggests that the gambling activity is commercial in nature. The difficulty is that the employment of such criteria by individual officers may lead to disparity in practice and, even where practice is consistent, may involve basic policy questions which are not raised and thus not considered or resolved./ Complaints may originate from neighbors who are disturbed by the noise or from wives who are either concerned over the monetary losses of their spouses or resent their absence from home. Should a police agency allow itself to be "used"

---

16. For an interesting case study growing out of an unarticulated policy of nonenforcement against bingo in churches and synagogues, see Logue & Bock, *The Demotion of Deputy Chief Inspector Goldberg* (Inter-University Case Program, No. 78) (1963).

under such conditions? Does the fact that enforcement takes place only when there is an insistent complainant constitute a desirable pattern of action?

The tests used in practice to determine whether the game is "commercial" rather than "social" also raise important policy questions which have not been resolved. Social gambling in a slum area assumes a different form than does social gambling in a middle-class neighborhood: a number of men commonly get together in a private apartment, placing comparatively small bets on a dice game. Such activity is endemic to such an area. When the police investigate such games they typically find that the participants cannot identify each other. The gambling is therefore viewed as not being "social" and thus is considered properly subject to enforcement. Yet, considering the pattern of life in such an area, is there any reason to characterize this behavior as more reprehensible than that engaged in by a group of men involved in a poker game for some financial stakes at a local country club? Pursuant to present practices, the participants in the dice game will generally be arrested, searched, transported to a lock-up, detained overnight, and brought before a judge the following morning. The net effect of such actions for the police seems obvious: relationships with the residents of the area, which typically are already very strained, are further aggravated.

The police action with regard to the dice game in the slum area is often in response to complaints from neighbors who are disturbed by the game. It may also be a response to the general police concern, based on prior experiences, that dice games in such areas frequently end in fights, which in turn sometimes result in homicides. Intervention by the police therefore is viewed as serving a crime prevention function. But neither the attitude of the community nor the relationship of the dice game to more serious crime is studied and evaluated. As a consequence, the current police practice gives the appearance of being the product of improper class or racial discrimination.

The police treatment of aggravated assaults raises issues of a different character. This type of offense comes to police attention more routinely because it frequently occurs in public, the victim or witnesses seek out the police, there is a desire for police intervention before more harm is done, or simply because the victim desires police assistance in acquiring medical aid. Even though the perpetrator is known to the victim in a high percentage of these cases, however, there frequently is no arrest or, if an arrest is made, it may be followed by release without prosecution. This is especially true in the slum areas of large urban centers and is due primarily to an unwillingness on the part of the victim to cooperate in a prosecution.

If the parties involved are related or are close friends, the victim is frequently unwilling to establish the identity of the assailant, attend show-ups, view photographs, or even answer questions truthfully. If the victim does cooperate at the investigation stage, he may still refuse to testify at trial and may even express a desire that the assaulting relative or acquaintance be set free. Due to the frustrations police officers have experienced in handling such cases, they often take less than the expected degree of interest in pursuing a prosecution when there is any early indication of reluctance on the part of the victim to participate in the prosecution. In some jurisdictions, the accumulated police experience results in an early decision not to prosecute and, in some cases, not to arrest.

It would be possible for the police to prosecute more frequently those persons who commit assaults by resorting to the issuance of a subpoena to compel the attendance of the victim at trial, assuming the judge would be willing to compel the victim to testify. This procedure, however, is seldom used. Given the high volume of cases and the competing demands upon a police agency, the path of least resistance is to acquiesce in the desires of the victim. Such acquiescence is often rationalized on the ground that the injured party was the only person harmed and the community as a whole was not affected by the crime. These cases can be written off statistically as clearances—which are viewed as an index of police efficiency—and thus the most immediate administrative pressure is satisfied.

There is some question about the relationship between current police practice in slum assault cases on the one hand, and the amount of crime and the community's attitude toward police on the other. If the criminal justice process has some deterrent value, why would it not deter assaultive behavior in the slum area? To what degree does an awareness of the attitude of the police toward assaultive conduct result in the formulation of negative attitudes on the part of slum residents toward law and order in general? What is the impact upon the residents of such an area when an attack by a slum resident upon a person residing outside the area results in a vigorous prosecution?

Today, these and other basic policy questions which can be raised are not dealt with by the police. Routine practices are not examined in the light of overall enforcement goals and, as a consequence, may very well serve to complicate rather than solve important social problems. Were the police to review their current practices, they might well conclude that, insofar as assaults, for example, are concerned, it is desirable to base police decisions to arrest on such criteria as the nature of the assault, the seriousness of the injury, and the prior record of the assailant, rather than primarily on the degree to which the victim is willing to cooperate.

Selection of Investigative Methods

In the past few years, increasing attention has been given by legislatures and particularly by courts to the propriety of current police detection and investigation methods.[17] Nevertheless, there remain many areas in which the determination as to the investigative technique to be used is left to the police. For example, neither legislatures nor courts have yet reflected much concern with the propriety of police use of "undercover" or "infiltration" techniques, surveillance, or other methods which afford an alleged offender an opportunity to commit a crime in a manner which will make evidence of his offense available to the police. If the present trend toward judicial rule-making continues, it is not at all unlikely that current investigative practices thought by police to be proper and effective will be subject to increasingly specific rules. This has already occurred with respect to in-custody investigation, which is now specifically controlled by the *Miranda* decision. Whether this will occur with respect to other police practices will depend in large measure upon whether the police can develop policies which differentiate the proper from the improper use of particular investigative practices and can see to it that improper methods are not used as a matter of informal departmental policy or by individual officers out of either ignorance or excessive zeal.

Field interrogation is illustrative of important police investigative techniques which may or may not survive attack. Police have generally argued that their right to stop and question people is essential, especially with respect to those persons who are observed in an area in which a crime has just been committed. With several exceptions, however, there has been little effort made to provide individual officers with carefully developed guidelines so as to assure that such interrogation is sparingly and carefully employed under conditions that justify its use.

The use of field interrogation as an investigative technique is complicated by the fact that it is a part of the total preventive patrol program—which is a current response by police in large cities to the demand that the "streets be made safe." Preventive patrol often involves stopping persons using the streets in high-crime areas and making searches of both persons and vehicles. The purpose of this technique is not only to talk with individuals who may be suspected of having recently committed crimes but, more broadly, to find and confiscate dangerous weapons and to create an atmosphere of police omnipresence which will dissuade persons from attempting to commit crimes because of the likelihood of their being detected and apprehended.

It is probably true that a program of preventive patrol does reduce the amount of crime on the street, although there has been no careful effort to measure its effectiveness. It is also apparent, however, that some of the practices included in a preventive patrol program contribute to the an-

---

17. The extent to which legislatures and courts have addressed themselves to three specific areas of police investigation—the conduct of searches, the use of "encouragement," and the stopping and questioning of suspects—is explored in McIntyre, Teffany & Rotenberg, *Detection of Crime*, 1967.

tagonism toward the police felt by minority groups whose members are subjected to them. A basic issue, never dealt with explicitly by police, is whether, even from a purely law enforcement point of view, the gain in enforcement outweighs the cost of community alienation.

The continuation of field interrogation as a police investigative technique depends upon whether the police are willing to develop policies which carefully distinguish field interrogation from street practices which are clearly illegal and to take administrative steps to demonstrate that a proper field interrogation program can be carried out without it leading also to an indiscriminate stopping and searching of persons.

The Decision Not To Prosecute Individuals Who Have Been Arrested

While in some states it is the practice to take all arrested individuals before a judge, it is standard procedure in others for the police to release some individuals prior to their scheduled court appearance. Drunkards are often given their freedom once they are sober; juveniles are often released after consultation with parents or a social service agency; and in large urban areas, narcotic addicts and small-time peddlers are often released with a grant of immunity in exchange for information leading to the arrest of more serious violators.

Where it is the practice to release some drunkards without charging them, eligibility for release tends to be based upon such factors as appearance, dress, reputation, place of residence, and family ties. The process is generally intended to separate the common drunkard from the intoxicated person who "knows better" but, in the judgment of the police, simply had "one too many." Whether this kind of distinction adequately serves an enforcement or social welfare objective is not entirely clear. Certainly police, who are daily confronted with the problem of the drunkard, ought to give continuing attention to whether defensible criteria are being employed and, perhaps more important, ought to lend support to and participate in an effort to develop ways of dealing with the alcoholic which are more sensible than the current arrest and release programs.

Criteria have been formulated in some communities to assist police in deciding whether a juvenile offender should be released to parents, referred to a social agency, or brought before the juvenile court.[18] In other communities, however, such decisions continue to be made by the police without an articulated basis and the decisions often reflect the use of such

---

18. See, for example, Chicago Police Department, Youth Division, *Manual of Procedure* (1965).

indefensible criteria as the child's color, attitude toward the police, or parental status in the community.[19]

The practice of releasing some narcotic addicts and peddlers in exchange for information or cooperation raises other complex issues. Persons involved in narcotics control assume that the investigation of narcotics traffic requires the accumulation of knowledge from those who are involved in the distribution or use of such contraband and that convictions cannot be obtained without the help of informants who cooperate in return for immunity. The potential for abuse in pursuing this practice makes it critically important that the standards for extending an offer for immunity and for measuring cooperation be uniformly and fairly applied. There is, moreover, a need for continual evaluation of the practice to determine whether the gain derived from it really justifies the costs which are involved.

The Issuance of Orders to Individuals Regarding Their Movements, Activities, and Whereabouts

The public, whether as pedestrians or motorists, generally recognizes the authority of the police to direct their movements in traffic. There are many other situations, however, in which police regularly tell people what to do under circumstances where police authority is less clear. For example, police order people to "keep the noise down" or to stop quarreling—usually in response to a complaint from a neighbor; direct a husband to stay away from his wife when they have had a fight; order a young child found on the streets at night to go home; order troublesome "characters" to stay out of a given area; and tell persons congregated on street corners to disperse.

Police generally assume that congregating on a street corner is likely to give rise to disorderly conduct, especially if such assembling takes place outside of a tavern, if those assembled are intoxicated to varying degrees, and if there is heavy pedestrian traffic which is likely to be blocked by the congregating group. The technique ordinarily used by police in such a situation is to order the persons to "move on," thus presumably minimizing the risk of a group disturbance. There is a tendency, however, for this technique to become standard operating procedure as applied to all groups that congregate on sidewalks and street corners, without regard to the varying character of the groups. For example, in some cultural

---

19. See, for example, Piliavin & Briar, "Police Encounters With Juveniles," 70 *Am. J. Sociology* 206 (1964); Goldman & Nathan, *The Differential Selection of Juvenile Offenders for Court Appearance*, in National Research and Information Center, National Council on Crime and Delinquency (1963). For an overall view of the police function in the juvenile process, see Wheeler & Cottrell, *Juvenile Delinquency: Its Prevention and Control*, 28-31 (1966).

groups, congregating on the streets is the most common form of socializ-
ing; and in some congested areas of a city, the corner is used because of
the absence of adequate public recreational facilities. For police to respond to these situations in the same manner as they respond to the situation involving an intoxicated group outside a tavern may not serve any
real enforcement objective and may instead strain the relationship between the police and the residents of those areas in which the street corner
is the place of social and recreational activity.

The practice of ordering people to "move on" is one which has major
implications and warrants more careful use. In confronting the question
of what should be their proper policy in dealing with congregating
groups, the police would have an opportunity to give attention to why
groups congregate, to distinguish those congregations which create risk of
serious disorder from those which do not, and to relate police work to
other community programs designed to create positive social and recreational opportunities for persons who now lack these opportunities.

The Settling of Disputes

A substantial amount of the on-duty time of police officers is devoted to
the handling of minor disputes between husbands and wives, neighbors,
landlords and tenants, merchants and customers, and taxicab drivers and
their riders. Relatively little importance is attached to the handling of
such matters by police administrators, particularly those in large urban
areas. The patrolman who responds to the report of such a disturbance
may inform the parties of their right to initiate a prosecution, may undertake to effect a resolution of the dispute by ordering the parties to leave
each other alone (as, for example, by advising an intoxicated husband to
go to the movies), or may use some other form of on-the-scene counseling.
The approach taken in each case is a matter of choice on the part of the individual officer.

Important policy questions are raised with respect to the way the police
handle all disputes and, in particular, to the way they handle domestic
disturbances. Yet there has been no systematic effort made to measure the
results which may be obtained under the alternative methods which
police use, nor has there been an effort made to develop more adequate
referral resources (such as social agencies) which might, if they existed,
provide a basis for a positive police program for dealing with such
disputes. In an effort to develop adequate policies to guide the actions of
the individual patrolman, police agencies should compile several relevant
facts: how often the same families become involved in disturbances that
require police intervention; how often the husband or wife swears out a
complaint; the disposition of such cases and the impact that varying
dispositions have in preventing future disturbances; the number of serious

assaults or homicides which result from domestic disturbances and whether these follow a pattern which might enable a patrolman to identify a potentially dangerous situation; and the kinds of cases which can be referred with positive results to existing community resources for dealing with family problems.[20]

Through the process of careful evaluation of existing practices and experience, the police can acquire a competence which should enable them to develop more adequate follow-up procedures in the domestic disturbance case. This added competence should increase the value and effectiveness of the emergency intervention function of the police and should, in the long run, reduce the heavy burden that is presently placed on the police in dealing with this type of recurring social problem.

The Protection of the Right to Free Expression

None of the functions which the police perform illustrates the sensitive and unique role of the police in a democratic society as well as that which is involved in the safeguarding of the constitutional rights of free speech and assembly. Police frequently are called upon to provide adequate protection for a speaker or demonstrating group that wishes to exercise the right to express one's opinions—opinions that are often unpopular and which are often voiced in the presence of a hostile audience.

Many urban police agencies have not developed and formulated policies to guide police action in such situations. Although the issues involved in recent demonstrations reflect many factors which are beyond police control, it is nonetheless a fact that the manner in which police respond to demonstrations will determine, in large measure, whether violence will break out and, if it does, the degree to which the resulting conflict will escalate and spread.

The problem is a particularly difficult one because police officers may themselves identify more with maintaining order in their community, especially to prevent disorder created by outsiders, than with their basic responsibility to protect the right of free expression of social and political views. For example, the officer in a police district which consists of a white neighborhood may view a Negro march through the neighborhood in favor of open housing as a threat to both public order in the district and the values of the very people in the neighborhood upon whom the officer depends for support in his day-to-day work. In rural areas or small cities the population may be relatively homogeneous and thus the police officer can be responsive to all of the local citizens without this producing con-

---

20. The techniques that are used by police in handling domestic disturbances were the subject of a research project conducted with the cooperation of the Chicago Police Department by Raymond I. Parnas, a graduate student in criminal law at the University of Wisconsin.

flict. But a very real conflict may develop for the officer in a large urban area, since such areas are typically made up of communities which differ in economic, racial, religious, or other characteristics. The officer who protects the right of free expression of ideas may be protecting an attack upon the very segment of the community with which he identifies.

In order for the police to respond adequately and consistently in the highly tense situations which arise from political and social demonstrations, there obviously must be a careful effort on their part to work out, in advance, policies which will govern their actions. This development of policies must be coupled with an effort to communicate them to individual officers in a way which will give each officer a basis for identifying with the protection of freedom of expression as an important enforcement objective. In addition, an effort must be made to articulate such policies to the affected community so that the public will understand the reasoning behind police actions. This, in itself, can serve to lessen the likelihood of major disorders.

Implementation

Since police agencies do not presently have the capacity to fulfill the kind of policy-making role that has been outlined in this article, implementation of this program will require numerous adjustments in their existing procedures, orientation, and staffing. The nature of these requirements is discussed in detail elsewhere,[21] but their general character will be summarized here.

As a prerequisite, it will be necessary for the police to develop a systematic process for the identification and study of those aspects of their operations which are in need of attention. Police administrators must take the initiative in seeking out the problem areas by analyzing complaints, by observing the results of police activities as reflected in the courts, and by the various other procedures available for analyzing the functioning of their respective departments. It is essential that the police develop a research methodology for exploring the kinds of problems that are likely to be identified—a procedure that equips them to clarify issues, to identify alternatives, to obtain relevant facts, and to analyze these facts in a manner that provides a basis for the development of a departmental policy. The end product must include clearly articulated criteria that will serve as guidelines for police officers and that will be open to public view. Flexibility being one of the major values in administrative policy-making, it is important that provision be made for the periodic reconsideration of

---

21. See President's Commission on Law Enforcement and Administration of Justice, *Task Force Report: The Police*, Ch. 2 (1967). With specific reference to the need for controlling police conduct, see H. Goldstein, "Administrative Problems in Controlling the Exercise of Police Authority," 58 *J. Crim. L.C. & P.S.*, June 1967.

those policies which are adopted so that adjustments to new developments can be effected and corrections may be made of deficiencies which become apparent after functioning under existing policies.

A police agency which accepts policy-making responsibility must develop more adequate systems of control than now exist to assure compliance of its personnel with the policies adopted by its administrators. The agency must also expect and should welcome responsible outside review of such policies as a protection against arbitrary policy-making.

Numerous changes will be required in existing patterns of leadership, personnel selection, training, and organization in order to equip the police to fulfill adequately their broader responsibilities. It is important, for example, that police leaders be provided with an education that will allow them to grasp fully the unique function of the police in a democratic society and that will enable them to support the overriding values relating to individual liberty which often conflict with their attempt to achieve the goal of maximum efficiency in the arrest and successful prosecution of offenders. It is important also that patrolmen, in their training, be provided with a professional identification that is supportive of the proper role of the police and that aids in developing a willingness on their part to conform with administrative policies.

The progress realized in the law enforcement field in recent years, especially in the area of training and education, contributes significantly to achieving some of these objectives. Such efforts, however, have suffered for lack of an adequate definition of direction and purpose. The potential of current improvement programs would be vastly increased if those programs were related to the need for the police to develop their own capacity to formulate and implement law enforcement policies. Incorporating this requirement as an objective would serve to provide such programs with the kind of focus for which the need has long been apparent.

DISCRETION: THE ESSENCE
OF PROFESSIONALISM*

Police managers no longer live in a stable world of consistency. They now face almost endless and very rapid change.

Increased technology is producing changes. The economy is undergoing change. Society's norms are in flux. Court decisions are so inconsistent as to seem capricious. Our whole socio-political climate is undergoing important and often disquieting changes.

Police administrators are hard put to find the means to inject stability into their commands. And stability is necessary if we are to maintain a stable, peaceful society with a minimum of crime and social upheaval.

Yet, in the midst of this present instability, there is an area of police thought and action that remains surprisingly unchanged, amazingly untouched by the rapid fluctuations around us. One area of inflexible stability. That area is demonstrated in the consistency with which police steadfastly cling to the fable that they enforce the law—all of the laws—with impartiality, with neither fear nor favor and without the exercise of real, individual discretion by subordinates.

We seem convinced that purely objective, impartial, non-discretionary actions are wanted and required by the public we serve. Yet we all know full well that such ministerial, non-discretionary enforcement is impossible and always has been.

The simple fact is, police officers must make and do make literally millions of discretionary decisions every day, all across this land. We could not operate otherwise. A policy of full enforcement is both undesirable and unachievable.

Any casual observer who has ever been in a lawyer's office realizes that all those books cannot be memorized. Thus all laws cannot be fully enforced. The majority, in fact, are not even known by the police who hold responsibility for their enforcement.

A policy requiring police to enforce all statutes and all ordinances would mean an arrest for every arrestable violation— regardless of the wishes of the community, the intent of the legislature or the total ob-

---

* C.E. Pratt, "Discretion, the Essence of Professionalism," *Law and Order*, October 1981, pp. 46-50. Reprinted by permission.

solescence of the statute and despite the fact that no successful prosecution is probable and, if it were, that no sanction would result.

While nearly every police department publicly professes such a policy, the typical officer on the street exercises discretion by overlooking minor and insignificant violations. He opts for individual warning and advice where he feels it is warranted or would be more productive than an arrest. Holding an unenforced violation over an informant's head is often a means to gain his cooperation in catching "bigger fish."

These are discretionary decisions made daily in most police departments. They are necessary exercises of discretion if the officer is to do his job—if society is to be effectively served and if the jails and courts are not to be totally inundated with unproductive arrests.

Such decisions are the very essence of the exercise of professionalism by police.

As A.J. Reiss pointed out in his report "Discretionary Decision Making and Professionalism of the Police," "it appears that police exercise command in most situations largely through the exercise of the person in the role. The more 'professional' the person in that role, the more likely authority will be regarded as 'legitimate' and the more likely the officer will exercise authority legitimately."

A police officer must exercise authority with sufficient legitimacy and professionalism to withstand later review by peers, superiors and the courts and public.

Summoned into any situation the officer must quickly size up the affair and determine the proper action (or reaction)—totally based upon self-discretion. A series of discretionary judgments of major importance in the lives of others as well as the officers, are required.

Without discretion there can be little or no effective policing.

Police managers wanting to do a better job providing more and better service within reasonable financial restrictions, must recognize that discretion exists. They need to utilize its existence productively, to channel and manage it.

The police profession is unlike any other. They alone are authorized to use force against their fellow citizens. They must be prepared to use that force wisely and justly in a manner unlike any other group.

Reiss stated, "The teacher is faced with unwilling pupils, the psychiatrist with a resistant patient, and the judge with a hostile witness or defendant." They all turn to the police who must cope with any and all such clients, regardless of circumstances and on unfamiliar ground; often on the client's "turf" where the client is comfortable and the officer is not, where the client is relatively secure and the officer is "at risk."

It is remarkable that a police officer only occasionally makes the headlines with an indiscretion. Out of the millions of these decisions made daily, only a relative handful turn out wrong. It becomes even more amazing when we realize that the average police officer has only 12.4 years of education upon which to draw.

As good managers seeking the most of the best from traditionally inadequate resources, we should admit that individual discretion is at the heart of most of what we do. We should educate and inform the public so that they are consciously aware of it and can give their approval to it.

The reason those old ladies caught playing bingo weren't jailed should be stated. Why police gave a verbal warning of a traffic violation instead of an arrest, and the reason they elected to keep an errant husband out of jail in favor of counseling, should be told.

Let the public know that the police are serving them as wisely, as well and as economically as we know how. When we do well it is because we exercised discretion well. When we fall short, it is often because we exercised discretion poorly.

The public can and will understand, if we give them the truth. They will support us in what we are doing. If for no other reason than the simple fact that we—as the thin blue line—are all they have. But mostly because they believe in us and want to have faith in us.

After the importance of police discretion is recognized it can be channelled into a tremendous force. The petty rules and regulations restricting police to a traditional low efficiency can be reduced.

Those communities with a reduction in serious crime, with an increase in felony arrests and substantial recovery of property with reductions in armed robbery, are departments that allow and encourage the practice of discretion.

In a few cases this encouragement was a planned action, taken as one phase of a contemporary mode of management. In most cases, the "freeing up" of discretion has been ancillary to a change in management method, often a necessary outgrowth of a bigger program and coincidental to it.

August Vollmer realized the importance of individual discretion. He insisted upon personnel of a caliber suited to its exercise, and encouraged officers to exercise discretion.

Of course, there are those who argue that the open exercise of police discretion will produce abuses, corruption, bribes and all the other negatives that the press delights in reporting. But little exists to support such a notion.

Traditionally, we have stifled discretion and sought uniformity by creating and enforcing rules of procedure and codes of conduct. Ostensibly, this was meant to prevent police corruption and abuse.

Yet it is a widely accepted truth that the departments with the thickest rule books are the departments with the most corrupt histories and traditions.

We have produced gargantuan rule books with notoriously little success. Those who are corruptible will be corrupted. And they often employ rules compliance as a screen for their acts.

Kenneth C. Davis in his work on discretionary justice, points up the need for discretionary acts being brought into the open; being given recognition as both necessary and desirable by police and public.

Herman Goldstein and Egon Bittner—along with many others—have proposed the same "airing out" of this subject. Unfortunately, most of these learned writers go astray when, in final analysis, they suggest that as we allow freer exercise of and recognition of discretion, we must also provide rules of conduct for that exercise which are comprehensive and detailed, in order to assure that corruption is prevented.

Such an act would be tantamount to the elimination of discretion and would therefore be counterproductive.

Experience indicates that discretion should be exercised within clearly stated parameters or "outer limits" beyond which no officer may stray. Including—though not limited to—a clear statement of violations that must produce firm enforcement, violations that always require an arrest; the limits of prosecutorial and judicial tolerance; and the precise conditions when mortal force may be employed.

Those parameters should be "engraved on stone" and should be accompanied by a clearly stated philosophy. Rooted in that philosophy, wide latitude for the exercise of discretion should be permitted.

Supervision then becomes primarily a personnel selection process and an ongoing training process that will enable each individual to perform to maximum ability.

When an individual's exercise of discretion appears less than effective or seems to be straying too close to the "outer limits," instruction in better methods and better ways to exercise discretion to help fulfill the department's philosophy and the public's needs and desires may be instituted. In those rare instances where the opportunity so afforded is refused, the officer can be eliminated.

Such management methods have been a success. To cite one, a more than 50 percent reduction in targeted serious crimes and a sevenfold increase in successful case-closings during the first year of implementation was noted. A continued solid improvement followed over a four-year period.

August Vollmer started it many years ago, and proved its efficacy. Other police administrators have followed his lead with the very results that make them outstanding.

In view of the ever-increasing demands being made upon police it is apparent that managers must find better ways to cope; better methods by which to do more with shrinking assets. Allowing each officer to perform to the maximum—freed of needless, often outmoded and usually stressfully suffocating rules—may be the best path to follow.

If all of this is not sufficient, look at yet another valid reason for employment of individual discretion by officers.

Police officers frequently demand "professional" status. The public expects "professionalism" of us. There are many definitions of professionalism. One, however, stands out: a professional is one whose discretionary advice and guidance we accept due to his acknowledged expertise.

The very essence of professionalism is centered in our acceptance of guidance or advice based on knowledge and wisdom greater than our own. Which is, of course, precisely what the public does in dealing with police—voluntarily or otherwise.

The average citizen recognizes that the officer has access to special knowledge, special information; that he has the ability to make decisions based upon that knowledge and the authority to back those decisions with force, if needed. This is not vastly different from a doctor-patient relationship or a lawyer-client relationship. And it is all based upon discretion.

It is time that police practitioners recognize that discretion is a fact of life; that it is commonly practiced; that it is in fact the heart of most good police work.

Having recognized this, it is time we learned to control, guide and develop discretion as one of our most useful tools in providing more police service to an ever changing society.

Chapter 3
THE POLICE USE OF DEADLY FORCE

Introduction

A serious issue facing our society is the use of deadly force by police officers.[1] According to the Vital Statistics of the United States, police officers have killed an average of one person per day since 1970.[2] Furthermore, the ratio of police killed to police killing has remained approximately 1 to 5.[3]

At the same time, according to Kobler, police are the "only representatives of governmental authority who in the ordinary course of events are legally permitted to use physical force against a citizen." Other agencies of state power rely upon request, persuasion, public opinion, custody, and legal and judicial processes to gain compliance with rules and laws. Only the police can use firearms to compel the citizen to obey. The police are also in a special category in that they are sworn to enforce the law at all times, on or off duty in most jurisdictions, so that their access to firearms is constant and legal. The possibility of excessive use of firearms in the course of police duties and thus the power of life and death over the citizen is facilitated by the unique legal definition of the powers and responsibilities of the police in our society.[4]

Although a sizeable number of killings by police officers may be

---

1. National Institute of Law Enforcement and Criminal Justice, "Use of Deadly Force by Police Officers" (1979).
2. Larry Sherman, "Homicide by Police Officers: Social Forces and Public Policy," grant proposal (1977).
3. Arthur L. Kobler, "Police Homicide in a Democracy," *Journal of Social Issues*, Vol. 31, No. 1 (1975), p. 164.
4. Ibid., p. 163.

71

justifiable and necessary, one report (in which 1500 incidents between 1960 and 1970 were examined) has suggested that one-fifth of the homicides studied were questionable, two-fifths unjustifiable, and two-fifths justifiable. According to sociologist Albert J. Reiss, Jr., the homicide rate by police officers has been rising at a rate that is not commensurate with population growth and furthermore, the persons killed are disproportionately minority persons.[5] Some authorities have also claimed that racism is a major factor in these results inasmuch as the laws which set forth the written standards for acceptable police behavior and conduct as well as the judicial apparatus set up to enforce such standards are established and administered by persons with interests and perspectives representative of white Americans.[6] Consequently, the very structures of the legal system, according to Louis Knowles and Kenneth Prewitt, not only reflect the prejudices and ignorance of white society but tend to operate to the disadvantage of the culturally different.[7] To support this argument, statistics are cited from the National Center of Health Statistics, U.S. Public Health Service, which note that of the 376 civilians killed by law enforcement officers in 1973, 79 percent were black.[8] In addition, another study on police killings of civilians found that the police-caused death rate for blacks from 1958 to 1968 was consistently nine times higher than that for whites.[9] One theory is that the friction between the police and minority communities stems from the overwhelming whiteness of most police departments.[10]

To complicate the situation, studies have also shown that police are more likely to exercise force against members of their own race. According to Reiss, 67 percent of citizens victimized by white policemen in his sample were white and 71 percent of the citizens victimized by black police were black.[11] He further theorizes that "though no precise estimates are possible, the facts just given suggest that white policemen, even though they are prejudiced toward Negroes, do not discriminate against Negroes in the excessive use of force. The use of force by the police is more readily explained by police culture than it is by the policeman's

5. Ibid., p. 165.

6. Louis L. Knowles and Kenneth Prewitt, "Racism in the Administration of Justice," *Race Crime and Justice* (Pacific Palisades: Goodyear Publishing Company, Inc., 1972), p. 13.

7. Ibid.

8. Catherine Milton, et al., *Police Use of Deadly Force* (Washington, D.C.: Police Foundation, 1977), pp. 4-5.

9. S. Harring, T. Platt, R. Speiglmann, and P. Takagi, "Management of Police Killings," *Crime and Social Justice* (Fall-Winter 1977), pp. 34-43.

10. Ibid., p. 14.

11. Albert J. Reiss, Jr., "Police Brutality," *Crime and Justice: Volume II*, eds., Leon Radzinowicz and Marvin E. Wolfgang, p. 304.

race. . . ."[12] Reiss noted that in all cases, two facts stand out: (1) all victims were offenders; and (2) all were from the lower class.[13]

Reiss' theory is further underscored by Fyfe's study in which he found that not only were blacks and Hispanics disproportionately represented in police shootings of civilians but that possibly due to their location and assignments, the black and Hispanic New York police officers were far more likely to have fired their guns on duty as well as off duty than were white officers.[14]

There are also legal aspects of the problem that must be examined. State laws regarding use of deadly force by police officers differ substantially, but basically they fall into three major categories: common law, forcible felony rule, and the Model Penal Code approach.[15] Under common law, a police officer may be justified in the use of deadly force under the following circumstances: self-defense, prevention of the commission of a crime, recapture of an escapee from an arrest or from a penal institution, stopping a riot, or effecting a felony arrest.[16] Twenty-four states still adhere to the common law justification for the kinds of felonies for which deadly force may be used; seven states have adjusted the Model Penal Code approach which restricts the use of deadly force to violent felonies. And the remaining twelve states do not have justification statutes limiting an officer's use of deadly force.[17] Furthermore, the definition of felony differs from state to state.

Kenneth J. Matula has stressed that the decision *to use* deadly force is rare to nonexistent in the career of most police officers. This decision, however, is a very complex, multi-faceted, and often an instantaneous process. There are four critical and complex elements to this process:

1. *Perception.* The officer forms a "mental set" regarding the situation. This mental set is a product of several factors including:

a. Information received through police radio, roll call, lookout notices, conversations with other officers.

b. The officer's senses of observing and hearing a scene.

c. Information provided by interested citizens.

d. The officer's professional knowledge and skills developed through training and intuition.

---

12. Ibid.

13. Ibid.

14. Lt. James J. Fyfe, dissertation, *Executive Summary Shots Fired: An Examination of New York City Police Firearms Discharges.* Police Academy, New York Police Dept. (1978), p. 2.

15. Gilbert G. Pompa, Director of CPS, DOJ speech entitled, "Police Use of Excessive Force: A Community Relations Concern," presented to the National Black Policeman's Association on August 25, 1978 in Chicago, Illinois.

16. Larry Sherman, "Homicide by Police Officers," p. 21.

17. Gilbert G. Pompa, "Police Use of Excessive Force," p. 11.

e. Personal attitudinal bias with respect to a set of circumstances or individuals.

2. *Evaluation.* The officer compares his perception of the situation against several other factors:

a. Departmental guidelines controlling the use of deadly force.

b. State law regarding deadly force.

c. Immediate risk of harm if deadly force is used as well as possible consequences if deadly force is not used.

d. The availability of alternative methods of coping with the situation.

3. *Decision.* The actual commitment to use or not to use deadly force is based upon:

a. The totality of the officer's knowledge about the scenario.

b. The limit and extent of his power.

c. Risk involved.

d. Available alternatives.

4. *Action.* If deadly force is to be used, the officer must exercise the highest degree of care, proficiency, mental and physical calmness, and unflinching determination to achieve the immediate objective of stopping a life-threat.

Keep in mind that this very complex process may be completed in a matter of a few seconds. The consequences of the final action have grave legal, physical, and emotional implications that extend far beyond the moment of action for all parties involved. For the officer, the action could result in:

1. Lifelong psychological trauma.

2. Severe administrative sanctions.

   a. Suspension.

   b. Dismissal.

3. Severe legal consequences.

   a. Criminal action in state court.

   b. Civil action in state court.

   c. Criminal action in federal court.

   d. Civil action in federal court.

(Even in the case of an injured crime victim, the civil action for failing to take advantage of the authority to use deadly force.)

For the officer's family, the action could result in:

1. Mental strain from "second guessing" the decision.

2. Trauma from waiting for legal and administrative rulings.

3. Threat of physical retribution.

For the city and its constituted authorities, the action could result in:

1. Vicarious liability damage suits.

2. Riots.

For the victim, the action could result in:
1. The end of life.
2. Serious injury.

For the victim's family, the action could result in:
1. The loss of a loved one.
2. The loss of a family provider.
3. A drastic change in life-style.
4. Hatred.[18]

James J. Fyfe has pointed out that:

Ironically, it is important to provide information on police use of deadly force because it is employed so infrequently and is, thus, often regarded as insignificant and not problematic. True, every violent death is a tragedy and, in comparison to deaths by execution, deaths at the hands of the police occur with great frequency. Since 1967, we have executed five convicted murderers in this country; estimates of the numbers of people shot and killed by police in the same period are between 4,000 and 8,000. There is, of course, no reliable way to estimate the number of people wounded or missed by police bullets during those same years. Thus, in comparison to deaths by execution, deaths by police use of deadly force are a phenomenon of enormous proportions.

From another angle, however, the frequency of deadly force looks quite small. There are 17,000 police departments in the United States, and American police have killed somewhere between 4,000 and 8,000 people over the last 15 years. Thus, arithmetic indicates that most police departments have killed nobody over the last 15 years. There are nearly a half million sworn police personnel in this country, and they encounter thousands of potentially violent situations every day; but even the greatest estimates of killings by police indicate that fewer than one in 60 officers have killed anybody over the last 15 years. Further, the limited data available suggest that most police shootings take place in large cities, so that rates of police killings in America's small jurisdictions are probably far lower than this one in 60 aggregate rate.[19]

Police "killings" and the legal complexities surrounding their use of deadly force are further compounded by the fact that an increasing number of police officers are the victims of felonious assault or murder.

The following account illustrates the dimensions of this problem:

Ninety-one local, county, and state law enforcement officers were feloniously killed in the line of duty during 1981. This 1981 total was

---

18. Kenneth J. Matula, *A Balance of Force* (Gaithersburg, MD.: I.A.C.P., 1982), pp. 2–5. Reprinted by permission.
19. James J. Fyfe, *Readings on Police Use of Deadly Force* (Washington, D.C.: Police Foundation), pp. 7–8. Reprinted by permission.

down 13 percent from the previous year when 104 officers lost their lives.

From 1972 through 1981, 1,110 officers were slain. As shown in the table below, fewer line-of-duty deaths were reported in 1981 than in any other single year during the 10-year period.

Year	Number of victim officers
1972	117
1973	134
1974	132
1975	129
1976	111
1977	93
1978	93
1979	106
1980	104
1981	91
Total	1,110

Geographic Locations

In 1981 as in previous years, more officers (43) were slain in the country's most populous region, the South, than in any other. Eighteen officers were killed in the North Central States, fourteen in the Western States, thirteen in the Northeastern States, two in Puerto Rico, and one in American Samoa (see Table 1).

Of the 91 officers slain during 1981, 88 were from 77 different local, county, and state law enforcement agencies in 30 states. As indicated above, the remaining three were from Puerto Rico and American Samoa. None of the slain officers were employed by federal agencies.

Among the states, California, with eight officers slain, lost the most officers in line-of-duty deaths. The States of New York, Florida, and Mississippi followed with six officers killed in each.

Circumstances Surrounding Deaths

Responses to all types of disturbance calls (family quarrels, man-with-gun calls, bar fights, etc.) claimed the lives of nineteen officers during 1981. (See Table 2.) Seventeen officers were slain by persons engaged in the commission of a robbery or while in the pursuit of robbery suspects, and six lost their lives at the scene of burglaries or while pursuing burglary suspects. Fifteen were killed while attempting arrests for crimes other than robbery or burglary.

Twelve officers lost their lives while enforcing traffic laws. Ten were killed while investigating suspicious persons or circumstances; nine were ambushed; two were slain while handling mentally deranged persons; and one was murdered while transporting a prisoner.

Types of Assignment

Sixty-eight of the 91 officers killed in 1981 were on vehicle patrol duty when attacked. Of the remaining victim officers, 10 were detectives or on special assignments and 13 were off duty but taking appropriate police action at the time they were slain.

Thirty-eight of the 78 officers who were on duty when killed were alone and unassisted at the scene of the fatal incident.

Weapons Used

Firearms were the weapons used in 95 percent of the murders of law enforcement officers during 1981. (See Table 3.) Sixty-nine of the officers were slain with handguns, 12 with rifles, and five with shotguns. The officers' own firearms were used against them in 12 of the killings.

Of the five officers slain with other weapons, two were struck by vehicles; one was stabbed to death; one was killed with a blunt object; and one was drowned.

Thirty-three of the officers who met their demise in 1981 attempted to utilize their service firearms while in contact with their assailants, and 27 discharged their service weapons. Fifty-three percent of the officers killed by firearms were within five feet of their assailants at the time they were shot.

Profile of Victim Officers

Eighty-nine of the officers killed during 1981 were male and two were female. Breakdowns by age showed that 33 were 30 years of age or younger, 38 were 31 through 40 years old, and 20 were over the age of 40. (See Table 4.) Seventy-seven of the victim officers were White, thirteen were Black, and one was a native of American Samoa. Their average years of service was eight, and 73 of the officers were in uniform when slain.

Persons Identified

Law enforcement agencies cleared 81 of the 91 murders of officers which occurred during 1981. In connection with these crimes, 125 offenders were identified, 96 percent of whom were male. (See Table 5.) Of all suspects identified, 41 percent were White, 58 percent were Black, and the remainder were of other races. The assailants ranged in age from 15 to 79, and the average age was 30 years. Seven percent of the offenders were under the age of 18, and 46 percent were between 18 and 30 years of age.

As can be seen from the accompanying chart, the majority of the assailants were not first offenders. Seventy-three percent had prior arrests, 54 percent had previous convictions, and 47 percent had been arrested for violent crimes, such as murder, forcible rape, etc. Forty-nine percent of the offenders had at one time been paroled or given probation following criminal convictions, while 26 percent were on parole or probation at the time of the police killing in which they were involved. Persons having prior arrests for narcotic charges made up 26 percent of the total offenders, while 14 percent of the assailants had previous arrests for assaults on law enforcement officers.

During 1981, 13 offenders were justifiably killed either at the scene of the police killing or in ensuing confrontations. Three of these assailants were killed and an additional nine were wounded by the victim-officers themselves. Two of the offenders committed suicide.[20]

The following articles discuss the administrative and legal aspects of policy utilized in the control of police deadly force.

---

20. William H. Webster, *Crime in the United States 1981* (Washington, D.C.: F.B.I., 1982), pp. 309-311.

Table 1 — Law Enforcement Officers Killed, 1981

[By geographic region and division and population group]

Geographic region and division	Total	Group I 250,000 and over	Group II 100,000 to 249,999	Group III 50,000 to 99,999	Group IV 25,000 to 49,999	Group V 10,000 to 24,999	Group VI under 10,000	County, State Police and Highway Patrol
Total	91	23	5	9	2	6	16	30
Northeast	13	6	.	.	1	2	2	2
New England	2	.	.	.	.	2	.	.
Middle Atlantic	11	6	.	.	1	.	2	2
North Central	18	4	1	2	.	.	2	9
East North Central	10	3	1	.	.	.	1	5
West North Central	8	1	.	2	.	.	1	4
South	43	9	2	5	1	4	9	13
South Atlantic	18	6	1	3	.	1	3	4
East South Central	16	2	1	.	1	2	4	6
West South Central	9	1	.	2	.	1	2	3
West	14	4	2	1	.	.	1	6
Mountain	6	1	2	.	.	.	.	3
Pacific	8	3	.	1	.	.	1	3
Puerto Rico and American Samoa	3	.	.	1	.	.	2	.

Table 2 — Law Enforcement Officers Killed, 1981

[Circumstances by type of assignment]

Circumstances at scene of incident	Total	Type of assignment								
		2-officer vehicle	1-officer vehicle		Foot patrol		Detective, special assignment		Off duty
			Alone	Assisted	Alone	Assisted	Alone	Assisted	
Disturbance calls (family quarrels, man with gun)	19	7	2	6	......	......	......	1	3
Burglaries in progress or pursuing burglary suspects	6	......	6	......	......	......	......	......	......
Robberies in progress or pursuing robbery suspects	17	3	3	4	......	......	......	1	6
Attempting other arrests	15	1	4	3	......	......	1	5	1
Civil disorders (mass disobedience, riot, etc.)	......	......	......	......	......	......	......	......	......
Handling, transporting, custody of prisoners	1	......	......	......	......	......	1	......	......
Investigating suspicious persons and circumstances	10	2	6	......	......	......	1	......	1
Ambush (entrapment and premeditation)	5	1	3	1	......	......	......	......	......
Ambush (unprovoked attack)	4	......	1	1	......	......	......	......	2
Mentally deranged	2	......	......	2	......	......	......	......	......
Traffic pursuits and stops	12	2	10	......	......	......	......	......	......
TOTAL	91	16	35	17	......	......	3	7	13

Table 3 — Law Enforcement Officers Killed, 1981

[By type of weapon]

Type of weapon	Number	Percent
Handgun	69	75.8
Rifle	12	13.2
Shotgun	5	5.5
Total firearms	86	94.5
Knife	1	1.1
Bomb	....	....
Personal weapons	....	....
Other (vehicles, etc.)	4	4.4
Total	91	100.0

Table 4 — Profile of Victim Officers, 1981

Total victim officers	91
Under 25 years of age	12
From 25 through 30 years of age	21
From 31 through 40 years of age	38
Over 40 years of age	20
Male	89
Female	2
White	77
Black	13
Other race	1
Hispanic ethnicity	7
Non-Hispanic ethnicity	84
Average years of law enforcement service	8
Less than 1 year of service	4
From 1 to 5 years of service	31
From 5 through 10 years of service	30
Over 10 years of service	26
Average height	5′ 11″
In uniform	73

Table 5 — Profile of Persons Identified, 1981

Total persons identified	125
Under 18 years of age	9
From 18 to 30 years of age	57
Male	120
Female	5
White	51
Black	72
Other race	2
Hispanic ethnicity	21
Non-Hispanic ethnicity	104
Prior criminal arrest	91
Convicted on prior criminal charge	67
Prior arrest for crime of violence	59
Convicted on criminal charges - granted leniency	61
On parole or probation at time of killing	32
Arrested for prior murder charge	9
Prior arrest for narcotic drug law violation	33
Prior arrest for assaulting policeman or resisting arrest	18
Prior arrest for weapons violation	57

ADMINISTRATIVE AND LEGAL ASPECTS OF A POLICY TO LIMIT THE USE OF FIREARMS BY POLICE OFFICERS*

All police chiefs face one decision in common: what restrictions should be imposed on the amount and type of force used by their officers? Nearly everyone is aware of instances of police brutality and the flagrant misuse of force by some over-zealous officers. These situations are relatively easy to deal with, because they represent clear violations of departmental rules and criminal law. This discussion does not cover such blatant abuses of force, rather it focuses on those situations where regulations, laws, and circumstances are not so clearly defined.

The first consideration must be the question of what constitutes deadly force. It is generally defined as that amount of force that is likely to produce death or serious bodily injury. While the use of the police baton, fists, or feet sometimes produces the issue of deadly force, incidents in which a suspect is shot by an officer are always considered to have involved deadly force.

The primary legal question is clear: was the use of force reasonable? To be considered "reasonable," the force used must have been no more than was necessary under the circumstances. When a firearm is used, the burden of proof rests with the officer to show that there were no other reasonable alternatives available. In addition, reasonable force implies that the crime involved must have been a felony and, at that, a dangerous one—murder, voluntary manslaughter, forcible rape, felonious assault, arson, robbery, or burglary. With the exception of self-defense by the officer, killing or deadly force cannot be used when the crime involved is a misdemeanor.

The high value placed upon a human life in our society and the increasing number of crimes that are considered felonies have caused a gradual circumscription of the power of police officers to use deadly force. Even those jurisdictions which still allow a rather wide use of deadly force in a number of felony crimes require that the element of danger must be clear.

* Kenneth R. McCreedy and James L. Hague, "Administrative and Legal Aspects of a Policy to Limit the Use of Firearms by Police Officers," Vol. XLII, No. 1, *Police Chief*, January 1975, pp. 48-52. Reprinted by permission.

The situations in which an officer is most likely to use a firearm are: (1) while effecting the lawful arrest of a felon, (2) while preventing the escape of a felon, and (3) while preventing the commission or consummation of a felony. In the first situation the officer may use deadly force in self-defense, the life of a fellow officer or some other person. In the second case deadly force is permitted under certain circumstances. In most jurisdictions, escaping from an institution is usually considered a dangerous felony. However, merely escaping from an officer raises the issue of the dangerousness of the crime as well as the availability of less lethal alternatives. In situation 3, the officer must prove that the commission of a felony was imminent.

There is a discernible trend in law enforcement to limit substantially the use of firearms in cases where a significant danger to bystanders exists.

The above discussion encompasses the legal framework within which the policy decision concerning the use of deadly force must be made. While the variations of circumstances and conditions are endless, any policy must be consistent with legal requirements and prohibitions. Even the absence of a stated policy is a form of policy. In the past when officers were given a few broad guidelines and told to use their good judgment, the controlling factor became norms established by the officers themselves as the result of street experience. These guidelines were simply a knowledge of the consequences of improper action, and considerable emphasis was placed on individual decision making.

Available Alternatives

Before beginning to examine the condition under which a policy decision concerning the use of firearms should be made, we should first explore the available alternatives.

1. *The officers are armed and told to use full discretion.* Little attempt is made by the chief to define the circumstances under which such force should be used. The chief must rely on the training and competence of the individual officers. Normally, this condition exists because of a lack of any stated policy.

In many respects, this alternative is the most unfair. It requires the officer to bear the responsibility of his/her decision (which certainly must ultimately be done), but it fails to provide the necessary guidance to make that very important decision.

2. *The officers are armed and given partial discretion.* In this instance, officers are given rather detailed guidelines and considerable training. Such a policy may limit the use of firearms to situations where it is necessary to save the officer's life or the life of some other person. The exercise of discretion would cover circumstances where a reasonable possibility exists for further injury or death involving other persons.

This policy begins to circumscribe the use of force, but still allows the officer to exercise some discretion in unusual circumstances. It also shows the officers that the chief is willing to help them make the decision and to share the responsibility for that decision.

3. *The officers are armed and given no discretion.* When no discretion is given, officers are instructed to use their firearms only in defense of their lives. This means that unless a life is immediately in danger, deadly force should not be used. With this policy, the only decision the officer is required to make is whether or not a life is immediately in danger. Such a condition is fairly easy to identify.

This alternative is beginning to gain some popularity because of the advent of multi-agency communications systems, greater inter-agency cooperation, and the use of helicopters to reduce the possibility of escape. Because of modern technological improvements, much of the necessity for immediate action has been removed.

4. *The officers are unarmed and thus the decision does not become an issue.* This is the system that has long been practiced in England, where the bobbies have traditionally not been armed. This alternative is generally not acceptable in this country because of the frequency with which firearms are involved in calls for police service (not only shootings, but threatening and brandishing of firearms, carrying concealed weapons, etc.); and the frontier mentality dictates that the "law man" is the one who "won the West" with a six-shooter and a lightning fast draw. Many people still view the image of a policeman as incomplete without the gun. Perhaps in the future, when the technology is perfected, the use of nonlethal weapons will become the predominant policy.

From the above alternatives, it can be observed that as the chief's control of the officer's discretion in the use of firearms increases, the officer's discretion decreases.

Participants in Policymaking

There are many participants or actors who play a part in the decision as to what policy should be implemented.

1. *The police chief.* With the chief rests the ultimate decision as to what policy will be instituted. Influence stems from many factors, not the least of which is personal experience as an officer. The decision is further influenced by the present role—decisionmaker. The chief cannot be guided solely by his own experiences or by his desire to facilitate the interests of his officers. He must also evaluate the opinions, desires, and demands made by each of the other actors.

2. *The police officers.* Each officer will have his own opinion based primarily on three factors. The first is the officer's own experience using firearms while enforcing the law. Secondly, he will be influenced by his

training and perceptions of his own capabilities. The last factor is the norms and opinions of his peer group. Often, these norms are not based on actual conditions but only on what "could" happen. The officers either individually or in concert will have considerable influence because they are the ones to whom this policy will apply.

3. *The city council or other legislative unit under which the police department must operate.* Members are the elected representatives of the people. They express the views of their constituents or, at least, are conscious of their attitudes and feelings. These officials, in most cases, also have the power to remove the chief from office if they feel he is not doing his job properly. For these two reasons, they are very important actors whose opinions must be considered when establishing a policy on the use of firearms.

4. *Courts.* Both local and appellate courts may become involved directly or indirectly in implementing policy. On a case-by-case basis, the reasonableness of the officer's use of a firearm will be determined by the courts. Whether or not there are legal consequences is also a judicial responsibility. This responsibility includes both civil and criminal liability. The officer's use of his firearm may be criminal if the force is found to be excessive and, therefore, unreasonable under the circumstances. In addition, depending on the status of sovereign immunity in a particular jurisdiction, there may also be civil liability if negligence can be found. There will certainly be liability for state and local officers when, in the federal courts, they are found to have acted unreasonably and thus to have deprived citizens of their federal statutory or constitutional rights. This liability not only applies to the officers involved, but may also include the police administrators who were negligent in the formulation and implementation of policy and training.

All courts, and particularly those at the appellate level, see their role as one of supervision over police activities. Consequently, judges make policy for the police by deciding whether police procedures are consistent with the due process and protection of rights of those who are arrested. There is widespread debate about the relative impact of judicial control over police policy making; however, it is difficult to measure accurately this influence.

5. *Interest groups.* These are able to apply pressure to city officials and to the police chief directly by protests and newspaper articles as well as indirectly through legal pressure in the courts. These various interest groups may represent all sides of the same issue simultaneously, so in many respects they may only serve to further complicate the situation.

Interest groups have a quality which sometimes makes their effect more pronounced than it should be. Many interest groups are formed literally overnight, last for a few days, and then dissolve only to be reborn again under a different name. Because of this transience and because of the general secrecy of membership, the exact size of the group represented cannot be determined. The same is true of the rich and politically powerful within the city. The extent to which others share their opinions is also difficult to determine, even though they themselves often exhibit tremendous influence.

6. *Chief's own peer group.* Every chief is involved to some extent with police chiefs from other cities through conventions and professional associations. The opinions and particularly the experiences of the other chiefs will influence other members of the group.

The above list composes the major actors involved in the chief's policy decision. Others may be involved to a greater or lesser degree in other specific situations.

Other Considerations

Political environment. Any consideration of a policy which limits the use of firearms by police officers cannot be extricated from the political environment in which it is made. The nature and strength of local politics will often dictate many of the policy decisions that are made.

Community values are part of this political climate. The degree to which criminality is legitimatized by the members of the community will influence their values and attitudes toward such a policy.

Actual policy versus stated policy. In many police organizations, there is a significant gap between actual policy and stated policy. The actual policy may be a conscious process or it may occur almost accidentally. The classic example of the actual versus stated policy dilemma is the suggestion box. A chief can proudly point to the suggestion box on the wall and exclaim that he actually solicits the opinions of his officers. He may or may not be aware that the first suggestions that were submitted were either ignored or, if enacted, some other ranking member of the department took credit for the idea. In actual practice, then, the suggestion box could be welded shut and no one would notice.

The same is true with regard to a policy covering the use of firearms. The chief may state that he favors the use of discretion by his officers; but when officers are indiscriminately disciplined for what they perceive to be minor violations (called scapegoating),·then the actual policy becomes significantly different from the stated policy.

Environment of the policy. The decision to use a firearm is normally implemented in the heat of a conflict. As such, the decision is not the result of a thoughtful or even necessarily a rational process. In the final analysis, the officer will do what his instincts tell him to do in any given situation. The policy will only be enforceable after the fact, and by that time irreparable damage may have been done.

Enforcing such a policy seems to include training to make the officers' actions predictable in a given situation. The FBI developed a "Hogan's Alley" to test the agents' reactions and abilities to make life or death decisions. The agents are required to walk down a street, and as they walk targets appear in doors and windows of various buildings. Some of the figures pose no threat to the agents (woman holding a baby), while others are an immediate danger (criminal with a shotgun). The agents are judged on their ability to respond correctly to each given situation. Other experiments have been tried to judge the same accuracy of reaction. The results show that some officers do have better reactions than others. Just how much continued practice will improve faulty reactions is not known, but it appears that short of actual shootings there are few ways to train persons to make these kinds of decisions once the usual "moral and policy" aspects of the use of firearms have been covered.

Predictability of officer contacts with others. Part of the purpose of policy is to introduce a degree of predictability into the behavior of the person to whom the policy applies. A policy which limits the use of firearms by police officers would serve to make their conduct more predictable when interacting with others. As with any other issue, there is more than one point of view.

First is the opinion that if a person had done no wrong, he has nothing to fear from the officer. Community relations studies and experiments have found that this is not always the case. Often, those who have done no wrong still react in fear because of the perceived unpredictability of the officer's conduct. Many people would doubtless find comfort in knowing that the officer's discretion was limited and that he would only use his firearm in certain narrowly described circumstances.

On the other hand, to some this restriction may make the officer's conduct too predictable. If a person who has committed some serious crime believes that the only barrier to escape is a footrace with the officer, he may be willing to chance it. After all, at that price, it would be worth the gamble. If the price is increased to include the possibility of death, that alternative becomes less desirable.

Conclusion

Total use of discretion by police officers is more an indication of failure on the part of the chief than of a sincere belief in the judgment of his officers. This is not an area where no policy can exist. Even in the absence of policy, the norms and experiences of the officers, coupled with judicial decisions, will establish some type of policy, albeit informal.

The most appropriate solution, based on the total benefit to the community and the need to provide guidance and support for the officers, is a policy which severely limits the use of discretion but one which also acknowledges that exceptions are possible. Other than for the obvious situations, such as in defense of a human life, the use of firearms by officers is difficult to justify.

Such a policy for officers would give them absolute guidelines to follow and would also assure them of administrative support if they were within that policy. The chief would not have to decide the rightness and wrongness of a particular incident based on some flexible and intangible scale. A guarantee of support for officers should outweigh any disadvantage that such a policy would create.

If the advantage of not making the officer's actions predictable to the criminals is felt to outweigh the reassurance offered to the public, then the policy when established need not be publicized. On the other hand, if a public benefit is desired from the policy, then it could become a valuable public relations tool. The police department would receive the benefit of a reputation for decisiveness, while the public would be more aware of the parameters of police conduct.

A policy which limits the use of firearms to essentially life-or-death situations also raises several other questions which each administrator must answer before he enacts the policy.

1. *What is in defense of a life or what is a dangerous felony?* How much danger does a felony have to pose, or how much danger does someone have to be in? For example, is the officer's life in danger when he confronts a person who is armed, or when that person actually draws the weapon, or is it necessary to wait until that person fires the weapon?

2. *Does the threat have to be real?* On occasion, perceived threats seem to be real at the time but later are proven to be false.

3. *What will be done in a borderline case?* What action will be taken in cases where the justification was not as strong as it should have been?

4. *Who will review the incident?* Presuming that such incidents will occur, it is necessary to decide who will review the incident and decide whether or not the use of deadly force was justified. Involved in this process is deciding what will be done in instances that are beyond the policy but not violations of law. If no action is taken when violations occur, the effect will be to expand the parameters of the policy.

5. *Methods of determining violations of policy.* When a shooting occurs, it should be investigated immediately. The problem is by whom. Many people feel that to have police officers from the same police department investigate a shooting in which a person was killed by a fellow officer is asking for abuses of the authority. In some cases, this is probably true, especially in smaller police departments where everyone is known to everyone else.

The most advantageous solution is to have the incident investigated by some other nearby investigative agency. For example, if the incident occurred in a city, it might be investigated by the state police or prosecuting attorney's investigative staff. In this way, competence is maintained while the personalities are removed.

When the investigation is completed, the results should be evaluated by some independent agency beyond the control of the police department and representative of the people.

There are several such mechanisms already in existence. The grand jury and, in some states, the coroner's jury are both beyond the control of the police department and are composed of a random cross-section of the community. These juries rotate at regular intervals so there is little chance of co-optation occurring.

A third alternative is a civilian review board, but it is the least desirable of the choices. A CRB too often ends up on one side of the fence or the other. If it decides in favor of the police officer, then the community may lose faith in its judgments. If it decides in favor of the community, then the police officers perceive the board as being hostile to law enforcement. This dilemma can be avoided by using either of the two existing juries.

Summation

Deciding to enact a policy which would limit or restrict the use of firearms by police officers is a necessary but difficult task. It is one that cannot be avoided; some policy will always exist, even if it is only informally. A police chief has an obligation to the members of the department and the community to provide guidance and support. This can best be accomplished by the articulation of a definite and fair policy.

The road to such a decision is not, however, without its crossroads; and at each intersection, the police executive must decide which way to proceed.

Because there are several hundred-thousand police officers in many different police agencies, and daily they interact with millions of persons in various communities, the potential for conflict is great. The more easily that conflict can be resolved, the better the goal of law enforcement will be served.

INVESTIGATION OF THE USE
OF DEADLY FORCE*

You are the chief of police in a small middle-class community which enjoys the luxury of little violent crime.

One of your officers is on routine patrol in a residential area in the early hours of the first watch. He sees a young man furtively leaving the back door of a darkened home, carrying a box. The officer approaches the young man and orders him to freeze. The young man drops his box and runs from the officer.

The officer gives chase, but the young man widens the distance from his pursuer. The officer, fully within the limits of state law, tells the young man to stop or he will shoot. The young man keeps on running.

The officer yells again, and the young man suddenly turns, a "shiny" object in his hand. The officer fires, hitting the man in the chest. The officer calls for an ambulance; upon reaching the nearby hospital the young man is pronounced dead.

He is later identified as a sixteen-year-old community resident with a minor juvenile record. The shiny object recovered at the scene is a chrome flashlight. This incident, in a normally quiet community, is certain to send shock waves, pro and con, throughout the community.

Under the present law of many states, the subject was observed by the officer to be committing the forcible felony of burglary. Under such statutes, the officer was justified in using deadly force, both as self-protection and to prevent the subject's escape. Under such statutes, the officer's actions were justified.

Investigation

Each such use of deadly force, however, calls for thorough investigation of the officer's actions. There are several reasons for such investigation. First, public accountability demands an investigation of such police action. Second, from the standpoint of internal control, the officer's actions must be subject to review. Third, and perhaps most important, a

---

* Peter J. Donnelly, "Investigation of the Use of Deadly Force," *The Police Chief*, Vol. XLV, No. 5, May 1978, pp. 24-26. Reprinted by permission.

thorough investigation protects both the department and the officer involved from unjust criticism.

A deadly force investigation parallels a normal homicide investigation in that the principles of preservation of the crime scene and physical evidence must be adhered to. At the scene, one officer, preferably of command or supervisory rank, should be in charge, assigning duties to those under his command as is the case in an ordinary crime scene investigation.

The first consideration at the scene should be, of course, to secure medical aid for the injured. Even though the victim's death may be readily apparent to a lay observer, he should still be transported to the nearest hospital as quickly as possible. This is done for two reasons: to secure competent medical examination of the victim and to safeguard the department from future criticism. The placement of the body at the scene can be photographed or outlined before removal, and examination of the body may later take place at the hospital, morgue or funeral home. Here, maintaining chain of custody and preservation of the evidence is paramount; and an officer should accompany the body to insure these procedures.

An officer should be assigned to safeguard the scene and control access to it. Photographs should be taken as soon as possible. They should show all aspects of the scene and follow as closely as possible the sequence of events. Particular care should be given to the gathering of physical evidence such as blood, spent bullets, and prints, using a grid search method or other systematic pattern. The officer's weapon should be inventoried for ballistic comparison with any recovered bullets.

An officer or two should be assigned to locate and segregate witnesses to the incident. Written statements should be taken from eye and circumstantial witnesses. Do not rely on third-person summaries of oral witness interviews; written statements preclude changing stories at a later date. The general area of the scene should be canvassed for witnesses. The names of everyone contacted should be recorded and it should be noted whether they saw or heard anything. This again helps prevent "surprise" witnesses appearing with "eyewitness" accounts. The witnesses, in general, should be asked if they were physically in a position to see or hear what happened.

Detailed reports should be received from all involved department personnel as soon as possible, covering their actions in the incident. The involved officer's rights as a public employee do not prevent the submission of an official report regarding official actions taken.

A re-enactment of the incident may be valuable in clarifying points and indicating further avenues of investigation. The re-enactment should duplicate the actual events and setting as closely as possible.

Liaison with other agencies who have an interest in the incident should be quickly established to prevent duplication of effort and conflict of jurisdiction. In many areas, the state's or district attorney is notified of police shooting incidents and immediately begins a separate investigation. It is the duty of the police officer in charge of the investigation to cooperate and coordinate with such personnel, such as making witnesses available for on-the-scene depositions.

The initial offense which led to the shooting should also be thoroughly investigated, just as if the offender were apprehended and facing prosecution. In my hypothetical case, the burglary investigation should not be dropped in favor of the shooting investigation. The burglary investigation should proceed as usual, including processing of the burglary scene and inventory of the missing or recovered property. The burglary case report should then be made part of the shooting investigation file.

Treatment of Officer

There are several special considerations which must be given attention in a deadly force investigation, particularly regarding treatment of the officer involved. Police officers react differently following shootings. Some officers view it as part of the job, something that had to be done. Such an attitude should not be regarded as callous; it may be a product of the officer's past experience and training. Other officers may be upset and in need of immediate counseling by their partner, commanding officer, clergyman, or some other professional. In cases where serious emotional upset is evident, the involved officer's family should be briefed as to what the officer is going through. Relief from normal duties may be necessary in such cases. In many other cases, the officers may be exhilarated, telling and retelling their role in the incident. Such behavior is not boasting, but rather a manifestation of the natural excitement the officers feel.

Unless there is some indication of impropriety, the officer involved should not be suspended or placed on restricted duty pending the outcome of the investigation. If there is no impropriety apparent or emotional disturbance on the part of the involved officer, such action serves no real purpose other than to possibly create a feeling of "guilt." If such action is taken and publicized, undue suspicion regarding the officer's actions can be created in the eyes of the public and the officer's peers. Do not suspend or place an officer on restricted duty unless there is a need to do so. While remaining on duty, however, the involved officer should not take part in the shooting investigation, other than completing reports and making a statement.

In a departure from normal investigative procedures, the involved officer is interviewed as soon as possible in the investigation. This is done because the spontaneity of an immediate statement increases recall of details and credibility, and prevents the possibility of a "manufactured" account later on.

In some instances, the involved officer is often viewed as an accused. This is especially true in instances where the officer is required or requested to make a formal statement to a state's or district attorney. Prior to making such a statement, the officer must be advised of Constitutional rights regarding self-incrimination and right to counsel. In administrative or departmental inquiries, the officer should be advised of the nature of the inquiry and personal rights and responsibilities under civil service statutes. In such inquiries, if there is a possibility of criminal prosecution because of misconduct by the officer, the full *Miranda* warnings must be given. If the preliminary investigation discloses a question about the officer's actions in the incident, then the appropriate guidelines regarding the rights of the accused must be followed.

Media Relations

Handling of news media coverage of a shooting incident calls for a sense of timing and an understanding of the media's role regarding the inquiry. Information should not be prematurely disclosed to the news media. Such information should be withheld when it is felt that its release would jeopardize the investigation or expose the department to civil liability. When it is appropriate to release facts, the press release should recount the incident as it occurred. The release may include a brief statement about the legal guidelines regarding the use of deadly force.

In no instance should the release try to "sell" the public on how much of a criminal the victim was. Relating the victim's past record or amplifying the crime involved in the incident serves no purpose and hurts the surviving members of the family. The press release should, of course, be distributed equally to all members of the media; playing favorites here could have a disastrous consequence. The police administrator should not be alarmed, and indeeed should expect, sensational headlines such as "Cop Slays Teen Burglar."

The possibility of a civil suit arising out of a shooting incident should not be overlooked. Each bit of evidence is gathered with the view that it may eventually be presented in court. More simply stated, the investigation should be done properly the first time. As new evidence and witnesses are discovered, even though some time after the original investigation, there should be no hesitation to thoroughly examine the new material and include it in the case file. Information such as major witness discrepancies, which may cast doubt on the justifiability of the shooting, should never be excluded from the case file, just as such information should never be left out of an ordinary criminal investigation. Again, the need for accurately recording witness statements as soon as possible cannot be overemphasized.

Conclusion

In conclusion, consider the importance of preparation. A coherent, flexible standard operating procedure regarding shooting investigations is extremely valuable. Without such an SOP, a police department must "play it by ear" in a sensitive investigation. In the same vein, clearly understood and often repeated firearms use policies are also vital to a police department. What may be legally justifiable may be unacceptable in a practical social context. Therefore, many departments are restricting firearms use to situations involving armed felons, while statutes may allow such force to be used against escaping felons. The police administrator would do well to keep abreast of case law regarding use of deadly force. What may be legally justifiable may also expose a police department to civil liability in the eyes of a jury.

POLICE USE OF DEADLY FORCE*

Despite concerns about establishing an increased basis for civil liability, the clear trend across the country seems to be toward the adoption of department firearms use policies, generally narrower than either the statutory or decisional state law that is applicable. All of the seven sample departments have formal policies and most of those policies have been adopted within the last few years.

It is not a simple matter, however, to categorize firearms use policies as "restrictive" or "permissive." Oakland, for example, instructs its officers not to shoot at fleeing burglars.[1] Indianapolis imposes no such restriction. But in Indianapolis the officer who fires at a fleeing felon must have *positive knowledge* that the person committed a felony, while in Oakland the officer needs only *reasonable belief.* Thus, on one hand, Oakland has the more restrictive policy, while, on the other Indianapolis has.

Most firearms policies are really the sum of many components, each addressing a particular set of circumstances in which an officer might consider firing a weapon. Depending on local attitudes and the pattern of shooting incidents in a particular city,[2] the firearms policy may be unusually restrictive when it treats one type of situation and yet unusually flexible when it treats another. For example, former Oakland Chief C.R. Gain decided to change his department's policy on burglary after examining how the courts were treating persons charged with that offense:

> Considering that only 7.65 percent of all adult burglars arrested and only .28 percent of all juvenile burglars arrested are eventually incarcerated, it is difficult to resist the conclusion that the use of dead-

---

* Catherine H. Milton, Jean W. Halleck, James Lardner, and Gary L. Albrecht, *Police Use of Deadly Force* (Washington, D.C.: Police Foundation, 1977), pp. 38-64. Reprinted with permission.

1. See Table 1 at end of article. Oakland policy restrictions apply to the felony categories of burglary and auto theft only.

2. Frequently, written firearms guidelines evolve as a response to public outcry and media coverage surrounding some particular shooting incident. In 1974, a new set of written guidelines in Port Arthur, Texas, followed the killing of a youth after he was stopped for speeding. In 1975, a new set of guidelines in Cleveland, Ohio, followed the police killing of a 20-year-old motorcyclist.

ly force by peace officers to apprehend burglars cannot conceivably be justified. For adults, the police would have to shoot 100 burglars in order to have captured the eight who would have gone to prison. For juveniles, the police would have to shoot 1,000 burglars in order to have captured the three who would have gone to the Youth Authority.[3]

Although the Oakland department prohibits the shooting of burglars and auto thieves, it says nothing, at least officially, about other non-violent felonies, such as grand larceny. It is reasonable to assume that if an Oakland police officer did shoot a person who had committed a grand larceny, the department would adopt a rule to prevent such shootings in the future.

Indianapolis is the one city among those we visited with no written firearms policy at all beyond a restatement of state law. Birmingham, however, had no deadly force policy until March 1975. Because Alabama was one of those states without a statute establishing when an officer may use deadly force, the previous guiding principle of the decisional law was a 1915 Alabama case in which the court approved the use of deadly force to apprehend the operator of an illegal whiskey still as he ran from the premises.

Where guidelines have been formulated, the policies vary widely among departments. Some are decidedly narrower than the governing state law; some merely reiterate the law. Portland, for example, has a policy identical to Oregon law except for a single opening paragraph of general philosophy. Some policies are precise and technical; some are laced with statements of morality and strong rhetoric. Some policies amount to only a few paragraphs; some run on for pages. Until 1968, one southwestern department with more than 100 sworn members had the following policy on the use of a firearm (quoted in its entirety):

"Never take me out in anger; never put me back in disgrace.[4]"

A southern department had eight pages of its rules devoted to uniform specifications and allowances, yet had less than one page on the use of firearms:

Unnecessary and careless handling of firearms may cause accidents, and the drawing, aiming, or snapping of firearms within Police Headquarters, or in other places, is forbidden.

Samuel Chapman, writing for the Task Force Report on the Police, also noted other similar policies:

---

3. Charles R. Gain, "Discharge of Firearms Policy: Effecting Justice Through Administrative Regulation," unpublished paper.

4. Samuel G. Chapman, *Police Firearms Use Policy*, Report to the President's Commission on Law Enforcement and Administration of Justice (Washington, D.C.: U.S. Government Printing Office, 1967).

- Officers shall not intentionally fire their guns except as authorized by law.

- Leave the gun in the holster until you intend to use it.

- Shoot only when absolutely necessary to apprehend a criminal who has committed a major felony.

- Never pull a sidearm as a threat, and if it is drawn, be prepared to use same.

- It is left to the discretion of each individual officer when and how to shoot.

Before June 1975, the policy in Cleveland, Ohio, provided simply that "Officers and members should use only such force as necessary to effect the arrest and detention of persons."

This great variety, Chapman remarks, "reflects, in far too many instances, a failure on the part of police administrators to provide adequate guidance for officers faced with situations where they must decide instantaneously whether or not to use their firearms in discharging their official responsibilities."[5]

A common feature of many firearms policies is that they *appear* to be more restrictive than they really are. The Kansas City Police Department, for example, on the first page of its firearms order, states: "An officer is equipped with a firearm to defend himself or others against deadly force, or the threat of imminent deadly force." Two pages later, the policy authorizes the use of deadly force against certain fleeing felons regardless of immediate danger.

The Los Angeles policy (and, modeled on it, the Birmingham policy) hints that while officers may use their firearms to apprehend fleeing felons, they should exercise discretion. "It is not practical," the Los Angeles Police Department manual states, "to enumerate specific felonies and state with certainty that the escape of the perpetrator must be prevented at all costs, or that there are other felonious crimes where the perpetrator must be allowed to escape rather than to be shot. Such decisions are based upon sound judgment, not arbitrary checklists."

In Washington, D.C., the written policy holds that an officer may use deadly force to apprehend a suspect in a felony involving "an actual or threatened attack which the officer has reasonable cause to believe could result in death or serious bodily injury." The Washington policy is a restatement of the common-law rule of self-defense, which provides that the law of self-defense is a law of necessity. The necessity must be, in appearance, a reality, and must appear to admit of no other alternative before the taking of life will be excused as justifiable on the ground of self-defense.

---

5.   Ibid.

The following sections describe a variety of approaches, as articulated in department policies, to specific circumstances in which the use of a weapon might be considered. Certain aspects of weaponry are discussed as well.

Self-Defense and Defense of Others

Every policy gives the officer the right to use deadly force in self-defense or in the defense of others. Some policies say just that; others stipulate that firearms may be used only "when all other available means have failed" (Oakland), require a threat of "serious bodily harm or death" (Detroit), or specify that the danger must be "immediate" (Kansas City).

Fleeing Felons

In all seven cities there was some provision for the use of deadly force to apprehend fleeing felons. There was, however, considerable variation in the felonies covered. Some departments itemize specific felonies justifying deadly force, whereas others list the felonies that do not justify such force. Still others state only that the felony committed must itself have involved the actual or threatened use of force (or deadly force); and some departments authorize deadly force in the apprehension of any felon, without qualification.

Where distinctions are made among particular felonies, one offense likely to be excluded is auto theft, presumably on the rationale that most auto thieves are juvenile joyriders. In large cities, a similarly tolerant attitude, although to a lesser degree, seems to be developing toward burglars (while burglary continues to be viewed in rural areas as an implicitly violent crime, every bit as reprehensible as armed robbery).

In the majority of the sample cities, department policy forbids the use of firearms against fleeing burglars; Birmingham and Indianapolis are the exceptions. A very few police departments have drafted policies that virtually forbid the shooting of fleeing felons, regardless of the felony involved. The proposed new San Jose, California, firearms policy states: "The discharge of firearms is never justifiable solely for the purpose of apprehension.... A police officer may use deadly force when all other reasonable means have failed and the officer honestly and reasonably believes that such force is necessary to protect himself or another person from death or great bodily injury." San Jose's policy has not yet been put into effect because of a dispute with the police officers' association there.

San Diego's policy says much the same thing, adding only that an officer may use deadly force "to apprehend a violent person who is known to be armed and dangerous and who cannot be apprehended without risking loss of life or serious injury." It is somewhat difficult to reconcile this clause with another section of the San Diego policy that reads: "Firearms are not to be used. . . to fire at any person fleeing to evade arrest." Which passage would apply, for example, to a situation in which an armed bank robber was running away from the police and about to make good his escape?

Juveniles

Many departments have different standards for juveniles and adults; typically, officers are instructed not to fire at juveniles except in defense of a life. The problem is that it is not always easy to distinguish juveniles from adults; there are few departments that have gone as far as Kansas City, where the policy states: "The Officer will be required to prove that his judgment in the matter of age was reasonable. If there is any doubt as to the age of the subject, the officer should not shoot."

The Birmingham policy's stricture on shooting at juveniles seems slightly less emphatic. "An officer generally should not shoot at a fleeing felon whom he has reasonable grounds to believe is a juvenile. However, when the escape of such a suspect can reasonably be expected to pose a serious threat to the life of another person, then, under these circumstances, an officer may shoot to prevent the escape of such person. . . ."

In Detroit, most police officers feel that they are not to shoot at fleeing juvenile felons. The policy, in fact, makes no mention of juveniles; the only written reference to juveniles is contained in a training and information bulletin: "[I]t may be well to point out that over seventy percent of UDAA's (car thefts) and larceny from person (purse snatching) is committed by juveniles. Neither of these crimes, in most instances, are of such grave nature as to necessitate the use of an officer's firearm."

Innocent Bystanders

One of the points that more extensive firearms policies tend to cover, and briefer policies do not, is the risk to innocent bystanders. No department is known to demand that its officers refrain from shooting *in self-defense* because of a danger to bystanders. But when the purpose is to make an arrest or prevent an escape, the officer may be instructed not to fire in the direction of uninvolved citizens. The Oakland policy, for example, says that in such situations "firearms shall not be discharged if the member has reason to believe, based upon the attendant circumstances, that the discharge may endanger the lives of passersby or other persons not involved in the crime from which flight is being made or attempted."

Shooting from or at a Moving Vehicle

Shots fired from or at a moving vehicle are widely discouraged for two reasons. First, there is an obvious danger to innocent persons in the area if the driver should lose control of the car. Second, such shots are notorious-ly ineffective. Rather than imposing an outright ban on shooting in these situations, however, departments dealing with the question generally restrict use of firearms to clear cases of imminent danger or merely stress the need for special caution.

New York City has an unusually strong provision: "Discharging a firearm from or at a moving vehicle is prohibited unless the occupants of the other vehicle are using deadly physical force against the officer or another by means other than the vehicle." Officers frequently justify firing at automobiles by testifying that the occupants have attempted to run them down. The New York policy may reflect a suspicion that such claims are often exaggerated or fabricated; from a practical point of view, an officer actually about to be struck by a car could probably find a more promising method of insuring personal safety than the use of a firearm.

Warning Shots

All seven of the sample cities prohibit the use of warning shots in their firearms policy itself, in a supplemental bulletin, or verbally. In explain-ing such a prohibition, some police officials talk about the risk that a shot intended as a warning may strike an innocent person; privately they may fear something else—that officers shooting at a suspect and missing will claim they were merely firing a warning shot, and thus avoid answering for their actions. In addition, officials point out, warning shots rarely ac-complish their purpose, especially if suspects know officers will not or cannot actually shoot them.

Drawing and Display of Firearms

Most departments, taking the view that there are circumstances when drawing or displaying (pointing) a firearm is reasonable and firing it is not, have omitted the subject from their firearms policies altogether. Only a few policies go into the question of when an officer should draw a weapon. The Indianapolis policy (following the wording of Indiana law) begins: "No officer will draw or discharge a firearm except . . ." and then lists the conditions which apply equally to either act. The Pasadena, California, policy takes a slightly different approach: "Firearms shall be removed from holsters only when the officer reasonably believes that he will have to discharge the weapon. . . ."

While neither of these provisions is unambiguous, both might prompt objections from many veteran police officers if narrowly interpreted. It is common practice for officers to draw their weapons upon arrival at the scene of a holdup or burglary, or on checking out a possible suspect in a violent crime. Certainly, no officer wants to enter a bank or liquor store where a holdup alarm has sounded without weapon drawn. Similarly, no officer wants to confront a reported armed suspect in any alleged offense, yet to display a weapon in these circumstances would seem to go against the Indianapolis and Pasadena policies.

One proposed model policy suggests "allowing the draw but preventing the display." The author, Paul M. Gilligan, believes that it is caution enough for officers to hold a gun alongside their legs. Pointing or aiming, however, "must not be allowed without an accompanying legal justification for the actual use of deadly force."[6]

It is true that officers who point their guns indiscriminately may, at best, unnecessarily frighten and offend people and, at worst, bring about a violent incident. But the job of a police officer is unpredictable, and some would argue that if having their firearms in a ready position can reduce the risk inherent in certain situations, then police should be given that right, even at the sacrifice of ideal police community relations.

A plausible compromise, for a department wishing to restrain the display of firearms without putting its members in jeopardy, is a provision such as that contained in the Dallas, Texas, policy:

The policy of this Department permits the drawing and/or displaying of firearms when:

1. An officer, in the exercise of sound judgment, has reason to fear for his own personal safety and/or the safety of others (this includes but is not limited to the search of a building for a burglar, a robbery in progress) or

2. The offender is suspected of having a deadly weapon in his possession. (The intent of this provision is to permit the officers to protect themselves and others *and* to avoid the necessity of actually having to use a firearm when the threat of doing so might accomplish the purpose.)

Shotguns

Nearly all big-city police departments use shotguns, but not all departments issue them to patrol officers. In some jurisdictions only superior officers or members of special units are equipped with shotguns.

The need for a shotgun arises when police anticipate confronting an armed subject or group of subjects at close range. Whether a department should issue shotguns to all its members or have one in every car is a difficult question. It is expensive to train hundreds of police officers in the use of a shotgun, and dangerous to put one in the hands of an untrained person. In addition, the widespread use of shotguns frequently makes for bad public relations. Finally, because shotguns have to be left inside

6. Paul M. Gilligan, "Police Policy Formulation on Firearms: Some Considerations," *The Police Chief* (May 1971).

vehicles during many, indeed most, police calls, there is always the risk of theft.

In one city surveyed, an officer observed a subject breaking into a basement window, chased him, ordered him to halt, and fired at the subject with a shotgun from a distance of more than 200 feet. Although the shot struck its mark and a burglar was thereby apprehended, such an incident raises at least two questions: First, wasn't there a substantial risk to innocent persons from the expanded shot pattern over so great a distance; and second, would the officer, if not carrying such a heavy and cumbersome weapon, have been able to apprehend the suspect without the use of any firearm?

Since the time of our site visit, Portland has put shotguns in patrol cars, a step prompted by an alarming increase in armed attacks on officers. This step was taken, however, only after considerable thought and planning, resulting in a set of procedures and policy guidelines that tell officers when and when not to take shotguns with them on assignments. Each patrol car is equipped with a shotgun mount but the weapons are issued only at the discretion of supervisory officers.

Second Guns

In two of the seven sample cities, it is not uncommon for officers on duty and in uniform to carry a second or "back-up" weapon. Detroit expressly permits the practice. Indianapolis, at the time of our visit, tolerated it despite a regulation that could be interpreted to the contrary. In July 1975, a revised general order was put into effect in Indianapolis which specifically stated that "officers wishing to carry a second gun may do so providing it is a departmentally approved weapon and remains concealed from public view."

The rationale for a second gun, presumably, is that it will protect officers should they be disarmed, run out of ammunition, or have mechanical difficulties with the primary weapon. But there are many possible pitfalls. First, the practice is likely to make it harder to prevent the improper carrying of "drop guns"—weapons carried for planting on a suspect in order to build a case or justify a police shooting. In a department in which no additional firearms are permitted, the sight of a second gun protruding from an officer's pocket will be cause for immediate investigation by a passing superior. In cities such as Detroit and Indianapolis, where second guns are allowed, the passing superior might reasonably assume that such an extra gun was merely an officer's back-up weapon.

In addition, the practice may cause an officer to be less cautious— perhaps to take unnecessary risks rather than call for assistance. It could also hamper the investigation of an incident by making it harder to trace a bullet to an officer's gun.

Finally, by leaving so important a question as the carrying of a second gun to the discretion of the individual officer, a department risks reinforcing the belief of many rank-and-file officers that desk-bound command officials have no idea what it is like out on the street. If officers are allowed to decide for themselves what weapons they should carry, why not decide for themselves when to use them?

Structure and Language of Firearms Policies

Many police firearms policies seem poorly organized, badly worded, or both. Sometimes, apparent conflicts within a policy may be the result of a department's attempt to say two things at once—one thing to officers for their own information and another thing to the courts for the handling of incidents gone awry.

In some cities, it is difficult even to locate a complete copy of the firearms policy, which may be split among several department orders issued over a period of years. Oakland's provision against shooting fleeing burglars, for example, is contained in an order separate from the main firearms policy. Policies also can be long and confusing. The Kansas City policy, the longest of those studied, was written immediately after the shooting of a 15-year-old prowler, an incident that generated considerable controversy, and may, therefore, be reflecting the trying circumstances in which it was conceived.

Some firearms policies are far too complex or the language too convoluted to be of practical use to police officers. For example, the Dallas policy, composed mostly of excerpts from Texas law, includes among its many sections and subsections the following:

(c) A peace officer is justified in using deadly force against another when and to the degree the peace officer reasonably believes the deadly force is immediately necessary to make an arrest, or to prevent escape after arrest, if the use of force would have been justified under Subsection (a) of this section and:

1. the actor reasonably believes the conduct for which arrest is authorized included the use or attempted use of deadly force; or

2. the actor reasonably believes there is substantial risk that the person to be arrested will cause death or serious bodily injury to the actor or another if the arrest is delayed.

Some policies, or parts of them, are heavily philosophical. A one-page order issued by a former chief of the Indianapolis department in 1974, for example, concludes with the following paragraph:

The Indianapolis Police Department values life so highly that each individual member is sworn to give a substantial portion of his or her own life at great risk to make certain that all other lives are safeguarded. The fabric of civilization and law which makes possible enjoyment of life and property in our community is worthy of careful and certain defense.

Not only is the precise meaning of this passage unclear, but some officers could find its moralistic tone patronizing. As impressive as such discursions may be to outsiders, their impact on the conduct of police officers is questionable.

Conclusion

Our survey of the literature, the law, and recent court decisions, as well as a review of shooting incidents in seven cities has left us with the strong feeling that police departments should adopt written firearms policies. The administrative objective in adopting a formal policy is twofold:

1. Control over police use of firearms and protection of the community. Although no study has yet extensively documented the impact of formal policies on the rate or nature of police shootings of civilians, it stands to reason that the desired result is more likely to come about if the intent of a police administrator is conveyed in a clearly written document that lets officers know what is and what is not permissible behavior. A formal policy also tells the community what standard of conduct it can expect from the police department.

2. Reduction in the number and degree of adverse results from both criminal and civil litigation arising from shooting incidents. These benefits can be expected to flow not only to individual police officers but to the department and to governing agencies. A clearly stated policy removes much of the uncertainty that can surround many situations confronting both individual officers and department administrators, and will certainly help to resolve subsequent legal issues that may arise after a shooting incident.

It is not enough, however, just to commit a policy to paper. If police officers are to respect the departments which employ them, it is important that rules be (and be perceived as) clear and reasonable. Firearms policies, and policies in general, should be written for use on the street rather than for public relations or for after-the-fact insurance against liability. The best way to accomplish this seems to be to examine other departments' firearms policies and perhaps to borrow elements from "model" or existing policies, adding whatever provisions seem appropriate for the individual department in light of local and state statutes and local community needs.

Table 1 —Comparative Elements in Departmental Policies

	Oakland	Birmingham	Detroit	Kansas City	Indianapolis	Washington, D.C.	Portland
Shooting of fleeing burglars permitted?	No	Yes	Yes	No	Yes[2]	No	No
Auto thieves?	No	Yes	No	No	Yes[2]	No	No
Fleeing juvenile felons?	No	Discouraged	Discouraged[3]	No	Yes[2]	Yes	Yes[1]
Warning shots permitted?	No	No	No	No	Prohibited by unwritten rule	No	No
Must officer have positive knowledge or reasonable belief that suspect has committed a felony?	Belief	Belief	Known "as a virtual certainty"	Belief	Certain knowledge	Belief	Belief
Does policy include caution on firing at or from moving vehicle?	Yes	No	Yes	Yes	No	Yes	No
Carrying an off-duty firearm (in jurisdiction)?	—	—	—	Optional	Mandatory	Mandatory	Optional
Are officers permitted to carry "second guns"?	No	No	Yes	No	Yes	No	No

1. The Portland policy includes a clause not taken into account here, authorizing use of firearms against *any* fleeing felon if, "under the total circumstances at the time and place, the use of such force is necessary."

2. The policy includes the proviso: "[after] all other reasonable means of capture have been expended."

3. The subject of juveniles is discussed obliquely in supplemental training bulletin.

SPLIT-SECOND DECISIONS:
SHOOTINGS OF AND BY CHICAGO POLICE*

The empirical and legal study on which this summary is based is the product of three-and-a-half years of research by the Chicago Law Enforcement Study Group, an independent, nonprofit, criminal justice research organization sponsored by 25 legal, social service and community groups.[1] Extensive data on shootings of and by Chicago police officers were collected from a number of sources, the most important being the Chicago Police Department's internal investigative files. These files had never been voluntarily opened to persons outside the official law enforcement system prior to this study, and the Chicago Police Department deserves praise for having the courage to cooperate with this research in the face of pervasive official secrecy about police shootings.

The Study Group's purpose in seeking access to these highly confidential files was two-fold: (1) We wanted to describe comprehensively the phenomena known as "police shootings," possibly dispelling myths held by the community, the media, and police officers alike; and (2) We hoped our analysis and recommendations would provide information that could be of use in reducing the number of shootings of and by police—both in Chicago and elsewhere.[2]

The importance of such research need not be stated at length: Regardless of the justifiability of shootings by police, such incidents sometimes have societal consequences far beyond the injury or death of the shooting victims. Gilbert Pompa, Director of the U.S. Justice Depart-

---

* William A. Geller and Kevin J. Karales, *Split-Second Decisions: Shootings of and by Police* (Chicago: Chicago Law Enforcement Study Group, © 1981 by William A. Geller), pp. 1-3, pp. 8-9 and pp. 13-14. Reprinted with permission of the authors.

1. The efforts of our staff and sponsoring organizations were greatly facilitated by a large and talented group of advisors, most of whom donated their services.

2. The applicability of our findings and recommendations outside of Chicago is uncertain since our data concern only Chicago events. But we think it safe to assume that police administrators in other large cities will find much that is pertinent to their experiences in our recommendations. This is not to suggest that our data are comparable to data concerning use of deadly force by other police departments. A multiplicity of definitional differences would make such comparisons extremely misleading.

ment's Community Relations Service, recently called police shootings "the most volatile and potentially divisive force in the nation today." Police-involved shootings have played key roles in triggering several of America's disastrous urban riots, Miami (1980) being the most recent.

The scope of our inquiry may be delineated briefly. In using the term "deadly force," we mean only shootings. The study encompasses all shootings of and by officers of the Chicago Police Department reported to have occurred within the city limits from January 1, 1974 through December 31, 1978. In addition, the numbers of civilians shot by police during 1979 and 1980 are presented, but no data were collected on the characteristics of these individuals or the incidents in which they were shot. Both on- and off-duty and unintentional shootings are included. Encounters in which shots were fired at or by police but in which no person was hit are not part of the data set because there was insufficient time to collect such information. We agree with other researchers that the ideal subject of research on police shootings is the officer's decision whether to pull the trigger, not the fortuitous result that a person was struck by a bullet. The best approach to examining this decision would involve comparing instances in which police used their guns with those in which no shots were fired. Within the narrower confines of this study, 650 qualifying incidents occurred from 1974 through 1978. In these incidents, 523 civilians were shot by police and 187 police were shot by civilians, by themselves, or by their colleagues. The characteristics of these incidents and their police and civilian participants were computer analyzed.[3]

In thinking about the results of this analysis, it is important for the reader to keep in mind the nature of our data. Although civilian accounts of the shootings analyzed are reflected to some extent in the source documents, our data are based for the most part on statements by the officers involved in the shootings either as shooters or victims. Accordingly, some degree of "reporting bias" may taint the data. A large number of the variables we analyzed are very likely to have been reported accurately (e.g., the age, gender, race and degree of injury—wounded vs. killed—of the civilian and police participants in the shooting incidents, the officers' unit, duty status and experience in the Department.) On the other hand, some other variables (e.g., degree of threat or danger to officer) may be less immune to reporting bias. For example, it would certainly have been possible for officers to exaggerate the degree of danger they felt at the time they shot a civilian. Such exaggeration could stem from a conscious or unconscious desire by the shooting officer to legitimize self conduct in one's own mind or to avoid discipline for a questionable shooting. Because it

---

3. The principal analytic techniques relied upon were simple cross tabulations and correlations, using the "SPSS" standard program. Time and resource constraints precluded us from using multivariate statistical techniques.

was impractical for us to independently attempt to verify the police accounts of these shootings, we have no way of knowing how often such
reporting bias may be present in our data or what patterns, if any, it
might follow—except that it almost certainly would put police officers in
a favorable light. Indeed, it would be unusual if police officers were ex-
empt from the human tendency, exhibited by most workers in most job
settings, to try to place their own conduct in the best possible light when
under the scrutiny of their employer. While any reporting bias is a source
of concern, we are convinced that a cautious and thorough examination
of police records is far more enlightening and beneficial to the public than
a continuation of virtually complete public ignorance on the subject of
police-involved shootings. Despite any limitations of scope and reliability,
this data base is one of the most comprehensive that has been developed,
and affords the public with our first panoramic look at the deadly force
issue in Chicago. Further, findings that reveal room for improvement in
police practices are that much more credible if based on data that give the
benefit of the doubt to the police.

This summary has the same structure as the full report, but excludes
summaries of the background chapters reviewing the "historical/legal
context" of police shootings and the prior and contemporaneous research.
Some tables from the report are combined and simplified in this summary
to highlight their key elements.

Shootings of Civilians—A Typology

Figure 1 presents an original typology of the reasons Chicago police officers gave their superiors for shooting civilians from 1974 through 1978.

In all, 523 civilians were shot by police, 85% intentionally and 14%
unintentionally. The vast majority of the intentional shooting victims
were shot, according to the involved officers, because of their use or
threatened use of a deadly weapon against the officer or another person.
Seventeen percent of the victims were shot when offering no resistance
other than flight, although all 89 of these individuals were reportedly
suspected of having just committed a "forcible felony," a key statutory
prerequisite to an officer's use of deadly force to effect arrest. Nearly half
of all these "fleeing forcible felon" shootings involved suspected
burglaries. Of the three types of unintentional shootings identified—accidental, mistaken identity, and stray bullet—the first is clearly the most
common, accounting for 10% of all civilian shooting victims.

Shootings of Police Officers

As with shootings of civilians by police, we have categorized the shootings
of police officers. The following typology, depicted in Figure 2, specifies
the intent and identity of the perpetrator.

Figure 1 — Typology: Reasons Given by Police for Shooting Civilians in Chicago, 1974-1978

(N = 523 Civilians shot)

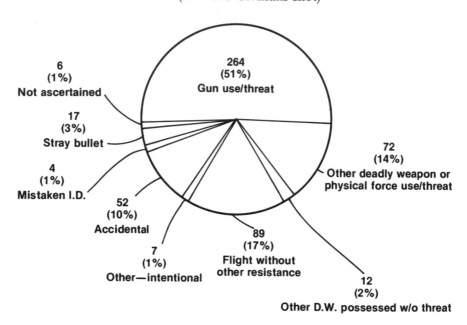

Shootings of officers by civilians accounted for 58% of all of the 187 officers shot, while at least 38% of the victim officers were shot by themselves or their colleagues. Shootings of officers by themselves or by other officers, with the exception of 11 suicides or attempts, were always reported to be unintentional events.

Most of the officers were shot while off-duty (52%). This was true of 44% of the officers shot by civilians, 75% of those who accidentally shot themselves, 100% of the suicide/attempts, but only 25% of the officers shot by other officers. Three explanations are offered for this high percentage of off-duty events: (1) There is a high number of self-inflicted shootings, which are primarily an off-duty phenomenon; (2) Officers consider their responsibility for off-duty police action to include aggressive intervention in crime situations; and (3) A number of officers (primarily Black) live and spend their off-duty time in high-crime areas of the city.

Figure 2 — Typology: Chicago Police Shot, 1974-1978

(N = 187)

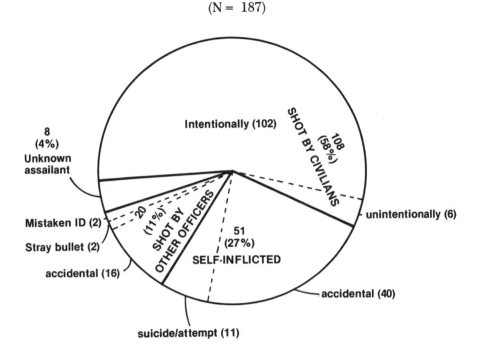

Despite an initial assumption that shootings of police and shootings by police would be fairly strongly correlated over time, the data have indicated that they are not. While shootings of police by civilians remain relatively constant over time, police shootings of civilians display wide variation. The correlation coefficient obtained for quarterly frequencies of both types of shootings from 1974 through 1978 was + .15, a very weak positive value, indicating that neither type of shooting causes the other on a systematic basis. For an individual officer, however, the risk of being shot may affect individual likelihood of shooting a civilian.

We also looked at departmental initiatives that may have had an impact on shootings. The frequencies of Officer of Professional Standards "adverse" findings in *non*-deadly, excessive force cases and the 1977-1978 deadly force in-service training were examined. We found a moderately strong "negative" correlation (− .64) between O.P.S. decisions recommending discipline for uses of non-deadly force and shootings of civilians by police. Thus, as the frequency of one variable increases, the frequency of the other decreases. If disciplinary decisions are indeed the causal factor in this relationship, discipline for officers' use of non-deadly force may help control police use of deadly force.

While it is possible that the 1977-1978 in-service deadly force training helped produce the reduction in shootings in 1978, the impact of this training is subject to question, for several reasons. For example, training urged restraint in shooting fleeing burglary suspects, but shootings of this type did not significantly decrease in 1978. Further, examination of variations in types of shootings over time suggests that shootings may fluctuate without regard to any departmental initiatives to control them. "Defense-of-life" and "non-defense-of-life" shootings were found generally to increase or decrease together. This may suggest that the substantial decreases in shootings in 1976 and 1978 stemmed from fewer opportunities for shootings during those years, rather than from police avoidance of whatever shootings they could avoid.

Recommendations—Shooting Control Strategies

Drawing on our data, literature review, and consultation with police trainers and administrators, we have identified strategies for reducing the number of "avoidable" shootings by and of police officers. These control strategies are by no means the only reasonable ways to work toward this goal, but they seem to be promising ones. A number of these strategies or variations of them are already being used by some police departments, including the Chicago Police Department. We urge police administrators to give serious consideration to employing all these techniques in their ongoing efforts to control police shootings.

General considerations bearing on the avoidability of shootings are presented, including the following: (1) the degree to which the officer's or another person's life would be immediately endangered if the officer did not shoot; (2) the availability of alternative, less violent means of capturing a suspect; (3) the extent to which the officer can obviate use of deadly force against a potentially violent suspect by using better search and field interrogation techniques or by maintaining cover and still controlling the situation until a non-lethal capture can be accomplished; (4) the degree of risk to bystanders which might be posed by police use of deadly force; (5) the reliability of information upon which the officer's irreversible decision to shoot is made; and (6) the extent to which officer carelessness, nervousness, bad gun handling habits or other "correctable" factors were largely responsible for the shooting.

On a number of these dimensions, a sizable number of shootings by police officers would seem to be avoidable. Many such shootings are prompted by civilian conduct that does not immediately jeopardize the lives of officers or the public (nonviolent flight being a prime example). Others seem to be the result of poor gun handling habits (carrying cocked revolvers, carelessness in gun cleaning, etc.). In many cases, we believe that greater tactical and human relations skills could have given officers the "strategic edge" necessary to permit them to resolve a potentially violent encounter without firing their weapons or placing themselves in grave danger.

The control strategies we recommend fall into four basic areas: policy development, policy enforcement, personnel practices, and training and weapons. Because it is the most controversial, we devote somewhat more space in this summary to the first approach.

Policy development. We recommend the adoption of a "defense-of-life" shooting policy. Recognizing that amplification is required on a number of points (e.g., shooting as a last resort, reasonableness of the officer's perception of danger), we suggest the following as the core message of the policy: A police officer is justified in using deadly force only when such force is intended to defeat a present threat to the officer's or another person's life. This policy is supported on a number of grounds, including the following: (1) It justifies shootings based on information easily and instantly available to officers in the field—their honest perceptions of immediate danger—rather than on generalizations about the future dangerousness of persons suspected (rightly or wrongly) of having committed any one of a series of enumerated felonies; (2) The recommended policy, which admittedly is based to an important extent on value choices, would not inhibit police officers from shooting when they honestly felt it was necessary to protect their own or someone else's life; (3) The shooting of a person who is not immediately jeopardizing someone's life may be discovered, too late, to have been prompted by misinformation about the shooting victim's prior or likely future conduct. Even if predictions about the future "dangerousness" of a fleeing suspect are based on accurate information about past behavior, research suggests that such predictions are likely to be woefully inaccurate; (4) Policies which do not restrict shootings to defense-of-life situations permit the killing of people for the *possible* commission of crimes for which they would never be executed if convicted; and (5) Very often, "lethal capture" of non-threatening suspects fails to accomplish its ostensible purpose—to take a criminal suspect alive and bring him to trial. To the contrary, the use of deadly force without necessity to defend life has engendered widespread resentment of police, especially in minority communities, making the broad spectrum of police work that much more difficult.

Policy enforcement. No policy is any better than its enforcement. The Chicago Police Department's Office of Professional Standards and a "shooting review panel" that would focus less on discipline than on prevention of future shootings are promising enforcement techniques. A number of practical issues, such as possible expansion of civil and criminal liability for wrongful or unnecessary police shootings, need to be creatively addressed in connection with the proposed shooting review panel. Such a panel would need to collect different kinds of information on shootings than is currently collected for disciplinary purposes and would need to treat police officers as "expert witnesses" on the question of how to improve Departmental policies, training, supervision and operations so as to both obviate shootings and ensure officer and public safety. Among other promising policy enforcement techniques are several which concern field supervision, communication by headquarters to district-level administrators of information about patrol officers who are "violence prone," and review of police shootings not only by the Police Department but by local and federal officials and, with appropriate safeguards, by private entities.

Personnel practices. Officers should be hired, promoted, and commended or disciplined with an awareness that, while "toughness" is critical to the police role, so is non-violent problem solving. Psychological screening tests and routine monitoring of officer behavior should be used to the extent that they can help separate officers who would properly exercise their discretion to use deadly force from those who would not.

Training and weapons. Training is recommended in three basic areas: policy, human relations techniques, and tactics for the use and *non-use* of weapons. A tactical exercise is described which helps officers learn how to use cover and positioning to maximize their chances of resolving tense situations without unduly exposing themselves to danger. Other areas for improvement are identified, including two: (1) Officers could be better trained in when "heroic" action on their part is commendable and when it could prove counter-productive; and (2) an *outdoor* police training facility, currently lacking in Chicago, would expand the capacity of Departmental trainers to prepare police officers to be more effective with less bloodshed.

Several recommendations are also made concerning weapons, including: (1) increased range practice and instruction in the handling of service revolvers and other guns; (2) greater restrictions on the types and possibly the number of handguns officers can carry; (3) modification of service revolvers to preclude "single-action firing," a method which involves cocking the weapon and has been responsible for a number of accidental shootings of civilians and police officers; and (4) exploration of the extent to which modern, "less-lethal weapons" can be used, as they are in other police departments, to effectively facilitate the non-lethal capture of certain kinds of criminal suspects.

Chapter 4
REVIEW OF POLICE CONDUCT

Introduction

The police function as society's mechanism for maintaining ordered liberty. Unquestionably the police are at the cutting edge of society's ills. Consequently their conduct is under constant scrutiny.

In many instances police conduct becomes embroiled in the political process and alleged police misconduct becomes a political issue. The romanticists become the champion of human rights and are in conflict with the pragmatists who are concerned about controlling crime.

The problem (review of police conduct) must be viewed in the total context that acknowledges the complexity of our society. The police are not responsible for the economic and political conditions that exist today nor are they equipped to deal with the multitude of issues that are clearly beyond their control.

When pondering only one aspect of police misconduct—police brutality—then consideration should be given to the opinion of Kenneth J. Mathulia[1] who points out that:

> The police have often been cited as the scapegoat cause of many of our community ills. The police have been accused of precipitating community disturbances in Houston, Miami, Chicago, Flint, and Philadelphia; yet, each of these major disturbances has been thoroughly studied and has resulted in similar conclusions: "disturbances do not erupt as a result of a single triggering or precipitating incident.[10]"

We do not intend to suggest that the police share *no* blame for the ills of our society; we merely want to place them at their rightful plateau in the hierarchy of concerns.

---

1. Kenneth J. Mathula, *A Balance of Forces* (Washington, D.C.: I.A.C.P., 1982), pp. 7-8.

Over 10,000 civil rights violations charging brutality by police are being reported to the Justice Department every year. In 1977, for example, there were about 12,000 complaints of which about 3,500 required investigation; some 50 were presented to the Grand Jury resulting in litigation of about 25 with convictions in about 16 cases.[11]

Can the conviction of 16 police officers for brutality out of an estimated 500,000 be considered a national problem? Or, is police brutality merely an over-used cliche rendered almost meaningless because of its being applied to everything from murder[12] to a police officer's using gentle persuasion to move a group of loitering juveniles? Is it possible that a few bureaucrats are using emotional and frustrated minorities to generate sufficient controversy from which to build an empire?[13]

---

10. An investigative panel appointed by the Governor of the State of Florida to determine cause of the Miami riots of May 17-19, 1980, concluded causes to be facism, neglect of and negative action against Blacks, perception of racism by Blacks, poverty, poor housing, functional illiteracy, the criminal justice system, complaints of police brutality, inadequate recreational facilities for the young, political deprivation and hard core delinquency. (*New York Times*, Dec. 1, 1980).

"The experience of the Community Relations Service supports the National Advisory Commission (disorders do not erupt as a result of a single so-called triggering or precipitating incident). It has been the product of CRS assessment in Chicano disorders at Moody Park in Houston, the Puerto Rican disorders in Chicago, and Black disorders in Miami, Florida; Flint, Michigan and Philadelphia, Pennsylvania." (Remarks of: Gilbert S. Pompa, Director, Community Relations Service, U.S. Department of Justice at the Peter W. Rodino Institute, Nov. 6, 1980.)

11. Assistant Attorney General Drew Days III in a speech to the 115th Session of the FBI National Academy, November 1, 1978.

12. The alleged killing of Arthur McDuffie by officers in Dade County, Florida; the alleged drowning of Joe Campos Torres by officers in Houston, Texas.

13. Statement of the United States Commission on Civil Rights, "Police Practices and the Preservation of Civil Rights," July 9, 1980. Recommendation: (1) The Congress approve the hiring of additional personnel for the criminal section of the Civil Rights Division of the Department of Justice in order to make it possible for the department to handle cases involving alleged violations of civil rights by police effectively and expeditiously. (2) The President and Congress urgently address the need for the services of the "Community Relations Service" and provide for an expansion of its staff and resources so that the important work it is doing in mediating police-citizen conflicts can be extended.

In the eyes of most police administrators, the effectiveness of law enforcement rests on the relative autonomy which society has invested in the police. Therefore, any demands made for public review of police misconduct are typically regarded as intrusions upon that autonomy and as threats to effective law enforcement. Such demands are also viewed by many administrators as an attempt to politicize the police. This is especially resented because, during the last quarter of a century, police agencies have gained relative freedom from partisan political interference. It is commonly felt among police administrators that when officers become subject to public review for their actions they will become, once again, instruments of pressure group politics. Finally, it is feared that public analysis of police conduct by review boards or other similarly constituted bodies will erode officers' morale by stripping away the self-contained authority to both discipline and control misconduct among the ranks.

There are other objections to public review of police conduct. One of the major contentions is that review boards threaten administrative authority. Management theory in all aspects of public administration repeatedly supports the position that a chief administrative officer is responsible for the conduct of his agency; concomitant with this responsibility is adequate authority. Dispersal of this formal authority will reduce the decisive and dramatic characteristics that are essential aspects of agency leadership.[2]

Compromise and conciliation are essential if this critical problem is to be resolved. The Michigan State study visualized two distinct alternate possibilities for the police:

1. They can refuse to initiate any changes and be prepared to tolerate decreasing public respect and suffer increased violence; or

2. They can admit some fallibility, welcome criticism, compromise a little, and objectively initiate considered changes in an effort to enhance public support and avoid violence.[3]

The proposals for review of police conduct can be categorized as follows:

Internal Review.

Civilian Review Boards.

The President's Commission pointed out that:

> ...formal machinery within every police department for the investigation of complaints against police activity or employees is an absolute necessity. It is also important that the complainant be personally informed of the results of the investigation and the disposition of the complaint. Every large department has machinery of some kind for dealing with charges of misconduct by its members,

---

2. For detailed discussion of administrative authority, see John M. Pfiffner, *Public Administration* (New York: The Ronald Press Company, 1967), pp. 212-216 and Peter Blau, *The Dynamics of Bureaucracy*, 2nd Ed. (Chicago: University of Chicago Press, 1962).

3. Michigan State University, A report submitted to the President's Commission on Law Enforcement and Administration of Justice, *A National Survey of Police and Community Relations, Field Surveys V* (Washington, D.C.: U.S. Government Printing Office, 1967), p. 256.

whether those charges originate inside or outside the department. It typically consists of a board of high-ranking officers or, in some cases, nonsworn departmental officials, that investigate the facts of alleged dereliction and make a recommendation to the departmental administrator. He properly has the authority and responsibility to take disciplinary action. When this kind of machinery is fully and fairly used it succeeds both in disciplining misbehaving officers and deterring others from misbehaving.

If the complainant remains dissatisfied with the disposition of the case, there are other avenues of appeal outside the police agency: the local prosecutor; the courts; elected officials such as councilmen or the mayor; the state's attorney general; the U.S. Department of Justice; and various civil rights or human relations commissions. While all of these are traditional institutions of legal redress they are frequently too formal, awesome, or geographically far removed for the often bewildered citizen. Some of them lack the machinery or resources to process grievances. Some can take action only if a criminal law has been violated. But many of the grievances that constitute acts of misconduct will not qualify as a basis for criminal action.

In going beyond the established legal procedures, the Commission finds it unreasonable to single out the police as the only agency that should be subject to special scrutiny from the outside. The Commission, therefore, does not recommend the establishment of civilian review boards in jurisdictions where they do not exist, solely to review police conduct. The police are only one of a number of official agencies with whom the public has contact, and in some cases, because they are the most visible and conspicuous representatives of local government, they may be the focus of more attention than they deserve. Incompetence and mistreatment by housing, sanitation, health, and welfare officials can be as injurious to citizens as mistreatment by the police and should be equally subject to public scrutiny. These officials, like policemen, are public servants. In view of the increasing involvement of government officials in the lives of citizens, adequate procedures for the consideration of such individual grievances as citizens may have against such officials are essential to effective government. So far as possible, it is desirable that such procedures be established within the governmental agency involved. To the extent that such procedures are ineffective or fail to inspire general public confidence, including the confidence of those who may have legitimate grievances, further recourse is essential. The form that such further recourse should take is dependent on local needs and government structure.[4]

---

4. The President's Commission on Law Enforcement and Administration of Justice, *The Challenge of Crime in a Free Society* (Washington, D.C.: U.S. Government Printing Office, 1967), p. 103.

The National Advisory Commission on Civil Disorders considered the problem of grievance mechanisms and recommended the following:

1. Making a complaint should be easy. It should be possible to file a grievance without excessive formality. If forms are used, they should be easily available and their use explained in widely distributed pamphlets. In large cities, it should not be necessary to go to a central headquarters office to file a complaint, but it should also be possible to file a complaint at neighborhood locations. Police officers on the beat, community service aides or other municipal employees in the community should be empowered to receive complaints.

2. A specialized agency, with adequate funds and staff, should be created separately from other municipal agencies to handle, investigate, and to make recommendations on citizen complaints.

3. The procedure should have a built-in conciliation process to attempt to resolve complaints without the need for full investigation and processing.

4. The complaining party should be able to participate in the investigation and in any hearings, with right of representation by counsel, so that the complaint is fully investigated and findings made on the merits. He should be promptly and fully informed of the outcome. The results of the investigation should be made public.

Although we advocate an external agency as a means of resolving grievances, we believe that the basic need is to adopt procedures which will gain the respect and confidence of the entire community. This need can, in the end, be met only by sustained direction through the line of command, thorough investigation of complaints, and prompt, visible disciplinary action where justified.

5. Since many citizen complaints concern departmental policies rather than individual conduct, information concerning complaints of this sort should be forwarded to the departmental unit which formulates or reviews policy and procedures. Information concerning all complaints should be forwarded to appropriate training units so that any deficiencies correctable by training can be eliminated.[5]

A study of this problem completed by the National Commission on the Causes and Prevention of Violence emphasized that:

...since internal review has been uniformly sluggish, some kind of outside pressure must be brought to bear to induce voluntary correction of illegal and otherwise abusive police conduct. Mandatory injunctions issued by federal district courts are too cumbersome for this purpose and are susceptible to complete disruption of the internal review mechanism. The civilian review boards are doomed to futility

---

5. The National Advisory Commission on Civil Disorders, *Report of the National Advisory Commission on Civil Disorders* (Washington, D.C.: U.S. Government Printing Office, March 1, 1968), p. 163.

since they pit the aggrieved citizen against the police department in a formal adversary proceeding; in short, someone always wins and someone is always resentful. The ombudsman, on the other hand, shifts the focus from dispute resolution to evaluation of the department's grievance response mechanism. Yet, since the primary goals of an effective complaint mechanism are to provide an objective forum and encourage its use, individual grievances must remain in the forefront, and their dispositions must be publicized.

What is needed is a hybrid of the ombudsman and the external review agency, whose operation would have the following attributes:

1.   The primary responsibility for police discipline must remain with the police department itself.

2. There must be an easily accessible agency outside the police department, which processes citizen complaints in their inception rather than on appeal from the police.

3. In each case, this agency should:

(a) make an independent investigation of the complaints;

(b) publicly exonerate the police if the complaint is groundless;

(c) in cases of misunderstanding or minor abuse, attempt to resolve the dispute through an informal conciliation meeting;

(d) if efforts at conciliation should fail or if the police behavior was unacceptable, make recommendations to the Department regarding discipline or ways to relieve tension;

(e) keep each citizen complainant aware of the disposition of his complaint.

4. On all matters, the agency should keep the public aware of its actions and the Department's response to its recommendations and should publish periodic reports and conclusions.

5. So as not to single out the police for special oversight, the agency should be responsible for processing citizen complaints not only against the police but also against other basic governmental service agencies, such as those responsible for welfare and employment.[6]

The National Advisory Commission on Criminal Justice Standards and Goals pointed out that internal discipline in police agencies often is crisis-oriented. Most agencies simply react to employee misconduct. They do a good job of investigation after incidents have occurred, but they do little to prevent them.

The key question police chief executives should attempt to answer concerning employee misconduct is, "Why?" Police supervisors must ask themselves, "What could have prevented the employee from engaging in this particular act of misconduct?" The answer should be made an integral part of the written recommendation for each complaint adjudica-

---

6. The National Commission on the Causes and Prevention of Violence, *Law and Order Reconsidered* (Washington, D.C.: U.S. Government Printing Office, 1970), pp. 393-394.

tion. The police chief executive, even though ultimately responsible for internal discipline, should not bear this diagnostic responsibility alone. It is the responsibility of all employees to seek ways to maintain a disciplined police agency.

Although preventive measures may not automatically produce disciplined performance, they may provide the impetus for the development of self-discipline. A self-disciplined employee will save a police agency time and money by reducing the necessity for much of the administration of internal discipline.

Preventive programs differ as much as the police agencies that run them; therefore, each agency must analyze its particular problem and innovate. Most of the preventive programs used by the few police agencies active in this field are controversial. The utilization of these programs is not a panacea for police misconduct. Neither are they blueprints for successful programs. Police misconduct is the result of many factors and cannot always be foreseen, discouraged, or circumvented. But a great deal of misconduct can be prevented by police agency programs and policies.

Each of the national studies cited in the preceding discussion has proposed a different solution for the difficult problem of police misconduct and its control, but it remains to be seen whether or not these or other recommendations as discussed in the following articles in this section will prove to be acceptable to the police profession and the community.

COMPLAINT PROCEDURES: VARIATIONS ON THE THEME OF CIVILIAN PARTICIPATION*

It is clearly apparent that if the police do not take a vigorous stand on the matter of internal investigation, outside groups—such as review boards consisting of laymen or other persons outside the police service—will step into the void.

The legitimate use of force, or the threat of force as a method for imposing constraints on citizens who have violated the law or are considering deviating from the norms of society, is one of the basic monopolies of power that citizens defer to their government. Of the government agencies that share this monopoly, the police are not only the most visible but are generally given the most power to exercise this task. Until fairly recently (the last 20 years), the police were afforded a good deal of latitude in their methods of law enforcement and order maintenance. This degree of freedom has been altered somewhat with the Warren Court placing legal restrictions on the police and the various national commissions recommending internal changes in police departments. Despite these efforts, one problem continues to exacerbate critics of police: the apparent inability of the police to assure the public that they are capable of policing themselves.

At issue is the process employed by most police departments for handling citizen complaints regarding questionable police conduct.[1] These accusations can involve illegal activities or improper conduct. Traditionally, this has been the sole responsibility of the department because it is considered the most efficient method of regulating police. The department receives the complaint, investigates the issue, and then determines an appropriate sanction if the officer has not been exonerated. The rationale frequently given for using this method, in addition to the claim that it is efficient, is that only police understand the complexities of the law enforcement task. Thus, like other professionals (such as doctors,

---

* Richard J. Terrill, "Complaint Procedures: Variations on the Theme of Civilian Participation," *Journal of Police Science and Administration*, Vol. 10, No. 4, 1982, pp. 398-406. Reprinted with permission.

1. The International Association of Chiefs of Police developed a manual entitled *Managing for Effective Police Discipline* (1977).

lawyers, and teachers), they should be given the responsibility of policing themselves.[2] This argument is enhanced further when one examines the prevailing organizational philosophy of most police departments. Police departments are typically quasi-military establishments that subscribe to the classical organizational principles enunciated in the theories of Frederick Taylor and Max Weber. When transferred to the police context, these theories suggest that control must come from within the department to assure discipline among the rank and file, accountability to the chief, and maintenance of morale within the force.[3] Thus, the most common type of control of police behavior is an internal one.

Adherence to this total in-house process has been the subject of increased criticism. Allegations against departments include: discouraging citizen complaints by acting hostile to the complainant when a charge is filed; a lack of objectivity in the investigation of the complaint by allowing the accused officer's immediate unit to investigate the matter; failing to provide formal adversary hearings which often results in secrecy and the lack of procedural safeguards for both the accused and the victim; and the unwillingness of some departments to impose meaningful discipline on officers found guilty of misconduct. Citizen involvement in the police complaint process is being suggested as an alternative to monitor the procedure and to assure some semblance of fundamental fairness.

This article examines two issues:

1. Are the views commonly put forth by the police, who oppose any external type of control over their mechanisms for misconduct, valid?

2. Have new mechanisms been established in recent years that permit citizen involvement in the complaint process?

One caveat is in order. There has never been a national opinion poll that suggests that the majority of citizens are displeased with police policing themselves. Most of the concern has been voiced by groups like the American Civil Liberties Union, the National Association for the Advancement of Colored People, or by students of the criminal justice system. In the near future it is unlikely to expect significant agitation nationally from citizens favoring an external system of review as the trend toward a more conservative climate of opinion in this country will undoubtedly discourage or resist such a movement.

---

2. In recent years, much has been written about whether or not the police occupation has professional standing. I tend to agree with Wilson (1968:283) that police work is more a craft than a profession. In any event, a person's relationship with one of the traditional professions (medical, legal, and educational) is based on a freedom to choose such professional services. People do not have that choice with police.

3. A number of books and articles have been written discussing the problems of retaining the classical theory of organization to police departments. Among the articles. Cordner (1978) and Hudson (1970) offer a concise analysis of the problem.

Nevertheless, history is replete with ideas that lacked the support of a majority of people but eventually gained widespread acceptance. This will probably be the fate of proponents of citizen involvement in the complaint process. Despite this seemingly dismal prediction, civilian participation in the process is a contemporary issue that many departments will have to address themselves to in the 1980s. This is especially true for those cities that have the potential for outbreaks of civil unrest similar to those that have already occurred in Philadelphia, Houston, and Miami.[4]

Police Opposition to External Review

During the past 20 years, the police have voiced strong opposition to the use of civilians in the complaint process and have offered a number of arguments to support their position. It is important to examine these arguments to determine the extent to which they are valid.[5]

1. *Due to the nature of their job, the police are apt to have a number of false accusations brought against them, especially by those who have been arrested or issued a citation.* Thus, the number of valid instances alleging police misconduct is probably not as great as it might appear. Although plausible, this argument should not detract us from the implicit point of view that police subscribe to, which is that only they are capable of weighing and determining the truth of citizens' statements. The police have not cornered the market on such wisdom, for if they had we would have abolished the jury system long ago.

2. *Given the variety of tasks that police are expected to perform, often under stressful circumstances, mistakes are bound to occur.* Police argue that some mistakes can be alleviated by more rigorous recruitment campaigns and with improved techniques in basic training and continuing education programs. Many departments are making sincere efforts at improving recruitment, selection, and training. The movement in a few states to require the certification of all peace officers is another positive approach. Unfortunately, it is improbable that these efforts alone will eliminate the problem central to this article.

3. *Aggrieved citizens, especially those who believe their civil rights have been violated, have recourse to the criminal law through prosecutors and grand juries and can also seek redress through civil claims.* Ideally, the law and the appropriate judicial institutions should be effective sources to seek redress. In reality, however, they have fallen short of the mark. Much has been written on this point. Among the reasons frequently

---

4. See the United States Commission on Civil Rights. For some of the scholarly treatment on this problem, see Fogelson, Friedrich, Reiss, and Westley.
5. The following arguments were cited by Black and the International Association of Chiefs of Police.

given for this ineffectiveness are: (1) the availability of tort remedies is limited; (2) the resolution of civil remedies is frequently slow; (3) complainants are often unwilling to initiate a suit because of a lack of personal funds; (4) there is a scarcity of witnesses for corroborating complainants' statements; (5) plaintiffs are unlikely to receive a sizable recovery for damages; (6) local prosecutors are unwilling to prosecute because they rely upon a positive working relationship with the police department; and (7) judges and juries are more apt to believe the officer than the complainant, who is frequently poor, has an unusual lifestyle, or has a criminal record. Moreover, by suggesting that the citizen turn to the court to seek redress, the police are assuming that most complainants want to sue or prosecute the police. Although the number of suits filed against the police has risen dramatically in recent years, the police are missing the point regarding the intentions of many citizens who file misconduct charges. Many allegations are not appropriate for such formal courtroom proceedings and a substantial number of citizens are not interested in seeking that kind of redress.

4. *By instituting a civilian review board, the police would be unable to fight crime effectively.* Implicit in this argument is a belief that the crime rate will increase. Following the urban riots of 1964, J. Edgar Hoover concluded "that where there is an outside civilian review board, the restraint of the police was so great that effective action against the rioters appeared to be impossible,"[6] This charge was refuted by officials of the Rochester and Philadelphia civilian police advisory board.[7] However, when pressed to substantiate his conclusion Hoover did not respond.[8] Furthermore, because of the very nature of the causal inferences, weak correlational statements are frequently hazardous. Since no statistical data were presented to support the claim that police efficiency would be hampered in fighting crime, and since crime rates continue to increase nationally without review boards, the authors of such a claim were desperately grasping at any illogical straw that happened to be blowing in the wind.

5. *Review boards would demoralize the police to the extent that an increase in resignations and retirements would leave the citizens unprotected.* This never materialized in the 1960s, and given current job market considerations, it is highly unlikely that it would occur today.

6. *Review boards would interfere with the authority of the chief, thus making it impossible for him to control the disciplinary mechanism of the department.* This rationale is interesting for three reasons. First, in both Philadelphia and New York, where review boards were established, the

---

6. *New York Times*, September 27, 1964.

7. *New York Times*, September 28, 1964.

8. For an extreme rightist position on civilian review boards, see Dieckmann (1965).

commissioner was always the ultimate dispenser of discipline. Second, the Patrolmen's Benevolent Association in New York City, which successfully convinced voters to reject the review board in 1966, had requested in 1959 the creation of a "committee headed by a civilian to review (the commissioner's) decisions against policemen." Third, in light of the Knapp Commission (1972), a strong argument could be made for civilian review of alleged police corruption and misconduct.

7. *Review boards are composed of citizens whose fields of employment and interest are unrelated to law enforcement.* In the case of New York City, this statement is historically incorrect. Three members of the review board were from the department. Two had a total of 50 years' experience in law enforcement, while the other was a former assistant United States attorney. In the case of Philadelphia, the argument is equally fallacious if one accepts the notion that lawyers and professors of criminology have an interest in law enforcement.

8. *Civilians are both unqualified to judge police and are likely to be biased against them.* If civilians were the sole judge of police practices, there might be a modicum of truth to the first of these charges. Neither the New York nor Philadelphia review boards were established in this manner. Regarding the latter point, police concern over a potential civilian witch-hunt was unfounded in the case of Philadelphia (Coxe 1965). When Niederhoffer (1967:189) examined the New York Police Department's trial room procedure, he concluded "that at least 80 percent of the patrolmen are firmly convinced that if they appear as defendants in the trial room, they will automatically be considered guilty regardless of the merits of the case." One could conclude that police perceive themselves, at least in New York, as being treated unfairly under an internal review scheme.

9. *Review boards are not answerable to a higher authority.* This statement is also inaccurate. Members of review boards are usually appointed by the mayor. Thus, they serve at the mayor's pleasure.

10. *Review boards will interfere politically with police operations.* If the police are concerned that there would be a return to the flagrant political abuses that existed in the nineteenth and early twentieth centuries, one might join them in their fears.[9] But *Tammany Hall* appears to be dead, and the science of public administration has offered significant insights on the management of local government. Thus, it is highly unlikely that police departments will encounter the kinds of political problems that plagued previous eras. There is, however, another kind of politics that the police might be fearful of. It involves the notion of impos-

---

9. For a history of the problems of politics in policing, see Fogelson (1977), Reppetto (1978), and Walker (1977).

ing a check and balance system on the bureaucratic structure of local government. The International Association of Chiefs of Police (1965:8) did argue that police review boards "represent a form of control which is entirely alien to the American concept of democratic process." Such statements merely reinforce the argument that police should be encouraged to seek a college education and preferably one with a liberal arts emphasis. Heading the list of required courses should be a seminar on the history, meaning, and present-day implications of the eleventh book of Montesquieu's *The Spirit of the Laws*.

11. *The history of review boards proves that they do not work.* One could concur with this statement in light of the demise of the Rochester (New York) and Philadelphia boards. But on closer analysis, one could argue that such a statement is far too simplistic in that it fails to consider the circumstances under which the review boards were disbanded. In the case of Rochester, the court voided the powers of the review board on the grounds that the city ordinance was illegal (Ark 1966). The court was not making a judgment on the utility of the board. The New York City board, operational for only 4 months, was rejected by the electorate (Black 1968). The Patrolmen's Benevolent Association vigorously employed many of the arguments cited above in its campaign to convince citizens to oppose the review board. It has also been pointed out that "the confused wording [of the amendment] worked in favor of those who wanted to abolish it (Black 1968:214). Obviously, it was impossible for the electorate or the Patrolmen's Benevolent Association to make an objective judgment on the effectiveness of the review board.

Philadelphia was the only city that utilized a review board for a significant length of time. In 1958, Mayor Richardson Dilworth created the Police Review Board (it was renamed the Police Advisory Board). The board, which was composed of citizens, was mandated to hear citizen complaints and recommend sanctions to the police commissioner. The police department was given the responsibility to investigate the charges. The board functioned until 1967, when the newly elected Mayor James Tate chose not to retain it.[10] During its existence, the board was confronted with a number of problems, which were not of its making. Among the obstacles were: (1) a lack of funding, (2) an inadequate staff, (3) a lack of publicity, (4) an indifferent attitude to its work by the city administration after 1961, and (5) the mayor's unwillingness to meet with the board to resolve differences (Coxe 1965:184-185).

Spencer Coxe, the executive director of the Philadelphia branch of the American Civil Liberties Union, has suggested that the board's most effective years were from 1960-1962. He pointed out that "[t]he board was able to dispose of most of the complaints without a formal hearing

---

10. For a history of the Philadelphia board, see Coxe (1961, 1965), Hudson (1968, 1971).

through the cooperation of police inspectors and captains" (Coxe 1965:181). Moreover, "[t]he board has never recommended dismissal from the force, though it has recommended a psychiatric examination to determine an officer's fitness" (Coxe 1965:181). Of particular importance was the fact that "[i]n a number of cases, the complainant was less interested in having the policeman punished than in some more tangible redress. For example, complainants illegally arrested frequently asked only that the record of arrest be expunged, and the Board often recommended this" (Coxe 1965:181). Coxe (1965:182) concluded that

> the board, through conciliation and hearings, (1) has vindicated policemen who have been unjustifiably accused of misconduct, and has helped civilians understand the extent of police authority, (2) has obtained redress for civilians with legitimate grievances, (3) has contributed to the enlightenment of members of the police force as to the limits of their authority, and (4) has helped reveal and correct objectionable departmental practices and policies.

Although these sketches of police review boards are admittedly brief, it is difficult to conclude from this information that history has proven review boards a failure. In fact, there is reason to believe that with adequate support they could have succeeded. The real failure rests with the police, city administrators, and some segments of the public who are either indifferent to or fearful of any change that could lead to improved police-community relations and a fundamental fairness in the police complaint process.

The aforementioned agruments opposing civilian review boards were frequently utilized during the 1960s when interest in such boards reached a peak. Today, many police administrators and line officers remain committed to all or some of these arguments, despite the fact that many are illogical, invalid, incorrect, unsubstantiated, and overly simplistic.[11] Not all city and police administrators concur with these arguments, however. In recent years, a few cities have implemented a police complaint process that includes civilian participation.

Civilian Involvement in the Complaint Process

Central to the controversy surrounding civilian involvement in the complaint process is the extent to which citizens should be permitted to participate (Terrill 1980). The complaint procedure consists of a number of steps: reception of the complaint, weighing its merits, investigating the case, determining its validity, and deciding to impose a sanction if the officer has not been exonerated of the charges. The purpose of this section is

---

11. Many of these arguments were expressed at the "Police Internal Affairs" conference held in Cincinnati, November 8-9, 1979, and at the National Institute on Police and Community Relations held at Michigan State University, October 19-22, 1980.

to review how citizen involvement in the complaint process has been instituted in four cities: Chicago, Kansas City, Berkeley, and Detroit.

Chicago

In 1974, Police Superintendent James Rochford established the Office of Professional Standards for the Chicago Police Department. Letman (1980) has suggested that the news media were instrumental in the development of this office. The office is part of the superintendent's personal staff. Three lawyers, reporting directly to the superintendent, administer this office whose staff of civilian investigators were former military personnel or investigators with other units of government.

The office is mandated to:

1. receive and register all complaints against Department members.

2. coordinate all resources of the Department and the total effort of the Office of Professional Standards toward the investigation of excessive force complaints and other complaints as directed by the Superintendent.

3. refer to the Commander of the Internal Affairs Division, or his designate, all complaints against Department members which are not to be investigated by the Office of Professional Standards.

4. conduct a comprehensive investigation into the circumstances of each complaint which it is required to investigate.

5. review instances of injury or death of a person involving alleged action of a department member and conduct an independent investigation when warranted.

6. establish and maintain liaison between the Superintendent and the Office of the United States Attorney, the Courts, bar associations, other law enforcement agencies, and community groups in matters concerning excessive force or corruption.

7. review all cases which recommend the separation of a Department member. Upon approval of the recommendation by the Superintendent, the Office of Professional Standards is responsible for the thorough and legal preparation of the cases for presentation to the Chicago Police Board.

8. safeguard the Complaint Register and allow access only to:
a. the Superintendent or the assistant deputy superintendent on duty,
b. the Executive Assistant to the Superintendent,
c. the Administrators of the Office of Professional Standards,
d. the Deputy Superintendent for Inspectional Services,
e. the Commander of the Internal Affairs Division,
f. inspectors,
g. the Commanding Officer, Complaint Section, Internal Affairs Division,

h. the Department Advocate, and

i. any other member of the Department designated by written order of the Superintendent.

Therefore, the Office of Professional Standards is not the sole investigator of complaints; that is a shared responsibility with the Internal Affairs Division. Furthermore, the office does not hear complaints or impose sanctions. The task of hearing complaints is performed by the Complaint Review Panel, generally composed of a lieutenant, sergeant, and a member of the same rank as the accused. The panel also advises the superintendent on appropriate disciplinary actions. Administrators of the Office of Professional Standards, along with the Commander of the Internal Affairs Division or the deputy superintendent for inspectional services, review disciplinary actions.

Thus, Chicago has introduced a limited in-house civilian review mechanism.

Kansas City

Kansas City's Board of Police Commissioners created the Office of Citizen Complaints in 1970. The office's civilian staff is primarily responsible for coordinating the complaint process. It receives all complaints either directly or as a result of them being forwarded to the office from the police department. These generally involve allegations of unnecessary or excessive force, abuse of authority, discourtesy, or ethnic slurs. If the director of the office thinks the complainant can be conciliated, he may elect to do so. If the issue is resolved in this manner, the case is closed. In all other instances, the director will forward the complaint to the Internal Affairs Division for investigation. Following the investigation, the case is returned to the Office of Citizen Complaints. The director may attempt conciliation of the issue at this time. If the mediation is successful, the director will forward his recommendation of settlement to the chief of police. All investigations are classified by the director as being substantiated, unsubstantiated, unfounded, or closed. The director must forward his reasons for such a classification to the chief of police. Although the director can recommend to the chief disciplinary action, the chief has the authority to impose a sanction. Although Kansas City has instituted a civilian complaint unit that is separate from the police department, the office has not been given total independence in handling citizen complaints.

Berkeley

The police department of the city of Berkeley, California, has what might be called a typical procedure for handling civilian complaints. Through an in-house process, the department receives, investigates, hears, and disposes of all complaints. However, if the complainant is not satisfied, the citizen can appeal the matter before the Police Review Commission. This commission, composed of nine commissioners, was established in 1973, with each member of the Berkeley City Council appointing one commissioner. The Police Review Commission is mandated to perform two functions: (1) reviewing police department policy, practices, and training, and making recommendations to the city manager and the city council; and (2) investigating and holding public hearings on complaints against the police. Regulations for handling such complaints are as follows:

1. receive complaints and register them after they have been reduced to writing and signed by the complainant.

2. conduct an investigation (the Commission has one Investigator)

a. interview the complainant and the employee of the police department

b. advisal of constitutional rights to those interviewed.

3. complete and submit a written report to the Commission.

Following the investigation, a Board of Inquiry hears the case. The board is composed of three members of the Police Review Commission. The board reviews an investigation and can either dismiss the complaint, if there is a unanimous vote to do so, or it can call for a hearing. Unless all parties agree that the hearing should be conducted in an executive session, the hearing is open to the public. Members of the board, the complainant, and the officer who is the subject of the complaint can call witnesses, introduce evidence, and ask questions of witnesses called by the other party. Attorneys may represent the parties, but they are not required to attend the hearing. The investigator for the commission is also eligible to call witnesses and introduce evidence.

Once the hearing is completed, the board deliberates and votes. The actions of the board are based on a majority vote and dissenting members can express, in writing, the reasons for opposing the action. The board then publicly announces its decision and sends its recommendation to the Police Review Commission for confirmation. Because the commission and its Board of Inquiry are advisory bodies, they can only recommend to the city manager, chief of police, and the city council an appropriate action for resolving the complaint. Thus, Berkeley has devised yet another scheme that enables citizen involvement in the review of complaints against its police.

Detroit

In 1973, the Detroit Charter Revision Commission created the Board of

Police Commissioners. The board is composed of five members who are appointed by the mayor following their approval by the city council. The board has been authorized the following responsibilities:

1. In consultation with the chief of police, and with the approval of the mayor, establish policies, rules and regulations;

2. Review and approve the departmental budget before its submission to the mayor;

3. Receive and resolve, as provided in this chapter, any complaint concerning the operation of the police department;

4. Act as final authority in imposing or reviewing discipline of employees of the department;

5. Make an annual report to the mayor, the city council, and the public of the department's activities during the previous year, including the handling of crime and complaints, and of future plans.[12]

The board's involvement in citizen complaints is still considered in the evolutionary stage because it was not until late in 1978 that Mayor Coleman A. Young directed the board and the chief of police "to begin immediately a planned program for finalizing the implementation of the city charter provisions regarding the respective responsibilities of the Board of Police Commmissions and the Chief of Police."[13]

Procedures have been recently developed in accordance with the city charter and are also consistent with the agreement between the city of Detroit and the Detroit Police Officers Association, and the master agreement between the city of Detroit and the Detroit Police Lieutenants and Sergeants Association (Board of Police Commissioners 1980). This includes the appointment by the Board of Police Commissioners of an executive secretary, who serves at its pleasure, and coordinates the activities of the board. The board also appoints a chief investigator and staff, who possess the requisite skills and experience to conduct investigations.

There are three types of complaints that the board entertains: original complaints, inquiry review, and appeals. Original complaints can be filed with the police department, office of the chief investigator, Board of Police Commissioners, or with other government agencies, such as the mayor's office or ombudsman. All complaints are then forwarded to the executive secretary of the Board of Police Commissioners. If the complaint cannot be resolved informally, it is turned over to the office of the chief investigator.

The initial investigation is usually conducted by supervisory staff of the precinct involved in the complaint. These investigations must first have the approval of the precinct commander and the Professional Standards

---

12. Detroit City Charter, Chapter 11, Police, 7-1103.
13. City of Detroit Executive Office, Executive Order No. 10, December 4, 1978.

Section of the police department. Investigations which are not conducted at the precinct level are handled by the office of the chief investigator or the department's Professional Standards Section. If the office of the chief investigator conducts the investigation, a copy of the findings is sent to the executive secretary, who informs the board of the findings. The board then advises the chief of police or a departmental trial board.[14]

An inquiry review is a request of the Board of Police Commmissioners to review a completed citizen complaint investigation. Grounds for such a review must be based upon the citizen's belief that some error or omission is present in the original investigation. Thus, one cannot request a review simply because of dissatisfaction with the outcome of the case. If sufficient grounds to reopen the case exist, the office of the chief investigator will follow the complaint procedures for investigating and processing as if it were an original complaint. (Detroit Police Department n.d.).

An appeal is a complete reinvestigation of a citizen complaint by the Board of Police Commissioners. It is only granted if the original investigation contains errors or omissions to warrant a full investigation, and it is conducted by the office of the chief investigator. Procedures are similar to those utilized in an inquiry review.

Another type of appeal exists that involves the Board of Police Commissioners and deals with disciplinary actions taken against a member of the police department. It was previously mentioned that members of the department are disciplined by the chief of police or a departmental trial board. But the Board of Police Commissioners has the right to review disciplinary actions by hearing them on appeal.[15] The Board of Police Commissioners can:

(a) In disposing of an appeal under Section 7-1107(2), the authority of the board shall be limited to affirming or setting aside the discipline and loss of pay imposed by the chief.

(b) In disposing of an appeal from the trial board decision, the authority of the board shall be limited to:

(i) affirming the decision of the trial board;
(ii) setting aside or reducing the penalty imposed by the trial board;
(iii) remanding to the trial board for additional testimony;
(iv) granting a new hearing before the trial board.

(c) Decisions of the Board shall be in writing and shall contain a plain and concise statement of reasons and shall be announced publicly.

Thus, Detroit's Board of Police Commissioners is empowered to receive complaints, monitor the investigation or conduct it personally, and can

---

14. Detroit City Charter, Chapter 11, Police, 7-1107.
15. Ibid.

affirm or set aside disciplinary actions imposed by the chief of police or a departmental trial board.

Although the methods employed by these four cities are not totally free from criticism, they are sincere attempts to utilize civilian participation in the complaint process. The initial response from citizens appears favorable. More in-depth study and analysis is necessary to determine whether or not these review mechanisms have a positive impact on police community relations and improve the policies and procedures of the departments.

Conclusion

In 1968, the Kerner Commission "cited deep hostility between police and ghetto communities as a primary cause of the disorders" that occurred during the summer riots. Recent events in Philadelphia, Houston, and Miami indicate the problem still exists.[16] One of the factors that exacerbates such stress is the inability of the police to assure the public that they are capable of policing themselves. Permitting citizen involvement in the complaint process will not completely alleviate these existing tensions. However, with economic indicators forecasting bleak conditions for the 1980s, any sincere attempt to diminish the frustrations and anger people vent toward some of the agents of government is advantageous.

City officials and police administrators must remember that citizens have deferred police powers to the government. This is a deferral of power based on trust, but this does not mean citizens have forfeited their right and obligation to assure fundamental fairness in the justice system. As Justice Brandeis pointed out in another context:

Decency, security and liberty alike demand that government officials shall be subjected to the same rules of conduct that are commands to the citizen. In a government of laws, existence of the government will be imperilled if it fails to observe the law scrupulously. Our Government is the potent, the omnipresent teacher. For good or for ill, it teaches the whole people by its example. Crime is contagious. If the Government becomes a lawbreaker, it breeds contempt for law; it invites every man to become a law unto himself; it invites anarchy. To declare that in the administration of the criminal law the end justifies the means—to declare that the Government may commit crimes in order to secure the conviction of a private criminal—would bring terrible retribution.[17]

Civilian participation in the review of complaints against the police can only assist in the reduction of contempt for the law and the administration of justice.

---

16. Footnote 4, supra.
17. Olmstead v. United States, 277 U.S. 438, 485 (1928).

THE INTERNAL AFFAIRS UNIT:
THE POLICEMAN'S FRIEND OR FOE*

The title of this article suggests that there is some question about whether or not the Internal Affairs Unit (IAU) is a friend or foe of the rank and file police officers. Even raising such a question would tend to offend the sensibilities of those police administrators who have worked so diligently to create and staff highly efficient, impartial, and well-organized Internal Affairs Units. The facts are, however, that in too many instances the rank and file members of a police organization are sometimes suspicious and hostile towards their departments' IAU. This suspicion and hostility results in some cases because of certain questionable practices employed by the personnel of the IAU. In other instances, it may occur because a vast majority of an agency's personnel do not really understand the purpose or need for such a unit.

In April 1974, Charles Otero, a 27-year veteran of the Tampa Police Department, was appointed as that agency's chief of police; and he set as one of his top priorities the creation of an Internal Affairs Unit. Among the many administrative considerations in building this unit was the need to create and to maintain a positive image of this unit in the eyes of the community and his officers.

In previous years, the assignment of internal investigations within the department had not been made with any high degree of administrative consistency. No specific unit was designated as being solely responsible for such investigations, the assignment of internal investigations was not systematically made, and there was no systematic method of filing the results of the investigations. In addition, those individuals who were ultimately assigned to conduct such investigations had no written policies or procedures to guide their investigative actions. Thus, in retrospect, it is not surprising that there was a lack of uniformity in the quality of the internal investigations conducted and a lack of uniformity in the methods employed to conduct these investigations. Such administrative shortcomings can have a very serious, deleterious effect upon morale, and can create considerable suspicion and animosity towards both the chief ad-

---

* Leonard Territo and Robert L. Smith, "The Internal Affairs Unit: The Policeman's Friend or Foe," *The Police Chief*, Vol. XLIII, July 1976. Reprinted by permission.

ministrator and those individuals responsible for conducting such investigations, regardless of how fair and impartial they try to be.

Prior to the creation of the Tampa Police Department IAU, serious questions had been raised about certain questionable tactics being employed by some individuals assigned to specific internal investigations. In addition, there was concern that some previous investigations may have been politically motivated; thus, a negative stigma tended to be attached to both the individuals and the responsibilities associated with such investigations. Hence, the Tampa Police Department wanted to accomplish a number of things. First, it wanted to create a unit that would be well organized, highly efficient, and scrupulously fair and impartial in its investigations. Second, it wanted this unit to be trusted and respected by department members and community citizens.

In an effort not to waste time and energy in remaking the proverbial wheel, numerous law enforcement agencies of similar size were contacted and requested to provide administrative data about their Internal Affairs Units. The response was overwhelming, and the subsequent administrative data that were provided were invaluable in developing the foundation upon which the Tampa department eventually built its IAU. Interestingly enough, the one bit of information that was not readily available was specific information about the administrative techniques that could be employed to reduce the negative reactions sometimes fostered by rank and file officers towards the IAU and its personnel. No doubt this was given serious consideration by many police departments, but this issue was not raised in the information collected. In an effort to address himself to this important issue, the newly appointed police chief initially distributed a carefully worded general order which provided a broad overview of what the newly created IAU was intended to do and equally important what it was not expected to do.

The second step was to create a policy and procedure that provided both clear-cut and comprehensive guidelines for the members of the IAU and the members of the department. The policy and procedure that was finally developed was not created in an administrative vacuum, and direct employee participation was encouraged and solicited. In the final analysis this participation was significant in formulating the organizational documents which now govern every phase of all internal investigations.

Administrative Overview

The following IAU guidelines which are presently employed by the Tampa Police Department were formulated based upon Florida State Law,[1] recommendations of the National Advisory Commission on

---

1. Policeman's Bill of Rights, enacted by the legislature of the state of Florida, effective October 1, 1974.

Criminal Justice Standards and Goals, and recommendations by key agency personnel.

1. Rights of Law Enforcement Officers While Under Investigation. Whenever a law enforcement officer is under investigation and is subject to interrogation by agency members, for any reason which could lead to disciplinary action, demotion, or dismissal, such interrogation shall be conducted under the following conditions:

(*a*) The interrogation shall be conducted at a reasonable hour, preferably at a time when the law enforcement officer is on duty, unless the seriousness of the investigation is of such a degree that an immediate action is required.

(*b*) The interrogation shall take place either at the office of the commander of the investigating officer or at the office of the Internal Affairs Unit or police unit in which the incident allegedly occurred as designated by the investigating officer or agency.

(*c*) The law enforcement officer under investigation shall be informed of the rank, name, and command of the officer in charge of the investigation, the interrogating officer, and all persons present during the interrogation. All questions directed to the officer under interrogation shall be asked by and through one interrogator at any one time.

(*d*) The law enforcement officer under investigation shall be informed of the nature of the investigation prior to any interrogation, and shall be informed of the name of all complainants.

(*e*) Interrogating sessions shall be for reasonable periods and shall be timed to allow for such personal necessities and rest periods as are reasonably necessary.

(*f*) The law enforcement officer under interrogation shall not be subjected to offensive language or threatened with transfer, dismissal, or disciplinary action. No promise or reward shall be made as an inducement to answering any questions.

(*g*) The formal interrogation of a law enforcement officer, including all recess periods, shall be recorded, and there shall be no unrecorded questions or statements.

(*h*) If the law enforcement officer under interrogation is under arrest, or is likely to be placed under arrest as a result of the interrogation, the officer shall be completely informed of all his constitutional rights prior to the commencement of the interrogation.

(*i*) At the request of any law enforcement officer under investigation, he shall have the right to be represented by counsel or any other representative of his choice who shall be present at all times during such interrogation whenever the interrogation relates to the officer's continued fitness for law enforcement service.

2. Representation on Complaint Review Boards. In the event a member requests a complaint review board and the circumstances are of a nature to permit the convening of said board, it shall be organized as follows: A complaint review board shall be composed of a five-member board with two members being selected by the administrator, two members being selected by the aggrieved officer, and the fifth member being selected by the other four members. The board members shall be law enforcement officers selected from within the agency.

3. Civil Suits Brought by Law Enforcement Officers. Every law enforcement officer shall have the right to bring civil suit against any person, group of persons, or any organization or corporation or the heads of such organizations or corporations for damages, either pecuniary or otherwise, suffered during the performance of the officer's official duties or for abridgement of the officer's civil rights arising out of the officer's performance of official duties.

4. Notice of Disciplinary Action. No dismissal, demotion, transfer, reassignment, or other personnel action which might result in loss of pay or benefits or which might otherwise be considered a punitive measure shall be taken against any law enforcement officer unless such law enforcement officer is notified of the action and the reason or reasons prior to the effective date of such action.

5. Retaliation for Exercising Rights. No law enforcement officer shall be discharged, disciplined, demoted, or denied promotion, transfer, or reassignment, or otherwise be discriminated against in regard to his employment, or be threatened with any such treatment, by reason of his exercise of his rights.

Selection of Personnel

The selection of personnel is a key factor in the success and acceptance of the IAU. This was a high priority item in the creation of the IAU of the Tampa Police Department, and it was generally agreed that certain factors were absolutely essential in the selection process. These were outlined as follows:

1. All personnel serving in the IAU must be volunteers. (Because of the nature and sensitivity of the work involved in the IAU it was believed that it would be unwise and unfair to assign someone to this unit who did not have a genuine desire to serve in it.)

2. The personnel who serve in this unit must have demonstrated in their previous performance that they possess a high degree of investigative skills. (This was considered an absolute prerequisite since there was little doubt that the members of the unit would be called upon to conduct a wide range of investigation both of a minor and of a serious nature.)

3. The individuals selected to serve in this unit must have excellent reputations both among their peers and supervisors in terms of their in-

tegrity and overall performance as police officers. Since the members of the unit would be called upon to investigate their fellow officers it was deemed important that they themselves not have been found guilty of serious official misconduct in the past. A failure to consider such a factor could later result in charges of administrative hypocrisy.

4. All IAU personnel must become totally familiar with those state statutes, department policies, and procedures which are related to internal investigations (mastery of this body of knowledge would assure that there would be no inadvertent legal or administrative errors occurring during the internal investigative process.)

5. Members of the IAU must be proficient in interviewing and interrogation techniques.

6. A knowledge and understanding of the local communities' ethnic minorities is absolutely essential since, for a variety of social, political, and economic reasons, many citizen complaints will initiate from this group of citizens.

Rotating Tours of Duty

The Tampa Police Department takes the position that there are certain positive advantages to be gained by rotating personnel periodically who are assigned to the IAU. (Investigators will serve a maximum of 24 months.) This approach will have a tendency to foster acceptance and respect for the internal discipline system because of its greater employee participation. Second, it will develop a cadre of investigators who can be used in the future if additional manpower is needed. Third, it should minimize the possibility of alienation from peers and supervisors.

The Use of the Polygraph

The polygraph is employed only after a complete and thorough investigation fails to obtain adequately all of the facts needed upon which to make a final decision in a specific case. Thus, for example, if a complaint is filed against a police officer by a citizen and it is apparent that either the complainant or the officer is not being completely truthful about the facts of the case, then both parties are requested to submit to a polygraph examination. Thus far there have been no instances where both the officer and the complainant involved in the same case have refused to take the polygraph. If the police officer refuses to take the polygraph and the charge is serious enough, the officer can be dismissed.[2] One Tampa police officer who was recently dismissed for his unwillingness to submit to a

---

2. George J. Roux, Jr., Department of Police, City of New Orleans Civil Service Commission, Case No. 440-A, decided September 6, 1968.

polygraph examination challenged the department's right to dismiss him for refusing to submit to a polygraph examination. Following his appeal, a decision by the local civil service board upheld the department's action. On the other hand, if a complainant refuses to submit to a polygraph examination, the officer is still requested to submit to one. In 1974, the Tampa Police Department began to utilize the polygraph as a preemployment screening device. Thus, many Tampa police officers are now quite familiar with the procedures involved in polygraph examination, and it is strongly suspected that this has had a tendency to reduce any unwarranted fears that might have otherwise arisen regarding the use and operation of the polygraph.

Disclosure of Internal Discipline Statistics

The National Advisory Commission on Criminal Justice Standards and Goals has recommended that police agencies should maintain the confidentiality of internal discipline investigations, although complete records should be maintained. However, the disclosure of internal discipline statistics does not violate the confidential nature of the process, and such disclosures are often valuable because they tend to dispel allegations of disciplinary secrecy voiced by some community elements.[3] The Tampa Police Department has wholeheartedly endorsed, accepted, and operationalized this recommendation not only for the reasons cited by the National Advisory Commission on Criminal Justice Standards and Goals but also because it tends to reduce the rumors and misinformation that may occur internally. Hence, although all of the specific details of an investigation are not normally revealed to the general public or to the total police department (except in certain rare and extraordinary circumstances), the Tampa Police Department distributes a monthly summary of activities of the IAU. Thus, the record is available both within the community and within the agency for all to see. Naturally, the availability and distribution of these monthly bulletins will not totally eliminate all suspicion about the IAU operations, but it will do much to minimize a major portion of it.

New Employee Orientation

In addition to providing department-wide distribution of the monthly summary of complaints the commanding officer of the IAU appears before all new police officers attending the police academy. A four-hour block of time is set aside to advise the new officers of the purpose and responsibilities of this unit. The investigative personnel of the IAU are

3. *National Advisory Commission on Criminal Justice Standards and Goals* (Washington, D.C., U.S. Government Printing Office, 1973), p. 479.

also introduced, and certain professional background information is provided on each. A comprehensive orientation is given relating to those state laws, civil service rules and regulations, and departmental rules and regulations which pertain to police officers' rights, internal discipline procedures, and so forth. Sufficient time is allowed for a question and answer period. This method of informing new employees about the IAU tends to reduce the types of negative misconceptions that result when little is known about such units.

In-Service Employee Orientation

Since the IAU was a newly created unit in the Tampa Police Department, it was necessary to provide a certain degree of orientation to older employees also. The vehicle employed to provide this orientation was a departmental closed-circuit television. The TV presentation consisted of a series of the most common types of questions that had been raised or could be raised about the administrative duties and responsibilities of the IAU. The questions were presented to and answered by the commanding officer of the IAU. This type of openness and candor can do much to reduce unnecessary fear or concern about a department's IAU.

Conclusion

The Internal Affairs Unit is an administrative tool and the extent to which it is useful and effective will depend upon the skills and integrity of the chief administrator and the personnel responsible for carrying out the duties assigned to the unit. The IAU is a double-edged sword which may be used by the chief administrator to make plain through sanctions his intolerance to employee misconduct, but equally as important it allows the police agency to defend the lawful and proper conduct of employees in the performance of their duties. Caution should be exercised to assure that the first point is not overemphasized by police administrators at the expense of the second.

Chapter 5
POLICE UNIONIZATION

Introduction *

Police unions you say? Do we really have such a thing; are our police organized? The answer is a big bold YES—yes to the point that, as a recent survey has indicated, 73 percent of all police employees are represented in their employment by some form of union or association.[1] Then you may ask—what are these police unions, how strong are they, how were they organized, what is their legal status? This [introduction] will present a brief overview of the historical development of police unions and will provide some generalized answers to these questions.

Before examining these issues very extensively, a firm definition of the word "union" is needed. For our purposes, a union will refer to any organization which represents or seeks to represent employees for the purpose of discussing with management (or employers) matters relevant to wages, hours, work conditions, and other terms of employment. In the area of police organizations, the term "union" by this definition will refer to a vast variety of organization and association structures. These shall be discussed in more detail later.

The History

Many law enforcement educators use the example of the Boston Police Strike (1919) as the first showing of organized labor among police. However, there were organizations and strikes among police prior to this time.

---

* Joseph D. Smith, "Police Unions: An Historical Perspective of Causes and Organizations," *The Police Chief*, Vol. XLII, No. 11, November 1975. Reprinted by permission.

1. "Labor Management Policies for State and Local Government," *Advisory Commission on Intergovernmental Relations,*" (1969).

As early as 1889, the Ithaca, New York, police force, consisting of five officers, walked off their jobs because their pay had been reduced from $12 per week to $9 per week. In 1897, a group of "Special Police" in Cleveland, Ohio, petitioned the American Federation of Labor (AFL) for a local charter. Significant in labor history is the fact that at this time the AFL rejected this bid for a charter on the grounds that it was settled with the chief's agreement to trades association to organize the police, anymore than they could organize the military. The Fraternal Order of Police (FOP) formed its first local in 1915, although until the 1930s the FOP was basically a social-benefit type of association. Last, but far from least, both in size and cause, is the 1918 police strike in Cincinnati, Ohio. Here was a situation of four officers being discharged for their attempts to organize a meeting to discuss a salary increase of $300 per year. Four hundred and fifty officers walked off their jobs when these four were discharged as a protest of the chief's denial of their attempt to meet as a collective body and to discuss job conditions. This strike was settled with the chief's agreement to reevaluate his discharge decision.[2]

This brings us up to the disastrous occurrences of 1919. Early in the year, the AFL, now having recognized the vast potential in organizing the police, opened its door to applications for police locals. The AFL was immediately swamped with a total of 65 applications, and by the summer of 1919, there were 37 locals chartered with a total membership of over 4,000 officers.[3]

In the Boston Police Department, wage and work conditions were very poor—there were dirty station houses, officers had to purchase their own uniforms, wages could not support a family man's economic needs, and the workweek ranged from 78 to 90 hours. Since officers were unable to get answers to their grievances, they decided to form their own union. The Boston Social Club was formed and received one of the AFL charters. This action was in violation of city policy, and nineteen of the union leaders were discharged. The other officers were outraged, and on September 19, 1919, a total of 1,117 officers (from a total strength of 1,544) went on strike.

The actions of the strikers brought public outrage, and there were comments such as those of Massachusetts Governor Calvin Coolidge: "There is no right to strike against the public safety by any body, anywhere, any time." President Wilson argued, "A strike of policemen of a great city, leaving that city at the mercy of an army of thugs, is a crime against civilization."

---

2. "Police Labor Relations," IACP, *Public Safety Labor Reporter* (1973), p. 2; "Police Collective Bargaining, 1900-1960," *Public Employees Relations Library (PERL)*, IPMA, vol. 18, pp. 1-6.

3. "A Union of Policemen?" *American Labor* (Sept. 1969), pp. 53-59.

The net result of the strike was that all strikers were fired and replaced by new officers.[4]

Beyond the fact that over eleven hundred men lost their jobs as a result of the Boston Police Strike, the total effect on the community must be considered. Bostonians learned that a police strike is a terrible threat to the public welfare and safety. In September of 1919, losses due to property damage and theft were high, and even more important was the loss of life. The community discovered that it wanted no more such problems; and even though the union had been stopped, citizens did listen to the demands of the officers. The new officers were granted a $300 per year raise, they no longer had to purchase their own uniforms, and a pension plan was established.[5]

Perhaps the most important result of the Boston Police Strike has yet to be discussed—that is, the effect which it had on police organization attempts. The strike created such negative public opinion concerning police unions that the unionizing efforts of the lawmen virtually collapsed. Few officers were willing to challenge the administration and lose their jobs in an effort to bring in a union. Even those locals already chartered by the AFL went by the wayside. For the next twenty years, the great powers of an organized labor force in law enforcement were to lie dormant.[6]

A final point to the Boston Police Strike is the causative elements. There are two areas which should be examined: (1) the reasons for organizing and (2) the reasons for striking. The causes for organizing were that the officers could not get anyone to listen to their problems on matters of wages and job conditions. The cause of the strike itself is even more basic and can be found in all of American labor's attempts to organize; that is, the question of the right to organize and bargain collectively. There was no strike until the leaders were fired and the officers were told that they could not meet and speak as a collective body. The police unions had problems similar to all labor organization attempts in its early history, with the right of recognition being a major factor.

Even through the 1950s, the advancement of police unions was greatly restricted, although there was some organizational activity starting at the end of the 1930s. In 1939, the American Federation of State, County, and Municipal Employees (AFSCME—an affiliate of the AFL) opened its door to charter applications from police associations, in addition to the other state and local government employees who were invited into the organization. By 1944, AFSCME had chartered only 39 police locals, but this grew to 61 locals by 1951.[7]

---

4. John H. Burpo, *The Police Labor Movement* (Springfield, Ill.: Charles C. Thomas 1971), p. 4.

5. "Police Labor Relations," p. 3.

6. "Police Collective Bargaining, 1900-1960," pp. 1-6.

7. Ibid.

The public-employer resistance to police unions remained strong during the 1940s and 1950s. There are several noteworthy examples which should be cited. Among these are two outstanding 1943 court decisions from the state of Michigan: *FOP* v *Harris* (306 Mich 68) and *FOP* v *City of Detroit* (318 Mich 182). Both of these cases questioned the rights of the municipalities to pass down antiunion policy for the police; in both cases the courts found in favor of the municipalities. Following these decisions, in 1944, the Detroit Police Department went so far as to issue a general order against any organizational activity. In 1944 and again in 1957, the International Association of Chiefs of Police (IACP) issued strong statements against officers' attempts to organize their agencies. Even in 1959, public opinion was still negative on the subject, with a poll showing 55 percent of the population against police unions.[8]

Even with this much resistance, the foundation was laid during the 1950s for future activity in organizing the police. While management would not give in to "unions," they were willing to live with social, fraternal, and benevolent police associations.[9] These associations were the beginning; they eventually became involved in informal negotiations, even though in some cases management was a member of the association. The majority of these associations were not affiliated with any national organization. They were, in most cases, only citywide, although some were to grow into statewide organizations. Because these associations were local in nature, they tended to be quite powerful politically, especially those which eventually became active in negotiations.

The only national police organization to evolve out of this period was the International Conference of Police Associations (ICPA). This organization had its beginnings in 1953 when it brought together a number of local organizations. The ICPA soon grew to a strength of 150,000 members in approximately 150 local units. A problem exists with the ICPA in that it is only an "association of associations." It is not active in negotiating contracts for its affiliates; the ICPA is basically a service organization.[10]

During 1958-59, there were attempts by the International Brotherhood of Teamsters to charter police locals. The public pressure was so strong against this move that the Teamsters association was not to become active in police unions for another ten years. It is highly noteworthy that about a month after the Teamsters made its effort to organize the New York City Police Department, the commissioner announced recognition of the New York City Police Benevolent Association as bargaining agent for the officers.[11]

---

8. *Police Unions* (Gaithersburg, Md.: IACP, 1958), pp. 57-74.
9. "Police Collective Bargaining, 1900-1960," pp. 1-6.
10. "Labor Relations in the Public Safety Services," p. 27.
11. "Who Will Represent the Police?" *PERL.* vol. 18, pp. 12-13.

The Future

The 1960s and 1970s represent a time of greatly expanded activity both in organizing efforts and collective bargaining. What are the police organizations of this period and why do the officers feel the need to continue this activity?

Why does the new crop of modern police officers want to organize the police labor force? According to John Cassese, former president of the New York PBA, it is for better wages; these officers "want it and want it now."[12] The following increases have been noted over a period from 1939 to 1950:[13] police officers salary, up 52 percent; federal employees salary, up 83 percent; and consumer's price index, up 69 percent. But beyond the wage factor, there are a multitude of needs and complaints for which today's officers are now demanding answers.

First, there are the changes in work conditions; increased danger, increased pressure from politicians for law and order, and ever-increasing liberal attitudes of the court systems. The race riots and general public apathy have also placed added pressures upon the police officer. Not only is he asking for more pay for working with such conditions, he is also trying to bring these matters to the attention of the public (hoping they will react favorably and offer a solution).

Another problem is the loss of social status for the police officer. In many areas of large cities, he is the "man"—the immediate representative of the legal system—and must bring the law to bear on people. Officers argue that by organizing they will become more professional and draw attention to their situation, and at the same time, show just how important an element in society they are. Professionalization and unionization—will these concepts serve as working partners in bringing social status to the police?

A final point is consistent with the cry for professionalization. In recent years, the police have encountered a fast-changing legal climate; officers must be trained and retrained to do their jobs effectively. A number of states now have mandatory training acts which prescribe a specific amount of training for an officer (anywhere from 120 to 440 hours) before he can be sworn in and assigned to duty. Furthermore, an increasing number of agencies are requiring two years and even four years of college as a selection standard for the police officer job. Officers, by way of their unions, are demanding recognition, respect, and wages commensurate with the level of job difficulty, training, and education.[14]

Many of these causative factors are the same as those observed affecting unskilled laborers as they made their organizational bids in the 1930s. We

---

12. "A Union of Policemen?" p. 55.

13. "Why Policemen Are Joining Unions," *PERL.* vol. 18, p. 7.

14. Ibid.

know that the actions of the 1930s led to such organizations as the Congress of Industrial Organizations (CIO), the United Auto Workers (UAW), and the United Mine Workers (UMW); what are the organizations of today's police officers?

First, there are the numerous local organizations; these are not affiliated with any other association. These organizations present a variety of names, such as: Police Benevolent Association, Police Officers Association, Deputies Association, and others. No matter what the name, by our definition, the vast majority of these local independents are "unions." There are two basic factors which normally determine if a local will remain unaffiliated: (1) that the cost-benefit element of organizing and aiding a small local would be too low for any national organization, and (2) as noted before, many local independents have found themselves to be politically powerful within their jurisdiction and are therefore very capable of caring for their own needs.[15]

Next, we should look at the statewide organizations. Examples of such organizations include: Police Conference of New York, New Jersey State Patrolmen's Benevolent Association, Police Officers Association of Michigan, California Alliance of Police Associations, and Massachusetts Police Association. Some of these organizations have national affiliation, particularly with the ICPA, but many have remained independent statewide associations. In most cases, these state organizations are service organizations; very few of them become involved in collective bargaining for the affiliated locals.[16]

One authority points out that:

> Since 1978, when the then-25-year-old International Conference of Police Associations (ICPA) split apart over the issue of whether to affiliate with the AFL-CIO, there have been four police groups aspiring to national memberships: the FOP; the Boston-based International Brotherhood of Police Officers (IBPO); the National Association of Police Officers (NAPO), formed by ICPA members who opposed joining the AFL-CIO; and the International Union of Police Associations (IUPA), founded by the ICPA faction that did join the AFL-CIO.
>
> Each of these organizations spreads across the map in a different fashion. The FOP's 160,000 members are most numerous in the Northeast and Midwest. IBPO, with 20,000 members, is confined largely to New England, where it was formed, and to Florida and Texas; CLEAT is its largest membership group. IUPA is about the same.
>
> At the same time, there is a growing body of opinion that trying to

---

15. Harvey Juris and Peter Feuille, *Police Unionism* (Lexington, Mass., D.C. Heath & Co.), p. 27.

16. Ibid., p. 30.

put together a national police union is, at least now, a waste of time. "There is a strong gravitational pull toward decentralization" in police labor organizations, said Tim Bornstein, a specialist in public employee relations at the business school of the University of Massachusetts at Amherst. Collective bargaining is done at the local level, and "the only hard and fast rule" in labor organizations, Bornstein said, "is that power [in unions] tends to follow collective bargaining."

For that reason, some observers believe that statewide police federations, like the 35,000 member Peace Officers Research Association of California (PORAC), and the Wisconsin Professional Police Association (WPPA) have become the real hub of police labor activity. They are able to provide lawyers, negotiators and business agents for locals that would otherwise be too small to afford them, and can also lobby state legislatures and regulatory agencies.[17]

One might want to believe that the police unions are in good shape, but they presently have a problem. They are not "together." We find that some police unions are affiliates of larger organizations which have busied themselves with the labor problems of a number of occupations. Furthermore, in many agencies we see several organizations—one for patrolmen, one for sergeants and lieutenants, and one for the top managers. Finally, there are those police officers who maintain dual memberships; one with an organization which is social or fraternal and one with an organization which is active in collective bargaining.[18]

There are over 370,000 municipal officers and 44,000 state officers in the United States. Many of these officers are well trained and highly educated.[19] These officers have the potential to become a very powerful labor force, but again, time will be the final factor.

A notable prediction for the future is the growth of minority police unions. Of particular import are the black unions, such as the National Council of Police Societies which claims a membership of over 5,000 black officers.[20] Some of the black leaders are urging militancy in their concern to improve relations between black officers, the agencies, the public, and other officers. Also notable among minority police are women.

To close this section on the future for police unions, perhaps we can best look to the 1972 comments of former Detroit Police Commissioner John Nichols as he quoted the comments of two leaders of the police labor

17. Bruce Cory, "Police Unions Jockey For Position," *Police*, Vol. 6, No. 3, May 1983, pp. 13-14.
18. "Labor Relations in the Public Safety Services," p. 28 and "Who Will Represent the Police?" p. 14.
19. U.S. Department of Labor, Bureau of Labor Statistics, *Occupational Outlook Handbook*.
20. "Negro Police Ask for Equal Voice," *New York Times* (June 13, 1969).

movement: "Chiefs, superintendents, and commissioners are temporal. They'll change. The union is the only permanency in the department.[21] It is us (the union) with whom you will deal; we will make the policy!"

The remainder of this chapter addresses the critical issues of police strikes and the process identified as collective bargaining.

---

21. Police Unionism, pp. 1-2.

POLICE STRIKES*

Although strikes are forbidden in almost all states, in city ordinances and in police department regulations, police unions have not been deterred from participating in them, and they are one of the basic concerns of every administrator whose department is unionized.

It is important at the outset to realize that strikes don't materialize overnight. They build like a volcano, starting with small grumblings that grow into deep employee dissatisfaction. The dissatisfaction develops as a result of poor communication and management's lack of concern and appreciation for employees and for the work they do, to the point where all that is needed is an emotional issue to act as the spark for a strike to erupt.

During the Boston police strike of 1919, Massachusetts Governor Calvin Coolidge exclaimed: "There is no right to strike against the public safety by anybody, anywhere, anytime."

"Anybody" was once again the police, "anytime" became 1975, and "anywhere" became Albuquerque, New Mexico; Oklahoma City, Oklahoma; and San Francisco, California. These were the scenes of the major police strikes of 1975.

These strikes caused police unions to come under heavy criticism by the public, press, and politicians. When strikes occur, one can rest assured that the old adages from the Boston police strike will be resurrected. The sage words of Calvin Coolidge and Woodrow Wilson in 1919 will reappear in the newspapers of every city undergoing a strike by its police. President Woodrow Wilson will be quoted as saying: "A strike of policemen of a great city, leaving that city at the mercy of an army of thugs, is a crime against civilization."

A strike by police today is no less a crime against civilization than it was in 1919, if violence, rioting, and loss of life and property occur. Fortunately, the police strikes of 1975 did not have these elements of violence attached to them. However, this may not always be the case in the future. With cities throughout the country facing financial crises and, as a result, taking a harder line with municipal employees, it is not unlikely that more strikes may occur. As with any police strike, the potential for

---

* Richard M. Ayres, "Police Strikes: Are We Treating the Symptoms Rather than the Problem?" *The Police Chief*, Vol. XLIV, March, 1977. Reprinted by permission.

violence always exists. It is therefore imperative that we take a closer look at our approach and previous responses to these strikes.

A tougher position at the municipal bargaining table by cities may well be applauded and long overdue. But is the "hard line" approach the answer to labor disputes? Have we been attempting to treat the symptom, rather than dealing with the problem itself?

While police officers should be prohibited from striking, it is most disconcerting to note that when they do walk out, many police and city administrators, politicians, editorial writers, and news commentators seem to be concerned exclusively with ways of crushing the strike and have little or no interest in determining the underlying causes of it.

While it may well be necessary to administer harsh penalties for striking employees and to enact strong no-strike legislation, it is now recognized that these are not sufficient measures in themselves to insure labor peace in the public sector. I believe it is therefore important that we stop trying to treat the symptom, the strike, and begin directing our attention to the problem itself—the employee dissatisfaction which caused the strike in the first place.

If police administrators are able to identify the causes of police strikes, they will be better equipped to predict, avoid, and deal with such labor disputes in the future.

Interestingly enough, a careful analysis of the police strikes that have recently occurred reflects that there are some common variables that can be identified in each case. To illustrate, let us focus our attention on the Albuquerque and Oklahoma City strikes of July and October, 1975. I was fortunate to be able to visit these cities and prepare case studies of the strikes by interviewing the major participants—the mayor, members of city council, police and city administrators, labor leaders, and striking officers. Here are some of the findings that evolved from these case studies as to what caused the strikes, along with general guidelines and recommendations for preventing future ones.

Factors Causing Police Strikes

One of the first allegations heard when examining the causes of strikes is bad faith bargaining. This term, of course, can mean many things to many people, depending upon one's perception of the situation. In Albuquerque, cries of bad faith bargaining were heard back in 1973, two years before the strike actually occurred. Following tradition, the police were the first city employees to bargain with the administration. At this time, they accepted a salary increase less than that which they had requested, on the basis that there was no more money in the city budget. The police then watched the firemen and the blue-collar workers go on strike and receive what they perceived to be better benefits than those which they themselves had been given. Comments such as, "Look what the firemen received for going out on strike," and "Look what a good organization can do for its members," were soon heard around the police department.

By 1975, the police were anxious to cash in on the alleged promises by the city that they would be given priority treatment for having been the "good guys" during the last negotiations. Now, when the city refused to meet their demands, the police believed that they were not getting what they deserved, and that the city administration was obviously not bargaining in good faith.

In Oklahoma City, bad faith bargaining allegedly began when the city agreed to a Fraternal Order of Police (FOP) request to call for advisory arbitration to settle the wage-benefits dispute. Hearings were held and the arbitrators returned a decision almost totally in favor of the FOP stance, recommending a 10 percent across-the-board wage increase for the police.

Shortly thereafter, the city council voted 9 to 0 to reject the recommendation of the arbitration board in favor of a smaller pay hike of 7½ percent.

Although the officers admitted that the arbitration ruling was only advisory in nature, they were clearly upset and frustrated with the city's decision. The FOP had led its members to believe that the city had agreed to go to arbitration and would accept the findings. The police viewed the city's rejection as bad faith bargaining. As one officer stated, "The city had asked for arbitration and now they won't let us have it after the award was favorable to the men."

Another commonly heard explanation for police strikes is a breakdown in communications. A large number of grievances that come up to management are traceable to its failure to listen and to get the facts as to why the employee had the grievance.

Complaints often heard by patrolmen in the studies conducted were that they had no voice in management and that no one would listen to them. As the president of one of the unions stated, "The typical feeling among patrolmen is 'Isn't anyone listening to me—I am the one doing the work.' "

However, failure of police management to communicate with its employees is only one segment in the chain of events leading to the total breakdown in communications which precedes a strike. Examining the total labor relations process, we must also cite the failure of the city administration to communicate to the police as well as a lack of proper communication between the union and its membership.

The lack of experience and expertise of the union bargaining team is also cited as being a factor in causing strikes. In both Albuquerque and Oklahoma City, city administrators contended that the inexperience of the union's bargaining team, due to its rapid turnover of personnel and its inability to bargain professionally, helped to promote the strike situation.

A close corollary to this situation was the lack of experience and inability of the union's leadership in general. It was contended in both cities that the unions should have had better control over their members, and that they were irresponsible in presenting proposals that were impossible to deliver. This type of rhetoric on the part of the union leaders allegedly caused great frustration in the rank and file of the police department, particularly when the union failed to deliver at the bargaining table.

Another factor present in each of these strikes was that the city and union had failed to reach an agreement before the existing contract expired. This exerted even greater pressure on the respective representatives to reach some type of settlement.

A hotly contested election to determine the exclusive bargaining agent will also contribute to a strike atmosphere. In Albuquerque, the Police Officer's Association (APOA) was challenged by the International Brotherhood of Police Officers (IBPO); and in Oklahoma City, the FOP was faced with the Teamsters. In both of these situations, the incumbent organization was victorious, but it placed tremendous pressure on both the APOA and the FOP to come up with a good contract. They had to produce or else. It's like one of the officers put on his ballot in Oklahoma City, "The FOP. We'll give them one more year."

A form of employee dissatisfaction which always seems to be present prior to a strike is that which is caused by poor supervisory practices. This discontent is usually expressed by officers complaining about the lack of concern for employees by their supervisors and their unwillingness to communicate with them relative to the elements affecting their job.

Tied closely to poor supervisory practices is lack of administrative leadership. Many police officers view management as being too autocratic in its implementation of policy regarding transfers, promotion, and discipline. Being expected to blindly obey orders issued by autocratic administrators will cause tremendous employee dissatisfaction. This, coupled with what historically has been a laxity on the part of police and city administrators to recognize and pursue the economic and job needs of the workers, raises the level of employee frustration.

The lack of education and understanding on the part of the legislative body, including the city council, has also been cited as a catalyst for strikes. As one official stated, "Politics plays hell with the process, and creates misunderstanding and fears on the part of both parties which prevent close relationships between the city and union."

The media also plays an important role in the circumstances leading to a strike. It often over-emphasizes and allows an undue amount of unprofessional material to be printed. All of this leads to misrepresentation of the facts thus developing distorted public opinion and preventing the parties involved in negotiations from reaching an amiable solution.

As indicated, there are many causes for police strikes. It is important to note, however, that once these causes are present, and as the employee dissatisfaction grows and the frustration level increases, all that is then needed is an emotional issue to act as a triggering device to set off the strike. In both Albuquerque and Oklahoma City, the triggering device was identical—a rumor, unfounded, regarding the suspension of one of the union members. This rumor was an emotional issue which in light of all the other factors present led the men into taking that unthinkable step—a strike.

The police strikes in Albuquerque and Oklahoma City are not unique; many of the factors present in them are common in most strike situations. Hopefully, we can learn from these experiences and be able to formulate some guidelines based on the variables identified that will help city and police administrators prevent such labor disputes in the future.

Guidelines to Prevent Police Strikes

1. Police and city administrators must work towards developing an atmosphere of trust and cooperation that is conducive to good faith bargaining.

It seems to me that the fundamental difficulty with the usual collective bargaining is that both management and labor approach it as a win-or-lose proposition; consequently, each girds itself to do battle with the other. Both parties come to the bargaining table ready to reject as unreasonable the other's demands. By expecting these things and preparing for them, each sets a tone for a relationship which tends to bring about the conduct expected. As a result, an atmosphere of distrust is created in which good faith bargaining is practically impossible. We must learn to approach negotiations as a "cooperative enterprise," a win-win proposition, where both parties come away with some needs satisfied. This attitude, if adopted, would help create a climate more conducive to good faith bargaining.

2. Police administrators must get politically involved in areas that affect the efficient operation of their agencies.

In all too many cities, the police department has stayed aloof from or uninvolved in important political decisions having an impact on effective police service. The police executive today must begin to articulate department problems to the public and actively pursue the economic and job condition needs of his employees. If police administrators fail to get involved, the union will fill the void created by this leadership vacuum.

3. A more effective internal communications system must be developed in police agencies.

As the size of police departments increases, their executives tend to drift further and further out of touch with their employees. Police administrators must begin to give high priority to establishing fast, easy, up-and-down communications so that no one feels left out and ignored. The answer to eliminating job alienation lies in effective and sincere manager/worker communication in a climate of high trust and credibility.

4. Better communications and relations must be established between the police administrator and the city administration, including elected officials.

Police administrators must try to establish a closely coordinated relationship with the personnel director, city manager, mayor, and other officials responsible for carrying out employee relations policies. Labor relations policy meetings between these top level managers are advisable and essential if empathy and understanding for each other's problems is to be achieved. Moreover, there should be a constant interchange of information and ideas so that the city management team develops a coordinated approach when responding to the police union.

5. Better communications and relations must exist between the police administrator and his union leaders.

Recently, a police chief related that he never dealt directly with his union president. If they wanted to get a message to each other, they did so through a third party. This type of antagonistic approach can only complement conflict. A more preferable approach is to deal with the union in a spirit of cooperation. In this environment, labor issues can often be resolved with a minimum of conflict by utilizing the union and its president as a vehicle for communication.

It is also recommended, depending on the size of the agency and its manpower needs, that the union president be removed from all police duties, making his sole responsibility the operation of the union.

6. Efforts must be made to enhance more effective communications and relations between the union and the city.

In many cities throughout the country, the only time the city administration meets with its labor leaders is at bargaining time. Depending on the duration of the contract, a long period of time may elapse without any contact between the parties. It is, therefore, recommended that regularly scheduled meetings between the police union and the city be held to provide an opportunity to discuss matters of mutual interest and to open the lines of communication. These meetings would be neither a substitute for nor an alternative to collective bargaining, but would act to complement the collective bargaining process.

7. Police administrators must insist on representation of police management at the bargaining table.

The transactions that take place at the bargaining table constitute one of the most important personnel events of the police department, because they have impact on all phases of the management activity. It is essential that a police executive be represented during the entire process to protect management interests and to obtain important feedback on the progress of negotiations.

It is recommended that deputy chiefs or potential chiefs of police be appointed to represent the department in order that they may obtain valuable experience in and understanding of the labor relations process to aid them when they later become the top executive.

8. Efforts must be made to remove all supervisory personnel from the same collective bargaining unit as patrolmen.

At a recent meeting of the California Organization of Police and Sheriffs (COPS), a San Francisco labor attorney advised those present of the necessity for police officers to "consider the strike and reserve the right to strike." This, of course, he stated, assumes that the police bargaining unit is adequately organized and unified to effect such influence when necessary. "So, don't overlook any facet of the police department," he warned. "Remember, the fewer members in your bargaining unit, the more officers there are available to do your work if you should choose to strike."

For this very reason, it is recommended, that where possible, supervisors should not belong to the same bargaining unit as patrolmen. There is a strong bond that naturally develops between employees in the same bargaining unit due to the common issues that will arise. If there is a strike or job action, you want your supervisory personnel remaining loyal to management.

9. Training must be provided for police union leaders in the area of improving their negotiating expertise, leadership, and organizational abilities.

Ken McFeeley, former president of New York City's Police Benevolent Association, remarked at a seminar, shortly after being elected president, that it was a shock to be riding a patrol car one day and to find yourself the next day having breakfast with the Governor of the State of New York. We provide our labor leaders with little or no labor relations training, yet we complain vociferously about their ineptness and inexperience. It is recommended that we provide our union leaders with training to improve their negotiating ability. When management and labor can come to the bargaining table with equal expertise, the negotiations are going to operate more smoothly and productively. Furthermore, we often fail to recognize that the union president, as the head of his organization, is in a management position. It is necessary, therefore, that he obtain training in the area of management, leadership, and organization to help him to operate the union more efficiently. The better the union president can manage the union, the less conflict there is going to be within the department.

10. Training must be provided for police management supervisory personnel.

Training programs must be developed to foster a "management consciousness" among supervisors and to provide them with the expertise necessary to deal with problems of employee discipline, performance evaluation, motivation, and grievance resolution. This is one of the most important steps a police administrator can take to dissipate labor unrest. Supervisory personnel must be trained to become attuned to the needs of employees and see that they receive proper recognition and appreciation for the work that they do.

11. Mixed training programs should be provided for police and city administrators and labor leaders.

Recently, at a seminar on labor relations and collective bargaining in one of the major cities, the city council, heads of municipal agencies, and their labor counterparts all attended. The objective of this seminar was not to teach the attendees the principles of labor relations, but to open lines of communication and develop empathy. More seminars of this type should be conducted, where a cross-fertilization of ideas may take place, and representatives of the various segments of the public sector can get together and discuss matters of mutual interest outside of the bargaining process.

12. "Eleventh hour" bargaining and negotiation in the press must be avoided.

Someone once said that eleventh hour bargaining makes good headlines but poor contracts. Every effort should be made to avoid eleventh hour bargaining. There should be an early exchange of contract proposals and every attempt made to settle the contract before the existing one expires.

Unfortunately, the public news media seldom explores or explains the benefits of a negotiated contract to the community, but spotlights misunderstandings and mismanagement of both participants in the bargaining. The news media must be utilized in a more positive fashion by emphasizing the matters that the negotiating parties have agreed upon and by not dwelling on points of difference.

13. It is necessary to develop and update an effective strike contingency plan.

A strike contingency plan is a valuable tool to a police administrator. A well-publicized contingency plan may be a key factor toward deterring strikes and other related job actions. More importantly, it is essential, if the community is to be afforded interim protection during the strike, absence from violence, rioting, and increased crime. It also allows the administrator freedom from making hurried decisions in a time of crisis and provides devoted effort to the impartial ending of the strike.

Conclusion

In any strike, there are many factors and variables that are peculiar to a given situation. You will have to analyze your own particular setting. However, let me leave you with what is admittedly an oversimplified remedy for preventing police strikes and reducing labor/management conflict. It is this:

Find out what is the cause of employee dissatisfaction in your department and then work toward achieving equitable solutions conducted in an atmosphere of trust and cooperation.

COLLECTIVE BARGAINING*

The initial surprise that police officers desire collective bargaining through unionization has given way to its recognition as an established fact. Approximately one-third of all police employees are unionized. Although this percentage has increased slowly in the past decade, its significance is not reduced in view of the fact that collective bargaining for police employees is legally possible in only half of the states. However, there is very little doubt that police unions are permanent units in the police organization structure.

Also, there is no longer any mystery surrounding why police officers favor collective bargaining. The indications are clear; union representation is elected wherever police officers believe their status is being eroded or whenever they realize that their traditions and values are threatened.

The dynamic nature of collective bargaining in the police field has created many controversial issues. One of the most prominent conflicts has arisen over the question of "management rights" or "management prerogatives."

Collective bargaining identifies the process whereby the employer and employees, represented through a recognized union, negotiate a formal written agreement over wages, hours, and conditions of employment. Despite the increasing frequency of collective bargaining in public service, considerable controversy exists concerning its validity for the police profession. Both the proponents and opponents claim equal justification for their positions, but neither has attempted to project the value of collective bargaining to the future of police officers and the police profession.

Currently, as the scope of collective bargaining for police employees expands, the task of determining what is or is not bargainable (or what is a management right) has become increasingly difficult. Since the interpretation of management rights has been an arbitrable issue, management prerogatives are emerging as significant issues in police labor negotiations. Subsequently, administrators are reexamining the rights previously conceded to unions in an effort to regain control of their

---

* Daniel J. Bell, "Collective Bargaining: Perspective for the 1980's," *Journal of Police Science and Administration*, Vol. 9, No. 3, 1981, pp. 296-304. Reprinted by permission.

organizations. Recent decisions by labor arbitrators and courts have done very little to reestablish traditional management rights. The U.S. Supreme Court has defined management rights as only those rights "over which the contract gives management complete control and unfettered discretion."[1] The Supreme Court has concluded that in the labor contract, management must exclude specific management rights from the grievance procedure if they expect to prove that they have retained those rights.

Currently, however, it is the employees who ultimately determine the extent of management's rights. This occurs as a result of the lack of "absolutes" in management rights, and it is often the manner in which management rights are exercised that determines whether or not the employees will support them. Where employees believe that management has acted in a responsible manner, the question of whether these actions are unilateral has not been of primary importance. The exercise of management rights implies responsibility. Therefore, it is important for employees to believe that management has discharged its responsibilities in a fair and equitable manner and that their concerns are being appropriately considered. This has been especially true in the police field.

The concept of management rights has been referred to as "The Residual Theory," implying that some rights reside exclusively in management. Management rights in public employment have been much broader than those in private industry, for government views its policymaking role as sacrosanct, and they have not been anxious to share it with employees.

Management rights are derived from the concept of state sovereignty.[2] Few individuals would reject the necessity or desirability of some form of sovereignty in a democratic society. However, the extent of disagreement regarding the sovereignty issue and what its boundaries should encompass provide support for the perspective that sovereignty does not require to be, and in many locations is not, interpreted so narrowly as to preclude public employees' rights to collective bargaining.

If collective bargaining (or the right to strike under certain conditions) were shown to improve the efficiency of governmental activities, it would be irrational and undemocratic of the state not to increase its own benefits or deny to a segment of its citizens the same rights enjoyed by others.

---

1. United Steelworkers of America v. Warrior and Gulf Navigation Company, 46 LRRM 2416 (1960).
2. Specifically, the concept of sovereignty has been used to justify the denial of collective bargaining rights to public employees based on the unique nature of the power of the state. The state has the sovereign power, through law, to govern public employees' working conditions, and it is a unique power that cannot be delegated or otherwise diffused. In this context, a process such as collective bargaining can be considered irreconcilable with the concept of sovereignty, and therefore unlawful. Ohio Legislative Service Commission (1969:12, 21-22).

Therefore, the concept of "sovereignty" should include the democratic principles of labor negotiations that have been utilized in the private sector, so long as these principles, in practice, do not threaten the public's safety.

As management rights are examined, it is evident that the limitations that unions have imposed upon the exercise of management rights have varied tremendously from industry to industry, from organization to organization within the same industry, and even from location to location within the same organization.

There is a preponderance of evidence that police administrators have been losing their right to manage under collective bargaining procedures. Management has stressed that its primary purpose is to operate its organization as efficiently as possible. Police administrators have contended that they cannot operate their organizations like a town meeting, with endless discussion, debate, and voting before any action can be taken. Someone must have the authority to make decisions and provide organizational leadership. The typical manager in private industry and his counterpart in the public sector have become acutely aware of the gradual eroding of management prerogatives. Every year the unions demand something new, and conceivably, management could end up by being employees of the union.[3]

Public administrators are keenly aware that their prerogatives are fewer today than yesterday and were fewer yesterday than the day before, and they know without doubt who is reducing their prerogatives — labor unions.

Administrators are also aware that there is more at stake in the conflict over management rights than in the usual bargaining over wages and working hours. To the administrators, it is a matter of survival. If they are not allowed to make certain basic decisions free of union pressure, they cannot meet their responsibilities to the consumers whose requests for service are equally as valid on the organization as are the employees'. The same is true in the police service where the demands of the citizens are justifiably great.

Management's bargaining posture can be presented in the following manner:

1. In the course of negotiations, management has the right to refuse to negotiate on issues involving inherent managerial policy.

---

3. The essential lesson of New York City's entire experience is that there is no substitute for alertness on the part of the elected officials once they embark on the basically sound proposition that the city's best interests will be served by granting civil service unions negotiating rights comparable to those which prevail in industry. If managerial slackness, ineptitude, or politics blunt the relationship, the community will become captive of its unionized employees. Raskin (1972:122, 144).

2. Management has the right to make selective use of its wage surveys and other bargaining data to support its bargaining position.

3. Management has the right to resort to the press during negotiations. (The wisdom of this is questionable.)

4. Management has the right to say "no" to any unreasonable union demands.

5. During negotiations, public management has the right to demand a "quid pro quo" for any bargaining concessions which it makes. (If there is a wage increase, there has to be an equivalent increase in production on the part of the employees.)

6. Once a contract has been signed, management has the right to insist that all terms agreed upon during negotiations must be fully respected and carried out during the life of the contract.

7. Finally, management has the right, if not the duty, to prepare a strike contingency plan or to consider alternative means of delivering necessary government services should a work slowdown or stoppage occur.

Since it is doubtful that any list of management functions can be made all-inclusive, it should be understood that "management retains any other duties and responsibilities that properly belong to it."

Disputes involving management rights should not be subjected to arbitration; however, any grievance with respect to the reasonableness of the management rights may be subject to the grievance procedure.

Although collective bargaining improves communications and employee satisfaction with the organizational environment, management will find many of its prerogatives and freedom of action appreciably curtailed. The obligations incurred by the contractual relationship compel management to negotiate with the union as an equal in areas where it formerly had an unlimited choice of actions. This situation tends to produce managers with hostile and rigid attitudes toward unions and their members.

An uncompromising management attitude has prevailed in the police labor environment. It has been axiomatic that an uncooperative administrator can provoke police labor organizations to seize the initiative in seeking economic and employment benefits through collective bargaining or militant activity. Conversely, passive administrators have seen their employees achieve increased wages and also make questionable inroads into their administrative prerogative.

Management's View of Collective Bargaining

Where police administrators must participate in the bargaining process, there should be certain steps taken to ensure that the process will proceed smoothly. When problems do occur, solutions must be identified and implemented. Although such bargaining agreement is different, the process of discovering solutions is similar. Many problems arise due to management's lack of action or unwillingness to act when a problem is clearly evident.

In the past the administrators of public organizations, especially police departments, have claimed the ultimate right to make the decisions. But, in the recent decade, this power has constantly diminished due to the growing strength of the labor unions.

Police administrators are aware of the fact that it is their duty to protect the interests of government and the citizens; however, they have misperceived the concept to include "at the expense of the employees." Second, negotiators, as they bargain for the exclusive right to manage, must consider that without employees there is nothing to manage. The need to retain management rights to operate efficiently, utilize technology, and reduce labor costs is not synonymous with the right to dictate the lifestyle of the employees. Third, during contract negotiation, "management" should include all persons in supervisory positions. These individuals should be excluded from the employee's bargaining unit. Membership in both creates an unresolvable conflict of interests on the supervisor's part and reduces the quality of decisions which affect the employee, the union, and the written contract. If included, they will create additional dissension among the management group and lessen the impact of management's influence on the employees. Fourth, separate financial incentives should be available for both management and labor for exceptional contributions to the organization. The concept that government employees (including police) cannot or should not be motivated by financial rewards defeats the potential of recruiting and retaining qualified individuals for public service, a problem which the police have encountered for decades.

Collective bargaining in the police field has not developed due to one isolated incident. It has grown over the past decades due to numerous problems but generated from one general area — management; that is, the problem of the management itself.[4]

In part, the problem lies within the structure of government management (Pegetter 1975:16). The multilayered and often multiemployer organization tends to reduce status for the manager as well as the

---

4. Evaluation of police agencies indicated that the most important problems uncovered during a typical assessment were: (1) a lack of decisive leadership by the police chief executive; (2) failure of the police chief executive to understand his role and how to do his job; (3) poor organization of the agency; (4) lack of a management system and followup controls; (5) lack of training for personnel engaged in specialized activities; and (6) failure of the police chief executive to define and establish priorities and objectives. National Advisory Committee on Criminal Justice Standards and Goals.

employee. The reduction of status tends to produce negative attitudes toward labor negotiations and the union employees. Obviously, where negative attitudes are permitted to develop, they will have serious consequences for the acceptance and administration of any contractual agreement. Also, the manager's attitude may be deliberately destructive if they cannot identify with the contract as a positive management tool.

There are steps that can be taken to reduce the internal friction between management and union employees. First, there must be communication and participation in the decision-making process. In this circumstance it does not matter whether the union bargaining unit was voluntary or agency determined, input from the involved key personnel can be valuable and should be solicited on matters affecting their areas. This will tend to increase the acceptance of the union as an organization of responsible employees committed to the contractual agreement. A second method that may smooth the negotiating process is for each party to seek advice and counseling for the other's point of view.

Many situations may be resolved by the ceremonial contract signing by the administrators at the conclusion of negotiations. These steps to reduce internal conflict are only an overview of most situations. Where specific problems occur, they must be handled individually depending on their severity of conflict within the bargaining structure.

After the internal conflicts are resolved, guidelines for developing a positive management attitude toward the employees, their union, and the contract is necessary. A negative attitude is easily detected by employees, and they have taken advantage of this existing situation in their contract demands. To obtain a positive attitude, management must be fully prepared to present a program to the employees, one that is well thought-out and consistent with the overall goals of the police organization.

The best prepared proposal may be destroyed during its presentation by an unskilled individual. If the employer has a personnel or labor relations specialist, this person should represent the interests of management.[5] Where the employer does not have such a person, two alternatives are available: (1) employ a negotiator from outside the organizational structure, or (2) train a staff member in labor relations. Selecting a police supervisor to be trained for labor relations is almost certain disaster in the making.[6] The existing negative relationship between the employees and

---

5. Unfortunately, in contrast to their counterparts in the private sector, many public employers have not recognized the need to establish a distinct labor relations staff function as a permanent part of their organization. National Governor's Conference (1968:10).

6. Negotiations by operating officers have the disadvantage that operations personnel cannot afford to take time from their duties to engage in bargaining, and they are not necessarily capable bargainers. Nothing is more likely to produce bad bargains for employers than impatience on the part of management representatives to return to their regular assignments. Slichter, Healy, and Livernash.

management are normally responsible for the existence of the union. Therefore, bargaining with their "sworn enemy" merely increases the friction rather than reduces it. Bargaining, however, is an adversarial process, and each party should take steps to coexist.

Since contractual agreements are designed to be restrictive, there must be a reasonable search conducted to determine the long-range effects and costs before either the union or the administration agree on clauses or the total contract. Where management determines the dollar value of the union's proposals, they must also provide the rationale for either denying the proposal or requesting a reciprocal benefit of similar value. Considering all costs as direct or indirect will enable either party to ascertain the expense involved in all the aspects of the bargaining process.

One item that evades administrators is that the contract or its intent will often be misinterpreted or misapplied by first-line supervisors. Based on the degree of past friction and dissension in the organization, a liberal cost projection should be allowed for training supervisors. It is more economical to train supervisors than it is to defend unfair labor practice suits generated by their ignorance.

Collective bargaining was not intended to be the downfall of management rights. Both labor and management may receive benefits from the negotiations if each will learn the method to do so. With sufficient time expended in study and preparation, the police administrator can become well versed in contract management. In addition, the police officer's profession includes negotiating with citizens in practical situations. In the final analysis, negotiations are the crux of collective bargaining.

The Union View of Collective Bargaining

The most visible advocates of collective bargaining are the police employee organizations. Their primary concern has been the quest for: recognition of their organizations by management, increased economic benefits and employment conditions for their members, a voice in organizational policymaking, and professionalization of the police career field. Improved economic benefits have included: salaries, overtime, pensions, paid holidays, health insurance, and tuition reimbursement. Employment conditions have included: hours, workweeks, holidays and vacations, and sick leave.

The unions view collective bargaining as a necessary internal check against the misuse and abuse of power within the police bureaucracy. Opponents of collective bargaining would counter that this argument is invalid when applied to the police organization. Police organizations are viewed as unique because it is generally accepted that the service rendered requires employee discipline which is assured only by the military approach. This means exacting rules and regulations, also orders that flow from the top down. Police unionism alters this kind of management. Furthermore, persons who enter the police service appear to willingly accept the autocracy of military management as a basic condition for their employment. Also, they tacitly recognize military management as being ingrained in the operation of police organizations.

The management structure of police organizations has not prevented the formation of police unions and has done little more than facilitate the political control of their agencies. It is possible that administrative mismanagement and political scandals could be prevented through the internal balance of power of those in control. In addition, the communication channels created by police unions have the potential to expose facts for public attention which otherwise would remain secret.

Police administrators have feared that collective bargaining would threaten their ability to manage. This is partially correct. The police administrator's management ability is and has been in question. Collective bargaining, however, reduces their arbitrary decision-making power that has negatively affected the employees. Unions normally desire that any proposed departmental policies or programs be submitted to them for consideration and comment before being implemented. Police administrators have contended that this process places too much authority into the hands of the employees. In brief, the authority of the police administrator and internal departmental discipline are perceived to be threatened by collective bargaining.

Unions have stressed that they should have a direct voice in their organization's policies, as these policies directly affect the employees. In addition, police administrators have failed to heed the obvious need for strong, capable leadership. By not seeking improved financial benefits and employment conditions for their employees, management has created a leadership vacuum that has been filled by police employee organizations. If police administrators had recognized the importance of their position as a vehicle through which officers could attain their goals, the labor-management relationship in the police profession would not be in turmoil today.

Some administrators have considered the collective bargaining process to be illegal when utilized by the police organizations (or any safety force), primarily because the process carries with it the right to strike. During a strike, the processes of government service delivery are seriously curtailed. The possession of the right to strike (not the actual strike) distinguishes private employees from those in public employment; employee strikes are permissible for the private sector employee, but an act of mutiny in the hands of the public service employee. However, deprived of the right to strike, employees are denied essential sanctions, and there is no purpose served by affiliation with other factions of organized labor.

Collective bargaining has been perceived to be a threat to the neutrality of police officers. An officer's primary duty is to the public he serves. But, as members of a union, officers also owe an allegiance to that organiza-tion. Opponents of collective bargaining foresee the possibility of conflict of interest in this dual allegiance, with the temptation to place union loyalties above their police duties. However, since organized labor first entered into the police field, there has not been one instance where police officers failed to perform their duties as a result of being influenced by a sense of loyalty to a union. Neutrality is desirable to the integrity of the police organization.

A fallacy of the neutrality argument is that it demeans the ability of the sincerely motivated police officer to recognize the necessity for placing public service duties above union loyalty. A police officer who has been trained in and maintains the tenets of impartial, neutral police work will not be swayed by union affiliations. Any police officer who is swayed has not done so because of a feeling of primary concern for his union, but, rather, because of a lack of total commitment toward the chosen profes-sion. The factor that primarily contributes to the destruction of police neutrality are the employment conditions created by marginally qualified administrators.

An additional issue concerning collective bargaining is the threat it poses to the civil service merit system (or lack of merit system). Negotia-tions will normally concern personnel policy in employee evaluation, job classification, promotion, and training. Police unions have attempted to include merit system issues in collective bargaining. The economic con-siderations identified earlier are generally accepted as negotiable. However, the issues of recruiting, training, and promotion are perceived to interfere with the management prerogative. Management claims that employees are promoted on the basis of merit, and fears that employee organizations will gain control of the personnel system and demand that only members of their union be hired, in addition to forcing the standards of seniority upon the employer.

Adequately managed collective bargaining processes have the potential to enhance the merit system that has historically impeded the resolution of employee problems. Collective bargaining is a developing trend in police employee-management relations and must be recognized and managed. Through negotiation, the employer is required to examine personnel policies, establish grievance procedures to resolve employee dissatisfac-tions, and create improved lines of communication. Negotiation will also create a dual appraisal of the employment policies of the organization. Whether the resulting effect upon the merit system will be positive or negative is contingent upon the bargaining relationship between the police employee organization and the employer.

One stated purpose of employee organizations has been to further the professionalization of the police. It is advocated that through negotiated economic and employment improvements, higher qualified personnel will be recruited for police work, thus raising the quality of police organizations. Those administrators who favor collective bargaining have indicated that unions created a healthy environment for police professionalization by increasing morale, helping to prevent administrative corruption, and increasing the efficiency of the department through participation by employees in the decision-making process. This position is not widely accepted, as some propose that police employee organizations would not affect the professionalization process because unions operate on a local level and are concerned with employment conditions in a particular police agency. The concept of professionalization operates on a national level encompassing the police profession as a whole.

The union, as distinct from its members, will always attempt to preserve and extend its status and the status of its representatives. As a future objective, the union is undoubtedly desirous of participating in the affairs of any given operation to the point where it must be consulted on literally any matter affecting the welfare of its members. Opponents argue that unionism prevents the police officers from ever becoming professionals. For example, the union movement historically represented the unskilled and workers with craft skills of the blue-collar variety. The fact that there are no unions organized for professional status does not detract from this issue. Union affiliation certainly has no more bearing on a police officer than a milkman, office worker, or construction worker. Each has its place in contemporary society, and collective bargaining in labor is only a tool to correlate the welfare of citizens in any community.

Collective bargaining is a process based upon negotiation and consideration of the welfare and rights of the other party. Past experience has indicated that both police administrators and union representatives can easily become closed-minded. It is imperative that both parties be willing to meet and negotiate.

It is obvious that collective bargaining is an integral part of the police organization, at least for the time being. Both management and employee unions must make every effort to meet the identified objectives, keeping in mind that employees of a police agency are public employees whose avowed purpose is to protect the welfare of the community they serve. When this objective is maintained as being of paramount importance, bargaining will concentrate on the means to improve and professionalize the police, in order to best serve that function.

Conclusions

Viewing police administration in the broadest sense regarding management capabilities indicates that it is necessary to motivate police managers. There are several methods in which this might be accomplished. First, every effort should be made to impress upon public managers that it is their responsibility to represent and safeguard the interest of the governmental organization just as it is the duty of unions to represent public employees.

Second, negotiators in the public sector should be committed to the necessity of retaining the right to manage. In the long run, this is of primary importance if the public agency is to operate efficiently, utilize technological change, and reduce labor costs.

Third, all supervisors should be included as part of the management team (and excluded from the bargaining unit). Including supervisors in the bargaining unit will nullify the managerial group and weaken the role of supervisors as managers.

Fourth, police managers should be provided with financial rewards for outstanding performance which their counterparts in the private industry receive.

Within this perspective police unions should not be allowed to encroach upon exclusively management functions. Both managerial personnel and unions must adopt and abide by this fundamental principle. Also, one question should be answered as each union proposal is presented in the bargaining process, "Does this proposal prevent management from initiating actions necessary to implement in an efficient manner the public policy goals entrusted to it by law?"

One possible program that will lead to compatible labor relations is providing members of employee organizations a stake in management affairs. This undoubtedly will be difficult for many administrators due to the traditional philosophy of "we" manage, "they" follow orders. Implemented properly, providing employees with an opportunity to participate in the development of management policies, programs, and procedures will result in fewer management-employee conflicts without compromising the ultimate decision and policymaking authority that resides with the administrator. Since the administrators are responsible for the performance and quality of their organization, they should have the final word as to whether a particular decision, policy, or program will be implemented.

Police labor leaders are not in complete agreement with this line of thought and are convinced that the employees can and should contribute to the management process, since most policy decisions have a direct effect on them.

Police officers have accepted the union concept with the expectation that collective strength under written agreements will enable them to: participate in decision making which affects their personal and organizational futures, concentrate on public service without undue concern regarding their economic security, and create counterbalancing forces to offset the increased autocratic power of police administrators. Without achievement of these factors, police unions may not prevail. But these underlying conditions demonstrate that unionization is a value-laden process which reflects the police commitment to their profession. By utilizing unionism and collective bargaining, police officers have reasserted their values, personal and professional, not as alien concepts of the "industrial model" or "adversarial process" but in the perspective of professional pride.

Police officers, by nature, are not managerial adversaries. However, similar to other citizens, they are fully capable of determining when activities and conditions are strained in their organizations. Frequently, the strongest impetus for collective bargaining comes from police administrators whose demand for autocratic control of the employees and their personal lives are disguised under the catchwords of flexibility, accountability, and cost effectiveness. Arbitrary controls tend to inhibit personal growth and police professionalization by degrading the individuals they are attempting to manage.

Past police strikes, in many cases by police unions affiliated with the AFSCME and AFL-CIO, have been examples of desperation that illustrate the need for effective police labor organizations. However, police strikes are atypical; more typical are the hundreds of labor-management agreements that have been negotiated throughout the country without serious confrontation. In this perspective, collective bargaining is not new to the police profession. It develops when informal organizational structures fail to function. Under these conditions, collective bargaining becomes the vehicle whereby the employees secure, in formal agreements, what management had advocated was theirs.

Evaluation of a decade's experience with collective bargaining indicates that the early fears of the police administrators have been unfounded. For example, traditional management has not been displaced by unionization as previously predicted, but strengthened. In general, unions have attempted to replace procedures for consultation that had previously been informal, tacit, and verbal with procedures that are formal, explicit, and contractual. In some organizations, with underdeveloped systems of employee participation, unions have succeeded in increasing the influence of police officers in organizational decision making. However, they have not expanded the range of decisions beyond that which has been traditional to their organization's system of decision making. They have, however, increased many employees' level of participation.

Police officers have supported collective bargaining because they value their careers and their profession. They require security in their positions and a decisive role in the decision-making process within the police organization. The experience gained under collective bargaining during an era of economic uncertainty has produced something more — police officers for the first time can appreciate that their organized strength is an instrument for the economic, physical, and psychological survival of the police in society.

Police officers have been committed to the traditional labor-management processes, while they have made their employee organizations key elements in sustaining their efforts toward professionalization. However, the requirements of the police profession may have moved beyond the capacity of collective bargaining. This has been observable by organized employees' involvement in the political process, by reaching out to other community organizations, and by gaining public support for their labor movement. Simply, police unions, especially in politics, can accomplish many tasks that management is unable to perform. Above all, in the cause of the larger self-interest that transcends a single department, police employees can legitimately support their union activities before the public and supplement the role of organizational administrators.

The police union has been a proven instrumentality in the defense of the police profession. Administrators who have waged a continuing battle against collective bargaining should consider the consequences if they are victorious in their internal conflicts, for the external struggle for public support must thereafter be carried on with a divided staff and without management allies in the labor movement. In the past there has not been any record of police labor unions abandoning administrators in their mutual struggle for survival. Therefore, it is not logical for police administrators to win internal battles and lose the external war.

The controversy over management rights is a complex issue and not likely to be resolved in the next decade. Management should retain the authority and responsibility concerning certain rights, but must exercise these rights in a responsible manner if they expect to gain the cooperation of their employees.

Collective bargaining in the 1980s will experience many changes, only one of which may be its recognition as a method to preserve, improve, and expand the police profession.

Chapter 6
POLICE CORRUPTION

Introduction

The fact that official corruption does exist is amply supported by current evidence—but it cannot be allowed to continue. One of the most important needs in a democracy is integrity in government. Programs must be developed for the reduction of criminal opportunities in the public realm.

The National Advisory Commission on Criminal Justice Standards and Goals postulated that:

1. The corruption of public officials at all levels of government—federal, state, and local—is perceived as widespread by the American public;

2. Such corruption results in a staggering cost to the American taxpayer;

3. The existence of corruption breeds further crime by providing for the citizen a model of official lawlessness that undermines an acceptable rule of law.[1]

Corruption is not limited to its most egregious and sensational form—cash purchase of official favor. Corruption includes all of the circumstances in which the public officeholder or government employee sacrifices or sells all or part of his judgment on matters within the official purview in return for personal gain. Corruption thus defined includes a direct bargain—cash (or securities, a share in a business venture, or the promise of a future job on the outside)—in exchange for official action or inaction.

Corruption also includes more subtle arrangements in which the bargain is only implied. Such arrangements—frequently described as con-

---

1. National Advisory Commission on Criminal Justice Standards and Goals, *Community Crime Prevention* (Washington, D.C.: U.S. Government Printing Office, 1973).

173

flicts of interest—include any and all circumstances in which the officeholder or government employee is or may become the beneficiary of favor from persons with business that comes before the officeholder in an official capacity. Such conflicts of interest often involve the officeholder whose business or professional pursuits (e.g., insurance firm or law practice) service or represent those who may benefit from any official conduct.

Finally, corruption, as defined here, may flow from the electoral process itself. The payment, or promised payment, of campaign contributions in return for official conduct constitutes a bribe. Moreover, dependence on a source of campaign funding probably represents the most pervasive and constant monetary shackle on the judgment and action of the elected official.

In 1978 the federal government selected municipal corruption prevention (as a topic for training) as one of the most effective strategies for dealing with corruption. Figure 1 is a partial checklist that identifies indicators that allows one to conduct an assessment of the integrity-maintenance and corruption-risk condition of local government.

A simple and informal assessment of corruption in a community can be accomplished by talking to:

1. Taxi drivers.
2. Newspaper reporters.
3. Chamber of Commerce members and staff.
4. Lawyers.
5. Clergy.
6. Bar owners and bartenders.
7. Law enforcement officers (local, state, and federal).
8. Hotel help.
9. Homeowners association members.
10. Contractors.

Ask them:

Can I fix a ticket?
Where can I place a bet?
Who is the best zoning attorney?
How do I get a civil service position?
Can I get a girl for my room?
Who runs the gambling?
Who really controls this city?
Is this a good place to live?
How extensive is the drug problem?
What are the politics of this city?

How do I get a liquor license?
Is it difficult to open a business?
Whom do I see if I want to bid on a city contract?
How good is the Police Department?[2]

Figure 1 — Integrity Checklist Policy Toward Corruption

	YES	NO	DON'T KNOW
In your jurisdiction, do statutes and ordinances clearly forbid (and clearly define) bribery, extortion, and other forms of official misconduct?	—	—	—
Does your jurisdiction have an official code of ethics specifying what conduct is officially desired and what is officially prohibited?	—	—	—
Do these rules cover all elected officials, appointed commission members, department heads, and lower ranking employees whose duties may offer opportunities for corrupt acts?	—	—	—
In addition to prohibiting cash payments, do rules prohibit the acceptance of meals, gratuities, discounts, and favors from any individual or firm doing business with the city or county or subject to regulation by the city or county?	—	—	—
Do rules forbid engaging in private business on city/county time or using city/county materials or equipment for private purposes?	—	—	—
Is outside employment that conflicts with official duties forbidden?	—	—	—
Are officials forbidden to represent private interests in dealing with city agencies or take positions with firms they have previously regulated?	—	—	—
Do campaign finance laws set limits on contributions from individuals or firms doing business with the city/county?	—	—	—

For those questions that you answered "yes,"
additional factors to consider are:

2. Henry S. Dogin, *Maintaining Municipal Integrity*, Participant's Handbook (Washington, D.C.: Government Printing Office), pp. 61-62.

Are all personnel covered by the statutes, ordinances, and rules regularly informed of
what is required of them in the conduct of
their job?   ___ ___ _____

Are there mechanisms for detecting and deal-
ing with violations?   ___ ___ _____

Does every detected violation result in an appropriate disciplinary action or in pros-
ecution?   ___ ___ _____

A "no" answer to any question in this subsection indicates a deficiency;
the jurisdiction does not have all of the tools needed to combat corruption.

It is impossible to measure precisely the extent of corruption in America
today. But the presence of one especially virulent species—the influence
of organized crime syndicates on public officials—has been better
documented than most. As long ago as 1931, the National Commission on
Law Observance and Enforcement (Wickersham Commission) observed
that, "Nearly all the large cities suffer from an alliance between politicians and criminals." The link has been condemned by successive Attorneys General from Wickersham to Saxbe.

The President's Commission on Law Enforcement and Administration
of Justice noted that:

The millions of dollars ... (organized crime) can spend on corrupting public officials may give it power to maim or murder people
inside or outside the organization with impunity; to extort money
from businessmen; to conduct businesses in such fields as liquor,
meat, or drugs without regard to administrative regulations; to
avoid payment of income taxes or to secure public works contracts
without competitive bidding.[3]

The Commission went on to conclude that:

Today's corruption is less visible, more subtle, and therefore more
difficult to detect and assess than the corruption of the prohibition
era. All available data indicate that organized crime flourishes only
where it has corrupted local officials. As the scope and variety of
organized crime's activities have expanded, its need to involve public
officials at every level of local government has grown. And as
government regulation expands into more and more areas of private
and business activity, the power to corrupt likewise affords the cor-
rupter more control over matters affecting the everyday life of each
citizen.[4]

---

3.   President's Commission on Law Enforcement and Administration of Justice, *The
     Challenge of Crime in a Free Society* (1967), pp. 187-188.

4.   Ibid., p. 191.

No wonder, then, that a Harris poll revealed that 80 percent of the American people believe that "organized crime has corrupted and controls many politicians in the country."[5]

Charges of corruption, some of which already have led to convictions, have been brought against many officials throughout the United States. In one large eastern state at least 57 elected or appointed officials have been indicted or convicted on federal or state charges based on federal investigations. These officials include ten mayors, two judges, three state legislators, various local officials, and several state officials including two secretaries of state. Not all officials were charged while still in office. In another, smaller state, similar charges have been brought against at least 24 officials, including a former Governor, two state senators, a state attorney general, and several other state and local officers or employees.

Lincoln Steffens' mordant observation of over half a century ago—"The spirit of graft and of lawlessness is the American spirit"—is far from outdated in these post-Watergate days. But the American public's confidence in governmental "purity" was far from strong even before the disastrous disillusionment caused by Watergate. A study by the Center for Political Studies at the University of Michigan revealed that almost 30 percent of white Americans and almost 50 percent of black Americans believe that "quite a few of the people running the government are a little crooked."[6]

The direct costs of corruption are incalculable, but they are believed to be astronomical enough to support the wry observation of one high U.S. Department of Justice career official who stated that "when we finally stop payoffs to public officials at all levels in this country, we will have found the cure to inflation."

There is no dollar figure that can represent adequately the debilitating effect on human life of such activities as narcotics operations, extortion rackets, prostitution rings, and gambling syndicates that are permitted to flourish because of compliant and corrupt law enforcement.[7]

The Knapp Commission investigated the extent and nature of police corruption in New York City, reporting:[8]

> "We found corruption to be widespread"; that plainclothesmen participated in regular semi-weekly or monthly collections of payoffs

---

5. "Feelings of Alienation up Sharply in Past Year" (The Harris Survey, June 19, 1972); see also, "Public's Trust in Elected Officials has Diminished" (The Harris Survey, November 25, 1971).

6. Center for Political Studies, University of Michigan, "Election Time Series Analysis of Attitudes of Trust in Government" (Fall 1971).

7. National Advisory Commission on Criminal Justice Standards and Goals, *Community Crime Prevention*, pp. 205-207 and 267-269.

8. From Lawrence J. Dempsey, "The Knapp Commission and You," *The Police Chief*, Vol. XXXIX, No. 11, November 1972, pp. 20-29.

from gambling establishments; that narcotic enforcement officers received individual payoffs; that detectives carried out shakedowns of individual targets; that uniformed officers received regular payoffs from gamblers, bars, businesses, etc.; and that payoffs and bribes were not only to first-level officers, but were paid to sergeants and lieutenants.

The Commission reported that in the five of seventeen plainclothes divisions investigated in regard to police corruption, the investigation found a striking standardized pattern of corruption. They found that the officers assigned to plainclothes duty in the enforcement of vice and gambling laws participated in the collection of scheduled payments of graft amounting to as much as $3,500 a month from each gambling location and afforded each officer from $300 to $1,500 a month as his share (or "nut") of the so-called "pad" (payoff list money). Supervisors, sergeants and lieutenants and even higher officers received a share and a half, while newly assigned plainclothesmen had to wait two months for their first share.

The terminology for the receipt of police graft by narcotics officers was known as a "score," denoting a mostly one-time payment to an individual officer or partners, and ranged from minor shakedown payments to many thousands of dollars, with the largest narcotic payoff "score" uncovered by Knapp investigators to be $80,000.

The Commission reported that corrupt practices on the part of detectives not assigned to narcotic investigation, but to general investigative duties, took the form of shakedowns of individual targets of opportunity and although these "scores" were not of the usual high amount as found in narcotic cases, they not infrequently came to several thousands of dollars for each score.

The corrupt practices carried on by uniformed patrol assigned to normal patrol operations were reported to be the receipt of monies in much smaller payment amounts than those received by plainclothes-officers. Yet, when the number of smaller payments was totaled, it represented a serious corruption practice. It was reported that the uniformed patrol participated in gambling "pads" and received regular payments from construction sites, bars, grocery stores, and other business establishments. Although the payments received by uniformed personnel were small — mostly under $20 — they were reported to be so numerous as to add substantially to an officer's income. The Commission noted in its report that uniformed officers also received other payments, although less frequently, including those made from after-hour bars, bottle clubs, motorists for traffic violations, payments from tow-truck operators, money from cab drivers, parking lots, prostitutes, and defendants wanting to "fix" their court cases.

Another practice that the Knapp Commission found and reported to be widespread was the payment of gratuities by one officer to another in order to expedite normal police procedures and paperwork or to gain favorable assignments.

The Knapp Commission found that sergeants and lieutenants who were so inclined could also participate in the same kinds of corrupt practices as officers they supervised. And in addition, some sergeants had their own "pads" from which the officers who were working under the sergeants were excluded.

The Commission noted that although they were unable to develop hard evidence that superior officers above the rank of lieutenant were receiving payoffs, considerable circumstantial evidence and some testimony so indicated. It was reported that most often, if a superior officer was corrupt, a patrol officer would serve as "bagman" for making collections and would keep a percentage of the take as a collector. It was noted that because there was the possibility that the "bagman" might solicit and keep some moneys, although claiming to be collecting for the superior, it was extremely difficult for the Commission to determine with any degree of accuracy when a superior might be involved.

The Knapp Commission used two terms to describe the nature and significance of police corruption. These terms are "meat eaters" and "grass eaters."

A "meat eater" is a police officer who aggressively misuses the police powers for personal gain, whereas the "grass eater" is one who simply accepts payoffs that the happenstances of police work would throw his way. In describing these categories of police officers, the report noted that "although the meat eaters get the huge payoffs that get the headlines, they represent a small percentage of all corrupt officers. The truth is, the vast majority on the take don't deal in huge amounts of graft."

The Commission felt that the "grass eaters" are the heart of the problem; that because so great a number of police personnel is involved in this type of corrupt practice, its widespread nature tends to make the practice "respectable"; and that a code of silence exists among the police, with the effect that if any of them were to expose such corrupt actions, that individual would be branded as a traitor.

A recent newspaper article cited in a government publication pointed out that:

Suppose you are the sheriff of a small, rural county in south Georgia. You earn about $8,000 a year and have begun to wonder how you are going to send your kids to college. One day you are offered $50,000 to go into Joe's diner on the highway and have a cup of coffee. All you have to do is sit in the diner while a small plane lands in a cow pasture 10 miles away. If you simply don't notice the arrival of a million dollars worth of cocaine in a single-engine private plane at an isolated spot, all your financial worries will be over. Could you withstand this temptation? The Justice Department reports that with increasing frequency, small-town law enforcement officers are finding this kind of offer irresistible. . . .

A leading agent in the Fort Lauderdale office of the Drug Enforcement Administration has been indicted on four criminal counts involving the smuggling of drugs and obstruction of justice. FBI Director William H. Webster has cited problems not only with DEA officials but also among FBI agents and Justice Department prosecutors as well. He predicted indictment of some of these law enforcement officers in the near future. . . .

Can anything be done to stem this bribery, without which the drug trade would collapse? Of course, it helps to start with honest public officials, and most are. But with so very much money available to buy cooperation, there will always be sellers. Mr. Webster is wise to admit to problems within the bureau and express his determination to see that the offenders are prosecuted. The Justice Department and the DEA, to their credit, moved quickly to build an impressive case against the Florida agent. It is important not only that these cases be brought and won, but that they also be given maximum publicity. Prosecutions reinforce the ethical standards of those officers who cannot be bribed and, at the same time, serve as a warning to those who are tempted that they will be sought out."[9]

Consider Herman Goldstein's "Police Corruption: A Perspective on Its Nature and Control":[10]

Until recently, it has been almost impossible to generate open discussion of corruption by police themselves. If corruption was discussed at all, it was done privately, among officers who knew and trusted each other. Corruption was seldom referred to in police administration and law enforcement texts. It was rarely covered in any depth in police training programs or discussed formally at meetings of police administrators. Most strikingly, administrators of some of the most corrupt police agencies have publicly denied the existence of a problem. When confronted with evidence of wrongdoing, they have deemphasized the problem by dealing with the wrongdoers and claiming that they, like a few rotten apples, were exceptions in an otherwise clean barrel.

Today there is a greater willingness to discuss the problem. The session on police corruption at the 1973 meeting of the International Association of Chiefs of Police was among the most heavily attended of the entire conference. Articles on the subject are appearing in police journals. Several conferences have recently been held for the specific purpose of encouraging more open concern. But even at meetings called to discuss the problem, some participants try to divert attention from police corruption by insisting that it should be seen as only a part of the problem of corruption in the criminal justice system and society.

---

9. Anne R. Voight, *Justice Assistance News*, Vol. 4, No. 1, February 1983, citing an editorial in the Washington Post (nd).

10. The Police Foundation, 1975. Reprinted by permission.

Why is open discussion so difficult?

Cynics argue that those who are corrupt or potentially corrupt obviously have an interest in diverting attention from their own improprieties. Honest police administrators who have failed to control corruption have no desire to call attention to their failure. But these explanations do not account for the silence of police leaders strongly committed to rooting out corruptions or the silence of rank-and-file police personnel who themselves are honest.

One major reason for this unwillingness to discuss the problem is that it is difficult to do so without impugning the integrity of honest police personnel and contributing toward an already prevalent stereotype that labels all police corrupt. Many police officials feel that public discussion also undermines public confidence in the police in a manner disproportionate to the prevalence and seriousness of the corrupt acts.

There is little doubt that disclosure of a single instance of corruption in a large police agency adversely affects the reputation of the entire agency and makes all officers suspect in the eyes of a substantial segment of the community. This tends to be true even when an agency ferrets out its own corruption and when the disclosure reflects the agency's intense desire to rid itself of corrupt practices. Likewise, any effort by a newspaper, the mayor, a group of citizens, or even the police administrator to stimulate a public discussion of police corruption tends to besmirch the reputation of all police personnel. The effect sometimes extends beyond the agency involved. The most isolated instance of corruption may impugn the integrity of police personnel in agencies far removed from the area where the corruption is exposed. As a result, the low status accorded police is reinforced, the respect upon which their effectiveness depends is further diminished, and their own self-image suffers. Given the far-reaching and rather indiscriminate effects any ventilation of corruption has on the reputation of police and their morale, police inclination to suppress open discussion is understandable.

Apart from these considerations, there is a strong feeling among police that they have been made scapegoats, that because they are responsible for policing the conduct of others, some segments of the community delight in alleging police corruption. Some personnel even argue that certain elements of the community, by seizing every opportunity to paint the police as corrupt, hope to convince themselves that their own corruption is less serious.

A police officer learns a great deal about the corruption of citizens, such as how individuals exploit each other, and of the existence of a multitude of corrupt schemes in a community. Overt corruption may be witnessed in the prosecutor's office, in the courts, and in the relationships between lawyers and clients. It understandably angers one to know that institutions and professions which enjoy more prestige and status than the officer's are as corrupt, if not more corrupt, but that police are most commonly singled out for attention. What we now know in this Watergate era about corruption in government lends substantial support to these feelings.

Yet, understandable as the reluctance may be, it is impossible to deal in an innovative manner with corruption and to develop community support for confronting it unless the problem is fully discussed. Not addressing it openly will have an even more devastating effect than will the negative consequences of open discussion.

At the same time, it should be apparent that the police administrator who addresses the problem must, in order to maintain credibility with personnel, constantly acknowledge the extent to which corruption constitutes a problem elsewhere in society. This administration must argue convincingly that corruption elsewhere is no reason for tolerating it among police.

The executive also must guard against becoming a fanatic. The problem can arouse an emotional involvement that can be dysfunctional. Important as it is to address corruption, concern with it must be related to the magnitude of the problem in the given community and be balanced by concern with other problems.

Articles in this chapter have been selected in order to review the nature of corruption and consider programs that can contribute to overall police integrity.

REPORT ON POLICE CORRUPTION AND THE QUALITY OF LAW ENFORCEMENT IN PHILADELPHIA*

The Commission found that police corruption in Philadelphia is ongoing, widespread, systematic, and occurring at all levels of the Police Department. Corrupt practices were uncovered during the investigation in every police district and involved police officers ranging in rank from policeman to inspector. Specific acts of corruption involving improper cash payments to the police by gamblers, racketeers, bar owners, businessmen, nightclub owners, after-hours club owners, prostitutes, and others are detailed in the Report; more than 400 individual police officers are identified by first name, last initial, and badge or payroll number as receiving improper payments in terms of cash, merchandise, sexual services, or meals.

Corruption and political influence in the Police Department are problems which have plagued the force since its inception. In the 20th century alone, there have been three previous special grand jury investigations, each of which found widespread corruption within the Department. Difficult problems of integrity, political influence, and professionalism still continue, as the following summary of the Commission's factual findings indicates.

Liquor

The time, location, and means of selling alcoholic beverages in Pennsylvania are all subject to strict regulation under the Liquor Code. Many establishments operate in violation of the liquor laws to maximize profits, either by staying open past required closing times or having women solicit drinks from customers. Little social pressure exists in favor of the laws, but the Police Department has had to assume responsibility for enforcing those laws. In many instances, rather than enforce the Liquor Code, the police receive payments to overlook violations. More than 20 officers are identified as having received illegal cash payments from bars and approx-

* The Pennsylvania Crime Commission, *Commission Report* (Harrisburg, PA: Pennsylvania Crime Commission, 1974).

imately 50 from after-hours clubs. Additionally, more than 25 officers are identified as having been in after-hours clubs after the proper closing time. The Commission found widespread shakedowns of licensed liquor operators on the "Locust Street Strip" by members of the Philadelphia Police Department. The Commission discovered evidence that payments to the police were directly responsible for several illegal and open "bust-out" operations.

Eventually, one bust-out bar owner cooperated with the Commission's effort. He worked with the Commission for over a year and made tape recordings of conversations involving payoffs to police officers. During that time, he or his employees made direct payments to twelve police officers on a periodic basis. The tape recorded conversations which occurred during direct payoffs implicated another five officers. He testified concerning payoffs to two other identified police officers—one when he operated another bar and one when he had been arrested and was attempting to obtain expedited treatment at the Police Administration Building. He paid the police in a highly organized fashion, and his experience is a good example of the payoff system as it presently exists in Philadelphia.

To protect his bust-out operation, the bar owner paid an aggregate of $800 per month to policemen in every unit which had vice enforcement functions in his area. He paid each of the four uniformed squads when they worked the midnight to 8 a.m. shift; three of the squads received $35 and the fourth received $40. The "captain's men," who did plainclothes vice work for the captain of the 6th Police District where the bar was located, were paid $80 apiece each month. The plainclothes officers who did vice work for the inspector of the Central Police Division, the "inspector's men," also received $80 apiece each month. Their lieutenant received $100 per month, which was paid by the bar owner's manager. The manager also paid the inspector and his "bagman" each month—the bagman received $50 and took $100 to the inspector. Two members of the City-wide vice squad, the Chief Inspector's Squad, received $50 per month.

The Commission also uncovered circumstantial evidence of payoffs to police by three other bust-out bars. An officer who was picking up money from the cooperative bar owner commented, in tape recorded conversations, that the bar was only one of a series of stops. Also, other conversations occurred concerning payments being made by the other bars. A police witness for the Commission also confirmed that he had received payments from other operations on the Strip. Because of this evidence and because the bust-out activity continues in such a blatant manner with few arrests being made by the police, a reasonable conclusion is that the owners of those establishments are also paying for protection.

In addition to the Locust Street Strip, the Commission found that certain after-hours clubs routinely and systematically paid police in order to operate past prescribed closing times. After-hours clubs are private clubs licensed to sell drinks until 3 a.m., one hour past the normal closing time for bars.

A pattern of police activity occurred at the clubs which operated illegally after 3 a.m. Officers would enter the club at approximately 3:15 a.m., but make no effort to close it. They would then leave and subsequently return a few minutes before 4 a.m. and close the club. On occasion, an officer would remain at a club during the extra hour, and the bartender would continue to serve drinks in his presence.

This pattern of police activity occurred in all of the clubs for which the Commission has evidence of payments by the club to members of the Police Department. The cooperative bar owner tape recorded conversations with the managers and employees of several clubs in which the employees detailed payments to various police officers including the inspector of the Central Division.

The owner-operator of a Kensington club identified over 40 police officers that he had paid during the period from January, 1970, to September, 1972, including uniformed men up to the rank of lieutenant, two captains, two captain's men, two inspectors, and two inspector's men. The Kensington bar owner's identifications were corroborated by direct observation of payoffs by Commission agents, examination of a ledger the owner maintained in which he recorded police payments, and an examination of police assignment sheets. Incredibly, even after a widespread transfer of men in the 26th District and the East Division, the police did not miss a payment installment; the only result was a slight reduction in payment amounts. Thus, the uniformed squads received $170 each month until January, 1972, and then the new squads received $160. The captain and his men received a total of $110 per month prior to the transfer and $75 afterwards. The inspector and his men received a total of $80 per month prior to the transfer and $50 afterwards.

Illegal liquor sales outlets, "speakeasies," also operate in Philadelphia with both the knowledge and protection of the police. The Commission found two kinds of speakeasy operations: one operates on Sunday when state liquor stores are closed, and the other is similar to an after-hours club and is in operation seven nights a week.

The Commission discovered a typical Sunday operation in Germantown. Agents made numerous purchases from the speakeasy. One former police officer testified he had received steady payments from that speakeasy. The Commission also uncovered a bar which permitted lewd shows under the protection of a policeman moonlighting as a bartender, and a tavern owner who testified under oath that prior to selling his bar he paid the police between $300 and $400 each month.

The Commission thus found evidence of widespread payoffs to police officers from Locust Street Strip establishments, after-hours clubs, and speakeasies in order to conduct operations in violation of the liquor laws.

Even legitimate taverns were at times forced to pay to forestall being charged with having violated one or more of the numerous technical provisions of the Liquor Code. Clearly, segments of the Police Department, confronted with enforcing laws about which society cares little, selectively enforce the law for personal gain.

Gambling

The gambling laws prohibit conduct in which large numbers of people engage. The prohibition of gambling is unpopular and is certainly not of as great public concern as the enforcement of laws against such serious acts as burglary, robbery, rape, and murder.

The most prevalent forms of illegal gambling are numbers, horse bets, and sports bets. Commission agents made direct bets or observed bets at more than 200 illegal gambling locations. This does not include the numerous locations where agents saw all the indications of a gambling operation but did not observe or place a bet. An example would be a variety store where very few goods could be found on the shelves, and large numbers of people would enter the store for short periods of time during peak betting hours but rarely buy anything.

The Commission found direct evidence of ongoing illegal gambling in every police division of the City. Gambling operations were found in such places as candy stores, variety stores, restaurants, and bars. Police witnesses identified other locations which were systematically paying for police protection. The Commission documented payoffs to more than 25 police officers from gamblers. As a result of the work of the Commission's police witnesses and other investigations, there is evidence warranting more than 200 gambling raids and the arrests and indictments of more than 50 gamblers on bribery charges.

One of the Commission's more successful ventures was the infiltration of a medium size gambling network in West Philadelphia. The agents also became familiar with a nearby horse betting system on North 64th Street, as well as other gambling operations in the area. Because of their acceptance by these groups, Commission agents also placed bets with the largest operation in West Philadelphia which conducts business from a club on North 66th Street.

Because of the regularity, size, and openness of the business, widespread illegal gambling cannot exist over a period of time without the knowledge of the Police Department. Gambling has historically been tied to police corruption, and the Commission found the same ties exist today.

Each time police raid an operation, the disruption costs the gambler hundreds, and possibly thousands of dollars; consequently, a gambler is willing to pay to prevent the disruption. Confronted by an apathetic public, by gamblers who can evade arrest through the use of rice paper and the telephone, and by courts in many cases unwilling to impose a sentence of more than a small fine or probation, the police have become justifiably cynical about their ability to control a "crime" which few wish to control. However, Department policy demands vice arrests, and many times police officers turn the situation to their own benefit.

The Commission found that police officers throughout the City accept protection money from gamblers. The commission received sworn testimony from its principal police witnesses concerning many gambling locations giving protection payments to police. The Commission's investigation disclosed that the basic pattern of gambling payoffs involved a sum of money paid by a numbers banker to a policeman who acted as the bagman for his unit. The bagman then distributed the money to all the members of his unit who were aware of the illegal activity and who wanted the note. Uniformed squads were paid when they worked the 8:00 a.m. to 4:00 p.m. (day work) shift, every 24 days, with generally about $5 going to a policeman, $10 to the sergeant, and $15 to the lieutenant. Payments to plainclothes units may range from $15 to $50 per man paid through a bagman once each month, usually on the 1st or 15th. Plainclothes officers normally have a number of such regular notes.

The method for handling the payoffs can be well planned and hidden. For example, in West Philadelphia, a middle level gambler pays the uniformed squads $65 a month when they are on day work; he also delivers money for two smaller bankers, each of which pays $50. He also pays a total of $450 to one bagman for the captain's men and inspector's men.

The Commission uncovered other payoff patterns. Some gamblers pay by locations, with office men and writers making their own payments when necessary. Two principal Commission police witnesses gave sworn testimony concerning $5 and $10 notes they had received from many gamblers, usually through a bagman. One banker from South Philadelphia began working with the Commission and taped a payoff with a sergeant. The payoff occurred in a police car, and the police radio can be heard in the background. Other bankers pay their "edge off" houses a fee for police protection.

The Commission also discovered a substantial number of illegal gambling machines in the City. The machines were declared illegal in the late 1950's by the Pennsylvania Supreme Court. Distributors would not place them in the outlying counties but had no hesitation about installing them in Philadelphia. However, the Commission was unable to determine whether the existence of the machines was due to police laxity, ignorance, or payoffs.

A combined program of gambling law revision, adequate police training, and leadership on the corruption issue, as well as the deterrent of an ongoing, institutionalized investigative unit outside the Police Department specializing in integrity are necessary to fight corruption arising from gambling activities.

Prostitution

The Crime Commission investigation into prostitution and its relationship to police corruption concentrated in the Central and North Central Police Divisions. During the course of its investigation, the Commission located various centers of wide-open prostitution operations. Approximately seven police officers were identified as receiving cash payments to permit prostitution; eight others were alleged to have received or demanded sexual services from prostitutes in lieu of arrest. The Commission found that in certain selected localities within those areas, streetwalker and bar prostitute operations flourished due to police protection.

Commission agents received 62 separate solicitations in two limited geographic areas. In the North Central Division, streetwalkers, primarily black, frequent a two-block stretch of North Broad Street. They become known to both the police and the general public and obtain most of their clients from being in a place where prostitutes are "known" to be.

In the Central Division, Commission agents discovered wide-open and fast-moving prostitution rings at two bars at 10th and Race Streets, both within two blocks of the Police Administration Building. In addition, agents received solicitations at other bars in the area.

The Commission interviewed several of the bar prostitutes from the 10th and Race Streets area to determine whether they paid the police in order to operate so openly. Three of the women gave sworn statements that they were required either to solicit four drinks from their clients before they adjourned from the bar to a nearby hotel or to pay the equivalent of four drinks to the bar from the money they earned. It was their understanding that the money was used by the bar to pay police for protection. The witnesses had both observed and been involved in instances which corroborated their understanding. For example, when a prostitute was about to leave the bar with a client and saw a police car outside, she told the bartender. He went outside and the car left. Additionally, a procurer (pimp) who frequents one of the bars testified that he had observed the owner pass currency to a police officer inside the bar. As soon as the Police Department learned of the Commission's activity in the 10th and Race Streets area, the prostitution operations were closed down for a short period, according to one of the police witnesses who testified before the Commission.

A cooperative bar owner tape recorded a conversation with two officers in which they told him bar owners still pay the police for protection of their prostitutes. The same bar owner and his employees told the Commission that police protection involved not only payments of money but also free sexual services. The bar owner identified five police officers who received these services. One prostitute who worked at a Center City restaurant testified that she had sexual relations with police officers several times a week. She also told the Commission of an incident in which two police officers extorted $300 from her, part of which was used to pay for their dinners and a hotel room where they engaged in sexual relations with her. The prostitutes from the 10th and Race Streets area also testified that they were propositioned by police officers. When they did get arrested, an officer would offer to drop the charges if the female would engage in sexual relations with him.

The laws against prostitution, like those regulating gambling and the distribution of alcoholic beverages, are concerned with victimless crimes. The Commission found corruption usually attended the regulation of the conduct by the police.

Narcotics

In terms of patterns and regularities, narcotics related police corruption shares little with the other vice areas. The Commission discovered corruption in narcotics enforcement to be more of an individual than squad-wide activity. While the financial temptation is greater because of the extensive profits involved in narcotics traffic, the long standing law enforcement view of narcotics graft as the "dirtiest" type of corruption and the very nature of the narcotics transaction itself mitigate against systematic corruption. Nevertheless, the Commission received sworn testimony concerning police officers who allegedly have accepted, and in some cases, extorted money and narcotics from drug offenders interested in avoiding arrest. Approximately eight officers have been identified as being involved in narcotics related corruption, although an additional estimated fifteen unidentified officers were said to be involved. This does not include the incidents detailed by the special investigating grand jury.

The most common type of corruption appears to be the "shakedown," where an officer receives money, drugs, or other payment in lieu of arresting a suspected drug offender. An officer who makes a practice of narcotics shakedowns may patrol known drug use areas in search of a "score." When he sees an addict or a pusher, the corrupt police officer stops him as if to make an arrest. At the suggestion of the suspect or on his own impulse, the officer may come to some sort of understanding with the individual. The street addict, pusher, and addict-prostitute make particularly easy targets for the corrupt officer.

A former police officer testifying before the Commission estimated that in 65-70% of narcotics arrests, part of the drugs seized were not turned in as evidence but were kept for farming, paying addicted informants, sales, or personal use. Farming—the planting of evidence—is used to make or strengthen the case against a suspect. This conduct is often rationalized as a means of removing the trafficker from the street.

The Commission assembled evidence about the occurrence of shakedowns and farming in the 16th, 17th, and 18th Police Districts. In some cases, female addicts were allegedly threatened with arrest, beaten, or forced into performing sexual acts with the officers who had stopped them, while males were threatened, beaten, released, and told to "keep their noses clean."

One addicted drug dealer told of four incidents during the last two years when he was detained by police officers and lost more than $2,400. Another told of being detained during a drug raid in North Philadelphia and having all of his cash stolen. A third pusher, a woman, described various instances when officers allegedly obtained sexual services to forestall an arrest, mentioning three detectives and a lieutenant by name. The Commission has received allegations concerning fourteen other instances of Philadelphia police officers taking money, drugs, information, goods, or sex from suspects.

The Commission's findings in this area are supported by the investigating grand jury which unearthed similar examples of narcotics corruption. However, the Commission did not uncover the same widespread, systematic corrupt activity as in other areas of vice enforcement.

Business Notes

The Crime Commission found a broad spectrum of businesses, large and small, making illegal direct cash payments to the police; they included banks, insurance companies, automobile dealers, restaurants, supermarkets, jewelers, construction companies, vendors, country clubs, and moving companies. Businesses were found paying police officers in every one of the twenty-two police districts.

Most of the payments can be categorized as follows: (a) payments made in return for clearly improper acts by policemen, including providing on-duty policemen as private guards and providing confidential criminal records and intelligence information; (b) payments for proper police services rendered during the course of duty, including extra protection, police escort service, and quick response to calls; (c) gifts or payments made to incur "goodwill" on the part of the policemen; and (d) payments by businesses in response to extortionate demands by policemen or as bribes to overlook traffic, building codes, or other violations.

Although only a limited investigation of this matter was undertaken, the Commission uncovered identifying data on more than 200 police officers receiving cash payments from businesses. The names and badge numbers of 129 police officers who have received illegal cash payments were obtained, including one inspector, one captain, seventeen lieutenants, twenty-four sergeants, one corporal, and eighty-five policemen. Hundreds more such identifications would be obtainable through careful examination and correlation of police records with testimony of Commission witnesses. An estimated 700 policemen have received cash from just the businesses named in this Report in 1972-73. In addition, approximately 167 police officers were specifically identified as having received one or more free meals. An estimated 2,000 policemen have received free meals from just one restaurant chain in the above period.

The cash payments uncovered by the Commission are specifically punishable by dismissal and up to 90 days in jail under the Philadelphia City Charter and are potentially punishable as bribery under the criminal laws. The Police Department takes a strong official position opposing such payments, yet the Department never investigates them or punishes officers who receive them. Policemen thus generally refer to business payoffs as "safe notes" or "clean notes."

Police officers high in the chain of command are well aware of and participate in clean notes. Guard service at one company was arranged with at least the knowledge of the commanders of ten police districts. One instance was found in which an inspector in command of a police division was required to share Christmas notes by taking a case of liquor to a downtown staff meeting.

The amounts of money paid to the police for extra services provided to businesses range from $2 for an escort to the bank to $125 paid weekly for a full-time police guard stationed on business premises. Although the amounts of individual payments to police are often small, they can amount to a substantial investment of money. One business paid nearly $60,000 in cash and dispensed $70,000 worth of free meals to policemen in 1972. Another business paid cash to police officers at an annual rate in excess of $23,000.

The clean note presents a serious corruption hazard to any police department, despite the fact that often no criminal activity is being protected. Where police act as regular guards for specific businesses their services are effectively denied to the rest of the public. The Commission found that in the case of one fast-food chain, the services of the equivalent of 22 full-time on-duty police officers were devoted to protecting various business locations. These on-duty policemen were used in place of private guards at a substantial savings in cost to the company. However, the Philadelphia taxpayers lost the services of men who received a combined salary of about $264,000.

In addition to taking police services away from the public, this use of police as private guards was completely inefficient as a means of reducing crime. Close examination of crimes at protected and unprotected restaurant locations shows that the regular presence of on-duty police guards prevented, on the average, less than $13,000 in crime losses due to thefts per year, while the police protecting the stores were paid a combined public salary of about $264,000. At the four major supermarket chains in Philadelphia, extra police services also had no measurable effect on the crime losses of individual businesses.

Failure to enforce restrictions on clean notes thus has led to policemen being given assignments which afforded inefficient and ineffective protection to the public and has resulted in a distorted allocation of police resources.

An even more serious consequence of the clean note is that decisions on where to allocate police personnel are influenced by who is willing to pay extra for them, rather than where they are most needed. In effect, police services are open for bidding with the money going to individual police officers.

The receipt of clean notes also has an impact on the integrity of the individual police officer. The wide acceptance of illegal gifts causes everyone to be compromised to some extent. Some honest officers find them personally degrading and resent the assumption that they can easily be bought. Clean notes are also one means by which officers are tested by other officers who want to see if they will go along with the system. Even an officer who will not personally take a clean note learns that he must look the other way when his colleagues take them, or risk being an outcast.

In some cases where police officers receive a modest but steady clean note, they can become dependent on the extra income, causing them to look for other sources of notes if transferred. The note becomes an expected way of life, and officers may use the wide discretion at their disposal to bring non-paying individuals into line. For example, the Commission discovered that in certain sections of the City, vendors are systematically "shaken down" by the police. One fruit vendor testified before the Commission that he had been operating a fruit truck for the past twenty years and during that period he had to make regular payments to members of the Philadelphia Police Department in order to operate. During the five years that he operated an unlicensed stand at 20th and Johnson Streets, he paid at least $60 a month and at times as much as $75 a month to the police. Each of the shifts was paid $15—$5 for the sergeant and $10 for the sector car. He also usually had to pay $10 a month to an emergency patrol wagon. The vendor believed that everybody in the fruit business has had to pay the police at one time or another. The vendor finally stopped payments to the police in October, 1972, and several months later, his truck was confiscated by the police and shredded.

Police officers become so accustomed to receiving income from vendors they have actually been known to argue over the location of vendors. For example, a former police officer testified about a dispute between officers in the 22nd and 23rd Districts over the side of the street on which a vendor would illegally park. Each wanted access to the free food and cash that would be forthcoming.

Even occasional Christmas notes, free meals, or other presents given to create goodwill have an adverse effect. Although at first the effect of a gift to policemen or other public employees may be to create good feeling and marginally better service, in the long run the recipients grow to expect the presents as their just due. When they are not forthcoming, hostility is often created, and sol.c 'ation, or even harassment may take place and service deteriorates.

Car Stops

Police officers often receive cash from motorists who have been stopped for an alleged traffic or other violation. Small cash payments are made in return for failure to issue a ticket; larger amounts change hands when a driver is caught with a stolen car, numbers, drugs, or bootleg whiskey.

According to police witnesses, an expectation prevails among both policemen and motorists that the cash will be offered and accepted. Car stops are one of the first ways a rookie will be tested by his peers to see if he is "trustworthy" in terms of accepting notes. Many officers, according to Commission witnesses, do not solicit such payments but rarely refuse them if offered. Others, if they are aggressive, can make significant amounts of money through car stops.

Unprotected Property

Another common variety of police corruption, and one which offers no clear-cut remedy, is the taking of money or valuables from premises or individuals when the valuables are unprotected. This type of violation occurs when a building is open and unoccupied, presumably because a burglary has been committed. Similar to this practice is the confiscation of money or goods during a search, arrest, or detention of an incapacitated person.

The Crime Commission has received sworn testimony from a Philadelphia police officer concerning several incidents of police burglary that he personally witnessed. His accounts of these incidents indicate that such a practice is pervasive. Further evidence of irregularities which occur during arrests has been provided by a Philadelphia police officer and by individuals who have been arrested and have allegedly had money stolen from them while in the custody of the police. Although the Department promulgates regulations to prevent such occurrences, it is apparent that there is a substantial problem in the area of enforcement and detection.

Stolen Cars

The handling of stolen cars by the Philadelphia Police Department provides a further opportunity for corruption and misconduct. During the course of its investigation, the Commission found evidence of three types of police activity related to the handling of stolen cars. First, the Police

Department occasionally uses for its own purposes private automobiles and automobile registrations which have been impounded. Second, there is a general lack of security in the handling of impounded cars which has resulted in an inordinate amount of stripping of impounded automobiles. Third, there are indications that as a result of the stripping of cars at the Police Automobile Pound, insurance companies may have a practice of paying a "reward" to police officers for recovering cars and holding them at the district headquarters instead of sending them to the Pound.

The Crime Commission undertook an investigation of the Pound when a regional claims manager of an insurance company informed the Commission that a system of payments existed between one of its district claims managers and officers of the Philadelphia Police Department in order to secure the retention of recovered stolen vehicles at the district station and prevent the vehicles from being taken to the Automobile Pound. It was the company's experience that once a car went to the Pound it would be completely stripped of tires, wheels, radio, battery, engine, chrome, and grill.

On the basis of these allegations the Commission began a surveillance of the Pound and also subpoenaed representatives from five major insurance companies to see if the company's experience was unique or typical. However, at private hearings, officials of the complaining insurance company denied the payments to the Philadelphia Police Department had ever occurred. Representatives of other companies testified concerning poor security at the Pound and confirmed that on many occasions when they went to the Pound, they would see men surreptitiously working on cars.

Commission investigations also disclosed situations where tires were stolen from inside a locked trunk of a car that was in the sole possession of the Police Department, a car was totally stripped while in the Police Department's possession; and a car was stolen, recovered, but stolen again from the police before the owner could get to the station to claim the car.

Perjury

A Philadelphia police officer's conduct often leads to perjury and offering intentionally false statements in reports and in court. Perjury and intentionally false statements occur in the following contexts: officers swearing to false probable cause sections of search warrants for purposes of conducting a raid; officers falsifying the "evidence found" section of returned search warrants to hide evidence retained by the officers; officers planting vice evidence on suspects or searching them illegally and later lying under oath about the arrest situation; and officers providing false statements to protect themselves or another officer under suspicion of corruption.

Although no perjury is defensible, much police perjury is actually created and almost compelled by the Department's system of vice enforcement, which, despite officially stated policy, is in fact based upon arrest quotas.

The Commission has received sworn testimony concerning the above types of police perjury and false statements. A former Philadelphia policeman testified in detail about the course of events and conditions that brought him to a choice of perjury or testifying against a fellow officer.

Substantial evidence uncovered by the Commission indicates that a number of Philadelphia police officers committed perjury during sworn testimony before the Commission concerning their involvement in the illegal receipt of money from established businesses.

The Corruption Environment

The Commission's investigation has shown that systematic corruption exists in the Philadelphia Police Department. This condition results from the interaction of many factors, including the Police Department's attitude toward the corruption problem, the vice enforcement policy of the Department, various societal pressures on the individual police officers, and the reaction to corruption of other parts of the criminal justice system and the public.

A rookie policeman is assigned to patrol city neighborhoods with complex human problems that society has been unable to resolve. He is placed in difficult situations with almost unlimited discretion to exercise, virtually no guidelines for action, and little or no supervision. There are strong corrupting influences "in the street." His position exposes him to far more temptations than in other occupations. Public apathy to the enforcement of vice laws helps break down resistance to accepting gifts or bribes or ignoring violations of the law. Also, many practices such as tipping and doing favors that are accepted in the business community are not compatible with the police role. Thus, the police are subjected to conflicting pressures.

The attitudes within the Department to the corruption problem do not assist the individual police officer facing temptations and pressures from his peers. The Department takes the official position that corruption exists only in isolated cases and is a matter of individual conscience. This theory, known as the rotten apple theory, is an obstacle to any meaningful attempt to deal with systematic police corruption. It is impossible to fight successfully a problem that the leadership will not acknowledge exists.

To the individual policeman, the action of the Department leadership speaks louder than pious statements on corruption. Department spokesmen assert, for example, that taking clean notes is against departmental policy; yet, despite its prevalence and openness in the Department, there have been no investigations of the clean note problem by the Internal Affairs Bureau. With this type of official response, the burden of the corruption hazard is placed on the individual policeman without the

Department leadership doing its part to assist the individual officer face difficult temptations.

Another indicator of this attitude has been the failure of Department leadership to provide adequate training at the Police Academy to educate young officers about the corruption hazard. Many Crime Commission witnesses testified that the Academy failed to prepare young officers for the temptations that would arise once they are assigned to a district.

The Department's vice policy also contributes to the corruption problem. This policy is ineffective as a means of suppressing vice activity. According to Directive 8, the Department's official statement of its vice policy, all units are required to enforce the vice laws and to file various reports about vice activity. These reports are useless as a law enforcement tool. There is little or no correlation among the number of vice figures arrested, the identities of those arrested, and those listed on the vice reports. The Commission's investigation revealed that most vice reports are essentially recopied from year to year.

In addition to this reporting system, the Department has established vice arrest quotas, which emphasize the quantity and not the quality of the arrest. There is much pressure created at every level of the Department for vice arrests. The number of vice arrests made by a police officer is one factor used to evaluate his ability and performance. Yet the Department does not provide sufficient financial support and equipment to enforce vice laws in any effective way. These pressures for vice arrests and lack of support result in illegal conduct to meet the quota requirements.

The current vice policy of the Department, therefore, is not effective as a law enforcement tool but appears to exist as a shield for the Department leadership. Without the pressure for vice activity, very few arrests would be made. Corrupt officers would be content merely to collect their money from vice centers. Such conduct would become obvious to the public. With current policy, corruption is somewhat hidden from the public by the large number of vice arrests. These vice arrests are not effective against vice centers because the emphasis is only on arrest and not conviction thereby resulting in bad arrests and arrangements between corrupt police and illegal operators to satisfy the quota.

Not only Department policy but pressures created by a "policeman's lot" have an impact on an officer's resistance to corruption. As a young man puts on the police uniform, he becomes a different person in the eyes of many people. His presence creates uneasiness in many people. The paramilitary police organization places further pressures on him and his family. His working schedule isolates him from many prior friends. As a result, he turns inward to the police community. He thereby becomes more susceptible to peer pressures. There will be many pressures on the new policeman to be trusted and accepted by his fellow officers. When a man arrives at a new assignment, he will be tested by the older men to see his reaction to minor indiscretions. He will be told about places he can get the police price on food, clothing, and other merchandise. He will be assigned work which will produce the safe or clean note from a businessman. His reactions and attitudes to police problems and borderline conduct will determine the trust the older men have in him. Once the new man is accepted by the older men, he may be given a permanent sector assignment. When he patrols a permanent sector assignment, he will notice open illegal activity; he must begin to question what is happening. Such inquiry will usually determine whether he will become part of the system. As one officer testified, if he does not go along, he will be "walking the third rail" on subway duty.

For many reasons, there is great hesitancy on the part of police to turn in other police officers. Warnings from supervisors about internal security operations in the district clearly tell the policeman that he should not make any disturbance about activities of fellow officers. If one is caught, he should remain silent.

Systematic corruption of policemen does not occur in a vacuum. Officers succumb to pressures within the Department. Illegal conduct of fellow officers, and especially by superior officers, has a destructive impact on an individual policeman. In Philadelphia, police officers have seen the Police Commissioner held in contempt of court for "blatant disregard" of a court order. They have witnessed the Department leadership fail to take action against open and widespread violations of Department policy such as in the area of safe or clean notes. They see other public officers act in ways suggesting improper influence or corrupt behavior. They perceive the courts treating policemen as a special category of offenders. Very few police cases get to trial and fewer still are sentenced to jail. The general public seems complacent about corruption problems. Even though large segments of the population are victims of it, people generally do not come forward to protest about police corruption.

All of these various factors contribute to the corruption environment in which a police officer in Philadelphia must work. The Department leadership must acknowledge that corruption is a problem that must be dealt with openly and frankly before there will be any meaningful progress made towards eradication of systematic corruption. The attitudes of members throughout the Department must change to deal effectively with the corruption problem. At the Police Academy, the recruit should be educated about the corruption hazard. Commanders must be held responsible for the conduct of their men. There should be changes in the criminal laws to remove the police from attempting to enforce the unenforceable vice laws. The Commission's investigation established that vice laws cannot be effectively enforced without enormous commitment of resources in terms of support and supervision. Departmental policies toward the vice area should be modified to reflect realistically the conditions which exist in an urban community.

Control of the Police

The control of corruption and misconduct by police officers in Philadelphia lies for the most part in the hands of the Police Department itself. The District Attorney's office has shown itself to be ineffective at investigating the police and in fact is forced to rely upon the Police Department to assist in its investigations. The federal authorities also often refer allegations of corruption or misconduct by police officers to the Department, since there is not always a violation of federal law. Although some federal laws do prohibit police officers from taking bribes, the Commission is aware of very few police corruption prosecutions by the federal government in Philadelphia.

The internal control mechanisms within the Police Department are vague, fractionalized, and almost totally ineffective. The Department's attempts at controlling corruption are crippled at the outset by the attitude that there is no widespread or systematic corruption in the Department. Thus, there is little or no serious, active effort made to seek out evidence of corruption in the absence of complaints. Surveillance and exit interviews are conducted but produce few results. There has been no attempt to "turn" a police officer who has been caught and to have him work undercover to help improve the system in exchange for lenient treatment. There has been no attempt made to acknowledge the problem of corruption openly and to create an atmosphere within the Department which would allow honest officers to bring forward evidence of corruption without fear of retribution by their colleagues or their commanders.

The responsibility of investigating allegations of both corruption and police "brutality" (a catchword for improper and excessive uses of physical force on citizens) is shared by the commanding officers of the police officers involved and by the Internal Affairs Bureau. There are no written guidelines on who shall investigate particular matters and no special forms for recording allegations of police misconduct. Which unit investigates a complaint appears to depend on a number of various circumstances such as the source of the information, where it was received, the nature of the matter, and the amount of public attention it receives. According to the testimony of Chief Inspector Frank A. Scafidi, most investigations of corruption and brutality in the Police Department are carried out by the Internal Affairs Bureau, while investigations of lesser offenses are carried out by line commanders. Although complaints against police officers are required by police directive to be recorded, the forms used are the same as those for any matter which requires police action, and there are strong indications that the forms are not always filled out.

As the arm of the Police Department with primary responsibility for investigating corruption, the Internal Affairs Bureau is very weak. Under existing procedures it might never even learn of evidence or an allegation of corruption which turns up at the police district level since it might be covered up. Assuming the matter is duly recorded, the incident report would flow up the chain of command rather than be sent directly to the Bureau. Only if the matter is at some point determined to be sufficiently "serious" might a decision be made to bring in Internal Affairs investigators.

Assuming the Internal Affairs Bureau handles an investigation, there is little assurance the Bureau will conduct it vigorously and thoroughly. The officers assigned to the Bureau do not receive any special training in investigating corruption or in the use of undercover techniques. As previously stated, the Bureau has not attempted to exact cooperation from officers who are caught. The Department does not require police officers to submit to polygraph examinations during the course of internal investigations, although it makes frequent use of polygraphs in non-police investigations. Although the present policy is that a member assigned to the Bureau may remain as long as he wishes, Internal Affairs is not in fact a permanent assignment; and as a practical matter, an officer is subject to being transferred out if he displeases his superiors or an influential commander who may be the subject of an investigation. There is also no assurance that Internal Affairs investigators will not later be required to serve under or alongside officers they have investigated. Finally, the members of the Bureau receive no special rank, status, or pay to go along with the significantly different duties of their assignment.

During the course of its investigation, the Commission came across two incidents which illustrate the manner in which the Internal Affairs Bureau investigates evidence of corruption. In one case, a memorandum was sent from the District Attorney's office to Internal Affairs stating that a Locust Street bar owner had made tape recordings of payoffs to twelve police officers. One of the officers mentioned in the memorandum later testified before the Commission that his immediate commander was notified of the allegation by Internal Affairs and that the officer and his partner were questioned by the commander. At the end of that interview, the two officers were told to go to Internal Affairs the next morning. In the meantime, the two officers had an opportunity to discuss the matter and to make their stories consistent. They decided to deny the allegations. To assist them and to get advice, they also contacted a former policeman. The following day during the Internal Affairs interrogation of the two officers, the former policeman called a staff inspector in Internal Affairs and got a full outline of the evidence against the two officers. Later that day a representative of the Fraternal Order of Police called Chief Inspector Frank Scafidi, head of the Bureau, and was told the two officers need not be concerned since the charges would probably die a natural death.

These messages were immediately transmitted to the officers alleged to be involved, which fortified their resolve to deny the whole incident.

In another case, the Commission turned over to the Police Department massive evidence of police officers illegally receiving cash payments from businesses. Seventy-seven officers were identified by name and badge number and one hundred and six were identified by assignment, initials, or signatures as being apparently involved. The evidence consisted of documents and testimony. Thorough examination of relevant police records, together with interviews of all witnesses, could have resulted in criminal or disciplinary actions against several hundred police officers. However, the only action taken was that thirty files were "opened." One officer who was apparently deeply involved had been permitted to resign without charges placed against him. No effort was made to contact the business witnesses who testified or to interview additional witnesses. Furthermore, many police patrol logs which would have contained essential corroboration apparently were not examined and were routinely destroyed.

The weakness of the Internal Affairs Bureau is also illustrated by its lack of concentration on internal police matters. Several of its members were assigned during 1973, to conduct an ostensible investigation of corruption in other City agencies.

There is no question that given existing guidelines, attitudes, personnel, and organization the Police Department cannot effectively police itself. Efforts at internal control should not be abandoned; rather, they should be greatly strengthened and vigorously pursued.

DELPHI ANALYSIS OF POLICE CORRUPTION*

Numerous issues are of critical concern to police administrators, but none is more universal nor persistent than police corruption. Corruption is not unique to law enforcement; it occurs in other segments of government as adequately illustrated by Watergate. Lincoln Steffens at the turn of the century described the inability of reform governments to control corruption at the local level.[1]

The historical consistency of police corruption in the United States is legendary and closely parallels the corrupt political regimes that were prevalent in the nineteenth century as well as a significant portion of the current century. The police in many communities functioned as the military arm of incumbent political parties and actively supported corrupt activities.

The "economy and efficiency era" in the early part of the twentieth century did little to alter the patterns of police corruption. In the view of some experts, the efforts of reform were significantly stymied by the advent of prohibition. What little reform had been accomplished was immediately eradicated by public rejection of prohibition.[2] Breaking the law became a way of life, and the tentacles of corruption strengthened its stranglehold on many police officers and police departments.

The corruption of politicians at the municipal level fostered and nurtured political control of police departments. As emphasized by the Wickersham Committee in 1931:

> The well-known and oft-proven alliance between criminals and corrupt politicians which controls, in part at least where it does not wholly do so, the police forces of our large cities, might well be taken as a primary cause of police inefficiency.[3]

Lawrence Sherman has described the 20-year cycles of corruption and

---

*   Harry W. More Jr., "The Delphi Analysis of Police Corruption," *Journal of Police Science and Administration*, Vol. 8, No. 1, 1980, pp. 107-115. Reprinted by permission.

1.   Lincoln Steffens. *The Shame of the Cities* (New York: Hill and Wang, 1902).

2.   Richard Hofstadter, *The Age of Reform* (New York: The Vintage Books, 1960).

3.   National Committee on Law Observance and Enforcement, *Report on the Police* (Washington, D.C.: U.S. Government Printing Office, 1931), 5.

reform that have characterized the largest police department in the United States.[4]

The fact that corruption does exist in some police departments and has been a repetitive type of activity in many cities clearly places it as one of the major obstacles confronting many police administrators. A number of police agencies, such as Los Angeles, Oakland, and Kansas City, have been plagued by corruption in the past but now have outstanding reputations for integrity. Obviously something can be done about corruption, and substantial improvement can be achieved in the control and elimination of corrupt police practices.

An accurate appraisal and assessment of police corruption can only occur after there is some agreement as to what actually constitutes police corruption. In the past, studies of police corruption were primarily concerned with "the bad apple theory" and proposed the problem could best be remedied by dealing with the moral fiber of the police officer. The basic assumption was that the integrity of a department could be maintained by eliminating or prosecuting the officers who succumbed to the temptations of bribery or other illegal activities. In general, it was assumed this could best be accomplished through internal investigations by police department personnel.[5]

McMullen presented the following widely accepted definition of corruption:

> a public official is corrupt if he accepts money or money's worth for doing something that he is under a duty to do anyway, that he is under a duty not to do, or to exercise a legitimate discretion for improper reasons.[6]

Goldstein, in his 1975 study of the nature and control of police corruption, stated:

> police corruption means acts involving an authority by a police officer in a manner designed to produce personal gain for himself or for others.[7]

This definition was concurred with by Barker and Roebuck in their empirical typology of police corruption.[8] A broader definition was recently released by the International Association of Chiefs of Police in one of its studies concerning police corruption: "deviant behavior [is] behavior that

---

4. Lawrence W. Sherman, ed., *Police Corruption* (Garden City, New York: Doubleday Anchor Books, 1974).
5. Albert J. Reiss, *The Police and the Public* (New Haven: Yale University Press, 1971).
6. M. McMullen, "A Theory of Corruption," *Sociological Review*, 9(2) (July 1961), 183-184.
7. Herman Goldstein, *Police Corruption* (Washington, D.C.: Police Foundation, 1975), 3.
8. Thomas Barker and Julian Roebuck, *An Empirical Typology of Police Corruption* (Springfield: Charles C. Thomas, 1973), 9-10

violates normative expectations."[9] The study pointed out that corruption has begun to breed when a policeman receives, or expects to receive, an actual or potential unauthorized material reward or gain by virtue of his official position.

A concrete definition of police corruption is essential in order to ensure that it encompasses acts or misdeeds that fall into carefully specified categories. For the purposes of this study, police corruption was operationally defined as *any act involving the misuse of authority that resulted in a law enforcement officer receiving a material reward or violating criminal laws.* As emphasized by Goldstein, this allows one to eliminate from consideration police activities which involve a corruption of power, such as physical abuse or illegal searches and seizures.[10]

Material reward, the key element of the operational definition, must include the acceptance of free coffee and meals. while it is acknowledged such gratuities seem insignificant, there is reason to believe they create an atmosphere conducive to corruption. Under such circumstances, police integrity is compromised. This must not be allowed to occur if the police are to serve the total community instead of just special individuals or groups.

With this definition, noncriminal activities are incorporated; the parameters of corruption are clearly established; and the police administrator is provided specific boundaries.[11]

The Delphi Technique

The Delphi technique allows a number of individuals to communicate with each other anonymously regarding a complex problem. It is a positive system for facilitating the analysis of solutions and the development of decision options. It is a quasi-empirical forecasting technique developed by the Rand Corporation of California and deals with unknown quantities or factors such as future events. It is a means of arriving at working conclusions regarding a specific subject matter through the use of expert knowledge.

Individuals are chosen for inclusion on a Delphi panel by virtue of their knowledge, experience, and ability to project decision options based upon that knowledge and experience; hence, they are classified as experts. Individual participants are interrogated by a sequence of questionnaires in which the responses to one questionnaire are designed and structured around a particular topic; in this instance, police corruption.

---

9. William L. Tafoya, *Police Corruption* (Washington, D.C.: IACP, mimeographed, October 7, 1974), 6.
10. Goldstein, 3-5.
11. Ibid.

The resulting environment of the Delphi method is a communication process (as opposed to a poll), since individuals have the opportunity to change their earlier views and to benefit from the contributions of others. A clear-cut advantage is that the process eliminates psychological factor-bias.

The optimum steps in a Delphi sequence include:

Round 1

a. Panelists receive general instructions
b. Panelists respond with items (such as events, trends)

Round 2

a. Panelists receive list of items
b. Panelists respond with estimates (dates) for each item

Round 3

a. Panelists receive list of items
b. Panelists respond with revised estimates

Round 4

a. Panelists receive list of items and summarization of statements
b. Panelists respond with revised estimates, additional supporting statements, comments on statements of other panelists.[12]

Research Design

Two distinct groups of individuals who work within or act upon the criminal justice system were included in the panel for this study. The first group consisted of 75 police officials, and each group of experts were regionally represented according to the following geographical areas: Northeastern, Northcentral, Southern, and Western. A key element in the composition of this panel was the inclusion of individuals who had, in all probability, developed some expertise about the problem of police corruption and the trend(s) associated with this critical issue.

Each prospective panelist was sent a letter of participation request. Of the 100 individuals selected for the survey, the response was 72 (54 were police panelists and 18 were educational panelists). After waiting a reasonable period of time (to ensure adequate response to the questionnaire), some of the nonresponding panelists were contacted by telephone in order to obtain representation from each of the four major segments of the United States.

---

12. Joseph P. Martino, "Survey of Forecasting Methods—Part II," *Bulletin*, 11(1) (January-February 1977), 27. For detailed discussions of the Delphi Method, see: Norman C. Dalkey, *The Delphi Method: An Experimental Study of Group Opinion*, (Santa Monica: The Rand Corporation, RM-5888-PR, June 1969); A. Linstone and P. Turoff, *Delphi Method—Techniques and Application* (New York: Addison-Wesley, 1973).

Research Application

The total sample for the survey was utilized in order to establish a data base for the application of the Delphi method. The police officials and criminal justice educators were combined into one panel as a means of bringing together a broad background of knowledge and experience for generating a conceptual reaction to the complex issue of police corruption.

This panel responded to three open-ended questions:

1. What have been the significant trends concerning the extent and nature of police corruption and its control during the last 10 years?

2. During the next 25 years, do you anticipate these trends to continue in the same direction and at the same rates, or do you anticipate significant changes? Please explain.

3. Do you foresee any new trends in the control of police corruption emerging during the next 25 years? Please explain.

These questions were specifically designed to acknowledge the complexity of the subject and to initiate extended answers concerning the extent and nature of police corruption and its implications of control during the past and in the future. This process provided the opportunity for nonstructured responses that ranged from simple to multidimensional statements. This extended data base was then utilized as a means of developing a series of categories concerning trends and issues of the last 10 years and implications for the next 25 years. Subject categories were established in 9 areas for the period encompassing the previous decade, and 113 items were placed within these categories. Regarding the anticipated trends of corruption and the potential for their control over the next 25 years, 115 items were placed into 10 subject categories. This allowed for the summarization of the responses and afforded the panelists additional opportunities to respond to specific statements about past levels of police corruption as well as anticipated trends during the next 25 years. The panelists provided controlled anonymous feedback by placing in rank order specific statements of the characteristics of police corruption, potential methods of control, and items that would influence control of police corruption in the future.

Iteration of feedback in subject categories provided group consensus and identified trends. These trends were subjected to comprehensive inferential analysis, comparative evaluation, and conjectural development.[13]

---

13. Terry L. Cooper, "A Blue Future: Police Values and Police Power During the Next Three Decades," cited in Andrew A. Spekke, ed., *The Next 25 Years, Crisis and Opportunity* (Washington, D.C.: World Future Society, 1975), 251.

Level of Corruption

In the subsequent response to the specific issues and propositions, the police panelists numbered 44, and the educational panelists numbered 15. The responses for each group were analyzed, and there was adequate regional representation for the four geographical divisions of the United States. The initial responses of the panelists indicated that during the last 10 year period, 46.2 percent believe corruption had begun to level off, but 34.6 percent thought corruption, as a critical police issue, had increased. Anticipated by 78.4 percent of the panelists was the belief that corruption would level off and/or begin to decrease during the next 25 years. Interestingly enough, regional differentiation was not apparent in responses to either past or future trends of police corruption. These "experts" were generally positive in their view of corruption during the next quarter of a century, and there was a twofold increase in the number of panelists who foresaw a reduction in the level of police corruption.

Control of Corruption

With reference to controlling corruption, the respondents initially identified three major areas of significant influence: administrative control, control by the media, and control by "watchdog" groups. The respondents overwhelmingly identified administrative control (52.4 percent) as the most significant means of controlling police corruption. This was followed, in terms of importance, by watchdog groups (26.2 percent), and finally by control of the media (21.4 percent). During the subsequent evaluation process, the means of control were converted into the following four variables: internal controls and accountability, internal affairs units, exposure by mass media, and watchdog groups. In placing these in rank order of importance, the subsequent evaluators identified the area of internal controls and accountability as the most significant step toward potential control of police wrongdoing, followed very closely by internal affairs units. The third level of importance was identified as exposure by mass media followed by watchdog groups as having the least potential impact on the control of corruption in law enforcement agencies.

The overwhelming support of internal policing of wrongdoers and the rejection of external exposure and control reflects the desire for internalizing discipline or disciplinary control by members of the "select group." There is considerable data from the study indicating that the hierarchical and bureaucratic nature of police departments provides a means of inculcating honesty in its incumbents and ensures organizational integrity.

Acknowledging the difficulty of controlling police corruption, the panelists supported the view that control optimization can be achieved by instituting a managerial perspective of accountability. The organizational model for police efficiency was envisioned as epitomizing carefully delineated policies, procedures, techniques, and numerous review points.

Again, there was no significant difference in terms of regional responses to the rank ordering of importance of control variables for educational or police panelists.

Nature of Corruption

The specific nature of police corruption was found to be influenced by a number of variables: police corruption paralleled political corruption; police corruption reflected the moral values of the community; police corruption resulted in the nature of police work; police cynicism resulted in corruption; and political involvement resulted in corruption (Table 1).

Table 1 — Rank Order of Responses on the Nature of Corruption for the Last 10 Years

Categories	Rank Order
Paralleled political corruption	2.00
Less political involvement	2.63
Moral values of the community	2.80
Police cynicism	3.81
Nature of police work	4.18

During the subsequent evaluation of these propositions, the respondents overwhelmingly identified "politics" as being the most significant influence on police corruption. This was divided into two areas—police involvement in the total political process, and political corruption fostering and encouraging police corruption. The police are obviously a part of the American political scene; consequently, they reflect the political activities and processes occurring in cities throughout this nation. According to the respondents, they also reflect the moral values of the community. This was found to be the second most important variable.

The application of the rule of law in a democratic society requires acquiescence and acceptance by the majority of its citizens. When these laws are rejected by the majority, their enforcement becomes an unmanageable task; consequently, law enforcement officers and officials act accordingly. The corrupt community can only exist when the police have been corrupted. In a community that values high morals, the public will not tolerate or accept police corruption. Conversely, if the moral values of a community are low or nonexistent, an atmosphere that nurtures corruption is created in all parts of government, generating a popular position that "no law enforcement is good law enforcement." Overall, there seems to be some truth to the statement that a community deserves the type of police protection it has, and there is no reason to be naive enough to assume that the members of a police department should be any better or worse than the average individuals in the community.

The next most important variable identified by the subsequent respondents was the concept of police cynicism. Niederhoffer pointed out that:

> in the police system the typical adaptation to anomie is cynicism. Like resentment, it consists of diffuse feelings of hate and envy, the impotent hostility, and the sour grapes pattern, and is . . . a state of mind in which the anomie of the police organization as a whole is reflected in the individual policeman.[14]

While cynicism has not merited consideration as a primary conditioner of police corruption, on the basis of current social science knowledge, it must be considered as an important variable in the analysis of this topic.

The last factor identified from the data provided by the respondents was whether or not police corruption was a result of the nature of police work. Manning pointed out that the occupational culture of law enforcement allows for the formulation of the following postulates or assumptions:

1. People cannot be trusted; they are dangerous.

2. Experience is better than abstract rules.

3. You must make people respect you.

4. Everyone hates a cop.

5. The legal system is untrustworthy; policemen make the best decisions about guilt or innocence.

6. People who are not controlled will break laws.

7. Policemen must appear respectable and be efficient.

8. Policemen can most accurately identify crime and criminals.

9. The major jobs of the policeman are to prevent crime and to enforce the laws.

10. Stronger punishment will deter criminals from repeating their errors.[15]

Respondents in this case gave police work the lowest rating of all the variables that might impinge upon the critical topic of corruption. Needless to say, there is an occupational culture for the police, and even though it might vary from community to community, it still exists and must be acknowledged, although not given a great deal of weight as a corruption modifier.

---

14. Arthur Niederhoffer, *Behind the Shield: The Police in Urban Society* (Garden City, New York: Anchor Books, 1967), 98-99.

15. Peter K. Manning, "The Police: Mandate, Strategies, and Appearances," cited in Richard Quinney, ed., *Criminal Justice in America* (Boston, Little, Brown and Company, 1974), 175.

Corruption Modifiers

The panel of experts suggested that during the next 25 years, police professionalization would emerge as the most important factor in the control of police corruption. Of the data items, 33 percent dealt specifically with the concept of police professionalization; 38 percent of the items positively supported the concept of professionalization and served to reinforce and amplify the significance of this trend as well as to establish the interrelationship of training, supervision, and the quality of personnel. The data indicated that 64 out of 84 individual items specifically identified or reinforced the concept of police professionalization (see Table 2). Police administrators and justice educators definitely view police professionalization as being capable of responding to the critical problem of police corruption (see Table 3).

Table 2 — Initial Control Response of Panelists for the Next 25 Years

Categories Identified	Frequency of Identification
Professionalization	28
Training	12
Ethical education	4
Isolation	6
Personnel	12
Supervision	8
Society	9
Prosecution	13
Civilian control	7
Miscellaneous	16
Total	115

Table 3 — Subsequent Responses of Panelists Placing Categories in Rank Order for Control Trends in Next 25 Years

Categories	Rank Order
Police professionalization	2.36
Better supervision	3.81
Improved training	4.18
Ethical education	4.18
Stringent prosecution	4.27
Quality of personnel	4.45
Society will not tolerate	5.45
Civilian control	8.00

Conclusions

There is considerable data in this study to support the view that political corruption (and more specifically, the "political" involvement of law enforcement agencies) has contributed significantly to the corruption of law enforcement agencies. Political corruption fosters, nurtures, and encourages police corruption. In fact, there is reason to believe that a corrupt community will inevitably have corrupt police officials and officers. History also supports this study and mandates the need for ensuring police responsiveness to elected political figures and to the community.

The police are the enforcers of the laws, and they represent the society of which they are a part. To suggest that the police are not political is to ignore reality. The police are, indeed, political, and they are an important part of the political process. But at the same time, the police cannot (nor should they) become the "tools" of political machines.

Politics in and of itself does not need to reflect or lead to corruption. However, when corrupt politics and a corrupted police are identified, they *must* be rejected. Inevitably these characteristics will show up occasionally in our type of government. The police must be true "justice actors" and support the continuing search for justice.

Equitable justice is a concept that must permeate the police process, becoming a goal for all. However, the police process must never become more important than the individual and/or society.

The study further shows that police administrators and criminal justice educators perceive that police professionalization, improved quality of police personnel, improved training, and better police supervision will result in greater control of police corruption during the next 25 years.

The bureaucratic police organization can serve as the frame of reference for a police ideology that embodies all the concepts of freedom. Organizational effectiveness, rather than organizational efficiency, can overcome the inadequacies of Weber's bureaucratization and create "professional" justice.

Chapter 7
TERRORISM

Introduction *

Contemporary terrorism has migrated to industrialized societies in the seventies and now poses a real threat to several nations. Police and law enforcement agencies have become vulnerable to terrorism's twin characteristics—uniqueness and unpredictability—as they have responded to counter, neutralize, and suppress this criminal menace. Officials in West Germany, Italy, and France have been hit particularly hard this year, and "The Troubles" have continued in Northern Ireland. Japan has suffered several defeats abroad because of her concern over foreigners in skyjacking, as evidenced in the September, 1977, skyjacking by the Japanese Red Army, and several Latin American countries have already passed through a solid decade of terrorism. Not all terrorists, however, have been successful. Important defeats have been dished out by the Dutch and West Germans. More will be forthcoming as governments tailor their responses to counter terrorism.

It is widely recognized that a proper response by police and law enforcement officials is critical in winning the struggle. Unfortunately, less attention has been directed towards how this response should capitalize on terrorism's weaknesses. Too often police have had to react after a terrorist attack rather than to initiate their response beforehand. Understanding this phenomenon is essential in structuring a successful response to defeat terrorism and destroy its mystique of invincibility. This article discusses terrorist strategy and tactics, using a recent European example with the aim of contributing to that understanding, and advances some

* John D. Elliot, "Contemporary Terrorism and the Police Response," *The Police Chief*, Vol. XLV, No. 2, February 1978. Reprinted by permission of the International Association of Chiefs of Police.

tentative conclusions to guide the response of threatened governments.

Police and law enforcement officials are the most frequently targeted representatives of threatened governments. Terrorist propaganda begins usually with verbal attacks on the police, using the now familiar epithets, and may move through a phase during which uniformed police officers bear the full brunt of terrorist attacks on society. *"Las Violencia"* and the "Kill a Cop a Day" activities in Latin America are direct examples of how verbal abuse transitioned to murder. Yet, it takes a statement like that of Carlos' accomplice at the OPEC raid in December 1975 that she had just killed a "pig" to place this problem in true personal perspective. In this case, the Austrian policeman, Tichler, was summarily killed when he announced that he was a police officer in answer to her question.

Murder of police is a favorite tactic of terrorists in their attempt to create what Robert Moss terms a "climate of suspicion" in his book, *The War for the Cities*. Such murders are designed to erode the citizen's trust in his government to protect him. These tactics support a two-phase strategy. In phase one, terrorists strive to achieve a step-by-step increase of abusive power by police and law enforcement agencies until a right wing, authoritarian overreaction takes place among a bewildered public, frightened by its loss of liberty. In phase two, a public which has lost its liberties to a "police state" begins to fall into a "climate of collapse." Then, the urban terrorists expect to become cadre for the new political system.

Great revolutions of past history have relied on slowly winning a favorable degree of mass support for their success. Cuba's revolution was no real exception to this even though questions are still being asked about whether or not a "majority" supported it. That debate does not impact on this discussion simply because the active supporters were where they were needed most, regardless of their total numbers. This is brought out here because urban guerrilla warfare, as theorized and practiced by Ché Guevara and Regis Debraz, attempted to alter the classical revolutionary role of mass popular support. They argued that conditions could be created by a small dedicated group to start the revolution, and thereby awaken the masses who would then lend their support. Not everyone has agreed with their *foco* theory, but it is a key element in terrorist thinking and action today.

Contemporary terrorists in industrialized societies believe that small groups can bring the state to a "crisis of collapse" by applying the *foco* theory in an urban setting. This is particularly true for democracies where the freedoms of the individual citizen can be turned on the state by the terrorist with considerable effectiveness. These terrorists are organized for the long-term accomplishment of their objectives, even though the life span of many of them has proven to be relatively short. Terrorism becomes a way of life for them and takes on a parental sheen. Struggle is their only brother.

Contemporary terrorists operate even more clandestinely in urban areas than the classical rural guerrilla. Their surroundings have changed but their utmost concern remains the same: security. To ensure this, they even execute "backsliders" and have been observed to give their wounded comrades the *coup de grace,* as Carlos did in Paris. Their whole purpose in being is to strive for gains by their "political movement." No sacrifice is too great for its success.

Terrorists commit their illegal acts of violence for perceived political purposes and utilize a variety of tactics. Many of these have not changed since the invention of gun powder, but have been modified by the Latin American experience with urban guerrilla warfare. They include kidnapping, bombing, and assassination. Some of the newer modifications include skyjacking and holding diplomats hostage. It need not be pointed out that all of these are criminal acts and their frequency of occurrence has risen steadily over the past decade. By all indications, this trend will continue, particularly bombings, incendiary attacks, ambushes, and assassinations. Moreover, the seriousness of the threat will become worse as terrorists obtain more sophisticated weaponry and stronger international support from radical governments. These conditions combine to make the response of police and law enforcement officials much more difficult.

Contemporary terrorism does not present a new problem to police authorities because terrorist acts are essentially criminal acts employing criminal techniques. It does present a unique problem, however, because of its political ramifications, particularly in democratic societies. Laws in some countries have already been changed to increase their effectiveness against politically motivated violence. When this is done, it is essential that the public knows and understands the rationale behind the changes. Such adaptive changes alone will not suffice in a politically charged atmosphere. It is far more important to gain the willing support of an active citizenry for the police and law enforcement agencies. People can become a police multiplier in a democratic society also, as long as the government's response is built firmly on the rule of law.

Specific police tactics in direct response to the terrorist threat have proven just as innovative as terrorist tactics. A major limitation is the use of clandestine techniques by the police. Every democratic constitution serves as a basis for such restrictions, and some nations provide effective means for securing their existence by permitting techniques like electronic surveillance when properly authorized. In those cases, it seems to be the rule that when the police and internal security forces begin to operate like the terrorists and infringe on their own laws, they accelerate the move towards an overreaction desired by the terrorists. Terrorism may be a cyclical phenomenon, as some argue; however, the rule of law must be applied after terrorism passes or is defeated. By this is meant that the police and law enforcement agencies must rigidly adhere to the laws they are sworn to enforce. Obviously, this does not rule out the promulgation of stronger legislation to cope with terrorism. Several threatened nations have already done this.

Contemporary terrorism's organizational features present some additional unique problems that impact on the police response. Most important among these is the fact that many terrorist groups are organized in supporting networks. These are functionally oriented and include a command and control network supported by intelligence, communications, operations, and logistics. Essentially their role is to protect the terrorist before and after the crime. For example, when a cell is activated by command and control, the individual terrorists know little more than their own mission. Intelligence provides them with what they need to know about the target; logistics provides the essential equipment with which to carry out the mission. Afterwards the terrorists can rely on organized supporters and sympathizers to hide them and assist their escape. Ordinary criminals lack such organization, particularly in the post-operation phase of their crimes. This situation is made even more difficult for police in countries where a complete underground has been developed. Terrorists vanish to be "activated" on call. Many even hold ordinary jobs and live routine lives.

Very sophisticated computer technology is being employed now in several countries in checking for suspects and building authorized intelligence dossiers. Improvements have also been made in weaponry and communications equipment. Most importantly, significant progress has been accomplished on psychological bargaining techniques and anti-terror combat training. Several successful police encounters with terrorists are directly attributable to these efforts. But most direct success has been the result of long hours of detailed police investigation supported by helpful citizens.

But even when apprehended the unique features of contemporary terrorists continue to confront police and law enforcement agencies. Terrorists are politically motivated and are not affected seriously by fear of severe punishment for their crimes. Many even seem to welcome lengthy prison sentences so they can provide media representation for their cause. Placing terrorists behind bars is only the first step in the struggle, and experience has shown it to be a small step forward in some instances. It is now a common terrorist tactic to demand the release of captive cohorts simply by threatening destructive action. This occurs frequently on an international level with participation by a collection of multi-national terrorist groups. It is not always successful, nor does it always fail.

We also know that, once imprisoned, the terrorists will use every legal means at their disposal to frustrate legal proceedings. Frequently, laws designed to protect citizens within democracies are subverted to accomplish this objective. Terrorists may be assisted in these efforts by defense lawyers, intellectuals with benchmark reputations, and a variety of supporters and sympathizers among the general public.

Government response to counter these unique features of terrorism have proceeded along procedural and substantive plateaus of effort. On the procedural plateau, police and internal security forces are being trained, equipped, and motivated to protect both the apparatus of government and the citizens of the threatened society. Where appropriate, laws are being changed to preclude their subversion by terrorists, and legal procedures are being modified to halt their abuse. On the substantive plateau, massive efforts are in progress to communicate the extent of terrorism's actual threat to the society being attacked. In addition to describing various aspects of the terrorists and their activities, all changes to the process of law are fully explained to the public. Generally, these government efforts have met with success and resulted in a better informed public which supports actively the ongoing work of police and law enforcement agencies.

Today, West Germany provides the best example of how one industrialized nation has combatted terrorism. The struggle between Bonn and the terrorists of the Rote Armee Faktion (RAF) has been going on since the late sixties. The Red Army Faction is an extension of the original Baader-Meinhof Gang; and since the capture of the Gang's guiding elite in 1972, the RAF has ambushed the West German government in the cities using special action Kommandos for each operation. An overview of terrorism in West Germany with emphasis on current events is presented in the following section to provide some concrete examples of how one nation has structured its response.

Contemporary terrorists launched their 1977 offensive in West Germany by assassinating Siegfried Buback, the Federal Chief Prosecutor (equivalent to the U.S. Attorney General) in April. Police response was immediate and better coordinated than previously because of legal adaptations permitting closer investigative and executive relationships between Bonn's federal criminal agency *(Bundeskriminalamt)*, its office for the Protection of the Constitution *(Amt fuer Verfassungschutz)*, and the police forces of the various states *(Laender)*. Police powers are a *Laender* responsibility as West Germany does not have a federal counterpart such as the FBI in the United States.

The pressures of terrorism in the seventies have forced these separate police and law enforcement agencies to collaborate under increasing federal direction. Other specific adaptations have resulted in several changes to West German laws and the activation of special antiterror units. These cumulative changes have played a dynamic role in defeating the 1977 terrorist offensive thus far.

Two of Buback's murderers were apprehended in May with the help of an observant member of German society. This was the first of several defeats the RAF was to suffer during 1977. During the course of the search for Buback's murderers, the remaining "big three" of the Baader-Meinhof Gang—Andreas Baader, Jan-Carl Raspe, and Gudrun Ensslin—had been convicted of their crimes and sentenced to life imprisonment by the Stammheim court. (Ulrike Meinhof had committed suicide by hanging herself in her cell in May 1976). This sentencing was a most important defeat for the RAF. It further demonstrated that a democracy could respond to the terrorist threat and reinforce that response within the rule of law. Terrorist reaction was expected and not long in coming.

Terrorists responded to these setbacks in July 1977, by killing one of the most influential members of West Germany's financial establishment, Juergen Ponto. This signaled a new dimension to the struggle and served notice on all influential members of German society. This precedent was soon to have tragic consequences.

West Germany continued its efforts during the summer to round up the terrorists. Terrorist efforts were highlighted by an unsuccessful attempt to launch a rocket attack against the federal prosecutor's office in Karlsruhe and another hunger strike by the imprisoned terrorists. While police and law enforcement agencies amassed thousands of hours of overtime in their search, they also continued their coordination and training efforts. Parliamentarians debated new legal measures to defeat terrorism. This tension of expectation was rampant in early September when the terrorists suddenly stopped their hunger strike without explanation.

This charged atmosphere exploded when terrorists kidnapped Haans-Martin Schleyer, president of the West German Employers and Industry Federations, on September 5th. Negotiations were begun afterwards with the Siegfried Hausner Kommando of the RAF which demanded release of eleven imprisoned members of the Gang. This demand was expected, as was Bonn's response—stalling for time without concessions. While Bonn imposed a total news blackout, it coordinated searches in West Germany and with neighboring countries under the direction of a cabinet level crisis staff, capable of 24-hour-a-day response.

Bonn stuck to its hard line response, and the terrorists upped the ante on October 13th when "supporting" international terrorists skyjacked a Lufthansa aircraft with 87 passengers aboard in Mallorca. Demands of the four Palestinian terrorists also included release of the Gang. Bonn did not change its tactics in response to the terrorist's escalation of violence. In fact, after a six-day torturous odyssey through the Middle East, policemen of *Grenzschutz Gruppe 9* (GS G9 or Border Protection Group 9) stormed aboard the parked aircraft in Mogadishu, Somalia. Results of the rescue are well known and have met with worldwide approval. Particularly noteworthy for our purposes is the fact that the antiterror unit is composed of police officials. It is an excellent demonstration of how Bonn has structured its response to the uniqueness of the terrorist threat. An important factor is that employment of West German armed forces (the *Bundeswehr*) is reserved for special situations only, similar to those required for use of military forces in the United States and other industrialized societies.

Bonn's success was tempered by the subsequent suicide of three terrorists in Stammheim prison and the murder of Schleyer. Both events have given rise to several important questions that will impact on Bonn's response to terrorism as well as that of other industrialized societies. Parliamentarians in Bonn are debating fiercely over the need for additional antiterror legislation that would speed up terrorist legal proceedings and strengthen the ability of police and law enforcement agencies to combat terrorism. Activities also continue on the international level to produce specific antiterrorist measures at the United Nations and better means to coordinate police efforts across national borders. These efforts had not been as successful as desired in the search for Schleyer and later resulted in a round of mutual allegations. In spite of this, however, there was extensive cooperation among several European and Middle Eastern governments in the hostage rescue. Greater international cooperation is likely to be the future model.

Contemporary terrorists have responded to these activities by declaring war on West Germany. Immediately after the event in mid-October, attacks against "everything German" were launched in several European countries. Radical activities were particularly destructive in Italy and France, underscoring the support for the RAF by radical elements in these countries. Renewed terrorist efforts in West Germany itself are also expected in the near future. For the moment, propaganda activities are of primary concern as terrorists wager they can convert the radical fringe of communist party organizations, frustrated participants of citizen interest groups *(Buergerinitiativen)*, and sympathizers among the general public. It is obvious that the terrorist *foco* hopes to use the suicides of the "Stammheim Trio" as a rallying point for conversion of many new supporters to their cause. In this fashion more than an arithmetic increase in numbers is expected.

Terrorists hope to actually increase their threat potential and operational capability exponentially by fielding more terrorists, supported by more clandestine networks, than the government structure can successfully counter. With these tactics, they hope to achieve their strategy of forcing the government to overreact and precipitate a "crisis of collapse" during which they can take over.

Much of this is wishful thinking on the part of contemporary terrorists. They will experience some tactical success as they continue their offensive, but their strategy is doomed to failure unless Bonn departs from its thus far rigid adherence to the rule of law. West Germany's citizenry is alert to the terrorist threat and well informed concerning Bonn's response. Moreover, the majority not only supports the existing measures, but many are clamoring for harsher measures. Sustained terrorist success in such an environment is not possible. Terrorist attempts to win the general public to their side have failed miserably and will continue to fail as the police response becomes increasingly efficient. One may even advance the hope that many of those who now sympathize with the terrorists will emerge wiser from this experience and more actively support their government.

Contemporary terrorism has many weaknesses that are not effectively attacked by police and law enforcement agencies. Foremost among these is the terrorist myth of invincibility. Far too many societies have accepted this myth at face value when they should be organizing specific responses to combat the predictable characteristics of the terrorist threat. We have seen police success in countering specific acts of hostage taking, skyjacking, and bombings. These efforts have proceeded with a degree of success on the international level also, as is evidenced by the West German success at Mogadishu.

We need to now attack the general aspects of terrorism. Admittedly this is complicated by the oft-quoted thought that "one man's terrorist is another man's freedom fighter," but that must be recognized as merely part of the larger political problem. It can be resolved. Politics is terrorism's weak link in the chain of events used to lash out against industrialized societies. It is here that terrorism must be attacked first and hardest. Societies must illustrate the frailties of terrorism's political arguments for the general public and not tolerate criminal actions. This must be continued using all available media until everyone understands the terrorist threat and the police response. Terrorists are criminals, and this linkage must be strongly established in the mind's eye of every citizen. As long as this is not done, terrorists will continue to garner the advantages of their mystique and win converts.

Terrorists are criminals and must be punished for their crimes. Although every nation will not agree with a London newspaper's solution "to hang them, and hang them high," most will agree that they be imprisoned for criminal offenses. Politically motivated offenses are no less criminal. West Germany's recent experience demonstrates that no special privileges should be accorded these terrorists when being tried or imprisoned. Terrorists must serve their jail terms, and some assurances must be established that they will not return to terrorism when released.

Contemporary terrorists are certain to continue their attacks against established societies. Attacks against police and law enforcement officials will remain a prominent feature of their offensives. In the first ten months of 1977, returning to the West German example, six police officers (five German and one Dutch) were killed by German terrorists, as well as the chief prosecutor and several other persons. The fact that these officials are on the front line is underscored by the difficulties experienced by Bonn in appointing Buback's successor. Yet, responsible men like Dr. Kurt Rebmann will always be found in free societies. It is obvious that there are more available believers in democracy than those responding to terrorism's anarchic appeals to destroy the state.

Contemporary terrorism is destined for the same failure experienced by its classical precedents. Certainly, in the process of defeat we can expect terrorism to continue its rampages and escalate violence perhaps even to the level of nuclear blackmail. Terrorism's defeat will be complicated by the transitions that have placed it in a position to diversify its attack against any nation, while receiving international support from radical governments and possible assistance from communist intelligence agencies. We may take heart that the response is becoming equally diversified with increasingly stronger support from free citizens.

ANTI-TERRORISM: OPERATIONS AND CONTROLS IN A FREE SOCIETY*

An act of terrorism or a terrorist-like incident may occur almost anywhere. Obviously, it is impossible for law enforcement agencies to plan for every eventuality. As in other areas of operational planning, we have to think in terms of probabilities.

One important task that needs to be accomplished in the early stages of tactical planning is that of priority target identification. If we were planning for a war, we would identify certain high priority enemy targets and make tactical plans to carry out attacks on these selected targets. Counterterrorism target assessment is a reverse process whereby we identify those targets "at home" which have a high probability of being selected by terrorists or those who commit terroristlike acts. By identifying potentially attractive targets ahead of time, we are able to anticipate many of the major incident management problems which are unique to a particular target. Thus, we are able to determine in advance many of the response alternatives we will have if the attack takes place.

The Counterterrorism Target Assessment Form provides a means to systematically identify those potential targets which assign it a numerical rating based upon its value, potential for target selection, and vulnerability to attack. The target can be an individual, a category of individuals in a particular area, a building or other structure or facility, motor vehicles, aircraft, or anything else that may be targeted. (See Exhibit 1.)

The completed assessment forms are beneficial for further in-depth security and tactical planning as well as for the training of field commanders and special response forces.

The format can be very simple. Ours is typewritten on a legal size sheet of paper and reproduced. The information to be recorded is presented in condensed form at the right.

---

* John B. Wolf, "Anti-Terrorism: Operation and Controls in a Free Society," *Police Studies*, Vol. 1, No. 3, September 1978, pp. 35-41. Reprinted by permission.

Exhibit 1 — Counterterrorism Target Assessment Form*

COUNTERTERRORISM
TARGET ASSESSMENT

Target Name: .... Rating: ....
Location: ....
Type of Jurisdiction: ....

Category of Attack

Kidnapping   ☐   Armed attack   ☐
Barricade-hostage   ☐   Hijacking   ☐
Incendiary bombing   ☐   Assassination   ☐
Explosive bombing   ☐   Sniping   ☐
Letter bombing   ☐   Theft, break-in   ☐

Other action, specify. (Includes occupation of facilities without hostage seizure, shootouts with police, and sabotage):

....

Probable purpose of attack..
Probable method of attack...
Probable weapon(s) used...

Probable Category of Attacker(s)

Politically motivated-transnational ☐ Politically motivated-domestic ☐ Criminal deviant ☐ Mentally unbalanced ☐
Other, specify: ....

Probable Consequences of Successful Attack

Potential number of casualties....................................
Potential extent of property damage...............................
Estimate of economic consequences.................................
Estimate of political consequences................................
Other...

Prevention and Response

Existing attack prevention problems...............................
....
Anticipated incident management problems..........................
....
Anticipated special equipment requirements........................
....

---

* James M. Sands, "Counterterrorism Target Assessment Form," *The Police Chief*, Vol. XLV, No. 12, December 1978, p. 83. Reprinted with the permission of the International Association of Chiefs of Police.

Primary and alternate locations for field command post . . . .
. . . .
Primary and alternate assembly points for response force . . . .
. . . .

Target Priority

Target value (Circle one):

| 1 | 2 | 3 | 4 | 5 | 6 | 7 | 8 | 9 | 10 |

Low   High

Potential for target selection (Circle one):

| 1 | 2 | 3 | 4 | 5 | 6 | 7 | 8 | 9 | 10 |

Low   High

Target vulnerability (Circle one):

| 1 | 2 | 3 | 4 | 5 | 6 | 7 | 8 | 9 | 10 |

Low   High

Remarks (Continue on reverse) . . . .
. . . .
Assessment completed by: Date: . . . .
. . . .
        Signature

Rating. The rating is arrived at by adding the target value, potential for target selection, and target vulnerability figures together (highest possible rating is 30). Thus, targets with the highest ratings receive priority for security and tactical planning.

Target Value. To determine target value, consider intangibles as well as tangibles. Historical, cultural, symbolic, political, economic, military and psychological factors, as well as the value of human life, must be considered along with monetary value of the potential target.

Target Assessment. It is desirable that the target assessment be a composite resulting from a group effort. This provides an opportunity for brainstorming with valuable input by the group members who identify potential problems and develop appropriate responses in advance.

Today, in a world largely at peace, the terrorist, covered and concealed by a clandestine organization, is coercing people everywhere by perpetrating criminal acts on a regular basis in places specifically chosen for their vulnerability: an exclusive club situated on San Francisco's Nob Hill, the suburban Belfast home of a prominent financier, a limousine hesitating at a stoplight in Karlsruhe, a commuter train halted near a suburban station on the outskirts of Buenos Aires.[1]

Furthermore, a few of the world's most notorious terrorist groups are associated in a loose coalition which has slashed a trail of violence around the earth, and among their crimes are listed random murder, assassination, bombing of innocents, kidnapping, and hostage siege situations involving the elderly and young children. Among the operations, specifically staged by the terrorist for the singular purpose of obtaining maximum shock action and designed thereby to attract widespread exposure by the media, was the October 1977 joint operation conducted by West Germany's Red Army Faction (also known as the Baader-Meinhof Gang) and a splinter of the Popular Front for the Liberation of Palestine (PFLP) called the "Special Operations Group" who commandeered a jetliner belonging to Lufthansa Airlines.[2]

International Terrorist Coalition and Special Police Operations

For the release of their hostages, the Arab hijackers demanded, among other things, the freedom of the Baader-Meinhof leaders who were being held in maximum security prison cells in Stuttgart. However, ninety minutes before a threatened massacre deadline, a West German police unit, trained in commando tactics and known as Border Protection Group 9, stormed the hijacked airliner on an airport runway in Mogadishu, Somalia and ended a five-day, 6,000-mile terrorist episode by slaying four members of the "Special Operations Group" and freeing all 86 hostages unharmed.[3] Similarly, in July 1976, Israel's General Intelligence and Reconnaissance Unit 269 staged a lightning raid on the Entebbe, Uganda airfield and freed 61 Israelis and 43 French nationals held hostage by terrorists associated with the PFLP and the Red Army Faction and linked to "Carlos" an internationally sought terrorist.[4] The group headed by "Carlos the Jackal," a Venezuelan by birth, is a classic example of international terrorist cooperation as it includes Germans, Dutchmen, Latin Americans, and Arabs, and it has been involved in criminal activities in

---

1. "Radicals Bomb Swank Frisco Club," *The Star Ledger* (Newark, New Jersey), September 3, 1977, p. 3; "Financier's Home Bombed By The I.R.A. in Belfast," *The New York Times*, February 14, 1977, p. 6; "Motorcycle Gunmen Kill Bonn Official," *San Francisco Chronicle*, April 8, 1977, p. 1; and "Peronist Guerrillas Burn Train Near Buenos Aires," *The New York Times*, January 14, 1976, p. 4.
2. "Hijacking of Jet With 91 to Dubai Linked With German Kidnapping," *The New York Times*, October 15, 1977, p. 1.
3. "Terror and Triumph at Mogadishu," *Time*, October 31, 1977, pp. 42-44.
4. Terence Smith, "Israelis Staged Raid Rehearsal," *The New York Times*, July 9, 1976, p. 1.

Vienna (the seizure of the oil ministers), the Netherlands, the United Kingdom, and France.[5]

Antiterrorist Military and Police Units

The people of free societies have long demanded that military forces be wedded to the concept of minimum force in dealing with urban warfare and regard the commitment of federal military forces as a drastic last resort to be used only after the police and National Guard have used all of their own available force and are thereby unable to further cope with the emergency. However, international terrorism has caused democratic states to organize, train, and utilize specially skilled units of both their police and armed forces to suppress terrorist actions which are in progress.

Last October, following West Germany's rescue of the hostages at Mogadishu Airport, American officials revealed the existence of a United States Army strike force designed for use abroad and consisting of two battalions of Rangers. Constantly on alert, this strike force is geared for an instant response if the United States should be confronted with a crisis situation resembling the Entebbe or Mogadishu affairs.[6]

To deal with terrorist hijackers in the United States, the Federal Bureau of Investigation has created Special Weapons and Tactics (SWAT) Teams and almost all of its field offices have a specially organized group of five agents who train together once a month to meet emergency situations.[7] Additionally, in June 1976, the New Jersey State Police established a Helicopter Emergency Rappel Team (H.E.R.T.) to handle State Police tactical anti-terrorism, hostage, and civil disorder operations and to efficiently respond to requests for aid in remote or isolated areas.[8] Other State Police organizations now are developing units with a similar capability.

Although some Americans regard SWAT units as a "cure-all" for violent crime, others denounce the units as "shock troops" or "execution squads." The reasons behind the lack of complete public support for SWAT teams may be their military posture and the fact that their training closely parallels that of a military unit. However, the alternative to the police SWAT teams is specially trained military units whose use is difficult to reconcile with a democratic society's demand that minimum force be used to quell domestic violence.

---

5. Colin Smith, *Carlos: Portrait of a Terrorist* (New York: Holt, Rinehart and Winston, 1976), pp. 99-267.

6. Michael McGovern, "Ranger Force Poised For A Hijack," *The Daily News*, October 30, 1977, p. 2.

7. "F.B.I. To SWAT 'Em Here," *The Daily News*, October 30, 1977, p. 96.

8. New Jersey State Police Training Center, *Helicopter Emergency Rappel Teams* (Sea Girt, New Jersey: New Jersey State Police, 1977), p. 3.

Terrorism: A Worldwide Threat

However, some terrorist groups (i.e., Red Army Faction, California's New World Liberation Front, Fuerzas Armadas de Liberacion Nacional—F.A.L.N.) realize that their choice of a given strategy or tactic and its implementation require a strategic assessment. Uruguay's Tupamaro Insurgents referred to this evaluation process as the "coyuntura," a diagnosis of the political, economic, military, and organizational conditions of both the terrorist movement and the society in which it is enveloped. For the Tupamaros, therefore, the choice of every strategy and tactic was the result of a careful, rational analysis of the present and potential strength of their organization as well as of the general conditions and political climate of Uruguayan society.[9]

Imitating Tupamaro strategic thinking, members of the Red Army Faction hope that their violence will bring about an emotionally charged, indiscriminate, uncontrolled reaction so that they can denounce West Germany as a fascist dictatorship.[10] According to a Puerto Rican spokesman in New York City, F.A.L.N. strategists have decided that at the very least their bombings have reduced tourism to Puerto Rico and are dissuading American corporations from further investments on the island. According to Che Guevara and others, a stalled economy is the best condition for revolution.[11] Attempting also to foster an economic decline and attract sympathizers among the underprivileged, the New World Liberation Front [in September 1977] set off an explosive device at a swank San Francisco Golf Club and threatened to unleash a terror campaign against the city's tourist industry unless its demands for "decent housing for all" are met.[12]

Use of the "Coyuntura" by Police and Security Forces

In 1976, the Irish Republican Army (IRA), failing to ignite Catholics over the British government's abolition of political prisoner status for terrorists in prison, began to realize that its "coyuntura" no longer favored a sustained campaign of assassination, explosions, and car-bombings in Northern Ireland. Additionally, their "coyuntura" appears to have been usurped by the security forces as reflected in the growing number of

9. Arturo C. Porzecanski, *Uruguay's Tupamaros: The Urban Guerrilla* (New York: Praeger Publishers, 1973), pp. 11-12.

10. Craig R. Whitney, "Schmidt Warns Germany to Avoid An Excessive Reaction to Slaying," *The New York Times*, April 14, 1977, p. 43.

11. Michael Kramer, "Will Puerto Rican Terrorism Work Here," *New York Magazine*, January, 1976, pp. 5-6.

12. "Radicals Bomb Swank Frisco Club," *The Star Ledger* (Newark, New Jersey), September 3, 1977, p. 3.

suspects being arraigned before the Northern Irish criminal courts as well as a sharp rise in the number of convictions being obtained.[13]

Also, a substantial number of Catholic members of the Northern Ireland peace movement, particularly from the ghettos, which are the traditional havens of the I.R.A., have "turned informer" and are providing the security forces with reliable and accurate information over the confidential police telephones. Aware that the people of Northern Ireland had become weary of more than eight years of terrorism, the British security forces have apparently seized the initiative from the terrorists and consequently, the I.R.A., which once could mobilize up to 700 armed men in Belfast alone, at the time of this writing has difficulty in mustering 200 gunmen in all of Northern Ireland.[14]

Democratic States and Terrorism

The initial decisions and reactions of government to an urban terrorist threat are critical as they usually define the issues at stake, the presumed character of the anti-terrorist campaign, and the legitimate basis for any eventual termination of the struggle. But inherent within the framework of the liberal democratic state are factors which impede the collection of intelligence required by decision makers to shape the governmental response to a terrorist threat in its incipient stage. Officials of the Federal Bureau of Investigation, for example, complain that their agency has been too severely restricted in intelligence investigations following the 1976 public disclosures of allegations that F.B.I. agents burglarized the homes of militant political figures, leftist suspects, and anti-war radicals during the early 1970s.[15]

Controlling the Weather Underground Organization

The Weather Underground Organization (W.U.O.) was the primary target of Squad 47, a unit of the Internal Security Division of the F.B.I.'s New York City field office. Between 1970 and 1973, this squad, consisting of between 20 and 30 agents, conducted operations which were specifically tailored to uncover .clues to the whereabouts of some of the better-known members of the W.U.O. These fugitives had accepted limited aid from Cuban espionage agents operating in the United States and Canada and some technical assistance from North Vietnam. After the W.U.O.

---

13. Sean Duignan, "The 'Troubles' In Ulster May, Just May, Be Easing A Bit," *The New York Times*, October 16, 1977, p. 3E.

14. "I.R.A. Losing Catholic Support, British Say," *The Chicago Tribune*, October 27, 1977, p. 16.

15. Joy McIntyre, "F.B.I. Keeping Eye On N.J. Groups," *The Daily News*, March 24, 1977, p. 16.

went "underground" in 1970 and many of them were being sought by the F.B.I. on criminal charges, a group of Cuban intelligence officers from the General Directorate of Intelligence (known by its initials in Spanish as the D.G.I., Cuba's equivalent of the Central Intelligence Agency), assigned to the staffs of the Cuban Mission to the United Nations in New York and the Cuban Embassy in Canada, maintained contacts with them. Additionally, a few members of the W.U.O. had received training in practical weaponry, explosives handling, and guerrilla warfare in Cuba by Cuban military officers through the so-called "Venceremos Brigades." Consequently, Castro's Cuba has been the primary training ground and principal foreign supporter of W.U.O. terrorists who raised great havoc in the United States in the late 1960s and early 1970s. Thus, there was serious reason for the F.B.I. to be interested in the activities of any young American who had spent time in Cuba as a member of the "Venceremos Brigade," particularly those who were also active members of the W.U.O. Approximately 1,500 Americans, mostly college students, participated in Venceremos Brigades' activities in Cuba when travel to the Caribbean island was prohibited for United States citizens.[16]

Among the investigative techniques used by agents assigned to Squad 47 in their search for clues to the whereabouts of W.U.O. fugitives, such as Mark Rudd, Bernadine Dohrn, Kathie Boudine, and Cathy Wilkerson, were mail openings and surreptitious entries. Mail openings took place as agents used keys to remove mail from apartment mail boxes and then took it back to the F.B.I. field office in New York City, where it was steamed open, copied and then returned.[17] Surreptitious entries were made to photograph and search records and to place electronic listening devices. Undertaken by specially trained teams of F.B.I. agents, a surreptitious entry involved agents as lookouts, radio watchmen, and in various other stand-by roles as well as the person or persons who entered the premises.[18]

In August 1976, regardless of the linkage between the W.U.O. and hostile foreign governments which was established during the course of investigations conducted by American law enforcement agencies of radical and terrorist organizations, the F.B.I. removed from its intelligence division the responsibility for investigation of domestic extremist groups. Instead, responsibility for this matter was given to its investigative branch where they were treated "like all other criminal cases

---

16. John M. Crewdson, "F.B.I. Asserts Cuba Aided Weathermen," *The New York Times*, October 9, 1977, p. 1.

17. John M. Crewdson, "F.B.I. Reportedly Stole Mail in its Drive on War Foes," *The New York Times*, August 22, 1976, p. 26.

18. John M. Crewdson, "F.B.I. Burglaries Said to Be Focus of Major Inquiry," *The New York Times*, June 24, 1976, p. 1.

in that division." This change in organizational responsibility was necessitated primarily as a consequence of the sharp criticism of the "Bureau" by United States Congressmen and others who objected to its use of mail opening, surreptitious entries, and other covert tactics to combat terrorism.[19]

Royal Canadian Mounted Police Operations against the F.L.Q.

Similarly, Royal Canadian Mounted Police (R.C.M.P.) antiterrorist operations have been impaired by the trend to restrict law enforcement usage of covert intelligence collection methods and related police activities. During the 1960s and early 1970s, the security unit of the R.C.M.P. tried to combat the Front de Liberation du Quebec (F.L.Q.), which was involved in successive waves of bombings and bank robberies, efforts to establish guerrilla camps in the Laurentian mountains, kidnappings, and the assassination of Pierre Laporte, the Quebec minister of labor.[20]

Consequently, the security unit became the critical component of at least three distinct R.C.M.P. clandestine operations designed to furnish the Canadian government with accurate information for law enforcement purposes relative to the activities of the F.L.Q. and other organizations which shared its strategic objective of independence for largely French-speaking Quebec and also carried F.L.Q. members or their associates on their membership lists. These antiterrorist operations were code named Cathedral, the copying of personal mail; Featherbed, the building of dossiers on selected individuals; and 300, a program of warrantless entries.[21] Thus, in 1972, members of the security unit surreptitiously entered the premises occupied by the Agence de Presse Libre, a leftist news agency, and in 1973 they used similar methods to gain access to the Montreal offices of the Parti Quebecois for the purpose of seizing and copying its records.[22]

---

19. John M. Crewdson, "F.B.I. Chief Curbs Intelligence Arm In Command Shift," *The New York Times*, August 12, 1976, p. 1.

20. Robert Moss, *The War For The Cities* (New York: Coward, McCann and Geoghegan, Inc., 1972), pp. 112-113.

21. "Canada Mail Was Opened By Mounties," *The Star Ledger*, November 10, 1977, p. 50; Robert Trumbull, "Trudeau Faces Cover-Up Charges In Case Involving Illegal Break-In," *The New York Times*, June 3, 1977, p. 16; and "Quebec Liberals Say Police Raided Office," *The New York Times*, December 2, 1977, p. 12.

22. Robert Trumbull, "Quebec Party Data Stolen By Mounties," *The New York Times*, October 29, 1977, p. 7 and Robert Trumbull, "Questionable Acts of Mounted Police Reported in Canada," *The New York Times*, January 10, 1978, p. 10.

Apparently some Canadians, presently complaining about R.C.M.P. intelligence activities, have forgotten that the F.L.Q. succeeded in one of its tactical goals: "to bring the army into the streets and place in doubt the norms of democratic society." On October 16, 1970, Prime Minister Pierre Trudeau introduced the War Measures Act, and Canada, for the first time in its history, was placed on a wartime footing to face an internal emergency. Current restrictions placed on R.C.M.P. public security activities portend the future use in Canada of war measures.[23]

Information Gathering: Police Patrol Practices

During the past decade there have been many innovations designed to alter traditional American police organizational arrangements. One of these alterations, known as Team Policing, is designed to make the police officer a part and an accepted member of the community he serves and to encourage the people of a neighborhood to become important contributors to the social order. A team policing unit consists of an integrated group of patrol officers, detectives, and community relations specialists whose task is to acquire the help of the neighborhood in accomplishing the police mission.[24]

Additionally, police-sponsored crime prevention programs (Block Watchers, Neighborhood Watch, etc.) are also intended to encourage people to become alert to suspicious criminal activity and to report it to the police, facilitating thereby a police department's effort to control crime generally, and terrorism specifically, in all areas of a city.

However, the main problem confronting the police of a free society engaged in antiterrorist operations is the development of politically acceptable and legally permissible methods to gain reliable information about terrorists for immediate tactical use. Consequently, increased emphasis could be placed on the further development and cost reduction of computer-based police tactical information systems. These systems greatly enhance police patrol as they accomplish in minutes a series of record checks that once required as much as an hour or more to complete. Computerized police patrol operations, including routine and regular checks of all motor vehicles, would also seriously impede terrorist operations and thereby force the terrorists to place increased reliance upon the people of particular neighborhoods for services and support, a practice which could prove to be disastrous for them once team policing units have established a city-wide informant system. Last October, the West German Police, at-

---

23. Robert Moss, *The War For The Cities* (New York: Coward, McCann and Geoghegan, Inc., 1972), pp. 112-113.
24. Donald T. Shanahan, *Patrol Administration: Management By Objectives* (Boston: Holbrook Press, 1975), pp. 441-460.

tempting to track down the kidnappers of the Red Army Faction, applied many of the above-mentioned techniques.[25]

Thus, in a free society a terrorist organization is best controlled by the systematic application of routine police patrol, investigative and crime prevention techniques, provided that the police themselves are aware of the effective antiterrorist capability of a democratic policing service.

Information Gathering: Covert Police Methods

At a May 1976 meeting, the National Advisory Committee on Criminal Justice Standards and Goals published a report that outlined a variety of legislation intended to authorize anti-terrorist measures designed to help American society defend itself against terrorists. One of the recommended measures is the use of police tactics designed to cause havoc and chaos within a terrorist organization by infiltrating police officers into these groups, not merely to gather information, but to inhibit or provoke hostile activity among individual terrorists or cells.[26]

The F.B.I. has for years been engaged in special programs of disruptive techniques and surreptitious entries against racist organizations, the Ku Klux Klan particularly, and leftist political groups. According to F.B.I. officials, these activities are needed to combat subversive activities of a clandestine nature aimed directly at undermining and destroying the United States.[27] The F.B.I., however, is currently being studied by the Senate Select Committee on Intelligence Operations and many of its counter-subversive activities have, as a consequence, been curtailed.

Wiretapping and other forms of electronic eavesdropping are viewed with mixed emotions by many Americans who apparently see them as the epitome of an unjustified and nondirective invasion of privacy. Yet, court-authorized electronic surveillance fulfills a vital investigative purpose, especially in cases involving terrorism, where evidence from other sources is often simply not available. . . .

Police Intelligence Systems

In a free society, a public security intelligence unit must be particularly responsive to the legal principles and public policies that develop with respect to the collection, storage, and dissemination of domestic intelligence as their assessments are used by law enforcement agencies to

---

25. Paul Hoffman, "West Germans Hunt 16 Terror Suspects," *The New York Times*, October 21, 1977, p. 1.

26. Daniel Hays, "Terror And The Law," *The Star Ledger*, May 3, 1976, p. 1.

27. "F.B.I. Burglarized Leftist Offices Here 92 Times In 1960-66, Official Files Show," *The New York Times*, March 29, 1976, p. 1.

make the informed judgments and preparations required to police adequately the disorders, meetings, rallies, parades, and strikes that take
place in their jurisdiction. Therefore, to ensure that this vital task is completed without violation of civil rights, certain measures must be carried
out.

All police working in intelligence units, including undercover agents,
must be given intensive instruction in relevant constitutional principles. It
is urgent, also, that intelligence units draft, adopt, and enforce guidelines
and procedures for the recording and storage of information in public
security files and for the intra- and extra-departmental dissemination of
these data. Perhaps the most critical of the guidelines are those having to
do with the use of informants. The steps to be followed in the processing,
registering, and payment of informants must be clearly spelled out. It is
important, too, that a Criminal Source Control Office be created to
legitimize and ensure the most efficient use of intelligence obtained from
informants.

In order to control terrorism, police intelligence units must have
strategic and tactical analytical capabilities, as well as traditional field-
information collection units and sources. These requirements can be met
by establishing public security intelligence modules which are comprised
of a team of field investigators and a desk analyst who work together as a
unit and concentrate on a specific area of concern, such as right-wing or
left-wing extremist groups.[28]

National Intelligence Services

Intelligence is a vital prerequisite for antiterrorist operations. Therefore,
it is essential for nations to cooperate with each other in a systematic effort to pool information about terrorist organization and tactics. MI-5, a
British counter-espionage agency, for example, needs information which
could be supplied by the American C.I.A. regarding clandestine
shipments of Armalite AR-15 rifles to the I.R.A. and the Ulster Defense
Forces (U.D.F.), MI-5 most certainly has information which the Spanish
could use regarding alleged connections between the I.R.A. and Basque
terrorist groups (E.T.A.), and the French Territorial Surveillance Bureau
might also profit from MI-5's information on Breton separatist groups.
The C.I.A. undoubtedly could use any information supplied by foreign
intelligence services which links domestic American extremist groups to
foreign terrorist organizations. The West German Bundesnachrichten-
dent (BND), the equivalent of the American C.I.A., also might want to
exchange information on terrorist groups as it is the central depository for
information gathered by the special West German Police Kommando

28. John B. Wolf, *The Police Intelligence System* (New York: John Jay Press, 1978), pp. 1-4.

Unit which tracked down and captured the leaders of the Red Army Faction, who had connections with terrorist groups comprised of nationals from other countries.[29]

After the 1972 Munich tragedy, which illustrated that international terrorism had reached the point where innocent people anywhere could be victimized, the United States established a Cabinet Committee Working Group. The working group's function is (1) to ensure collaboration among U.S. agencies and departments with domestic and foreign responsibilities and (2) to recommend countermeasures that can close gaps in the security screen around Americans at home and abroad, as well as foreigners in the United States, whom the agencies represented in the working group help to protect. With respect to the task of protection, the working group relies heavily on the customary local and federal agencies. Thus, it is kept informed by the F.B.I. of the international potentialities or implications of domestic terrorist groups and uses the C.I.A. as an important tool in foreign incidents.[30]

The Antiterrorist Assessment and Response Group

Although the American public is largely against surveillance, data banks, dossiers, or any other facet of a long-term intelligence operation, intelligence is the only way we can learn about terrorist plans and predict terrorist acts. Consequently, there is a definite need for legislation to establish an Assessment and Response Group at a high level of the national government. The activities of this group would supplement the work of the Cabinet Committee Working Group and serve as an immediate information resource for other authorized agencies. It would not duplicate the work of the C.I.A., which is restricted by law from performing internal security functions. Nor would it supplant the F.B.I., which does not collect intelligence abroad or employ analysts with sufficient expertise in international politics to function in a strategic public security capacity. This new group would be staffed with people who know how to gather and analyze public security information from both domestic and foreign sources for regular dissemination to law enforcement agencies on a "need-to-know" basis.

The Antiterrorist Assessment and Response Group should contain three primary units: an assessment unit, a teaching unit, and a response unit. The assessment unit would receive information on terrorists from members of the Cabinet Committee Working Group, municipal law en-

---

29. John B. Wolf, "A Global-Terrorist Coalition—Its Incipient Stages," *The Police Journal*, October-December 1977), pp. 337-338.

30. U.S. House Committee on Internal Security, *Terrorism Hearings*, 93rd Congress, 2nd Session, May 8, 14, 22, 29-30, June 13, 1974, Part 2, pp. 3080-3190.

forcement agencies, and the response unit. It would then process this information for its own use and for dissemination in strategic reports to other agencies. The teaching unit would provide training for local law enforcement agencies in subjects relating to terrorism that are not currently taught by the F.B.I.

The response unit, composed of experts in such disciplines as management, law enforcement, psychology, and public relations, would travel to the site of a terrorist act whenever an American citizen or corporation is involved. Although fully respectful of the sovereignty and sensitivities of other nations, the jurisdictions of other agencies and, of course, the wishes of the victim, the response team would urge other governments to accept all the American resources that could be put at their disposal, including intelligence and communications. Additionally, the response unit would collect specific field information for the assessment team on foreign terrorist groups with the capability to infiltrate highly trained teams into the United States.[31]

Antiterrorism and the Police

Confronted with proliferating and increasingly sophisticated terrorist groups at home and abroad on the one hand, and the necessity to maintain the basic constitutional freedoms and safeguards that are the hallmark of a democracy on the other, the United States must develop programs and policies to combat terrorism. In America today, by virtue of a process of governmental debate and freedom of the press, it is fortunately almost impossible to undertake a program of pure repression. If we examine the political culture within which Americans function, it is evident that there exist well-defined convictions about what the government may or may not legitimately do and a broad consensus on the fundamental rights of man. Our democratic system is thus both a necessary and a sufficient limitation on the use of repressive force. Moreover, any illegal action by a democratic state is undertaken with peril since it can be manipulated by the terrorist to serve his own purposes. But Americans' desire to maximize individual freedom also blinds them to the dangers presented by terrorism and at times prevents them from seeing the necessity for deterrent action.

However, during the past five years the American police have gained increased sophistication in the areas of communication, mobility, and information gathering and consequently they have caused domestic terrorist groups to carefully regulate and restrict their membership. Some law enforcement officials believe that the F.A.L.N., for example, might contain

---

31. John B. Wolf, "Controlling Political Terrorism In A Free Society," *ORBIS, A Journal of World Affairs*, Winter 1976, pp. 1301-1302.

as few as twelve members. Consequently, the primary organizational requirement for urban terrorist groups now operating in the United States is to develop a structure that is impervious to penetration by the police yet sufficiently flexible to enable them to exploit opportunities for surprise. It is anticipated, therefore, that terrorism, providing the current state of socio-economic conditions in the United States remains relatively stable, will continue to be perpetrated inside this country by small groups knowledgeable in the techniques of terrorist organization and management, although police pressure will force them to adopt a more clandestine method of operation. Terrorist attacks, however, are apt to be conducted with increased efficiency and marked by a higher degree of technological sophistication designed to balance the increased effectiveness of the American police in the area of antiterrorist operations.

A BEHAVIORAL APPROACH TO HOSTAGE SITUATIONS*

Hostage seizures have been one of the most sensational and politically charged criminal acts of the last decade. Publicity surrounding these events has helped to generate an interest in studying what occurs between criminals and victims in such an environment. An interesting phenomenon observed in some of these hostage incidents is an intimacy that develops between a hostage and hostagetaker. This phenomenon is commonly called the "Stockholm Syndrome." The name comes from a bank robbery attempt in Stockholm, Sweden, on August 23, 1973. During the incident, a woman hostage had a conversation with the Prime Minister and stated her fear of the police. When assured by the Prime Minister of the desire for a safe resolution of the situation, she replied, "Of course they (the police) can't attack us. . . . He (the robber) is sitting here and protecting us from the police." This and other similar statements were widely reported by the media and were viewed as expressions of sympathy by victims for the criminals. Law enforcement officers who read accounts of the Stockholm incident noted still other cases in which certain hostages had expressed unusual sympathy for the criminal.

Although a great deal of discussion has been generated about the Stockholm Syndrome, much of this discussion has occurred in the absence of a body of known facts about the phenomenon. This article examines the Stockholm Syndrome and poses questions, the answers to which will clarify the importance of the syndrome in hostage situations. In addition, it suggests a behavioral analysis of the Stockholm Syndrome as an alternative to traditional ways of viewing the phenomenon, offers a variety of techniques of potential use to law enforcement officers, and concludes with recommendations for continued study of hostage situations.

The Importance of the Stockholm Syndrome

The Stockholm Syndrome is considered to be a positive and useful element

---

* W. Ronald Olin and David G. Born, "A Behavioral Approach to Hostage Situations," *FBI Law Enforcement Bulletin*, January 1983, pp. 19-24.

in a hostage situation because it may reduce the chance for the unprecipitated killing of hostages. Law enforcement officials have concluded that the longer the incident is prolonged, the greater the probability of a safe resolution, provided the hostage(s) and hostagetaker(s) have interacted favorably during the time period. Few explanations have been offered to account for this increase in safety except for rapport developing between participants.

The Study of the Stockholm Syndrome

The study of the Stockholm Syndrome is complicated by a myriad of data problems about hostage incidents. There are no requirements to report hostage situations to any central repository. As a result, there are few detailed summaries of the wide variety of hostage incidents that have occurred, and most of the relevant information is available only to the law enforcement agencies which actually handled the call. Few incidents have been investigated by the same personnel. This leads to inconsistent or even biased interviewing and reporting. There are no experimental studies of the occurrence of the Stockholm Syndrome. All of these conditions contribute to serious data interpretation problems.

Investigations of the Stockholm Syndrome have relied almost exclusively on postincident interviews of hostages about their recollection of events which occurred. Thus far, it is not clear that this method of study (i.e., interviews) has furthered the understanding of the Stockholm Syndrome or how the results of this method of inquiry have assisted law enforcement officers in resolving hostage incidents.

Theoretical Interpretations of the Stockholm Syndrome

Recent law enforcement literature suggests that the Stockholm Syndrome occurs when hostages and hostagetakers are isolated by authorities and there are:

1. Positive "feelings" from the hostages toward their captor(s);

2. Negative "feelings" toward authorities by both hostages and captor(s); and

3. Positive "feelings" returned by the captors to the hostages.

There is a widespread expectation that these three conditions may be enhanced in some circumstances by the actions of the authorities. Research has attempted to demonstrate that some of these conditions may be present in hostage situations. For example, a recent study by Mirabella and Trudeau indicated that fear and anger toward authorities were reported in 82 percent of the hostage incidents examined. Unfortunately, the reader is not told if this percentage is a normally occurring level of antipolice sentiment or if the authorities in these cases took specific steps to promote this hostage hostility.

The Stockholm Syndrome has sometimes been attributed to defense mechanisms, regression, weakness of the ego, and identification of the hostage with the aggressor. In fact, most law enforcement articles written about the Stockholm Syndrome rely on Freudian interpretations of "inner feelings" reported by the hostages and their captors. Few alternative interpretations have been offered. While the Freudian approach provides one explanation for a limited number of hostage incidents, it has not yet provided a framework to assist law enforcement personnel. To make such an approach useful, persons espousing *post hoc* analyses of the underlying personality dynamics of hostages and captors have to show how these analyses can be translated into guidelines for officers trying to resolve a hostage incident with lives at stake.

An Alternative View of the Stockholm Syndrome

Applied behavior analysis provides another perspective for the examination of hostage incidents. The focus of this approach is not on underlying personality dynamics, or ". . . on what people report they do, but on how they actually behave and the conditions under which the [behavior] occurs." The study of the Stockholm Syndrome, as an outcome of some hostage incidents, may also be facilitated by this approach. From this position, the Stockholm Syndrome is viewed as a particular way in which hostages and hostagetakers interact (e.g., they make positive statements concerning each other), and the interest shifts to the identification of conditions under which the Stockholm Syndrome phenomenon is observed.

Behavioral definitions of criminal acts are not a recent development. Researchers Sutherland, Jeffrey, Burgess, and Aker have all used a behavioral approach to describe the causes of criminal conduct. They agree with other behaviorists, such as Skinner, that there is a direct relationship between the environment and behavior.

In an attempt to clarify the importance of the Stockholm Syndrome for hostage incidents, there are several important questions to be answered. How often does the syndrome occur? Does occurrence of the Stockholm Syndrome actually increase the safety of persons involved in hostage incidents? Assuming that it occurs in a significant portion of hostage incidents and that it increases participant safety, one might then ask under what circumstances does the Stockholm Syndrome occur? Can it be facilitated? How? Is the Stockholm Syndrome more likely to occur in some hostage situations, such as those involving family members, and less likely to occur in others, such as in incidents of political terrorism? While many other questions might be asked, this brief list provides a starting point for understanding whether/how the Stockholm Syndrome will be of use to law enforcement officers.

Although there is little evidence that bears directly on the preceding questions, a review of the original incident in Stockholm, Sweden, makes it clear that the Stockholm Syndrome is a more complex phenomenon than was initially believed. The complexity in this case arises from the fact that all of the hostages and hostagetakers were subjected to the same police pressures, and yet, not all exhibited the Stockholm Syndrome. As defined earlier, the Stockholm Syndrome was observed only between one captor and some of the hostages. Thus, the phenomenon does not necessarily occur to all individuals exposed to virtually identical conditions. A brief summary of the Stockholm incident may highlight some of the problems in the case.

On August 23, 1973, Jan-Erik Olsson attempted to rob the Sveriges Kreditbank. The incident was prolonged after a rapid police response trapped the robber inside. The resulting incident lasted 131 hours. The other criminal participant in the situation, Clark Oloffsson, was delivered from prison to the bank as the result of a demand by Olsson to the police.

During the initial stages of the robbery, Olsson fired an automatic weapon inside and outside of the bank, wounding a police officer. He made demands and pointed his submachinegun at a woman hostage, threatening to kill her. When Oloffsson joined the group, the situation changed. Olsson no longer shouted, he allowed bindings on the hostages to be loosened, and the situation calmed. The hostages were moved into the bank vault. There was more shooting and another police officer was wounded. The police finally trapped the participants in the vault and shut the door. Police decided to drill into the vault, knocking out electricity and flooding the vault floor with water from the drill. There was more shooting. Human waste accumulated in wastebaskets. Authorities stopped delivery of food and water into the vault, forcing the hostages to strain the water on the floor through cloth to filter it before drinking. Local radio stations, which were being monitored by the hostages and hostagetakers, reported actions being considered by the police, including the use of nerve gas and assault. Hostages were subsequently tied into nooses so that if they fell unconscious they would strangle.

Not suprisingly, these conditions resulted in both the hostages and hostagetakers fearing the actions of the police. Further, some of the hostages had favorable interactions with Oloffsson who, in at least some instances, protected them from Olsson. Throughout the incident, the hostages feared Olsson. A positive rapport developed in this environment between the women hostages and Oloffsson. Strentz and Ochberg delineate this distinction. However, some of the literature and many speeches have widely misunderstood the circumstances and have suggested that the Stockholm Syndrome is a more generally occurring phenomenon than is probably the case.

These misunderstandings may be avoided by a simple restatement of the Stockholm Syndrome. The syndrome is the positive rapport which occurs between a hostage and hostagetaker when they both engage in interactions which are of mutual benefit and when the participants express greater fear of the police than of each other. This rephrasing may provide a better guide for actions taken by law enforcement personnel than the other explanations for the phenomenon. For example, a law enforcement supervisor faced with a hostage situation must make numerous decisions about which hostagetakers demands to honor during a negotiation. Should authorities negotiate for concessions in trade for additional weapons, ammunition, food, drink, alcohol, drugs, cigarettes, publicity demands, or a hostage exchange (substituting a law enforcement officer for a hostage)? In the past, a law enforcement supervisor would make these decisions based on past experience and common sense. Using the previous description of the syndrome, the supervisor should determine whether this decision would encourage interactions of mutual benefit to the participants? A supervisor would then examine the list of options and would probably negotiate for exchanges of food, drink, publicity demands, and cigarettes, while rejecting demands for weapons, ammunition, alcohol, drugs, or hostage exchanges. The first items could be expected to encourage rapport if delivered in a timely fashion; the last items probably would not. These individual interactions could possibly reduce the probability of injury to hostages.

Given the circumstances of the Stockholm Syndrome it seems likely that the occurrence of the Stockholm Syndrome depends upon specific participant interactions, and perhaps, the interactive styles of the individuals. Thus, some hostage situations are probably more amenable to the Stockholm Syndrome than others. For example, there might be a smaller likelihood of the phenomenon developing in kidnaping or politically motivated hostage seizures. Some terrorist incidents appear to have been deliberately structured by the terrorists to limit the possibility of any interpersonal relationships developing between hostages and their captors. Such actions have been used by the South Moluccan terrorists in the Netherlands and by the Japanese Red Army. Interpersonal relationships are inhibited by hostage segregation, blindfolds, language barriers, and other methods. Similarly, some hostages may avoid any potential for rapport with a hostagetaker by sleeping, performing repetitive actions, writing, etc.

In considering ways to promote the occurrence of the Stockholm Syndrome, it may be helpful to recognize that a hostagetaker's reponses toward hostages could be placed on a continuum which ranges from threatening behavior toward hostages on one end, through indifferent behaviors, to caring responses. The law enforcement response should always be designed to increase the likelihood of caring behavior by the hostagetaker. To accomplish this objective, negotiators should make judicious use of all available resources to reinforce the hostagetaker when he responds in a desirable way. Some resources may be provided (positive reinforcement) and others withdrawn (negative reinforcement) as a consequence of specific actions taken by the hostagetaker. Providing or withdrawing these resources must be coordinated between tactical and negotiations personnel.

A Behavioral Strategy for Law Enforcement Response

The initial actions taken by officers upon arrival at a hostage scene set the stage for the incident. It is of critical importance for law enforcement personnel to demonstrate immediate absolute control of the outer perimeter to establish the maximum limits of the hostagetaker's conduct. A hostagetaker may initially attempt to escape. A confrontation such as this requires that the authorities be able to use force if the escape attempt does not cease. The certainty and immediacy of punishment will assist law enforcement personnel in controlling the hostagetaker in many of the same ways it assists the hostagetaker in controlling the hostage. The options remaining to the hostagetaker are very limited. He may attack, do nothing, or surrender. Thus, the hostagetaker operates under conditions that closely resemble those of the hostage(s). The initial police objective should be limited to forcing the hostagetaker to abandon his escape attempts.

After tactically securing a hostage scene, law enforcement officers should allow time for the situation to stabilize. The initial confrontation between the hostagetaker and the hostage is the most dangerous time period for all participants. The hostagetaker will be operating under a variety of emotionally or politically charged reinforcers as a result of the failure to escape, the arrival of the police, the conditions of the hostage(s), etc. This may produce "frustrated expectation which refers specifically to a condition produced by the termination of accustomed reinforcement." These conditions are favorable to the introduction of negotiators on the scene.

Negotiators must be aware of the need for a direct, immediate relationship between hostagetaker caring behavior and reward. A negotiator must begin by modifying verbal behavior. Several different techniques may be used to do this. For example, differential reinforcement should be given during conversations. Positive comments by the hostagetaker should be responded to with warmth, understanding, and encouragement, while negative statements should be ignored. It is very important that the negotiation process be reinforcing to the hostagetaker so that there is a reason to continue talking. The more skillfully and appropriately a negotiator uses these techniques and the available resources to shape verbal behavior, the more likely negotiations will proceed toward the desired outcome.

The negotiator may ask specific questions or manipulate existing conditions in an attempt to force caring behavior between the hostage(s) and hostagetaker. The negotiator should always attempt to discuss the medical problems of the hostage(s). This gives the hostagetaker the opportunity to ask about or view the physical condition of the hostage(s). Naturally occurring physiological conditions, such as hunger, sleep, thirst, etc. may also be used advantageously.

Tactical unit personnel should be used to provide control over other resources which may be used to shape behavior. Food, water, medication, electricity, natural gas for heat, light, selected noises, obvious police activity, media releases, the threat of assault, and other options may be used to help manipulate environmental conditions at the scene.

In addition to activities and resources under the direct control of law enforcement personnel, there may be other significant aspects of the situation which could be influenced indirectly. For example, if a food box is delivered containing a plate of cold cuts and garnishes instead of readymade sandwiches, the result may be discussion, decisionmaking, compromise, etc., between hostage and captor. If these interactions provide the hostage with opportunities to behave in ways which are reinforcing to the captor (e.g., providing limited assistance), the potential for violence against the hostage may be lessened. Throughout the incident, hostages should be encouraged to behave in ways which would help them avoid violence. Some resources may be used to divert the hostagetaker's attention in the case of particularly threatening behavior toward the hostage. Spotlighting windows in darkness may illuminate the scene to the tactical disadvantage of the hostagetaker. Pounding on walls or drilling may give the impression of vulnerability or that an assault is imminent. These activities could then be terminated as a consequence of specific hostagetaker concessions. One important consideration suggested by the review of the original Stockholm incident is that the increasing level of sophistication of police tactical assault, i.e., silent drilling for eavesdropping, invisible police deployment, etc., may lessen the fear necessary to stimulate favorable negotiations during the incident. The judicious use of negotiators and tactical personnel to develop a coordinated, timely response creates the optimum conditions for a favorable resolution of the incident.

Conclusion

Although hostage incidents appear to have received increased attention in recent years, little is known about the dynamics of these situations, and there are only vague outlines to guide appropriate law enforcement response. The Stockholm Syndrome has been widely discussed as a significant outcome of many hostage incidents, yet almost nothing is known about how often it occurs, what causes it, or whether it actually enhances the safe resolution of hostage incidents, and if so, how to promote its occurrence. At least part of the problem appears to be related to how the Stockholm Syndrome has been investigated, and perhaps, the related theoretical interpretations of the phenomenon.

Behavioral theory offers many ways for law enforcement personnel to approach hostage situations. This study may lead toward the future development of specific techniques which may help control hostage situations. However, it is necessary to conduct further research before generalizations may be considered. Archival data should be collected and examined to define further the phenomenon of hostage(s) and hostagetaker(s) developing a favorable rapport and to validate statistically the assumption that the rapport is a useful conditon in hostage situations. Past incidents should also be studied to determine what specific actions were taken by hostages and hostagetakers. In describing these events, writers should be careful to note that the Stockholm Syndrome is only a label for the rapport that may develop between the involved parties, and it is not an entity which produces the rapport. The phenomenon can be observed and studied in the same ways used to examine other behaviors.

Several administrative steps may be taken to facilitate the study of the Stockholm Syndrome and hostage situations. A central repository for hostage information, perhaps at the FBI Academy, should be established and all reports of hostage incidents should be forwarded to that location. A more consistent reporting procedure must be established to guide data collection. This procedure should encourage:

1. A detailed, chronological police incident report;
2. Tape recording all negotiations while the incident is in progress; and
3. The completion of a detailed questionnaire by the participants.

This debriefing questionnaire should focus on the negotiator, tactical commander, witness(es), hostage(s), and hostagetaker(s). Using existing behavioral research methodologies and the detailed information which would be gathered by the system noted above, it may be possible to begin to evaluate hypotheses suggested by the incident reports.

Behavioral psychology provides a consistent, innovative rationale for viewing the dynamics of a hostage situation. This kind of analysis is a radical departure from the descriptive work done in the past. By identifying selected classes of behavior and using established techniques for bringing about behavior change, it may be possible to resolve successfully a higher proportion of hostage situations. By virtue of its empirical emphasis, behavioral psychology suggests strategies for appropriate law enforcement response and simultaneously suggests methods for evaluating the usefulness of many law enforcement techniques. It is the emphasis on observable events and the accompanying challenge to monitor and evalutate an assortment of techniques (which have been developed in other fields) that make behaviorial psychology a potentially useful tool for the study of law enforcement in general and the study of hostage situations in particular.

TERRORISM AND THE ROLE OF THE POLICE*

Terrorism has captured the attention of the contemporary American public. The rationale for the present focus on terrorism appears to stem from reasons that are relatively current in nature:

1. The speed and scope of news media coverage of terrorist events.

2. The advent of speedy and inexpensive transportation systems for the transportation and escape of terrorists.

3. The increasing belief that anyone, anywhere, is a possible victim of terrorists activities, intended or otherwise.

Current Definition of Terrorism

Terrorism has often been defined as mindless, senseless, violent acts. For the majority of cases, nothing could be further from the truth. Many definitions are presently in use. The following includes the majority of such acts.

Terrorism is the commission or threat of a criminal act for the purpose of furthering the goals of the terrorist group—material or political. The intended effects are fear instilled in the minds of others beyond just the immediate victims of the criminal act. Its psychological impact is designed to be out of proportion to its physical result.

The officer should make a distinction between what is currently called the "urban guerilla" and the terrorist. The urban guerilla's goal is revolution. The terrorist's goal is to focus public interest on a specific grievance. Both use terroristic means, but there is a distinct and important difference.

Another error is to believe that all terrorists represent a Communist point of view or are attempting to target an existing political power. Recent experiences around the world suggest that governments in power, of every political belief, often use terrorism to keep the people under their control.

---

* Earl W. Robitaille, "Terrorism and the Role of the Police," *Law and Order*, September, 1981. Reprinted by permission.

The Mind of The Terrorist

In dealing with any terrorist group the law enforcement officer must keep in mind three important factors that separate the terrorists from other groups involved in criminal acts.

1. Their *organization* is usually structured, regardless of the size of the group.

2. *Secrecy* is their best defense and they utilize it to its fullest.

3. They are highly *disciplined*. These three traits pose a real threat to law enforcement. When combined in an effort against an appropriate target, they often lead to overreaction by the police which is one of the aims of the terrorists. If police agencies are only reactive to terrorists' acts or threats and do overreact, the public feels that government agencies are unable to cope with terrorism. It turns people away from the efforts of the police and aligns them with the terrorists.

Terrorist Profiles

There have been numerous attempts to build profiles of the "average American terrorist" to aid the law enforcement officer in their identification. Such attempts have not been very successful. There is some commonality of characteristics, but not enough to build a usable profile. Some of the commonalities are:

1. Age — early 20's to 30's.

2. Sex — both male and female (some known groups with up to 70 percent females).

3. Education — some college through graduate degrees.

4. Religion — all denominations represented.

5. Race — all represented, but predominantly white.

6. Criminal background — almost without exception, no criminal record for violence prior to becoming involved in terrorist movement.

Contrast these characteristics with a recent profile developed on 350 known terrorists from 18 Mid-Eastern, Latin American, West European and Japanese groups:

1. Age — 22 to 24.

2. Sex — mostly unmarried males.

3. Education — partial college education (humanities).

4. Prior vocation — law, medicine, journalism, and teaching. (In Turkey and Iran most terrorists came from engineering and technical backgrounds).

5. Upbringing — from middle class to upper class families.

6. Recruitment — almost without exception, they were recruited into

terrorist activities on the university campus.

Law enforcement's ability to deal with terrorists depends on good intelligence and intelligence gathering methods so uniformed officers can be of greater assistance in reporting observations of their daily contacts to the intelligence section of theirs or allied agencies. Observations of the following can be of critical importance in determining if there may be a terrorist group in operation in your area.

Observations of groups or individuals in possession of:

1. More than one illegal weapon.

2. Any explosive materials or tools.

3. Chemicals used in bombs and incendiary devices.

4. Books, pamphlets or posters expounding on radical political points of view.

5. Maps or diagrams of possible targets. (i.e., military posts, utilities, police stations, etc.)

6. False identification.

7. Military training materials.

Officers should be alert for residences where many young adults and middle age types are living in conditions that suggest a commitment to a "cause" rather than comfort or material necessities. This is particularly true where items described above are in evidence.

Enforcement Considerations

Regardless of the threat posed to our society by terrorist groups, law enforcement personnel are obligated to operate within the framework of the law and the rules and regulations of their agency. The officers involved in cases pertaining to terrorists must remember their obligation to conduct themselves in a professional, unbiased manner, always acting within the framework of the Constitution in order to accomplish their assigned task.

With the possible exception of violent crimes against children, there are few other criminal acts such as those committed by terrorists that tempt law enforcement officers to step beyond the scope of the authority vested in them. There is nothing to be gained by law enforcement violating the rights of innocent citizens in the search for terrorists. In every instance where it has occurred, it has proven counter-productive.

Terrorists Countermeasures

Although intelligence is the agency's first line of defense against terrorist attacks, it has a number of serious limitations. One is the lack of precision of intelligence data. The second has to do with the appropriate concentration of intelligence efforts on the terrorist group. It is almost impossible to predict where and when terrorists plan to attack. Additionally, it is often difficult to determine which group of terrorists you will be up against.

Barring the ability to predict the target of the terrorist, police agencies should be prepared to set in motion those other actions that will lessen the personal and property damage.

One such step is to "harden the target," to use the military phrase. This means identifying as many potential terrorists targets as possible and then aiding in the provision of as many security precaution systems as possible (Guards, communications, closed-circuit T.V., fences, etc.) Make those targets so secure that the terrorist will elect not to spend the time and effort to make their attack at that point. It can be a very expensive and time consuming defense, as the steps to stop sky-jacking of commercial airliners by terrorists has proven.

There must be a plan to lessen the crisis caused by the act. This means the agency must be prepared to communicate its actions, must have the necessary resources in reserve (medical, shelter, military, utilities, emergency food, water, etc.) In other words, be prepared to meet all the needs of the victims, both alive and dead. This means operating humanely and efficiently to do the job and not lose the confidence of the public. All this presupposes prepared plans.

Conclusion

The impact of the psychological threat posed by the terrorist can be substantially diminished or overcome, but only through good intelligence, appropriate security measures and limitation of the crisis. These, coupled with contingency planning and good communications, are your best law enforcement tools.

TERRORISM: DOES IT AFFECT THE STREET COP?*

Most law enforcement officers are busy enough wondering how to get through the rest of their shift safely without having to worry about having some transnational, or even a domestic terrorist, cut their shift short.

With violent crimes on the increase, department budgets cut, and calls for services climbing inexorably, there is little time to ponder the effects of worldwide acts of terrorism and the impact they have on the local scene. Most officers have developed an "ostrich" approach to acts of terrorism.

We simply shake our heads when we read the grisly accounts of some far-off dictatorship "purging" it's intelligensia, or watch fuzzy pictures of blood spattered bodies on the evening news as the commentator tries to sound interesting while describing the next "junta." We go on, responding to silent alarms as we always have, or set up roadblocks, make high risk entries, and conduct "hot stops." We don't seem to comprehend the "why" or really the "who" . . . simply the "what."

To get the proper perspective, take a look at a few critical facts:

1. Since 1968, acts in international terrorism have grown from 142 to 709 in 1981, for a total of over 7,425 incidents.
(*Security Management magazine*, "Patterns of International Terrorism," September 1982, p. 148)

2. A third of terrorist targets were American.

3. There were 1,142 bombings and attempted bombings in the U.S. last year, causing 30 deaths and injuring 133. Six of the injured were law enforcement officers.
(FBI Bomb Summary 1981.)

4. 33 of the bombing incidents were claimed by terrorist groups
(FBI Bomb Summary 1981.)

5. Domestic Terrorists have killed and wounded police officers in this country, as late as Oct. 20, 1981. Some of those groups were thought to be defunct by many officers.

---

* Richard S. Michelson, "Terrorism: Does it Affect the Street Cop?" *Law and Order*, February 1983, pp. 42-45. Reprinted by permission.

6. Over 1,200 officers have been killed in this country in the last ten years.
(FBI Law Enforcement Officers Killed Summary 1981.)

7. Terrorist operations worldwide use bank robberies, kidnapping and extortion to finance their operations.

8. There is evidence of "linkage" between domestic groups and transnational groups.

During this same time frame we have seen a decrease in police manpower, severe budget cuts, and personnel layoffs. Training programs have also been cut.

Most officers regard terrorism as just something other countries have problems with, until something dramatic brings it smashing home.

October 20, 1981, Nyack, New York

Officers in the Nyack area were alerted to a robbery of a Brinks truck, about four miles away. Responding units set up a roadblock at the entrance to the New York State Thruway, something they had done many times before—the Thruway being a main artery leading out of the area. The suspects, described as black males, wearing ski masks, had fled the scene in a red van, but were observed switching vehicles to a "U-Haul" type truck. One Brinks guard had been killed and two others were wounded in the robbery.

Officers from Nyack spotted a "U-Haul" truck and stopped the truck before the entrance to the Thruway. They made contact with the white driver and white female passenger, later identified as Kathy Boudine of the Weather Underground, a fugitive wanted for bail jumping in Chicago in 1970 and the 1970 Greenwich Village Townhouse explosion, where a Weather Underground "Bomb Factory" exploded, killing three Weather persons.

As three Nyack Police Officers were interviewing the occupants of the truck, a Nyack Detective tried the overhead door, but could not get it to open. As he was walking back toward the truck's occupants, the rear door to the truck opened and six black males jumped out and fired with automatic weapons, killing two officers and wounding another. The weapons were an M-16, 9 mm's and a shotgun.

One of the officers managed to return fire and hit one of the suspects, but he, along with the other suspects, was wearing a bulletproof vest. The four Officers were armed with 357 Magnums and two shotguns. In a later shootout with officers, the suspect that had been hit, was killed still wearing the bulletproof vest. In his pocket was found the bullet fired from the slain Nyack officer.

At the Nyack shootout, police found the suspects had backup cars, two of which were recovered. The backup cars were driven by white males and females, members of the Weather Underground and May 19th Communist Organization. The vehicles were used to create diversions and provide escape to the black suspects by hiding them in the trunks of the cars. In related incidents, such vehicles have been equipped with an inside trunk release that allows the gunman to open and jump out if stopped by police. . . and open fire. The people involved were members of the Black Liberation Army, Black Panthers, Weather Underground and the May 19th Communist Organization. Many claimed such groups were long gone, distant memories of the turbulent sixties.

Some officers chose to ignore that some of these militant groups killed and wounded officers during those violent years. Considering that over 1,200 officers have been killed in the past ten years, it is easy to feel as though one is in the middle of an "urban war," with only the "thin blue line" pitted against the combined forces of the criminal element. Certain "underground" publications still advocate revolution and define police officers as legitimate targets to be "liquidated."

Until the Nyack incident, and the information that these groups have been involved in several other successful robberies, we tended to gloss over threats of terrorism, at least at the street officer level. Bomb technicians have had their share of the action, but the street "cop" has been relatively lucky. . . so far.

Financing Terrorism

Terrorists get the money to finance their operations from bank robberies, kidnapping and extortion. They are not thieves who steal on impulse. Usually they are very meticulous in their planning. They study their target, examine it very carefully until they find the weak link.

The targets are banks, key executives, top industrialists, governmental or military leaders, and armored cars. Also, police officers—from chief to patrolman—politicians, athletes, and other "newsworthy" types of people. Relatives of any of the above could be used in a kidnap/extortion plan.

It is not uncommon for terrorists to commit an act just for the publicity that it will certainly generate. The phrase "terrorism as theater" is very descriptive.

Most targets are symbolic. It is not really who they are, but what they represent. It's bad enough just with the "ordinary" criminals running around, much less having to deal with a group of trained commandos jumping out the door with automatic weapons.

Ulricke Meinhoff, of the infamous Red Army Faction, or better known as the Baader-Meinhoff Gang, had a comment about bank robberies, "For the revolutionary organization it means, first of all, a solution of its financial problems. It is logistically correct, since otherwise the financial problem could not be solved at all. It is politically correct because it is an act of dispossession. It is tactically correct because it is a proletarian action."

The Baader-Meinhoff Gang was responsible for 555 acts of terrorism in Germany.

Carlos Marighella, author of the MiniManual for the Urban Guerilla also reported on robbing banks, ". . . the armed struggle of the urban guerilla points toward two essential objectives: a) the physical liquidation of the chief's and assistants of the armed forces and of the police; b) the expropriation of government resources and those belonging to the capitalist, . . . and imperialists, with small expropriations used for the maintenance of individual urban guerillas and large ones for the sustenance of the revolution itself." This simply means—*kill the police and rob banks*.

Found distributed among the inmates of San Quentin prison was a booklet titled, "Urban Guerilla." It stated: "The most immediate assassinations which we should concern ourselves with is the destruction of police officers." "A pig is a pig—in uniform or out. It would be much easier to set up an off-duty policeman." "The man who approaches a policeman with a smile on his face and in an obviously friendly mood, (as witness the daring brother who took the head of the Japanese pig in Berkeley) has a far better chance of succeeding than a brother who walks up to the policeman with a look of scorn, hate and anger upon his face."

Domestic Terrorist

Terrorists indigenous to the U.S. cause their own wave of terror, either individually, or as members of organized, formal or informal, associations. The key is if they gather, meet, assemble, or act with the intent to steal, disrupt, destroy, or kill.

Examples range from the nebulous Mafia to the Hell's Angels; from the Croatians to the Armenians; the Ku Klux Klan to the Jewish Defense League; the Weather Underground, Black Panthers, Black Guerilla Family, the Nuestra Familia, and the Mexican Mafia; the George Jackson Brigade to the Soledad Brothers.

Nationalist groups operating in the U.S. are: Alpha 66, Omega 7, Puerto Rican FALN, the PLO and others. And don't forget the powerful prison gangs and narcotics traffickers, as well as organized street gangs. Each part of the country has it's own version of domestic terrorists. And there has been evidence of linkage to some of those groups, from transnational terrorists.

Perhaps the most difficult part of any officer survival issue is not to leave the impression that everyone is out to get you. While that is simply not true, the fact remains that officers will die, be wounded or injured, by some of the groups listed. Many officers will retire after 20 or 30 years, never having to fire their weapon in the line of duty, or having encountered a terrorist. But it is necessary to keep a high level of safety consciousness. Be "survival" oriented. Don't get suckered into the "routine" call.

Tactics and Training

In looking at the tactics that officers should master, several are crucial to survival. A tactically sound response to any crime-in-progress or silent-alarm call is critical. More officers are being shot and injured during these types of calls than in family disturbance calls.

Sound tactics, utilizing proper approach methods, the use of cover and concealment, and "invisible deployment," should be used on every call. Yet officers still screech up to the scene, siren blaring, slam the doors, and run blindly into their own death.

Another critical training area is the "hot stop" or felony vehicle stop. Emphasis needs to be on stopping vans, trucks, campers and especially rental trucks. It is a common tactic for terrorists, as well as criminals, to rent a commercial truck to transport personnel and weapons. Officers must know how to stop such vehicles safely. Even more crucial is how to clear the vehicle with the least risk to themselves.

The key to this type of stop is to maintain control as much as possible, and to stay behind the cover of the patrol unit.

Make suspects come to you. Have them exit one at a time, all from the same side of the vehicle, if possible. Make the rear of the police car the safety zone where you do your handcuffing and searching.

An interesting point was noted during training sessions in various cities. Once officers had "cleared the vehicle" and were about to search it, if they noticed movement inside indicating that someone was still secreted within, they still wanted to go up and search it. The suggestion that if they suspected someone was still inside, especially an armed suspect, they should not approach the vehicle, surprised many. They felt they still had to go up to the vehicle.

An alternative, short of a SWAT team entry, may be to use a chemical agent, such as a small "ferret." Or a police dog could be employed in certain situations. If you have stabilized the situation, time is on your side. Never just walk up to the vehicle.

High risk entries and searches is another important tactic that needs improvement. Proper approaches, use of high ground, cover fire, or at least someone covering your moves while you manoeuver into a tactically safe position, are more of a military approach than police, but are sound tactics. The rule is simple: Do not move from point to point unless someone is covering you.

This also holds true once you are inside a building moving from room to room. Training on spotting booby traps should be included.

A department policy on bomb threats, bomb searches, found devices, and explosions should be developed and tested. Ambush counter-measures should also be practiced. Effective stimulous-response shooting techniques should be mastered. Shooting survival courses need not be expensive or elaborate, just realistic and relevant to what is happening on the street.

Many departments have the philosophy, "why bother, nothing like that ever happens here!" Officers from all over the country have made the statement, and then they tell me of an incident that killed one or more of their officers.

Many departments rely upon on-the-job training in lieu of any professional training programs. Some only have academy level or basic training with little in the way of advanced officer courses, except for a roll-call type training session. One department even told its officers to take a correspondence course. More is needed for a defense against a vicarious liability suit for failure to adequately train officers.

A key to training is that it should be as realistic as you can make it. Officers need to experience bailing out of the patrol car during a hostile fire exercise. They should be able to come up with weapon drawn, behind cover, and return accurate fire—firing regulation or duty rounds. Wadcutters and reloads may save some money, but imagine your reaction if the first time you ever fired a department load was during a real firefight.

Over half of the officers killed are killed in the presence of a partner or a cover unit. Counting rounds and timing your fire so that both of you don't run out of ammunition at the same time is critical.

Yet in training session after training session, both officers run out of ammunition. There is an ominous silence as both frantically try to reload before their position is assaulted. Most departments cannot send officers to elaborate officer survival schools. Take a good look at the resources already in your community; military training facilities, community colleges, surrounding departments, shooting clubs, etc. Training need not be expensive, just practical and as realistic as possible.

Forecasting the Future

Terrorist activities aside, what else could be a possbile problem for law enforcement officers? Perhaps crowd control tactics, mass arrests, baton techniques, or dispersal of chemical agents in a tactical setting. The anti-nuclear movement could beat anything we saw in the 60s. Worldwide, it could dwarf the anti-war rallies and demonstrations. And who, again, will bear the brunt of the action? Police officers.

Are you ready for 800,000 demonstrators, with nearly 1,500 arrests?

One committee involved in a large demonstration recently was simply called, "The Committee for Civil Disobedience." Years ago, the Weather Underground named their newsletter and movement, "Prairie Fire". The term for what may explode across the world might be, "Groundswell," for that is what seems to be happening. Look at the lessons of Del Diablo, Livermore, New York and Washington, and others. And this could be only the beginning.

The purpose here is not to make officers paranoid, but to open their eyes a bit to what is happening. Remember the old adage that goes, "An ounce of prevention is worth a pound of cure."

There have been over 7,000 acts of terrorism since 1968. In 1980 alone, there were some 12.6 million dollars in property damage caused by terrorist bombing inside the U.S., with 34 deaths, and 160 injuries. These figures do not reflect crimes by biker or street gangs.

Add the organized protesters, leftist advocates, right wing extremist, "hate groups," volatile immigrant populations, narcotics trafficking, nationalist radicals and other disgruntled groups of individuals, and you begin to see the big picture.

Our tendency is to have a very myopic view of the world. Only when something tragic happens, do we react. Being reactive is the bane of law enforcement. Being proactive, or prepared, is not easy. And it is expensive. But considering the alternatives, it is crucial.

Chapter 8
STRESS

Introduction *

Historically, business and industry in the United States have been slow to identify and provide for the needs of workers. Largely because of the labor union movement, the U.S. worker has achieved a variety of benefits, ranging from increased wages to comprehensive medical care and retirement programs. The inclusion of mental health compensation as a significant management issue has evolved through a combination of union pressures and simple economics. A healthy well-adjusted worker means increased efficiency and higher production for the corporation. As a consequence, job-related stress "has moved from the nether world of 'emotional problems' and 'personality conflicts' to the corporate balance sheet. . . . Stress is now seen as not only troublesome but expensive."

Government and public service sectors generally lag behind industry or business in employee-benefit innovations, and the mental health issue is no exception. However, the private sector's recent concern with the wide-ranging effects of job-related stress on workers is beginning to be shared by criminal justice authorities — or at least by those in law enforcement. More and more literature on stress factors in policing is becoming available to the law enforcement executive for use in developing programs designed to help cope with and reduce stress among police personnel.

Stress in Law Enforcement

Police work is highly stressful, since it is one of the few occupations where an employee is asked continually to face physical dangers and to put his or

---

* Leonard Territo and Harold J. Vetter, "Stress and Police Personnel," *Journal of Police Science and Administration*, Vol.9, No. 2, 1981, pp. 195-207. Reprinted by permission.

her life on the line at any time. The police officer is exposed to violence, cruelty, and aggression and is often required to make extremely critical decisions in high-pressure situations.

Stress has many ramifications and can produce many varied psychophysiological disturbances that, if intense and chronic enough, can lead to demonstrable organic disease of varying severity. It may also lead to physiological disorders and emotional instability, that can manifest themselves in alcoholism, a broken marriage, and, in the extreme, suicide. Studies have shown that three-fourths of the heart attacks suffered by police officers are due to job-related stress. As a result, courts have ruled that a police officer who suffers a heart attack while off duty is entitled to workmen's compensation. Thus, even a superficial review of the human, organizational, and legal impacts of stress-related health problems should sensitize every administrator to the prevention, treatment, and solution of these problems.

Job Stress in Police Officers

In law enforcement, stressors have been identified in various ways. Researchers, such as Kroes, Eisenberg, Reiser, and Roberts have conducted extensive studies into law enforcement occupational stress, and although they do not group these stressors into identical categories, they tend to follow similar patterns. Most of the law enforcement stressors can be grouped into four broad categories: (1) organizational practices and characteristics, (2) criminal justice system practices and characteristics, (3) public practices and characteristics, and (4) police work itself.

Kroes, Margolis, and Hurrell interviewed 100 Cincinnati patrol officers about the elements of their job which they believed were stressful. Foremost on their list of items were: the courts (scheduling appearances and leniency), the administration (undesirable assignments and lack of backing in ambiguous situations), faulty equipment, and community apathy. Other items listed but not with so great a frequency were: changing shifts, relations with supervisors, nonpolice work, other police officers, boredom, and pay.

A survey of 20 police chiefs in the Southeastern United States confirmed these findings. These chiefs when asked about situations they believed were stressful for line personnel listed: lack of administrative support; role conflicts; public pressure and scrutiny, peer group pressures; courts; and imposed role changes.

While working with the San Jose Police Department, one researcher was able to identify numerous sources of psychological stress that were basically reflections of his personal observations and feelings while performing the functions of a patrol officer for approximately two years. Some of these sources of psychological stress were poor supervision;

absence or lack of career development opportunities; inadequate reward reinforcement system; offensive administrative policies; excessive paperwork; poor equipment; law enforcement agency jurisdiction isolationism; unfavorable court decisions; ineffectiveness of corrections agencies to rehabilitate or warehouse criminals; misunderstood judicial procedures; inefficient courtroom management; distorted press accounts of police incidents; unfavorable attitude by the public; derogatory remarks by neighbors and others; adverse local government decisions; ineffectiveness of referral agencies; role conflict; adverse work scheduling; fear of serious injury, disability, and death; exposure to suffering and agonized people, both physically and mentally; consequences of actions, their appropriateness, and possible adverse conditions.

It is rather interesting to note that an examination of the findings from a variety of police organizations tends to identify many of the same sources of psychological stress and similar reactions to it by police officers. This is true regardless of the geographical location or the organizational differences. The existence of these similarities is quite important, for it increases the possibility of creating programmatic solutions which have a high degree of applicability for a variety of law enforcement agencies that may on the surface seem to be dissimilar.

Stress Indicators

The Psychological Services Unit of the Dallas, Texas, Police Department has set forth (Table 1) its assessment of job-related stressors, the immediate response to stress, and the long-term response to stress. They have also developed a useful and practical guide to assist police supervisors in detecting the 15 most prevalent warning signs of stress (see Table 2).

Alcoholism and Police Officers

Alcoholism in government and industry is not only widespread but also extremely costly, a fact established most convincingly by many independent researchers. Some 6.5 million employed workers in the United States today are alcoholics. Loss of productivity because of alcoholism has been computed at $10 billion.

Although precise figures are not available to substantiate a high incidence of alcoholism among police, department officials have reported informally that as many as 25 percent of the officers in their respective departments have serious alcohol abuse problems.

Alcohol problems among police officers manifest themselves in a number of ways. Some of these are a higher than normal absentee rate prior to and immediately before the officer's regular day off; complaints of insubordination by supervisors; complaints by citizens of misconduct in

Table 1 — Short-Term/Chronic Stress Reaction

Job-related stressors	Immediate response to stress			
	Personality	Health	Job performance	Home life
Administration	Temporary increases in:	Temporary increases in:	Job tension	"Spats with wife"
Job conflict	Anxiety	Smoking rate	"Flying off the handle"	Periodic withdrawal
Second job	Tension	Headaches	Erratic work habit	Anger displaced to wife and children
Inactivity	Irritability	Heart rate	Temporary work decrement	Increased extra-marital activity
Shift work	Feeling "uptight"	Blood pressure	Etc.	Etc.
Inadequate resources	Drinking rate	Cholesterol level		
Inequities in pay and job status	Etc.	Etc.		
Organizational territoriality				
Job overload				

Job-related stressors	Long-term response to stress			
	Personality	Health	Job performance	Home life
Responsibility for people	Psychosis	Chronic disease states:	Decreased productivity	Divorce
Courts	Chronic depression	Ulcers	Increased error rate	Poor relations with other
Negative public image	Alienation	High blood pressure	Job dissatisfaction	Social isolation
Conflicting values	Alcoholism	Coronary heart disease	Accidents	Loss of friends
Racial situations	General malaise	Asthmatic attacks	Withdrawal	Etc.
Line of duty/crisis situations	Low self-esteem	Diabetes	Serious error in judgment	
Job ambiguity	Low self-actualization	Etc.	Slower reaction time	
Etc.	Suicide		Etc.	
	Etc.			

Reproduced by permission of the Psychological Services Unit, Dallas Police Department, adapted from Kroes, *Society's Victim*, p.66.

Table 2 — Fifteen Most Prevalent Stress Warning Signs

Warning signs	Examples
1. Sudden changes in behavior Usually directly opposite to usual behavior.	From cheerful and optimistic to gloomy and pessimistic
2. More gradual change in behavior but in a way that points to deterioration of the individual	Gradually becoming slow and lethargic, possibly with increasing depression and sullen behavior
3. Erratic work habits	Coming to work late, leaving early, abusing comp time
4. Increased sick time due to minor problems	Headaches, colds, stomachaches, etc.
5. Inability to maintain a train of thought	Rambling conversation, difficulty in sticking to a specific subject
6. Excessive worrying	Worrying about one thing to the exclusion of any others
7. Grandiose behavior	Preoccupation with religion, politics, etc.
8. Excessive use of alcohol and/or drugs	Obvious hangover, disinterest in appearance, talk about drinking prowess
9. Fatigue	Lethargy, sleeping on job
10. Peer complaints	Others refuse to work with him or her
11. Excessive complaints (negative citizen contact)	Caustic and abusive in relating to citizens
12. Consistency in complaint pattern	Picks on specific groups of people (youth, blacks, etc.)
13. Sexual promiscuity	Going after everything all of the time—on or off duty
14. Excessive accidents and/or injuries	Not being attentive to driving, handling prisoners, etc.
15. Manipulation of fellow officers and citizens	Using others to achieve ends without caring for their welfare

Reproduced by permission of the Psychological Services Unit, Dallas Police Department.

the form of verbal and physical abuse; intoxication during regular working hours; involvement in traffic accidents while under the influence of alcohol on and off duty; and reduced overall performance.

It has been further suggested that policing is especially conducive to alcoholism. Since police officers frequently work in an environment where social drinking is commonplace, it is relatively easy for them to become social drinkers. The nature of police work and the environment in which it is performed provides the stress stimulus.

Traditionally, police departments adhere to the "character flaw" theory of alcoholism. This philosophy calls for the denunciation and dismissal of an officer with an alcohol problem because recognizing the officer as a symptom of underlying problems reflects on the department. What is not considered is that alcoholism may result from the extraordinary stress of the job and that eliminating the officer does not do away with the source of stress.

Departmental Programs

There is no single "best way" for a department to assist its officers with a drinking problem but some agencies have enjoyed a fair degree of success for their efforts. For example, the Denver Police Department is now utilizing its closed-circuit television system to reach officers who are problem drinkers and encourage them to join the inhouse program. A major portion of the inhouse program is designed to persuade the problem drinker, having digested a sufficient amount of the educational aspect of the program, to enter the Mercy Hospital Care Unit and achieve the status of a recovering alcoholic.

Dishlacoff has concluded that it is the responsibility of the individual police agency and its administrators to recognize and accept the fact of alcoholism as a disease and to create a relaxed atmosphere and an inhouse program for the dissemination of information relative to this problem. As indicated earlier, the objective of such a program is ultimately to persuade individual officers to enter a care unit for treatment. The combination of unsatisfactory performance, excessive costs, and the almost certain progressive deterioration of the individual officer to the point of unemployability if the illness goes unchecked, creates a situation that conscientious chiefs of police should neither tolerate nor ignore.

An essential point to remember is that if drinking affects an officer's health, job, or family, immediate action is essential — the officer is probably an alcoholic.

Reports by the Denver Police Department indicate that the organization has benefited in specific ways since the implementation of their alcohol abuse program. Some of these specific benefits have been (Dishlacoff 1976:39):

1. Retention of the majority of the officers who had suffered from alcoholism.

2. Solution of a set of complex and difficult personnel problems.

3. Realistic and practical extension of the police agency's program into the entire city government structure.

4. Improved public and community attitudes by this degree of concern for the officer and family and by eliminating the dangerous and antisocial behavior of the officer in the community.

5. Full cooperation with rehabilitation efforts from the police associations and unions that may represent officers.

6. The preventive influence on moderate drinkers against the development of dangerous drinking habits which may lead to alcoholism. In addition, an existing inhouse program will motivate some officers to undertake remedial action on their own, outside the scope of the police agency program.

Suicide and Police Officers

Suicide as a problem for police officers is a bifurcated issue. Suicide among young police officers in not particularly common, but when it does occur it is frequently associated with divorce or other family problems. Among older police officers, suicide is more common and may be related to alcoholism, physical illness, or impending retirement. Although hard data are not readily available, there tends to be some speculation that suicides immediately after retirement may not be uncommon. Some researchers have suggested that police officers do not retire well. This fact is widely known within police departments, and it is not surprising to see newly retired officers becoming depressed and allowing their physical conditions to deteriorate. Like individuals in other occupations, police officers in general do not plan realistically for retirement. However, unlike other occupations, police officers are often deeply involved with their work until the actual moment of retirement. It is a shock to suddenly be estranged from a job that has occupied a major portion of one's life and has provided the source of so many social activities as well.

These losses can have devastating effects upon retiring or retired police officers, but unfortunately most police departments, unlike many major industries, have not yet addressed themselves to this problem which has no doubt led to an undetermined number of police suicides.

One study concluded that the data which are available indicate that male police officers are more likely to kill themselves than men in other occupations. For example, the suicide rate for members of the New York City Police Department from 1960-1967 was 21.7 per 100,000 per year. The rate from 1950-1965 was 22.7. This is higher than the suicide rate of

16.7 for all males in the United States during this period.

In reported suicide rates for males in various occupations in the United States in 1950, police officers had the second highest suicide rate of 36 occupations, 47.6 per 100,000 per year. Only self-employed manufacturing managers and proprietors had a higher suicide rate. Clergymen had the lowest rate (10.6). Six possible clues have been outlined to help comprehend the high police suicide rates. The clues are: (1) police work is a male-dominated profession, and males have demonstrated a higher successful suicide rate; (2) the use, availability, and familiarity with firearms by police in their work make for a high lethal factor with little chance for resuscitation; (3) there are psychological repercussions to constantly being exposed to potential death; (4) long and irregular working hours do not promote strong friendships and do strain family ties; (5) there is constant exposure to public criticism and dislike for "cops"; and (6) judicial contradictions, irregularities, and inconsistent decisions tend to negate the value of police work.

Some authorities believe that aggressive behavior does not stem from internal drives, but from societal frustration. In a sense they say that suicide and homicide are different manifestations of the same phenomenon. As acts of aggression, suicide and homicide cannot be differentiated with respect to the source of the frustration generating the aggression. Moreover, when the aggression legitimized by the aggressor is directed outward (other oriented) because of societal frustration, you have homicide. Suicides or self-oriented aggression, a consequence to frustration, becomes a residual category or aggression for which outward expression against others is deemed illegitimate.

In one study of suicides of 12 Detroit police officers who killed themselves between the period February 1968 through January 1976, Danto found that the group consisted of:

> ...young men, married and for the most part, fathers, and came with backgrounds of unskilled employment prior to their police appointment, or military service, high school education or better, and some stable family life as measured by parents who were married and who had created families. The majority of the officers were white and had not been employed as police officers for many years....
>
> The officers who committed suicide ... used firearms and fatally shot their heads and abdomens. Carbon monoxide was the second most common cause of death and many of the suicides, regardless of method, occurred in an automobile....
>
> The officers of the Detroit Police Department who committed suicide were different from the New York Police Department suicides. The Detroit group was younger, had less service time with the department, had a lower suicide rate within a police department, and less physical illness and police medical consultation

histories, and fewer were single. In some respects they were similar: many had a history of alcohol abuse and dependency, had picked primarily firearms as their suicide method, and had suffered marital disharmony prior to their deaths.

Neither study proves that the police officer is any more prone to choose his profession because of its opportunities to express aggression than anyone else in society. The rising suicide and homicide rates for nonpolice persons should attest to that. Furthermore, since women have become more violent in terms of crime, homicide and suicide, we know that we are dealing with a general trend rather than a masculine assertion or aggression conflict. . . .

By far and away the most upsetting problem for the suicidal police officer is his marriage. This marital discord is reflected both in the fact that the officer sometimes committed suicide following the murder of a significant person, but also killed himself in a location near to persons for whom he cared very deeply. To some extent, problems may be connected to his work because his hours are erratic, constantly subject to change, and the officer is subjected to danger which is beyond the reach of most civilian minds. . . .

It has been suggested that the police suicide phenomenon should be viewed from a psychological basis that emphasizes both the unique and multideterminant aspects of an individual's behavior as well as the societal influences on that behavior. The human being is a frustrated and status-oriented social animal not isolated from peers. In many ways the American police officer is like a health professional. Officers frequently come in contact with the behaviorally different and socially ill citizens of our cities as part of their life's work. Likewise, when they are suffering unrelenting anguish, they often fear the loss of their jobs (perhaps realistically so because of parochial attitudes toward mental health held by their department) if they seek treatment. Yet the closest analogy, unfortunately, linking the police and health professionals, is the reluctance of their respective colleagues to get them involved in treatment, in spite of their colleagues' awareness of their difficulties, because they may feel it is none of their business. A troubled police officer, like a health professional, is of no use to the public or to the profession if the officer does not seek treatment.

Stress and the Police Administrator

As any individual who has risen through the ranks of a police agency realizes, the types of problems and pressures encountered as an administrator are quite different from those encountered as a patrol officer. For either position, however, the end results of the stress can be equally menacing to the person performing the job.

The High Price of Success

One management expert has suggested that upward mobility in almost any type of bureaucracy tends to impose unique stresses upon individuals. These stresses occur in part because an individual often must sacrifice family relationships for career goals and because each promotion brings with it more responsibilities for the individual over wider ranging areas and increased numbers of subordinates. In addition, young men and women who ascend the organizational ladder rapidly tend to generate considerable envy from their peers who believe they have been unfairly passed over for promotion. Sometimes this envy manifests itself in negative interpersonal contacts between the superior and his or her less successful subordinates.

Upward mobility, regardless of age, carries with it certain risks. The higher one rises in the organization, the harder the fall if one should err. The errors that occur in the higher levels of police organizations are likely to be bigger, more costly, and more personally painful than those in the lower ranks. Because his or her errors are more obvious to a wider range of people, the individual becomes increasingly concerned about being viewed as incompetent. A person may also feel isolated as peers become subordinates and once gratifying relationships with them become modified or perhaps even dissolved. Moreover, at a certain point in the upward climb, usually close to the top, many executives experience a specific disappointment. Once having achieved a certain position, they discover that they still have the same frailties, inadequacies, and self-doubts except that now their younger and less experienced subordinates look to them for the answers to complex problems. Looking upward from the lower rungs of the hierarchy, subordinates often tend to view distant supervisors as omnipotent. They have a powerful impact on the organization and always seem to know what they are doing. When the younger person reaches these levels, he or she soon realizes that the giants were really human after all and that one does not acquire omnipotence merely from having achieved a certain position.

Pressure from Above and Below

Subordinates do not always view their police superiors with respect, admiration, and awe. Kroes, Hurrell, and Margolis, in their study of 30 administrators of the Cincinnati Police Department (12 captains and 18 lieutenants), found that there was a tendency for patrol officers to blame their immediate supervisor for stressful conditions, when in some instances these superiors have little or no control over the factor inducing stress. Being blamed unfairly for their officers' problems can cause considerable anguish and frustration to superiors who are genuinely concerned about the welfare of their subordinates. This anguish is especially acute when the superior has a limited range of alternatives, authority, and resources available to correct those situations or factors that are stress inducing.

Nevertheless, most police administrators do have some alternatives available that can be implemented within the framework of the organization's resources and budget. In addition to the creation of programs that assist police officers in coping with and reducing stress, considerable progress has been made in the selection and training of supervisory personnel who are better able to cope with the stress inherent in their responsibilities and who are also more sensitive to the needs of their subordinates.

There is considerable evidence, from the available literature, that police administrators throughout the country experience similar types of personal, organizational, and community-initiated stress-inducing problems.

Stress and the Police Family

A law enforcement career is much more than a job or occupation for the individual; it is a way of life for the officer, spouse, and family. A police officer's life becomes one of shared priorities between the family and the outside world where the work and functions are on an official basis. The officer brings the problems and frustrations encountered on the job home to the family, conversely, sometimes venting the frustrations, tensions, and hostilities engendered by an unsatisfactory home life on the public.

Administrators are starting to recognize that the spouse and family are significant contributors to the success or failure in a law enforcement career. Marital and family strife, discord and unresolved emotional problems affect a police officer's development, motivation, productivity, and effectiveness in ways we are only beginning to appreciate and understand.

The excessive psychological pressures on officers to maintain self-control on the job drain their energies and can leave them totally depleted and unable to cope with problems at home. The spouse and family who need and expect some time and attention in working out their own problems are confronted with a person who simply lacks the emotional resources to deal with one more stressful situation. Whether the problem is large and important or small and trivial is irrelevant to the emotionally depleted officer; the officer is unable to deal with it.

Problems in Police Marriages

Law enforcement marriages are susceptible to certain kinds of stresses inherent in the nature of policing. Erratic work schedules, job pressures, and the necessity for 24-hour availability are a few factors that can drive a wedge between officers and their spouses. There is considerable evidence that police officers as an occupational group have one of the highest divorce rates in the country, and divorce seems to be especially prevalent among young police officers.

Schwartz and Schwartz point out:

> In large departments, it is easy to find numbers of patrol officers who are on their third marriage before age 30. There is no particular mystery with regard to the breakup of marriages existing prior to entry into police service. Many police officers are married within a few years after finishing high school and typically neither spouses had any realistic notion of what police service would mean in terms of its effect on family life. Police agencies that provide any orientation or counseling for spouses are increasing in number but they are still the exception rather than the rule.

Earlier in this century, law enforcement personnel ranked thirtieth in divorce rates out of 39 job categories. Some occupations or professions ranked higher than police were physicians, lawyers, teachers, and salesmen. One explanation provided by Durner is that law enforcement officers during this earlier period constituted large numbers of Irish, Polish, and Italian Catholics. Thus, it seems reasonable to assume that traditional condemnation of divorce by the Roman Catholic Church kept the divorce rate from being a reliable indicator of the success or failure of law enforcement marriages. Some authorities have suggested that divorce rates are merely the tangible expression of a far greater problem, dissatisfaction in marriage, whether or not it ends in divorce. Expressed dissatisfaction among married people is identified as a more accurate indicator of the number of people who are living in a state of marital discord and aggravation than is the actual divorce rate.

In the case of the police officer, an unhappy marriage becomes a social disability because of the officer's role as a controller of society. There is an urgent need to identify and overcome difficulties leading to marital dissatisfaction in police officers, for the plight of the officer's marriage affects everyone — the officer, the family, the offspring, and society as a whole. Generally, a long period of poor communication, confrontation, and frustrations precedes the actual dissolution of a marriage.

Job-Induced Problems

Job-related pressures that are inherent in the law enforcement career were discussed earlier. Unusual working hours, scattered weekends, excessive overtime, court appearances, and the constant presence of a gun in one's everyday life are enough to cause significant stresses and problems in a marital relationship. Most of these are obvious pressures to which most couples are able to adjust. There are stresses, however, that can have long-range and lasting effects on a relationship. Many of them create problems that have never been encountered, or even imagined, by the couple until they are forced to cope with them following the marriage ceremony. In many instances, these stresses take their toll over an extended period of time, and neither party attends to the warning signals or is able to pinpoint the actual source of the difficulties.

Changing work schedules. Extensive disruption occurs in the family routine as a result of changing work schedules and may have an adverse effect on home life. Not enough time is spent with the children; weekends and holidays with the family are missed; the spouse dislikes and resents being home alone at night; and social events with friends and family are difficult to plan. Working overtime merely accentuates the problems of shift work and leaves even less time to spend with the family. The most important factor in all these missed opportunities is the lack of *shared experience* among husband and wife and children. The end result can be a loss of interest in one another and a resulting breakdown in communications.

Emotional exhaustion. The inability to function effectively and deal successfully with people's problems confronts the police officer daily. This constant barrage of unsolvable problems, along with the various negative situations with which the officer constantly comes in contact, leads to frustration and psychological exhaustion. By the time the officer gets home, all patience has been expended. Problems at home either seem insignificant or, at the other extreme, may serve to infuriate the officer. An outburst of displaced aggression may then be released upon the family. In any event, the family is the loser.

Negative public image. How other people behave toward us is a well-known determinant of social behavior. Most police believe that what they do is important, but they are also very conscious of the public's opinion of them. Public animosity and disrespect impose the negative label of "cop" on the officer. Such a label has adverse effects not only on the officer but also upon close friends and family relations.

Overprotecting the spouse and family. One police psychologist writing about male police officers, points out that "because of the trauma and degradation they observe each day, law enforcement officers also tend to become overly protective of their wives and families." The job teaches and actively encourages an individual to become extremely observant and to develop suspiciousness as a part of his working personality. Often, without realizing it, the police officer carries over these characteristics which are highly functional on the job, into his personal relationships to the degree that he becomes overly concerned about his spouse's and family's welfare. Wanting to know where his wife and children are, what they are doing, and who they are with at all times can impose irksome restrictions on the family. What the officer views as concern and love for his family can often be misinterpreted by his wife and children as a lack of trust and confidence on the part of an authoritarian husband and father who is not around most of the time.

Hardening of emotions. In order to function adequately on the job, law enforcement officers often find it necessary to suppress their feelings. There is little room on the job for anger, disgust, tears, or sadness. Emotional suppression enables police officers to avoid deep personal involvement in the upsetting and occasionally traumatic incidents they have to deal with on a daily basis. The "hardening" process, helps police officers perform unpleasant and distasteful but necessary tasks without any outward display of emotions. Unfortunately, it is impossible for the police officer to shed this stoic image with his uniform. Most officers bring this stoicism home to their spouses and families, who must try to relate to their impassiveness. Often the spouse is unable to see, or even remember, the formerly cherished personal qualities of her partner, which he now hides because his career demands it.

Sexual problems. Sexual problems between the officer and his spouse may be either a symptom or a cause of emotional conflict and estrangement, and often are both. Intimacy is an early casualty of the pressures the officer experiences. Once the harmony between marital partners has been shattered, it becomes exceedingly difficult to restore it. The consequence is a "vicious circle" in which frustration creates anxiety and self-doubt, which in turn results in further frustration. As one group of police psychologists points out:

> Sexual promiscuity can also be a problem when the parties, out of frustration, seek release outside of marriage. Some of the sexual problems emanate from factors relating to police work. For instance, the officer who works nights, whose wife works days, and both have different days off, encounter the basic problems of scheduling their sex life. In addition, if they also have children at home, the problem is exacerbated. Too frequently the couples do not put forth the effort to understand and tolerate these difficulties and to work out a compromise solution. Instead, they engage in open hostility toward each other and this creates feeling that in time can result in one or both partners seeking sexual partners elsewhere. This course of action, if discovered by the non-offending spouse, frequently results in the dissolution of the marriage.

Infidelity on the part of the officer or spouse is a common source of domestic discord. Infidelity appears to be far more common among male officers than among their wives. In those cases, where the wife finds out about her husband's extramarital affairs, confronts him, and threatens to leave him, he usually undergoes severe depression and attitudinal and personality changes, that can result in serious problems for him both on and off the job.

Identity problems. Traditional roles of men and women in marriage have undergone rapid changes in the past several years. Many women, no longer content to live in a world circumscribed by child rearing and housework, are asserting their fundamental rights to seek a broader set of opportunities outside the home for personal growth and self-actualization.

Marital problems may also result when the officer's wife believes that she has outgrown her husband and her social station as a police officer's wife. One case cited by a police psychologist concerned an officer's wife whose job involved circulating in highly sophisticated circles where her husband felt he did not belong: "This caused a serious strain in their relationship and they eventually sought counseling. If the officer's wife views his position as being one that does not have the degree of status or prestige she views as important to her own self-concept, then difficulties may emerge in the relationship.

Problems with the children. Children of police officers may encounter negative reactions and rejections from both peers and school teachers because of their father's occupation. Juvenile problems also seem to become quite prevalent when the children of police families reach adolescence. Although many of these problems are between the children and their parents, serious delinquency is not uncommon and may involve school truancy, vandalism, alcohol and drug abuse, rebelliousness, and various other kinds of misconduct.

Psychologists interpret the delinquent actions of police officers' children as the rejection of the authority represented by their father's occupation. According to Somodevilla:

> Many times it is apparent that the officer is overprotecting his children and creating such an inhibiting home environment that they rebel. This phenomenon is far more common with adolescents who may feel trapped and stifled by their parent's protectiveness and act out in a manner that reinforces the parent's reason for over-protecting them.

Once again, we see the familiar pattern of the vicious circle: the tighter the control, the more rebellious the juvenile becomes.

Marital Problems as an Administrative Concern

Until recently, law enforcement administrators have viewed marital problems among police personnel as a private matter involving only the officer and spouse. Fortunately, police executives are now beginning to view marital difficulties as an administrative problem. In acknowledgment of the magnitude and importance of marital problems and their far-reaching effects on job performance, some administrators have devised programs for solving, or at least reducing, marital problems within their organizations. As yet, however, these programs have not been implemented in the majority of departments. There is an urgent need to identify and overcome difficulties leading to marital discord and conflict among law enforcement personnel. The following suggests some programs for spouses of police officers that should help administrators reach this goal.

Orientation Programs for Spouses

An orientation program for police spouses should make police wives more aware and understanding of the many activities of the police agency. It should provide a comprehensive view of operations within the department, levels of command, and the day-to-day duties performed by law enforcement officers. This program should also enable the spouse to ask top police administrators questions concerning the department's function, the officer's job role, and off-duty requirements such as attending political rallies, doing volunteer work, and giving presentations at luncheon meetings. There should also be an honest effort given to presenting a realistic view of the law enforcement field and of the problems encountered on the job.

Interview Programs with Spouses of Police Applicants

As part of the investigation of a police applicant, an interview could be conducted with his wife at home to help determine the compatibility of the couple and their lifestyle to a law enforcement career. This interview should be only one determinant in the selection of law enforcement personnel because most pressures in law enforcement careers that result in marital problems are very difficult to foresee. From this interview, police administrators can gauge the willingness of the spouse to assume the burdens of a law enforcement marriage. Similarly, the spouse benefits by being able to ask questions about the job that her husband possibly cannot or will not answer.

Ride-Along Programs

Law enforcement agencies should implement a ride-along program to provide spouses with firsthand observation and knowledge of the law enforcement officer's occupational role. This type of program also helps familiarize the spouse with the police organization and its procedures.

Programs in Firearm Usage and Safety

Programs should be designed to introduce spouses to basic gun usage techniques and safety precautions since many wives are frightened by the presence of firearms in their home. Instruction in the proper use and care of handguns should be given to reduce this stress situation for many couples. The spouse should be given opportunities to actually fire a weapon. Such programs provide the additional benefits of reducing the risk of a family member being accidentally injured.

An Exemplary Program

Dr. John Stratton, psychologist for the sheriff's department of Los Angeles County has written about a program for spouses that was developed within this agency. Of the over 400 wives participating in the program, it was evaluated as *Excellent*, 62 percent; *Very Good*, 38 percent; *Good*, 5 percent; *Fair*, 0 percent; and *Poor*, 0 percent.

Though the spouses deemed all segments of the program valuable, they mentioned some aspects they believed were especially beneficial: the feeling conveyed that the department values the spouse as an important contributor, that their fears about firearms were allayed because they learned safety techniques and how to fire a gun, and that they were given the opportunity to experience patrol in realistic situations as opposed to what they generally saw on television and in the movies.

The following are some written responses from spouses who attended the program:

It helped me realize that I was not the only one having problems. It rather relieved the tension that had been building up inside. It was nice to air out problems that others had in common with you.

It lessened the fear that I have for this type of law enforcement work. The more you know about something, the less you will usually fear it.

The friendships that developed among the spouses were really great. It helped make spouses more enthusiastic toward their husband's work, which in turn makes it easier to understand problems that might be involved with their work. Also I know that I now don't feel "apart" or "distant" from my spouse's work experience.

There are obviously no simple solutions to the complex marital and family problems that afflict law enforcement personnel. The kinds of programs suggested are based on the premise that the spouse who understands her husband's work, the nature of its responsibilities, and the types of personality and behavioral changes it may cause will be more supportive, patient, and understanding, thus increasing the possibility of a successful marriage.

Though these programs are extremely beneficial, they should be supplemented by marriage, family, and personal counseling services obtained from specialists employed by the agency or by referral from professionals in the community.

Organizational and Individual Programs for Coping with Stress

The many suggestions made for reducing stress or learning to cope with it include the following methods, techniques, and programs:

1. More efficient pre-employment screening to weed out those who cannot cope with a high-stress job.

2. Increased practical training for police personnel on stress, including the simulation of high-stress situations.

3. Training programs for spouses so that they can better understand potential problems.

4. Group discussions where officers and perhaps their spouses can ventilate and share their feelings about the job.

5. A more supportive attitude by police executives toward the stress-related problems of patrol officers.

6. A mandatory alcoholic rehabilitation program.

7. Immediate consultation with officers involved in traumatic events such as justifiable homicides.

8. Complete false arrest and liability insurance to relieve the officer of having to second-guess his decisions.

9. The provision of departmental psychological services to employees and their families.

All the methods listed call for a firm commitment from both the individual and the agency or department. In this controversial area, one thing is certain; namely, efforts toward increasing one's effectiveness in coping with stress are less successful in the absence of close cooperation between the individual officer and the department.

Summary

It is quite apparent that some stress factors are unique to policing; others are comparable to the sorts of stress encountered in other occupations and professions; however, their meaning and significance for the present account lie in how they interact with the unique stress factors in policing to create special problems in how to cope effectively with the total stress situation.

There is little doubt that some unmistakable trends are developing in the study and prevention of stress-related problems in police work. It appears that, in the future, we will witness a greater number of law enforcement administrators directing their professional efforts and organizational resources toward the creation of services which can effectively deal with job-related health and personal problems. The organizational changes that result will manifest themselves in a number of ways. We can expect to see an increasing number of law enforcement agencies implementing psychological and psychiatric assessment of police applicants. This will be done in part to screen out the emotionally unstable applicant. Further, we will witness a dramatic increase in the number of law enforcement agencies that will make available to their personnel and their families inhouse professional mental health specialists as well as referral services to community-based mental health specialists. We will also see a greater number of inservice training courses on this subject for both patrol officers and supervisors to assist them in recognizing and coping with job stress and the ancillary physical and psychological conditions associated with it.

This trend towards greater organizational sensitivity is indeed a welcome change and certainly long overdue. Hopefully it will result in the reduction of alcohol-related problems, suicide, marital and other family problems, and premature retirements. In the final analysis the police officer, his family, and the organization will be the beneficiaries.

CRITICAL LIFE EVENTS SCALE
FOR LAW ENFORCEMENT*

Over the last several years, society in general and a number of professional fields in particular have shown an increasing concern over the concept and visible manifestations of stress, especially those arising from one's occupation. Among the professions where stress has been a special concern is law enforcement. As Burgin has summarized:

> ...From the perspective of the individual officers, stress manifests itself in physiological problems, such as heart disease, alcoholism, and other stress-related disorders. Psychological disorders and emotional instability are also outcomes of stress, as are broken marriages, overt verbal and/or physical hostility toward the public, and, in the extreme, suicide by the police officers.
>
> From the perspective of the police organization, stress takes its toll through: (a) losses of police officer efficiency, (b) complaints from the public, (c) lawsuits resulting from police malpractice, (d) compensation claims, (e) disability retirements, and (f) from burned-out personnel in supervisory and management positions who create still more stress in their subordinates, peers and commanding officers.

Inventories of Stressful Life Events

Since the effects of police stress pose such a serious problem for the law enforcement profession and particularly its administrators, there should be a means to gauge the magnitude of specific stressors. Yet, no search on police stress thus far shows more effort devoted to discussions of the existence and nature of the stress than to an evaluation of its magnitude. In medical and psychological research into stress as it affects the general population, however, one can find scales designed to measure the degree of stress and subsequent readjustment caused by specific life stressors.

As a result of previous research into stress-precipitated illnesses, Holmes and Rahe held that "a cluster of social events requiring changes in ongoing life adjustment is significantly associated with the time of illness

---

* James D. Sewell, "The Development of a Critical Life Events Scale for Law Enforcement," *Journal of Police Science and Administration*, Vol. 11, No. 1, 1983, pp. 109-116. Reprinted by permission.

onset." Efforts by Holmes and Rahe and other colleagues have indicated a common denominator relating each of these events:

> The occurrence of each event usually evoked, or was associated with, some adaptive or coping behavior on the part of the involved individual. Thus, each item was constructed to certain life events whose advent is either indicative of, or requires a significant change in, the ongoing life pattern of the individual. The emphasis is on change from the existing steady state and not on psychological meaning, emotion, or social desirability.

Because prior studies have only produced the number and types of events formulating this cluster, these researchers attempted to develop a scale judging the magnitude of these events. Using the Social Readjustment Rating Questionnaire (SRRQ) made up of 13 life events requiring adaptive behavior and arbitrarily assigning 1 (marriage) a score of 50. Holmes and Rahe utilized a sample of 394 subjects to rate the events on their relative degree of necessary readjustment. The mean value of the life events was subsequently formulated into the Social Readjustment Rating Scale.

In subsequent research, Holmes and Rahe were able to further utilize this scale to accomplish a more detailed understanding of the effects of stress on individuals. As Pilowsky (1974, p.128) summarized their work:

> This scale was then used to obtain a quantitive assessment of changes in the course of life and to investigate their relationship to illness. A "life-crisis" was defined as any clustering of life-changing events whose individual values added up to 150 or more "life change units" in a single year. . . . Further work established a linear relationship between the magnitude of the life-crisis and the risk of changes in health. It was also shown that the greater the life-change score, the more severe the illness which ensued. This sort of finding confirms the oft made clinical observation that illnesses, whether predominantly physical or psychological, occur in clusters, usually following a series of changes in life.

Since its development, the Social Readjustment Rating Scale of Holmes and Rahe has been applied to a variety of populations including Japanese, black, Mexican, and white Americans, Danes, Western Europeans, Swedes, medical students, and New Zealanders. In most of these studies, the researchers found that, when compared with the original Holmes-Rahe sample, their research "indicated essential similarities in their attitude towards life events, but with some interesting differences which reflect cultural variation." In criticism of the original study, however, several researchers noted that its major limitation "is its failure to discriminate between positive and negative events."

The relationship between illness onset and significant stressful events has been further documented by the research of Antonovsky and Kats, who found a significant relationship between the crisis score of patients and the onset of multiple sclerosis; by Brown and Birley, who contended that "both first and subsequent acute schizophrenic attacks were at times produced by clear-cut crises and life changes which most commonly occurred in the 3 weeks before the attack;" and by Cline, who found a significant relationship between the quality and magnitude of stressful daily events encountered in the training of officers in the armed forces and daily changes in health, attitude, effect, body biochemistry, and on-the-job performance. As a result of their study, Brown and Birley further suggested that the additive effects of stress events may be of particular concern in emotional disturbances and onset of illness.

Based on these research efforts, the development of a professional stressful life event scale can be hypothesized to be useful in dealing with stress in the law enforcement profession for two primary reasons. First, it should allow administrators and researchers to analyze and assess the stressful events faced by a law enforcement officer. Second, in its refined state, it should allow for better prediction and control of crisis points in an officer's life; those occasions where a buildup of stressful life events will adversely affect his ability to fulfill his occupational role.

Development of the Survey Instrument

The procedures utilized by Holmes and Rahe, that is, the compilation of a list of critical events, the assignment of stress values to these events by a study group, and the ranking of these events as a result of their mean values, would appear to be a logical approach to the development of a professional life events scale in law enforcement. Where Holmes and Rahe drew on their experience in psychiatry to develop the initial list of critical events, this research employed another method as being more empirically sound.

Early in the research process and in response to the criticism that the Holmes-Rahe Scale was not comprehensive enough, it was recognized that a large group of law enforcement officers, drawing from their diverse professional backgrounds, educational levels, and personal skills, could better provide a listing of stressful events than could a single researcher relying on limited experience and research. Thus, an open-ended questionnaire was designed and distributed to an initial survey group. The first part of that instrument gathered basic demographic information from each respondent; the second part asked the respondent to "list specific occupational events...that you see as the most positively and/or negatively stressful upon today's law enforcement officer." It was further emphasized in the instructions that the respondent need not have experienced any of the events which were listed.

This questionnaire was administered to 3 distinct groups of law enforcement officers: 250 officers attending a session of the FBI National Academy; 37 officers of a university public safety agency; and 49 members of a predominantly rural sheriff's department. Although each group may be viewed as a sample of convenience, specific reasons existed for the choice of each.

The FBI National Academy can be viewed as a logical selection for the administration of the initial questionnaire for several reasons. First, it houses under one roof, and within relatively easy access, a large number of potential respondents (250 officers per session). Second, the officers at each 11-week session are at least 5-year veterans who, from either personal experience or observation, should have a reasonably strong understanding of the specific problems which confront a contemporary police officer. Third, because attendees are selected from federal, state, and local agencies throughout the country, the sample offers a broad spectrum of the law enforcement profession in terms of age, race, education, size and types of department, professional expertise, and time in service and, consequently, should allow for the development of a more inclusive list of professional life events.

Yet the strong points of the FBI National Academy also foster its weaknesses. It is a highly selective school, both from the perspective of the agency nominating a candidate for its training and of the Federal Bureau of Investigation in its procedures for final selection of attendees. The criteria used for selection of attendees may, therefore, bias the list of stressful life events. This research assumed, however, that the size of the sample and the broad experiential level of the officers in attendance would reduce the effects of the academy's selectivity and allow for an adequate list of critical life events in the working world of a police officer; as a result, it closely parallels the approach used in an experience survey described by Selltiz (1959, pp. 55-9).

The university public safety department and sheriff's department were chosen for several reasons. First, both were easily accessible to the researcher. Second, the use of both allowed further input from the members of two specialized agencies on specific areas of stress they experienced. Third, the use of these agencies allowed some comparison and contrast with the responses from the more elite group of officers attending the FBI National Academy. Finally, particularly in the case of the university agency, a high return rate and a significant amount of quantifiable information were expected.

Of the preliminary questionnaires distributed, 281 (83.6 percent) were returned and utilized. As a result of the specific stressors identified by respondents on the initial questionnaire, and based in some measure on the researcher's experience as a law enforcement officer, a list of 130 items was developed for inclusion in the list of Critical Professional Life Events. Subsequent to the development of this listing of events, a variety of academic and professional law enforcement personnel reviewed the questionnaire for its content validity. With the input provided by this informal panel of judges, the listing was expanded to 144 events and prepared in full questionnaire form for distribution. To overcome another major criticism of the Holmes-Rahe instrument, the items of this scale were placed in order by the use of a table of random numbers, hopefully reducing the clustering of serious events at the beginning of the questionnaire.

Final Survey Instrument and Sample Selection

The final survey instrument included both a request for demographic information and the list of 144 Critical Professional Life Events. Respondents were instructed to rate each event from 1 to 100 in terms of professional stress readjustment in comparison with a designated constant event ("changing work shifts") with an assigned value of 50. For the purpose of this study, and based on the working of the Holmes-Rahe instrument instructions, stress readjustment in one's profession was defined as "the amount and duration of change in one's accustomed pattern of work resulting from various job-related events. . .it measures the intensity and length of time necessary to adjust to an event within one's professional life, regardless of the desirability of the event." Respondents were asked to carefully read through the entire list, then assign a value to each event based on the proportionate length and intensity of readjustment required when comparing that event to the designated constant. As an additional study variable, respondents were further asked to designate those events that they had personally experienced.

For the same reasons discussed earlier, the FBI National Academy was again chosen as the site for administration of the final questionnaire. With the cooperation of the staff of that facility, 2 sessions of the FBI National Academy, each containing 250 officers, were designated as the study sample. The final instrument was administered by staff of the academy's Behavioral Sciences Unit. To provide an additional group for analysis and comparison, a Virginia county police department (N-270) was also selected as a study sample, and the final instrument was disseminated through its Research and Development Section.

In developing their stress scale, Holmes and Rahe turned to the field of psychophysics for the best method of estimating the intensity of stress readjustment. That particular method, magnitude estimation, "has been used to gauge the consensus concerning the intensity or degree for such variable or strength of expressed attitudes, pleasantness, seriousness of crimes, and other subjective dimensions." Following a detailed review of the use of magnitude estimation of social sciences, Holmes and Rahe recognized the geometric mean to be the statistic of choice as the measure of central tendency. Similarly in this research, the geometric mean of each professional life event in the law enforcement scale was calculated, and the scores were ranked in descending order of magnitude. Standard deviations were also obtained for each event in order to evaluate the variability of scores within the events comprising the scale. Based on these geometric mean values, a Law Enforcement Professional Life Events Scale was ultimately developed.

Respondent Profile

Of a total of 770 questionnaires distributed, 378 (49.1 percent) were returned and used in the study. The typical respondent from the total sample was a married, Caucasian male, between 30 and 39 years of age, and having at least some college education. In addition, the majority of respondents (73.3 percent) indicated they had not been previously married (that is, were single or currently married to their only spouse); 22.8 percent had been married once, and 4.0 percent two or more times.

Although extensive comparison data are not readily available, the personal profile developed here would appear to parallel law enforcement officers in this country. Contemporary American law enforcement is, as a whole, still a predominantly Caucasian male occupation, with college graduates a significant although increasing minority and with the majority of its occupational population under the age of 40.

Surprisingly, in this sample the percentage of officers (26.7 percent) who were divorced at least once was significantly below that found by other research into the police divorce rate in Tacoma (82 percent) and Seattle (60 percent), Washington; and San Jose, California (60 percent). It was more similar to that discovered in Baltimore, Maryland (17 percent); Los Angeles (21 percent) and Santa Ana (27 percent), California; and Chicago, Illinois (33.3 percent). This particular statistic of police stress may have been scaled downward by the use of the FBI National Academy to provide the major portion of the study population. Most agencies would, in the opinion of this researcher, choose their most stable, productive officers for nomination to the FBI National Academy; such a selection process, which would reward the successful police officer with this benchmark in his career, might necessarily reduce the number of divorced officers in this program because, as DePue has explained:

> . . . most experts would agree that a stable family relationship is a significant contributing factor to a successful law enforcement career, an unstable relationship would most likely have the opposite result.

Additionally, the typical respondent in the total sample had been in law enforcement between 6 and 15 years; was primarily in middle management (sergeant, lieutenant, or captain); was assigned to either patrol, investigations, or administrative functions; and was a member of an agency best respondent-defined as "city" and lacking a stress management program. Again, due to the selection process of the FBI National Academy, the percentage of officers assigned to patrol (29.6 percent), those with less than 5 years service (2.1 percent), and those at entry-level rank (6.4 percent) are probably significantly underrepresented. Similarly, those with over 15 years "on-the-job" (35.7 percent), performing administrative functions (27.8 percent), or in supervisory and middle-level management positions (sergeant, lieutenant, and captain) (59.4 percent) are probably exaggerated.

From a stress-related illness standpoint, over half (52.1 percent) of the respondents indicated that they had experienced at least one of eight stress-related illnesses; the most commonly reported were digestive disturbances (25.4 percent) and increased alcohol use (22.8 percent). This data was strikingly similar to that developed during the preliminary questionnaire, in which 52.0 percent indicated that they had experienced at least one physical indicator of stress; 26.1 percent reported digestive disturbances; and 19.9 percent reported increased alcohol use. Such information indicates a commonality of stress-related diseases between two distinct samples of police officers (total N = 658) and implies the validity of contemporary concerns about such manifestations of stress. The percentages indicating that they had experienced two particular manifestations—coronary heart disease (1.3 percent) and increased alcohol use (22.8 percent)—were lower than expected. The former was in all probability due to the physical requirements for FBI National Academy admission. The latter may be due in part, again, to the selection process of the academy and in part to the reluctance of many persons, not just police officers, to accurately respond to such a question.

Analysis of the Professional Life Events Scale

In its final form, the values of the Critical Life Events Scale (Table 1) run from a high of 88 for the most stressful event, "violent death of a partner in the line of duty," to a low of 13 for the least stressful, "completion of a routine report." The rounding of geometric mean scores resulted in the assignment of the same whole-number value to many events.

As Table 1 indicates, the events reflecting over 60 points on the scale, and consequently requiring the greatest amount of readjustment, were concerned with violence or threatened violence, personnel matters, or ethical concerns. Included in these events were also "police-related civil suit" and "criminal indictment of a fellow officer," events which would seem to precipitate high stress. One other event—"assignment away from family for a long period of time"—ranked higher (14) than expected possibly because the majority of respondents, those attending the FBI National Academy, were away from home for 11 weeks, the duration of the

Table 1—Law Enforcement Critical Life Events Scale

Event	Value
1. Violent death of a partner in the line of duty	88
2. Dismissal	85
3. Taking a life in the line of duty	84
4. Shooting someone in the line of duty	81
5. Suicide of an officer who is a close friend	80
6. Violent death of another officer in the line of duty	79
7. Murder committed by a police officer	78
8. Duty-related violent injury (shooting)	76
9. Violent job-related injury to another officer	75
10. Suspension	72
11. Passed over for promotion	71
12. Pursuit of an armed suspect	71
13. Answering a call to a scene involving violent non-accidental death of a child	70
14. Assignment away from family for a long period of time	70
15. Personal involvement in a shooting incident	70
16. Reduction in pay	70
17. Observing an act of police corruption	69
18. Accepting a bribe	69
19. Participating in an act of police corruption	68
20. Hostage situation resulting from aborted criminal action	68
21. Response to a scene involving the accidental death of a child	68
22. Promotion of inexperienced/incompetent officer over you	68
23. Internal affairs investigation against self	66
24. Barricaded suspect	66
25. Hostage situation resulting from a domestic disturbance	65
26. Response to "officer needs assistance" call	65
27. Duty under a poor supervisor	64
28. Duty-related violent injury (non-shooting)	63
29. Observing an act of police brutality	62
30. Response to "person with a gun" call	62
31. Unsatisfactory personnel evaluation	62
32. Police-related civil suit	61
33. Riot/crowd control situation	61
34. Failure on a promotional examination	60
35. Suicide of an officer	60
36. Criminal indictment of a fellow officer	60
37. Improperly conducted corruption investigation of another officer	60
38. Shooting incident involving another officer	59
39. Failing grade in police training program	59

Table 1—Law Enforcement Critical Life Events Scale

Event	Value
40. Response to a "felony-in-progress" call	58
41. Answering a call to a sexual battery/abuse scene involving a child victim	58
42. Oral promotional review	57
43. Conflict with a supervisor	57
44. Change in departments	56
45. Personal criticism by the press	56
46. Investigation of a political/highly publicized case	56
47. Taking severe disciplinary action against another officer	56
48. Assignment to conduct an internal affairs investigation on another officer	56
49. Interference by political officials in a case	55
50. Written promotional examination	55
51. Departmental misconduct hearing	55
52. Wrecking a departmental vehicle	55
53. Personal use of illicit drugs	54
54. Use of drugs by another officer	54
55. Participating in a police strike	53
56. Undercover assignment	53
57. Physical assault on an officer	52
58. Disciplinary action against partner	52
59. Death notification	51
60. Press criticism of an officer's actions	51
61. Polygraph examination	51
62. Sexual advancement toward you by another officer	51
63. Duty-related accidental injury	51
64. Changing work shifts	50
65. Written reprimand by a supervisor	50
66. Inability to solve a major crime	48
67. Emergency run to "unknown trouble"	48
68. Personal use of alcohol while on duty	48
69. Inquiry into another officer's misconduct	47
70. Participation in a narcotics raid	47
71. Verbal reprimand by a supervisor	47
72. Handling of a mentally/emotionally disturbed person	47
73. Citizen complaint against an officer	47
74. Press criticism of departmental actions/practices	47
75. Answering a call to a sexual battery/abuse scene involving an adult victim	46
76. Reassignment/transfer	46
77. Unfair administrative policy	46
78. Preparation for retirement in the near future	46

Table 1—Law Enforcement Critical Life Events Scale

Event	Value
79. Pursuit of a traffic violator	46
80. Severe disciplinary action to another officer	46
81. Promotion with assignment to another unit	45
82. Personal abuse of prescription drugs	45
83. Offer of a bribe	45
84. Personally striking a prisoner or suspect	45
85. Physical arrest of a suspect	45
86. Promotion within existing assignment	44
87. Handling a domestic disturbance	44
88. Answering a call to a scene involving the violent non-accidental death of an adult	44
89. Change in supervisors	44
90. Abuse of alcohol by another officer	44
91. Response to a silent alarm	44
92. Change in the chief administrators of the dept.	43
93. Answering a call to a scene involving the accidental death of an adult	43
94. Move to a new duty station	43
95. Fugitive arrest	43
96. Reduction in job responsibilities	43
97. Release of an offender by the prosecutor	41
98. Job-related illness	41
99. Transfer of partner	40
100. Assignment to night shift duty	40
101. Recall to duty on day off	39
102. Labor negotiations	39
103. Verbal abuse from a traffic violator	39
104. Change in administrative policy/procedure	38
105. Sexual advancement toward you by a citizen	37
106. Unfair plea bargain by a prosecutor	37
107. Assignment to a specialized training course	37
108. Assignment to stakeout duty	37
109. Release of an offender on appeal	37
110. Harassment by an attorney in court	37
111. Administrative recognition (award/commendation)	36
112. Court appearance (felony)	36
113. Annual evaluation	35
114. Assignment to decoy duty	35
115. Assignment as partner with officer of the opposite sex	35
116. Assignment to evening shift	35
117. Assignment of new partner	34

Table 1—Law Enforcement Critical Life Events Scale

Event	Value
118. Successful clearance of a case	34
119. Interrogation session with a suspect	33
120. Departmental budget cut	33
121. Release of an offender by a jury	33
122. Overtime duty	29
123. Letter of recognition from the public	29
124. Delay in a trial	28
125. Response to a "sick or injured person" call	28
126. Award from a citizens group	27
127. Assignment to day shift	26
128. Work on a holiday	26
129. Making a routine arrest	26
130. Assignment to a two-man car	25
131. Call involving juveniles	25
132. Routine patrol stop	25
133. Assignment to a single-man car	25
134. Call involving the arrest of a female	24
135. Court appearance (misdemeanor)	24
136. Working a traffic accident	23
137. Dealing with a drunk	23
138. Pay raise	23
139. Overtime pay	22
140. Making a routine traffic stop	22
141. Vacation	20
142. Issuing a traffic citation	20
143. Court appearance (traffic)	19
144. Completion of a routine report	13

FBI National Academy session. A relatively high ranking (31) of that event by the county police subgroup indicates, however, that such a family separation is still a significant stressor, regardless of the current situation of the officers.

The events receiving 35 points or less, that is, those requiring the least amount of readjustment after the event, can also be broadly classified as involving community relations, or legal/judicial, administrative, and operational concerns. Each of these events, such as duty assignments, overtime duty and court appearances, can be defined as "routine" and, with two exceptions, "award from a citizen's group" and "assignment to decoy duty," had been experienced by a minimum of 65 percent of each subgroup within the total sample. It is highly likely that the regular occurrence of these common events reduces the perceived magnitude of the stress which they cause; it seems apparent, then, that repeated experience lessens much of the fear and frustration which fosters the stressfulness of life events.

An analysis of the rankings by subgroup indicated that the Virginia county police department ranked its most stressful events, "dismissal" and "violent death of a partner in the line of duty," with higher values than the values assigned to *any* event by either of the FBI National Academy sessions. More Arlington County police officers (7.9 percent and 27.0 percent respectively) had also experienced these two stressors than had officers of the other two groups. It is this researcher's opinion that much of this perception of the magnitude of these stressors may be due to the particularly heavy emphasis placed upon both the "job" and one's partner by line officers, for whom the risk and fear of losing either is often perceived as more real and potentially imminent than by personnel who are currently in investigation, supervisory, and administrative positions.

During the course of developing the scale, the percentage of respondents within the total sample and each subsample who had experienced a given event was determined. From the total sample, these percentages ranged from lows of 2.9 percent for "accepting a bribe" and 3.7 percent for "personal use of illicit drugs," to 59.8 percent for the standard, "changing work shifts," to a high of 96.0 percent for both "work on a holiday" and "making a routine arrest."

The standard deviation of geometric mean values ranged from a low 1.0947 ("passed over for promotion") to a high of 4.4861 ("vacation"). A significant majority of events (130) reflected a standard deviation between 1.1 and 2.5; in only three cases ("pay raise," "overtime pay," and "vacation") did the standard deviation exceed 3.0. With the elimination of extreme values through the use of the geometric mean, this scale becomes more reflective than the arithmetic mean as a measure of social concensus and, therefore, a more reliable analytic tool.

Implications

The successful development of a scale such as this has a number of practical implications for the field of law enforcement. First, in a more refined state, it should allow police administrators and personnel managers to analyze the stress of their officers, predict times of high potential for negative manifestations of stress within individual officers, and take appropriate measures to control that stress. Second, it should allow for the development of more comprehensive and improved programs of stress recognition and management within law enforcement agencies. Third, it can be used as an instrument to better educate police families, public officials, and the general public about the concerns, frustrations, and pressures of the officers who protect them.

Perhaps more significantly, this research has several implications for future research. First, continued administration of the final questionnaire to groups of police officers in their home departments or in larger educational/training situations such as the FBI National Academy or the Southern Police Institute should allow for refinement of the scale values. Additional review of the list of events by other officers, particularly those in specialized enforcement units, can assure the inclusion of the maximum number of critical events, reduce the number of events with identical scale scores, and increase the applicability of the scale to a greater number of officers and agencies. Such continued research should produce a more accurate assessment of the stress experienced in law enforcement as evaluated by its participants.

Second, significant differences noted in the mean values of the responses of the county police department from the responses of the two FBI National Academy sessions would indicate the need for further study. Such research should examine the stress magnitudes perceived by officers of differing ages, sex, race, educational background, agency of employment, type of assignment, and time in service. Hopefully, such efforts would allow for better understanding of personal and departmental factors underlying the phenomenon of police stress.

Third, the interpolation of this scale with the Social Readjustment Rating Scale of Holmes and Rahe could allow for a more detailed analysis of overall life stress experienced by a law enforcement officer. Such a comprehensive scale would take into account personal and job-related stressors which contribute to physical and psychological upset and could produce a more complete understanding of the interaction of occupational and home-life stress.

Finally, this research will allow subsequent researchers to retrospectively examine the relationship between specific stressors and physical or psychological manifestations in a manner similar to the efforts of Holmes and Rahe, Antonovsky and Kats, and Brown and Birley. To that end, a close examination of the work history of officers who have shown diseases of adaptation may pinpoint specific levels of stress which contributed to the onset of the disease. Such research would allow for an increased understanding of the cumulative efforts of stress and its impact on persons in law enforcement.

MANAGING POLICE BURNOUT*

The complexities of tasks and the many demands, responsibilities, and deadlines placed on law enforcement officers necessitate that they be fully functional throughout the workday. Each is expected to be energetic and self-motivated. The very nature of the job requires teamwork, yet each officer should also be somewhat independent and task oriented. Due to this necessary teamwork, officers are constantly evaluating each other. While supervisory evaluations are important, most officers agree that acceptance by, and recognition of, their peers is the ultimate goal and the one that provides the greatest amount of feedback and, consequently, job satisfaction.

When an officer fails to function at acceptable levels the label "an empty suit" is often applied. Officers resent having an individual like this on their squad. This officer has, in essence, "retired in place." The officer's only crime, one obviously tied with the officer's survival, is the failure to formally advise the department. This reference to retiring is in no way intended to imply that this attitude exists only in certain, older, age categories. It can be found at any age and at any stage of a career.

In many cases, this lack of energy and/or interest in one's work is the result of a condition popularly known as "burnout." Burnout is a common affliction to those employed in the human services. The police profession, like many others, is laden with job-related stressors such as role overload, role confusion/conflict, and low job satisfaction. While being a helping service, officers rarely receive positive reinforcement from those they help or protect. They live life in "the high-speed lane," responding to calls ranging from domestic disturbances to homicides; child abuse to kidnappings.

They confront human beings who are emotionally charged and often at their worst behavior. The officer must respond, on a routine basis, to situations others would consider emergencies.[1] There is an image to

---

* James T. Reese, "Life in the High-Speed Lane: Managing Police Burnout," *The Police Chief*, Vol. XLIX, No. 6, June 1982, pp. 49-53. Reproduced by permission of the International Association of Chiefs of Police.

1. James Q. Wilson, *Varieties of Police Behavior: The Management of Law and Order in Eight Communities* (Cambridge, MA: Harvard University Press, 1968), p. 24.

uphold and one must become psychologically hardened in such emergencies. Officers are not allowed to show natural human emotions such as fear, anger, or sadness while doing normal duty. This "image armor" becomes difficult to shed when worn so often. The police cruiser may leave the "high-speed lane" but the officer remains there emotionally, burning-out.

The responsibility to alleviate burnout and make this officer a productive member of the squad again is a management challenge. Discussed herein are definitions, causes, and symptoms of burnout, and some suggested remedies. A burned-out officer is not only nonproductive, but lowers the morale of the entire department. It is essential that managers accept the challenge and actively deal with the problem.

What is Burnout?

Burnout is much easier to observe than to define; however, a typical definition would include the following: "To fail, wear out, or become exhausted by making excessive demands on energy, strength, or resources."[2] Unfortunately, definitions such as this pay little attention to the emotional and attitudinal effects of burnout. Burnout often includes the psychological withdrawal from work in response to excessive stress or dissatisfaction; loss of enthusiasm, excitement, and a sense of mission in one's work;[3] and moving from an attitude of empathy to apathy.[4] It can be unscientifically measured by the extent to which a worker has become separated or withdrawn from the original meaning or purpose of the work. The employee begins to feel "locked" into a job routine, the joy of the job slips away, and there is a loss of concern for the people with whom one works. Burnout may be so gradual that the employee may feel nothing is wrong. The very nature and importance of the societal role of police makes the burned-out officers a major concern of managers.

Burnout has been referred to as a disease of overcommitment, ironically, causing a lack of commitment. The transactional definition of burnout defines three stages: (1) imbalance between resources and demands (stress); (2) immediate, short-term emotional response to this imbalance (strain); and (3) changes in attitude and behavior (defensive coping).[5] Burnout is in fact a counter-productive way of coping with occupational stress and emphasizes the use of intrapsychic defenses such as projection (blaming others), withdrawal, detachment (isolation of emotions), avoidance-oriented behavior (never being available), and a lowering of

---

2. Cary Cherniss, *Staff Burnout* (Beverly Hills, CA: Sage Publications, 1980), p. 16.
3. Ibid.
4. Jerry Edelwich, *Burn-out* (New York: Human Sciences Press, 1980), p. 164.
5. Op Cit. Cherniss, p. 18.

goals (to decrease the chance of failure). Police managers have a responsibility to identify burnout, determine its causes, and take remedial action.

Causes of Burnout

Burnout is one of many inappropriate responses to stress. The term stress refers to "the generalized, non-specific response of the body to any demand made upon it."[6] This non-specific response differs from one individual to another due to basic differences in personality traits, coping mechanisms utilized, and career-related goals and attitudes. Of importance is the number of stressors experienced by an individual or group and the duration of these stressors.

The time frame during which these stressors are experienced is also important, together with the perceived importance of them by the individual. A person serving in the position of a police officer, like others in law enforcement, is "required to handle many cases within a limited timespan. Investigating several cases concurrently, the detective receives numerous stimuli requiring work habits to be well organized and a masterful juggler of information. . . and, although working out of an office, one is continually thinking about cases. Ideals in solving cases are constantly with the detective. The office, then, is oneself."[7]

As a result of basic personality characteristics and career attitudes, many officers are able to handle this type of caseload without any problem while others look at the "juggling routine" involving their caseload as a hassle. This leads to discouragement and burnout.

Dr. Michael Roberts, San Jose, California, Police Department psychologist, refers to a primary personality feature of police officers as "responsibility absorption behavior." Dr. George Kirkham advises that this responsibility that the officers feel for people takes its toll. Testifying in Canada he stated:

> The police officer is unique, unfortunately unique in the whole criminal justice system in that he alone really has to confront the worst manifestations of human behavior as they are actually happening and as they are actually unfolding.[8]

Dr. Kirkham adds that the public expects all officers to be "super-cops," never emotional, always professional, never making mistakes, and always getting their man. In light of these beliefs, the

---

6. Hans Selye, *Stress Without Distress* (New York: J.B. Lippincott Company, 1974), p. 14.

7. John G. Stratton, "Police Stress and the Criminal Investigator," *The Police Chief* (February 1979), p. 23.

8. George L. Kirkham, testimony before The Royal Commission, Toronto, Ontario, Canada, 1/15/76.

public views "real cops" as woefully inadequate.[9]

Police departments, traditionally conservative organizations, are somewhat resistant to change, particularly by officer personnel. The term "change" has been used synonymously with stress. Law enforcement has undergone substantial changes which include, but are not limited to:

1. Turnover in executive policy-making posts.
2. Frequent rotation in supervisory personnel.
3. Policies regarding deadly force.
4. Adoption of affirmative action programs.
5. Perceived or actual lowering of entrance requirements.
6. Perceived or actual lowering of the department's public image.
7. Fluctuation in promotional policies and qualifications. Increased legal liabilities and civil suits.
8. Specializations such as SWAT and undercover.
9. Police unions.
10. Devaluing traditional police work.
11. Failure to adopt psychological services programs for officers.
12. Reduced manpower.

These changes (stressors), if they are perceived as threatening, all contribute as background sources for burnout in officers. Other stressors, which have been identified by officers on an informal basis while attending training at the FBI Academy are such items as public scrutiny, increased assaults on officers, budget reversals, limited range of income potential, lack of mobility, and lack of control of intradepartmental transfers. It has also been stated time and time again that there is no reinforcement for creative investigation in that it merely inundates the officer with paperwork, and excellence becomes expected, not rewarded.

The Symptoms of Burnout

"What's it all for?" "Why am I doing this?" "I hate to go to work!" "I have nothing to offer anymore." Statements such as these are frequently made by victims of burnout. They are not adjusting, or coping, well. They remain in a state of disequilibrium and strain to make it through the day. Often their attempts at coping are counter-productive. Studies have indicated that burnout correlates with other damaging indexes of human stress, such as alcoholism, mental illness, marital conflict, and suicide.[10] The alert manager may be able to intervene in a timely manner by looking for burnout symptoms. The many symptoms can be grouped in three

---

9. Ibid.
10. Christina Maslach, "Burned-out," in *Human Behavior* (September 1976), p. 16.

major categories: (1) emotional, (2) behavioral, and (3) physical.

Within the emotional realm of symptoms one finds apathy, anxiety, irritability, mental fatigue, and overcompensation or denial. The end results are officers who are restless, agitated, overly sensitive, defensive, preoccupied, and who have a great amount of difficulty in concentrating. These officers overwork to exhaustion or become suspicious paranoids. From the managerial standpoint, it is important to note that these same employees may become arrogant, argumentative, and insubordinate and hostile to orders and/or requests. Their feelings of insecurity and worthlessness have set the stage for their own defeat.

Behavioral indicators are often more easily detected. Among these are withdrawal or social isolation. These individuals are reluctant to accept responsibilities and/or neglect current responsibilities. They tend to act out their misery through alcohol abuse, gambling, promiscuity, and spending sprees. Much of this desperate acting out is a cry for help and should be recognized as such by managers. Administrative infractions such as being tardy for work, poor appearance, and poor personal hygiene may be observed. These behavioral indicators will be reflected in not only behavior at work but also within the family structure. This can lead to domestic disputes and child/spouse abuse.

The physical ramifications of burnout are extremely dangerous. The individual may become preoccupied with illness or may dwell on minor ailments. A manager may note frequent illness, monitored by the amount of sick leave taken, and physical exhaustion when the officer is on duty. There are many somatic indicators that include headaches, insomnia, recurrent awakening, early morning rising, changes in appetite resulting in either weight gain or weight loss, indigestion, nausea, vomiting, and diarrhea. These maladies are psychophysiological and are the result of excessive stress upon the individual.

Together with all these symptoms, the manager will see the employee's self-esteem dropping, and frequently, cynicism develops. Officers begin to feel and act like robots. They do as they are told, but no more. The manager is taxed to the limit trying to get a day's work out of the officer. Between the officer's depression, changing moods, and paranoia, the whole squad is affected. Due to this negative attitude, the officer may even feel guilty about collecting a salary. A responsible manager has an obligation to this officer, that squad, and the department to get the officer involved again. This is a difficult task and will not be accomplished overnight, but it is possible; burnout is reversible. It takes a mature manager, considerable thought, and some personal involvement to reverse burnout.

Coping Strategies and "Cures"

Prior to discussing possible remedies for the burned-out officer, it is necessary to understand the model of stress. An officer is confronted with a situation and almost immediately appraises it. Reaction is based solely on perception of the problem during the appraisal, and thereafter the officer's behavior is affected by this reaction. Thus, much of the problem lies in perception. A problem is perceived in the mind, analyzed, and then a decision is made.[11] A paradox exists in that perceiving situations in a positive, more favorable light, tends to alleviate stress and subsequent burnout. The more burned-out an individual becomes, the more negative and/or threatening the perceptions of situations; therefore, burnout is increased and reinforced.

Suggestions to remedy this situation begin with counseling. To motivate people in the work place, management must understand them, their values, and their motivations.[12] Managers should talk to the officer and attempt to assist in understanding the nature of the difficulty. The employee must be convinced of responsibility only for personal response to any crisis, not necessarily for the external factors that cause the burnout. Overload and/or overcommitment comes from outside—not within.[13] It is necessary to get the officer to recognize symptoms and to adequately cope, not self-medicate, drink, tranquilize, or withdraw. The manager in his role should move the officer from a helpless victim to an active participant.

In many cases change, while being a stressor, can be a very positive motivator. Even if this burned-out officer has been working the same types of crimes for years and is the expert, is it not better to energize the individual by involvement as a novice in something new than as an expert doing nothing? Another option is to let the officer use personal expertise to train other officers, perhaps recruits, in certain skills. Determine the date of the last in-service training program attended by this officer and find out possible interest regarding future training. It is important to note that change must come about in an orderly manner and not involve sudden upheaval.

In those cases in which burnout comes from trying to work off stress, suggest an outside activity or hobby to the employee. Emphasize the need for personal and family time as well as occupational time. The manager may suggest that the officer take a day or two off, or read some books on relaxation to help in decompression. It should be emphasized to the officer that failure to do this will not be viewed as employee failure to the

11. Walter McQuande and Ann Aikman, *Stress* (New York: E.P. Dutton and Company, 1974), p. 95.

12. E.F. McDonald, "E.F. McDonald Links Motivation and Incentives," *Training* (April 1981), p. 62.

13. Barbara Hendrickson, "Teacher Burn-out: How to Recognize it; What to do About it," *Learning* (January 1979), p. 38.

manager, but rather as self-failure.[14]

An important key to counseling in the work place is the ability to unlock the skills, attitudes, and motivations of the employee. Studies have shown that people are more diverse in their work values and motivational patterns than managers suspect.[15] A manager's success in determining what these values and motivations are and the ability to redirect and energize an employee will depend largely on this manager's counseling skills.

The term counseling, as it is being used here, may be interchanged with the term helping. While there are many theories, and subsequently approaches to helping, the manager in a police department will probably feel most comfortable with the client-centered approach. This approach "assumes that human beings are rational, good, and capable of assuming responsibility for themselves and making their own choices that can lead to independence, self-actualization, and autonomy."[16] This client-centered approach is founded upon an empathic relationship between the helper (manager) and the client (officer). It strives to allow the officer to experience spontaneity, genuineness, and here-and-now feelings.

Steps in Counseling

Most managers in the law enforcement profession are very familiar with step number one—initiation-entry. This step is an interview, a get-down-to-business approach of identifying issues and concerns. Counseling, however, adds a dimension to this interview technique. Rather than attempting to solve a case or learn facts which may lead to possible prosecution or other disciplinary forms of action, the interviewer/counselor must build trust, show genuine concern, and have some plan for helping the employee. With a proper initial interview, the manager should then be able to proceed to step two—clarification of the problem.

It is not unusual for an officer to present several different concerns or problems. The responsibility of the manager/counselor is to help sort and subsequently rank these concerns by priority. These priorities are established in concert with the feelings of the client (officer). By prioritizing the problems presented, step three—the structure for the helping relationship—becomes a natural involvement.

Having identified and clarified the presenting problem, the manager

---

14. Jay Haley, *Problem-Solving Therapy* (New York: Harper and Rowe, Publishers, 1976), p. 64.

15. McDonald, p. 62.

16. Barbara F. Okun, *Effective Helping: Interviewing and Counseling Techniques* (North Scituate, Mass: Duxbury Press, 1976), p. 96. See also Lawrence M. Brammer, *The Helping Relationship: Process and Skills*, 2d Edition (Englewood Cliffs, New Jersey: Prentice-Hall, Inc. 1979), pp. 52-66.

must now decide whether or not this is a problem in which help can be provided. If the problem presented is such that managerial skills are inadequate to help the officer, the manager should encourage assistance from another source. A referral such as this does not mean the manager has failed. Failure would be for the manager to pretend wisdom where it is lacking; to deceive himself by saying he understands the officers' values, beliefs, attitudes, defense, and coping strategies, as well as hopes and ambitions, when in fact he is doubtful; or to state unequivocally that the problem is solvable within the confines of their relationship. If the manager feels capable of helping, then this step includes stating clearly the limits of his assistance to include what he expects from the officer.

An intensive exploration of the problem becomes a necessary fourth step in those cases where the manager feels he can be of assistance in the resolution of the problem. While exploring this problem, the manager must continually assist in the development of trust, genuineness, and empathy, so that the officer will continue to feel free to explore self-awareness.

Following identification of the problem, the decision concerning whether the manager can help, and further intensive exploration of the problem, the manager is then at the final step—having to decide possible goals and objectives. Empathy becomes important at this point; it is not a helpful setting if the department's, or the manager's, needs are met while the officer's needs are secondary. In most cases, many goals and objectives become obvious. It should be a joint venture to determine which goals are feasible and what the conditions of obtaining these goals should be. It is also important to set immediate goals as well as long-range goals.

Once these steps have been fulfilled and goals and objectives determined, it then becomes the joint responsibility of this dyad to proceed at a reasonable pace in efforts to solve the problems. This manager/officer counseling model is not a new concept in police work.[17]

Of the many helpful suggestions possible to the burnout victim, they should include adequate sleep, exercise, proper diet, learning not to worry—to accept things one cannot change, and to always find something to look forward to each day. The employee should be encouraged to volunteer and be available for assignments and to attempt to continue personal and professional growth. Many times the manager may have to put these suggestions in the form of directives.

The emphatic approach is encouraged but does not always work with the burned-out officer. Often, the manager has to forcefully change the officer's position, attitude, or work structure in order to obtain results. A

17. Roger DuPue, "Turning Inward: The Police Officer Counselor" in Leonard Territo and Harold J. Vetter, *Stress and Police Personnel* (Boston, Mass.: Allyn and Bacon, Inc., 1981), pp. 304-313.

manager should also evaluate (if at all possible) whether the burnout symptoms are due to the problems of the individual or due to pathology of the working environment. If this can be determined, a more structured approach to the reduction of burnout is possible by concentrating on the appropriate stressors. It is important to remember that while many complaints will center on the department or the working environment as the cause of burnout, they may merely be scapegoats.

Conclusion

Thousands of intelligent, mature adults are employed in various law enforcement capacities at local, state, and federal levels. Thousands more compete daily for positions in law enforcement. More than ever, colleges and universities are teaching and/or offering degrees in the criminal justice field. Maybe the attraction is the fact that there are rewards in policing—satisfaction in living life in the "high-speed lane."

Prior to becoming a supervisor/manager, you may have personally suffered certain burnout symptoms. This can be very helpful and useful in your role as counselor in that you are able to empathize somewhat with the officer's feelings. You, however, as a supervisor are not immune to burnout. Burnout often becomes inevitable when the supervisor is forced to provide care for too many people. Managerial burnout is also treatable.[18] Perhaps it would be beneficial for you to reread this article with your personal situation in mind. *Remember, the best defense against burnout is personal growth.*

A great majority of law enforcement officers are self-motivated and believe that the reward of a job done well is to have done it. Yet, some officers still need assistance and guidance. Using the information provided herein, a manager can assist a squad to become more productive and satisfied. The benefits are many: people will begin, once again, to look forward to going to work; less time will be lost on sick leave; the squad will be rejuvenated and become more productive; your job will become easier as you act as a monitor rather than an initiator; and finally, your squad, and subsequently the department, will become a more efficient and better place to work.

---

18. Mark B. Sibler, "The Burned-out Manager: Hidden Organization Cost," *Pace Magazine* (Sept./Oct. 1978), pp. 14-17.

COPING WITH STRESS*

Law enforcement officers have had a number of occupationally related health problems throughout their history. With the use of automobiles and the fast-paced society, more health problems have arisen that could be attributed to the occupation. Authors such as Kroes (1976), Reiser, and Hageman have tried to categorize the various stressors. In this article, then, we are not so concerned with adding to the already growing list of stressors, but rather with identifying preventive measures that will help one to better manage the stressful moments. In this manner, then, one's health is healthier and one's life might be prolonged.

Physical Conditions

The physical condition of the officer should be a concern for the police administrator and for city officials who fund the operations. Sick leave, training costs for replacement officers, and disability payments are just a few of the more obvious cost factors. Other less obvious spin-offs are accident proneness, higher disciplinary actions, and general ineffectiveness. The general principle is people who are not feeling well do not act well and find it more difficult to be kind and considerate to others.

Stress is a condition of the occupation. Some stressors are controllable and some are not. One fact has been consistent in the earlier literature done by Cruse and Rubin and Grencik and Snibble. That is, the officer who is in good physical condition will have fewer health-related problems and will be better able to handle the situations that are stressful.

We believe the answer to the problem is adaptability to present situations. For instance, what good are big muscles to a supervisor who sits behind a desk all day when a sudden high-stress situation arises and a heart attack is suffered. The same events could be illustrated in a patrolman's situation time and time again. You have little control over your hours and the situations thrown at you, but you do have control over your body and how it functions.

Most physical fitness programs imply muscle strength. In reality, there

---

* Mary Jan Hageman, Robert B. Kennedy, and Norman Price, "Coping With Stress," *The Police Chief*, Vol. XLVI, February 1979. Reprinted by permission.

are three different kinds of physical fitness: (1) endurance, (2) flexibility, and (3) muscular strength.

Endurance should be considered a very important aspect of a physical fitness program. The officer may sit in the car or engage in other activities that require little exertion for long periods of time. The officer then may suddenly be required to chase a suspect on foot or engage in other activities that place strain on the heart and lungs. This type of activity is hard on the officer who is not in good physical condition.

Many activities are available to build up endurance. Any activity or sport that includes running or walking will help. Some of these activities include swimming, jogging, bicycle riding, golf, tennis, and walking. Jogging is one of the best exercises and one of the easiest to utilize. Yet 10 minutes of jumping rope is comparable to 30 minutes of jogging; plus, one can jump anywhere—even in an office. Walking briskly through a hilly area can provide almost as much exercise as jogging an equal distance. Walking, jumping rope, and jogging are exercises that require little expense compared to many other exercises. The only expense is for proper clothing which should include a good pair of shoes designed for running and a sweatsuit or shorts, depending on weather conditions. Space for these activities can be in a park, on sidewalks, or even up-and-down stairs in the stair-wells. All of these mentioned methods are good for almost all parts of the body. They are particularly good for the lungs as they increase lung capacity. The heart is also strengthened. Most of the muscles in the body are used and strengthened, especially the leg and lower body muscles. While the average heart rate is 70-80 beats per minute, the trained athletic individual's rates are as low as 30-40 per minute. The purpose of endurance exercises is to make the heart beat faster during exercises so that your body will lower the resting heart rate and thereby use less energy when it is not needed.

To test yourself, immediately following your exercising, wait one minute. Then, take your pulse. A good indicator of present level of fitness is the speed with which your pulse drops to normal after exercise. The pulse rate, therefore, should have dropped at least 10 beats. The quicker the heart rate drops after exercise, the better the physical condition.

Flexibility

Exercises to increase *flexibility* can be helpful in preventing lower back problems. They will allow the body to flex more and decrease back problems caused by sudden movements or twisting the body. These exercises are too numerous to attempt to list. Different exercises are necessary for different muscles and are illustrated in many good books.

Patrol officers and staff officers can do much to prevent lower back and neck disorders by following just a few simple rules. Try to reduce the sway or curvature of the spine when standing by consciously keeping the back straight. Stand when possible instead of sitting; however, long periods of standing "at attention" cause severe strain on the lower back. Long periods of standing should be done with one knee bent, preferably on a step or rail to ease the pressure on the lower back. If this cannot be done, one should occasionally get into a squatting position with one knee lower than the other. Using these suggestions will delay fatigue.

When sitting, attempt to have at least one knee higher than the hip and when possible, put feet up with knees bent. Officers in cars have a tendency to ride with the seat so far back that it creates a semi-reclining position which causes swaying of the lower back and the neck. Operate your vehicle with the seat forward enough so as to elevate the knees above the hips and thus cause the lower back to straighten. When dismounting the vehicle, swivel in the seat, and place both feet on the ground, and bend over to get out of the car.

When sleeping, you should avoid lying on your back or on your stomach as this causes swaying of the back and undue bending of the neck with resultant pressure on nerves in the spine. Sleeping should be accomplished by lying on one side with the knees drawn up which facilitates a straight-line effect on the spine. If sleep can only be accomplished on the back, pillows should be placed under the knees to elevate them enough to cause the spine to be flat on the bed.

One of the worst stresses on the back comes when you keep going after you are extremely tired. The back needs rest just as any other part of the body; if you burn the candle at both ends, the body will move from Selye's reaction stage to the exhaustion stage where, according to Selye, disks collapse and death ensues. The general rule is that proper exercise for strengthening the back is to keep loose flexibility. Constant stress causes tightening of back muscles and results in pain or a tight discomfort. Stretching exercises and sit-ups can help. Stretching exercises loosen up the back and sit-ups tighten the stomach and relieve pressure on the back.

Any back discomfort should not be disregarded as it could be a sign of big problems. When backache or pain in either or both legs or arms persists, contact your physician immediately. If back problems are corrected early, surgery or other drastic measures can be avoided.

If back problems from stress or overexertion (distress) become so serious that surgery is required, one can plan on six weeks to three months recovery time for light duty, and possibly a year to eighteen months for full recovery. Obviously, your back and the care you give it is not a minor thing.

Muscular Strength

Tests used by most police departments that have a physical fitness program are not of a type to accurately reflect an officer's physical ability to perform the necessary tasks related to the job or one's physical health. The testing that is done is usually testing of strength or of weight in relation to height.

Muscular strength above normal is not as important to the police officer as the other two areas of endurance and flexibility. If the officer wants to build up muscle strength, weight lifting is one of the best methods. Caution should be used in this type of program as overdevelopment can cause loss of some of the necessary flexibility. This does not mean that muscular strength is not important. Rather *physical fitness to us means adaptability, flexibility, accompanied by reasonable physical strength.*

Physical Fitness Programs

Most departments have some type of physical testing program on a one-time basis for hiring purposes; however, it is not continued past that point. We would urge department heads to pursue a physical fitness program with some sort of incentive to keep officers active physically throughout the ranks, with variations geared toward age and tasks. It is usually assumed that rookie officers stay in shape to perform their duties, but no program is available to assure that officers do so.

Programs for patrol officers should include more physical strength, muscle and back flexibility than staff officers. Staff officers should pursue exercise aimed at strengthening the cardiovascular function-endurance. Exercises such as walking, jogging, bicycling, and swimming are especially good for this purpose, but should be done sensibly and preferably after consulting a physician, especially if a long period of nonexercise has been the problem.

The officer starting an exercise program should use caution by entering the program gradually and not overexert. Overexertion can cause a heart attack or other serious illness. It is important to pace oneself so as to gradually build up one's system.

Incentive programs can be offered in the form of a punishment or reward system. Promotions or pay increases could be held up until the officer meets the standards. The officers could be offered a pay incentive for continuing a physical fitness program. No type of incentive system will work unless the officer can be motivated in some way to want to participate in the program. Educating officers and their spouses about pressures and techniques for coping with this distress might be part of the groundwork necessary to accomplish this task of personal motivation.

Another method of obtaining involvement in a physical fitness program is group participation at set times. This type of program works extremely well for recruit training classes since the recruits are all available at the same time without having to disregard other duties, but it can also be adapted for officers after graduation from recruit school. The department, for example, could assemble officers for group programs at the end of a shift and include the work in the "sweat room" as part of their job. Physical exercise is a much better approach to relaxation as opposed to drinking beer after a shift.

Lack of facilities is a problem in most police departments. There is seldom available space or money to set up a gym or exercise room. This problem could be met by furnishing the officers memberships in the YMCA or similar organizations who might even donate the memberships for publicity and good will. Another solution might be to try to obtain donated equipment if the department has available space to set up the equipment.

Any physical fitness program should be flexible enough to be tailored for the individual officer. The three areas it should cover are *endurance, flexibility* and *muscular strength.* The program should be of a type that the officer can utilize the parts of it that fit his particular needs.

In short, any physical fitness program should be designed to *fit the requirements of the police officer's job.* It should not require elaborate and expensive equipment. It should include *testing* to check the officer's physical condition and should offer an *incentive program.*

Tests to determine a police officer's physical ability to perform the job should use basic physiological measurements rather than strength tests. Heart rate and blood pressure tests are a much more accurate measurement of the officer's ability to perform the occasional physical aspects of the job. They can also indicate how one will handle stress. Physical fitness is more than just feeling or looking good—it can also be an insurance policy. An accident, an illness or an operation may fully test the resources of one's body. It is probable that the differences between a state of positive health acquired by daily walking and a state of passive existence (although one is diseased) may mean the difference between living or dying when confronted with a major illness or operation.

Diet

Another important area in which officers can minimize distress is in the area of diet. If an officer's body is likened to a car, it does not make sense to talk only about body repair without talking about the quality of gasoline—the food. Police officers are faced with a raft of "junk food" restaurants on their beats. Their accessibility coupled with the short time allotted for eating makes it easy for officers to grab a doughnut and go on. Leave the "junk food" for the junkies. White-refined sugar and flour products cause the pancreas to produce more insulin to digest the food which, in turn, causes the same bio-chemical responses in the body as a state of fright; i.e., adrenals produce more adrenalin, thyroid produces more thyroxin, heart beat is increased, etc. Alcohol, coffee, tea, cola and chocolate also affect the pancreas in a similar manner. When your body is high on "junk food" and other chemicals, the body is "worn out" and finds it hard to manufacture the needed internal bio-chemical responses to successfully aid you through the on-the-job stress situations.

To reduce stress, we recommend a low stress diet based on three rules:

1. Avoid intrusive foods like white-refined sugar and flour, alcohol, coffee, tea, chocolate, cola;

2. Minimize the factory chemicals by buying natural foods. Many ice cream products contain a form of plastic or clay. Our bodies have only 22 enzymes to digest food. None of the enzymes can handle plastics, hence these undigested particles become stored in the body as waste and clog the system;

3. Reduce the number of different foods per meal. Choose only three different food items per meal, i.e., hamburger, tomato and lettuce. Just as too many people with their demands in one day wear you out, so does having "too many different foods." Your body must consume more energy than necessary in the digestive process, leaving you less energy to function physically. If you run out of energy but still function, you place undue stress on the body.

To accomplish a low stress diet, we suggest several things. First, carry fresh fruits, vegetables, and nuts or seeds with you. Fresh fruit juices, milk, and water are all good substitutes for other more harmful drinks. Try to find a good place to eat on your beat or district that can provide more natural foods to which no chemicals (even sugars) are added. To partially offset the lack of better foods while on duty, the officer can make a special effort to eat better during off-duty hours. A note of caution: As in other drug addictions, when one withdraws from foods to which one is addicted, side effects such as headaches, irritability, and diarrhea, may become more noticeable. These side effects are of short duration. Some people, in order to avoid the uncomfortableness of withdrawing from coffee, will continue to drink a cup of coffee in the morning for that "headache." If they would just endure a few days totally without coffee, they will find the headache completely disappears. When you have been riding in your patrol car through traffic, you can become gassed by the carbon monoxide and other pollutants in the air. When the demands are slower, get out of the car and walk briskly, breathing in for one count and exhaling for three counts. This will help clear your head and your cravings for "junk foods."

Conclusion

We have discussed *physical fitness* and *diet*: things you can control to prevent more distress in your lives and to help alleviate the present stress. Both fitness and diet should be included in a program of employee fitness.

Chapter 9
POLICE PROFESSIONALISM

Introduction

Professionalism has long been an elusive goal of law enforcement. During the last decade considerable attention has been given to this topic, making it possible to say, without equivocation, that many police departments are on the threshold of professionalization.

The capacity and ability to move beyond this threshold is undisputable; however, there must be a concerted effort to build on the present foundation.

The embryo of a profession was conceived by the father of modern police administration, August Vollmer. He developed the first formal training school for police officers at Berkeley, California in 1908, reaching an agreement nine years later with the University of California whereby on-the-job experience could be combined with an academic education. The course included technical subjects along with liberal arts classes, thus leading to the creation, in 1933, of a criminology major. August Vollmer then joined the University staff as a Professor of Police Administration. It should be noted that he subsequently held a similar position at the University of Chicago.

Sparked by the success of Vollmer's efforts, educational institutions in various parts of the nation established programs leading to a major in criminology; but generally speaking, the growth of educational programs for law enforcement has been slow and sporadic.

The President's Crime Commission emphasized the need for advanced education when it stated that, "the quality of police service will not significantly improve until higher educational requirements are established for its personnel...." The complexity of the police task is as great as that of any other profession, and the performance of this task requires more than physical prowess and common sense:

It is nonsense to state or to assume that the enforcement of the law is so simple that it can be done best by those unencumbered by a study of the liberal arts. The man who goes into our streets in hopes of regulating, directing or controlling human behavior must be armed with more than a gun and the ability to perform mechanical movements in response to a situation. Such men as these engage in the difficult, complex and important business of human behavior. Their intellectual armament—so long restricted to the minimum—must be no less than their physical prowess and protection.[1]

"The need for highly educated personnel was recognized as early as 1931 in the report of the Wickersham Commission. But despite the admonition of that commission to improve low entrance standards, educational requirements remain minimal in most departments."

In 1961, a survey conducted of over three hundred police departments showed that 24 percent of those departments had no minimum educational prerequisite, while less than 1 percent required any level of college preparation.[2]

In one region of the country, the New England States, over 72 percent of the departments surveyed did not even require their applicants to have high school diplomas.[3]

"Although minimum educational requirements have not prevented some persons with higher academic achievement from pursuing careers in law enforcement, these exceptions are few in number. In a survey conducted of 6,200 officers in 1964, only 30.3 percent had taken one or more college courses and only 7.3 percent possessed a college degree.[4] A 1966 survey of over 5,700 police officers employed by police agencies in the metropolitan area of Detroit revealed that over 75 percent of these officers had not attended college.[5] In the Metropolitan Detroit survey, it was further shown that nearly 13 percent of the officers had not received high school diplomas. In many departments, particularly in New England and Southern States, a majority of the officers are not high school graduates. For example, a survey of one Connecticut department revealed that fifty-three of the eighty-five sworn officers had not com-

1. Quinn Tamm, "A Change for the Better" in *The Police Chief* (Washington: I.A.C.P., 1962), p. 5.
2. George W. O'Connor, *Survey of Selection Methods* (Washington: I.A.C.P., 1962).
3. Ibid.
4. George W. O'Connor and Nelson A. Watson, *Juvenile Delinquency and Youth Crime: The Police Role* (Washington: I.A.C.P., 1964), p. 79.
5. Michigan State University, Institute for Community Development, *Police Training in the Detroit Metropolitan Region: Recommendations for a Regional Approach* (Detroit: The Metropolitan Fund, 1966), p. 69.

pleted high school."[6]

The importance of advanced education is also emphasized in Stephen Kennedy's remarks:

> Sworn personnel, who, in various unpredictable situations, are required to make difficult judgments, should possess a sound knowledge of society and human behavior. This can best be attained through advanced education.
>
> A superior officer of any police department should certainly be conversant with the structure of our government and its philosophies. He must be well grounded in sociology, criminology, and human relations in order to understand the ramifications of the problems which confront him daily. He must understand what makes people act as they do and what impact his actions in the performance of duty will have on them.[7]

A Bureau of the Census survey revealed the following about the level of education of the nation's population:

1. Of all persons 25 years of age and over, 69.7 percent had completed four years of high school and 17.1 percent had completed four years or more of college.

2. Some 58.0 percent of the white males who are white collar workers have four years of high school education as compared to 42.1 percent of the black males. White females with four years of high school total 77.9 percent of the population while only 56.8 percent of black females are categorized as white collar workers.

3. Only 1.6 percent of the population are illiterate.

4. Of all whites, 17.8 percent have four years or more of college education as compared to 8.2 percent of blacks and only 7.7 percent of Spanish origin.

5. Among persons between the ages of 20-29 (prime recruiting ages for the police), 86.3 percent are high school graduates or have attended college.[8]

Additionally, statistics obtained from the Department of Health, Education, and Welfare indicate that the national education picture is

---

6. *Police and Fire Services of the City of Meriden, Connecticut* (Chicago: Public Administration Service, 1962), p. 121.

7. Statement of Stephen Kennedy, former Commissioner of Police, cited in Franklin M. Kreml, "The Role of Colleges and Universities in Police Management," *The Police Yearbook* (Washington: I.A.C.P., 1966), p. 40.

8. U.S. Department of Commerce, Bureau of the Census, *Statistical Abstracts of the United States, 1982-83*(Washington, D.C.: Government Printing Office, March 1983). For more recent educational studies see: U.S. Department of Commerce, *Social Indicators III* (Washington, D.C.: Government Printing Office, December 1980).

not static. During the decade of the 1960s, the proportion of the adult population that completed a high school education rose from 43 percent to 60 percent. During the same period, the proportion of high school graduates who enrolled in college rose from 50.1 percent to 59.8 percent and it is anticipated that it will reach 65 percent by 1979.

These educational statistics clearly indicate that the high school level of education is a questionable standard for the selection of police officers. The high school level of education no longer serves as an index of superior educational achievement; it is common throughout the nation.

The consequences of such a selection standard in an era of increasing educational achievement are discussed in the American Bar Association's draft of *The Urban Police Function*. In this publication, E. Bittner is quoted as saying that the net result of maintaining a high school requirement in a period of rising educational achievement is that police forces are drawn overwhelmingly from those in the third educational and social quartile of the population. Yet many leading police and criminal justice administrators and other government officials have urged that the best human resources be recruited for the police service.[9]

The high school education requirement has prevailed for many years. Initially, it served to identify individuals who possessed a superior level of education and often those with above-average mental ability. However, this is not as true today as it was immediately after World War II. Department of Health, Education, and Welfare statistics show that less than one-half of the 17-year-old population had completed high school in 1946. In 1969, this figure had risen to over 78 percent. Obviously, high school graduation has become a less significant factor in hiring personnel. The police once employed only persons with an above-average education; today they are employing persons with an average level of education that is fast becoming an inferior level.

There are those, however, who argue that while the population has caught up with and surpassed the police educationally, police work still does not require education beyond high school. If they are referring to the use of police officers to direct traffic, issue parking tickets, conduct permit inspections, perform clerical work, and drive tow trucks, perhaps they are correct. However, in more progressive police agencies such routine tasks are rapidly being turned over to civilian employees, paraprofessionals, and other governmental agencies. Thus, police officers are left with their more essential task which includes social control in a period of increasing social turmoil, preservation of our constitutional guarantees, and exercise of the broadest range of discretion—sometimes involving life and death decisions—of any government service. The need for police officers who

---

9. American Bar Association Project on Standards for Criminal Justice. *Standards Relating to the Urban Police Function*, March 1972.

are intelligent, articulate, mature, and knowledgeable about social and political conditions is apparent.

People with these traits, according to Charles Saunders in *Upgrading the American Police*, are more likely to be found on college and university campuses. Those who possess the requisite personal characteristics are more likely to pursue an advanced level of education, and a college education develops and imparts the requisite level of knowledge. Saunders further comments on the value of a college education:

> The reasons advanced for college education for the police are essentially the same as those used to justify higher education as preparation for any other career. They rest more on faith than on fact. Evidence does not firmly establish the necessity for 4 years of college for entry into any field.... Nevertheless, the worth of a general collegiate education for all youth of intelligence and ambition is unquestioned and the role of the 4-year liberal arts college in providing it is generally accepted as essential.[10]

David Geary, the former chief of police of Ventura, California, instituted a 4-year college degree requirement in 1966, with appreciable benefits: fewer personnel complaints against college-educated police officers, a lower rate of personnel turnover, and an overall reduction of 3 percent in the crime rate.[11]

A study of the New York City Police, *Police Background Characteristics and Performance*, revealed that officers with at least 1 year of college were very good performers and had fewer civilian complaints than average. The employees with college degrees demonstrated even better on-the-job performance; they had low incidence of all types of misconduct—except harassment, on which they were average—and took less sick leave. Generally speaking, the older, better educated officer received fewer civilian complaints than the younger, less educated officer.[12]

These findings were similar to the results of the 1968 Chicago study, Psychological Assessment of Patrolman Qualifications in Relation to Field Performance, which revealed that the highest rated group of tenured officers were those with significantly higher levels of education.[13]

Raymond Witte, former director of the evening division of Loyola University of New Orleans, in *Police Chief Magazine* reported on an ex-

10. Charles B. Saunders, *Upgrading the American Police* (Washington, D.C.: Brookings Institution, 1970).

11. David Patrick Geary, "College Educated Cops—Three Years Later," *Police Chief*, August 1970.

12. Bernard Cohen and Jan M. Chaihen, *Police Background Characteristics and Performance: Summary* (New York: Rand Institute), May 1972.

13. Melany E. Baehr, and others. *Psychological Assessment of Patrolman Qualifications in Relation to Field Performance* (Washington, D.C.: Government Printing Office), November 1968.

periment conducted in an anonymous police agency. Two similar patrol divisions were involved, one staffed with college-educated police officers, the other with officers with less education. The 6-month study revealed higher morale among the college-educated officers, less time off in the experimental division, and quicker response time.[14]

Reports in the *Journal of Criminal Law, Criminology, and Police Science* have indicated that college-educated police officers are not only significantly less authoritarian than noncollege-educated police officers, but also less authoritarian than college graduates in other fields.[15]

The National Advisory Commission on Criminal Justice Standards and Goals in 1973 stated that to insure the selection of personnel with the qualifications to perform police duties properly, every police agency should establish the following entry-level educational requirements:

(1) Every police agency should require immediately, as a condition of initial employment, the completion of at least 1 year of education (30 semester units) at an accredited college or university. Otherwise, qualified police applicants who do not satisfy this condition, but who have earned a high school diploma or its equivalent, should be employed under a contract requiring completion of the educational requirement within 3 years of initial employment.

(2) Every police agency should, no later than 1975, require as a condition of initial employment the completion of at least 2 years of education (60 semester units) at an accredited college or university.

(3) Every police agency should, no later than 1978, require as a condition of initial employment the completion of at least 3 years of education (90 semester units) at an accredited college or university.

(4) Every police agency should, no later than 1982, require as a condition of initial employment the completion of at least 4 years of education (120 semester units or a baccalaureate degree) at an accredited college or university.[16]

None of the above stated goals have been achieved. Certainly we have more educated police officers than we had in the past, but when law enforcement is taken as a totality, the educational level of officers leaves a great deal to be desired if law enforcement is to become a profession.

One practitioner pointed out:

The police occupation has consistently attempted to achieve a pro-

---

14. Raymond P. Witte, "The Dumb Cop," *Police Chief,* January 1969.

15. Alexander Smith, and others. "Authoritarianism in Police College Students and Non-Police College Students," *Journal of Criminal Law, Criminology and Police Science,* Vol. 59, No. 3 (September 1968).

16. National Advisory Commission on Criminal Justice Standards and Goals, *Police* (Washington: U.S. Government Printing Office, January 23, 1973), pp. 369-371.

fessional status. Resistance to formal education within policing tends to undermine the approach to professionalization. Traditional law officers are sometimes apt to ridicule academic accomplishments rather than accepting them as improvements within their chosen career.

Our society is composed of many professions in which college degrees are prerequisites to entry into a field, with graduate degrees needed for advancement. High standards of achievement are expected from these professionals and there should be no less a demand on police officers.

Yet, law enforcement holds fast to the adage of a high school diploma or equivalency as an entry level educational requirement, without any further academic accreditation required while employed within the field. Conventionally, a requirement of two to four months of peace officer training has prevailed. Then these "trained" officers are sent into the streets to combat every imaginable cultural inadequacy. The officer is placed outside a familiar environment to stabilize an emotionally charged situation and required to become intricately immersed in the lives of those involved. This is a supreme accomplishment for any person regardless of occupation or educational background.[17]

Important as education and an appropriate climate are to the establishment of a profession, there are a number of additional considerations which must be met. The United States Bureau of the Census has established the following prerequisites: "a professional worker is (a) one who performs advisory, administrative or research work which is based upon the established principles of a profession or science, and which requires scientific or technical training equivalent to that represented by graduation from a college or university of recognized standing, or (b) one who performs work which is based upon science or art, and which work requires for its performance an acquaintance with the established facts, or principles, or methods gained through academic study or through extensive practical experience, one or both."

Amplification of this definition was provided by J. A. Greening, who listed the following elements of a profession:

(1) An organized body of knowledge, constantly augmented and refined, with special techniques based thereon.

(2) Facilities for formal training in this body of knowledge and procedure.

(3) Recognized qualification for membership in, and identification with, the profession.

(4) An organization which includes a substantial number of the mem-

17. Lloyd L. Bratz, "The Educated Cop: Some Perspectives," *Law and Order*, March 1983, p. 19.

bers qualified to practice the profession and to exercise an influence on the maintenance of professional *standards*.

(5) A code of ethics which, in general, defines the relations of the members of the profession to the public and to other practitioners within the group and normally recognizes an *obligation* to render services on other than *exclusively economic considerations*.

Professionalization is accomplished through:

(1) Prescribed course of study, standardized and geared to one another in high schools, colleges, and universities.

(2) Application of prescribed methods in practice teaching, reading, briefing, etc.

(3) Post-graduate courses, prescribed and administered if a specialized field is selected.

(4) Internship for application of theory to practice for the purpose of developing skill.

(5) Acknowledgment and acceptance of self-imposed ethical standards of professional practice and personal conduct.

(6) Examination to determine fitness to practice and enter the profession.

(7) Continuous study and research for improvement and advancement of professional techniques and their application within the profession.[18]

The definition of a profession and the method of attaining that status provides a yardstick for measuring the present position of the police in terms of a standard of excellence. Outstandingly evident are a number of criteria that must be accomplished, including:

(1) Mandatory educational standards.

(2) Lateral transfer.

(3) Transferability of retirement credits.

(4) Ethical standards.

(5) Career development program.

(6) Certification of eligible professionals.

(7) Specialized literature.

(8) Continuous research.

*

The process of professionalism is in its incipience, and its attainment will only be possible if the police respond to the tasks at hand with zeal

---

18. J. A. Greening, "Report of the Committee on Professionalization of Police Service," *Yearbook of the I.A.C.P.* 1938-39, p. 20, cited in V. A. Leonard and H. W. More, *Police Organization and Management, Third Edition* (Brooklyn: The Foundation Press, Inc., 1978, pp. 658-659.

and determination. There are numerous stumbling-blocks that must be overcome; the three articles selected for this chapter discuss some of the changes that will have to occur before law enforcement can achieve professional status.

POLICE PROFESSIONALISM: A NEW LOOK AT AN OLD TOPIC*

The ways man has endeavored to protect himself and his property is a truly interesting and fascinating story. Traces are to be found in every organized society of some system of rules for the maintenance of peace and order. In the days of the Pharaohs, as in modern times, a group of men were needed to carry out the laws of society.[1]

In 1829, Sir Robert Peel, then prime minister of England, introduced into Parliament a bill providing for the organization of the professional police force, later to become known as the famed Scotland Yard. This was the first real attempt to professionalize police. American police departments today can trace their origins back to the ideas of Sir Robert Peel.

The view of police work has changed very little since the 1800s. An early student of police administration wrote:

> It is certainly not necessary and some have even maintained that it is not desirable that police patrolmen be men of large intellectual ability... (It is) extremely unlikely that, for the present at least, any considerable number of men who have enjoyed even a secondary education will turn to the police business.... The most important asset of the ideal policeman is unquestionably his physical constitution and condition.[2]

While this idea was expressed several years ago, it is still shared by many citizens as well as policemen today.

Despite the belief of some, the police service has changed, and by its very nature, is continuing to change. There is a nationwide awareness today that the police officer of the future is concerned with problems significantly different from those of his predecessor. But, to date, efforts to improve significantly local law enforcement agencies have been met with frustration. Only a few departments can point to any real breakthrough in this effort.

---

* Richard V. Mecum, "Police Professionalism: A New Look at an Old Topic," *The Police Chief*, Vol. XLVI, August 1979. Reprinted by permission.

1. V. A. Leonard, *The Police of the 20th Century* (Brooklyn: The Foundation Press, Inc. 1964), p. 1.

2. Leonhaul Felix Fuld, *Police Administration* (G. P. Putnam's Sons, 1909), pp. 90-91.

Change in police work has been made with the idea of improving the overall efficiency of the police, which would lead to the professionalization of police. But what is professionalism? How have other occupations acquired the social recognition of being "professional"? Are efforts to professionalize police going in the right direction? It is not intended to try and cover the many obstacles in the path toward the professionalization of police in this one short paper. It is, however, intended to discuss the elements of a profession, a map, a guide toward the desired outcome. Just how did medicine and law and the other professions of our society become professions? Can we relate these thoughts to the police occupation?

A task or a job does not suddenly become a profession. In tracing the history of several professions, definite patterns can be established. Certain professional elements generally precede other professional elements. As a child must learn to crawl before walking and be capable of walking before running, jobs must also pass certain criteria before being considered a profession. As a result it becomes possible to determine a time sequence to the elements of a profession.

Time/Element Sequence

The contrast between planned and accidental entry into a job is depicted in *Figure 1*. As a job progresses and acquires the various elements of professionalism, the number of accidental entrants into the job decreases. The ultimate takes place at the Time/Element Sequence (TES) #7. It is at this point when all entry into the job is planned. An example of this is the person entering dentistry. An individual desiring to become a dentist must first successfully complete a four-year college program involving biology

Figure 1—Time/Element Sequence and Linear Progression of the Task Development Towards a Profession

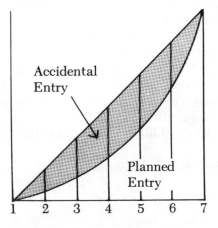

Percent of people (or entrants into a job area that is developing towards a profession)

Accidental Entry

Planned Entry

Level where all entry into the area is planned entry.

1 2 3 4 5 6 7

and chemistry courses while maintaining a grade point of at least 3.5 out of a possible 4.0. The competition is becoming much stiffer as many of the prospective dentists have completed their undergraduate studies with a 4.0, or nearly a 4.0 average. A four-year course of study in dentistry must also be completed and with the emphasis still on good grades and application procedures. After all the study and work involved in successfully completing eight years of school, the individual must now pass a state licensing examination and once successful, often he must go into debt to purchase the equipment necessary to perform in his occupation. It is indeed unlikely for an individual today to enter dentistry by accident. Can the same be said for police work?

Time/Element Sequence #1—The task-need-recognition stage. As shown in *Figure 1* TES #1 is the beginning of a job. The job begins to take shape as people realize the need for someone to actively perform various duties. The total job concept is far from being understood at this point; however, the basic job idealogy begins here. Law enforcement history reflects this, for as society began to regulate itself through laws, it became evident that the laws were of little value without enforcement. While societies have always had some kind of law, the key to establishing predictability within society is the enforcement of those laws. Thus, we can find law enforcement officers as early as 1947 B.C. enforcing the laws established by the Code of Hammurabi.

Time/Element Sequence #2—The definition of expected behavior stage #1. Though society realized the need for enforcement of their laws, little was known of the actual tasks involved in such a job. Because of the lack of a format, the first person to take a new job made that job for himself. It was up to these early experimenters to define the tasks and training needs. The lack of training facilities for a new job brings about the implementation of on-the-job-training and apprenticeship programs.

Training through apprenticeship and testing at the time of admittance to full membership were characteristic of the guild system. In the Middle Ages, surgeons and apothecaries, no more and no less than other vocations organized in this way, were thus trained and tested.[3] As the apprenticeship process continues, the beginnings of a small cadre of semi-skilled persons develops. With the advancement of knowledge and the raising of standards, the content of the courses of theoretical training will greatly increase.[4] Nowadays, apprenticeship is confined to practical instruction; and if there are no institutions in which the pupil can learn the theory, he must do so by private study.[5] Thus, apprenticeship is steadily losing

---

3. A. M. Carr-Sanders and P. A. Wilson, *The Professions* (Oxford at the Clarendon Press, 1933), p. 307.

4. Ibid., p. 375.

5. Ibid., p. 317.

ground before the universities and other training institutions.

Time/Element Sequence #3—The definition of expected behavior #2.
Persons on the job during this time are beginning to develop and collect a
common body of knowledge. They are determining the nature of the job,
and the job elements are beginning to be understood. Information about
the job begins to be collected and perhaps a job manual is prepared.
Figure 1 indicates the number of persons entering the job on a planned
basis is on the increase while accidental entry decreases.

Time/Element Sequence #4—The plan of study stage. The incumbents
of the job are beginning to develop a "plan of study" to prepare future job
entries as well as those already on the job. This is accomplished through
guidance manuals, seminars, local newsletters, or simply an exchange of
information between two persons doing the job. Education begins to play
an important role as police training schools and police academies are
developed to reach various new and improved methods of job techniques.
Training for the job begins to become formalized as it is introduced into
the public education system.

The advancement of a combination of education and training results in
society viewing the job more closely. As the appeal of the job increases,
there is an increase of planned entry into the job's labor force. Federal
and large metropolitan police organizations, for several years now, have
experienced large numbers of applicants for each police position
available. At the same time, the smaller agencies are having difficulties in
filling job vacancies with competent applicants. To say that education
and training are the only reasons for the discrepancies between the larger
and the smaller agencies would be in error; however, education and
training are found to be direct components of professionalism.

Time/Element Sequence #5—The restriction stage. As a result of society's increased recognition of the job, the quality of recruits is established
as a primary concern. Usually an organization or association is formed,
and the organization or association does the restricting. In 1852, lawyers
began restricting entry into their ranks with the Council of Legal Education, requiring that individuals pass examinations held by that body
before being called before the bar and accepted to practice law. In recent
years, several of the state's legislatures have enacted laws to provide for
police training councils. These councils are generally responsible for
restricting access of applicants into the police area, studying the duties
and performances required in police work, and advancing law enforcement toward a more professional stature.

During this time/element sequence, the job makes an impact on colleges and universities. There are several interesting comparisons which
can be drawn to illustrate the close tie that exists between education and
the professions. The most commonly identified professions of medicine
and law require extensive education.

While some may disagree with defining a mortician or a barber as a professional, both require licensing by the state and both require more education than most police officers must have. In some states, barbers are required to attend a barber college for one full year, pass the state examination, and go through a two-year period of apprenticeship. In order to be qualified to embalm the dead, the mortician must have the equivalent of an associate's degree, one year of a professional mortuary school, and serve one year in resident training before he may apply for the state board examination.

Education is an integral part of gaining the status of "professionalism," and if the police are to become professional, they must accept the requirements of some formal, higher education as a minimum standard for their occupation.

Time/Element Sequence #6—The control stage. Problems begin to develop as people who are not prepared for the job try to enter the field anyway. Thus, the restricting becomes more intense. A form of licensing is required of persons desiring to enter the job. The control is exerted by the state along with an association. There is also a noticeable increase in the public's requirement of accreditation or licensing of the person(s) entering the job.

Time/Element Sequence #7—The code of ethics stage. Thus far a system has been described which is designed to exclude altogether from the professions those who fail to pass certain preliminary tests. Such tests must inevitably be somewhat formal in character and take into consideration intellectual attainments rather than competence and integrity under conditions of actual responsibility. However, the quality of the service rendered is of the deepest concern to the client. He places his health and his fortune in the hands of his professional advisors, and he entrusts them with confidences of an intimate and personal kind. He is interested, therefore, not only in the technical, but also in what may be called the moral quality of the service.[6]

Enforcing Professionalism

It is unnecessary to study the charter or memorandum of every association, since they are very much alike. The more important unregistered professions have chosen the more important registered professions as their model, and have set out to penalize moral offenses, and not so much technical inefficiency. Chemists and druggists are examples of professions where people can be released from their positions for violations of technical procedures. The civil servants, such as police, are liable to be

---

6.   A. M. Carr-Sanders and P. A. Wilson, *The Professions* (Oxford at the Clarendon Press, 1933), p. 394.

dismissed at any time on any ground, and are subject to maintain a standard technical and moral competence. While observance of moral standards is of the utmost importance at present in police work, emphasis on the technical aspects in the police field appears to be on the increase. In the near future, we may find police officers being released from their job for the lack of proper technical efficiency as well as for the lack of proper moral conduct.

In 1957, the International Association of Chiefs of Police adopted a Code of Ethics for police. The Code is designed to provide police with a guide for patterning their professional behavior; however, in most professions there is the power to exclude from their ranks those who fail to conform to certain standards of conduct. While individual police departments may enforce their own departmental rules and regulations, these criteria cannot be brought to bear upon another police agency that does not have or does not enforce its own rules and regulations. Within the recognized professions such as medicine, dentistry, and law, an organization or board has been formed and given the authority to enforce the standards as set forth within their code of ethics. Punishment for performance considered contrary to the ideals set forth in their code of ethics is also decided upon by the organization or board.

A statewide police organization designed to represent all police in the state concerning the enforcement of a police code of ethics would require formulation by the state's legislature. This concept is not intended to punish a police officer twice for the same incorrect conduct. The strongest action the state organization could take would be to suspend or cancel a peace officer's state certification. Such action would prohibit an officer from performing police duties within that state for a period of time determined by the organization.

The seven stages of professionalism discussed above have taken a job from its conceptual beginning to a highly skilled and recognized profession. Time/element sequence #7 is not the end of the pursuit of professionalism. The professions are continuing to increase the requirements on individuals desiring to enter their professional ranks. More selective course requirements in college along with higher grades are evident.

Compensation

Generally, when the topic of professionalism for police is discussed by the peace officers themselves, money is also discussed simultaneously. The peace officer sometimes feels he should be compensated for his professional endeavors simultaneously with his professional actions; however, this has not been the case with the recognized professions of today. The increased compensation occurs after the attainment of the desired professional goals and public recognition of the professional advancements.

An example of this can be seen when comparing urban and rural police agencies. The large urban police departments, such as Los Angeles, Chicago, Philadelphia, and New York, have for a number of years supported and provided for police training and police training facilities for their peace officers. During this same period of time, the police agencies of rural America were receiving little if any police training. The urban communities are now beginning to recognize the professional accomplishments made by their police organizations and are compensating them accordingly. At the same time, the rural communities do not view their peace officers as being anything close to professional. They feel it takes very little skill to be a police officer, and the police are compensated accordingly.

For compensation of police to be increased to a professional level, the police must be considered totally as professionals. When the professional status of doctors is discussed, all the doctors in the country are considered with little or no thought given as to their location. A doctor in a rural area is as much a professional as the doctor in an urban setting. States providing law enforcement officers with equal accessibility to training, large and small agencies alike, are encouraging professionalized qualities of training throughout the state.

Several law enforcement agencies in the United States have demonstrated an advancement in their professional accomplishments and have obtained time/element sequence #6 while other agencies remain at time/element sequences #3 and #4. The opportunities for peace officer professionalization have increased considerably over the past few years. A greater attendance of law enforcement training is more prevalent now than at any other time in law enforcement history. The problems faced by law enforcement officers today are extremely complex and go beyond the skills required of his predecessor. It would appear, from all indications that today's law enforcement officer is on the verge of turning his job into a true profession.

INTEGRATED PROFESSIONALISM: A MODEL FOR CONTROLLING POLICE PRACTICES*

Since the establishment of the first police department in America, the public has intermittently been critical of the police. Police are periodically berated for both real and imagined abuses of their power and authority. Attacks on the police reflect the public's generally ambivalent stance toward its institution of social control. On the one hand, the citizenry fear disorder and crime (especially predatory crime) and recognize their dependency on the police for protection. On the other hand, the public fears the police, with its monopoly on force, and is particularly fearful that police power might get out of control. These citizen fears have historical roots which go back to our ancestors' experiences of subjugation by military and police forces in their European homes. In modern times, distrust of the police has continued as we witness political coups in other countries and the emergence of police states. Within our own country, concerns over police abuse are not without foundation—we need only consider disclosures of break-ins into private residences, spying and other criminal acts by the FBI, or charges against city police of brutality, beatings, and the murder of citizens.

Highly publicized examples of police abuse may represent occasional cases of malpractice; nonetheless, policing today needs to develop more effective ways to curtail its own illegal activities. What strategies might control and prevent police deviance? Do we need more punitive measures, more formal charges, and court trials; or is there a more positive way to approach the problem? Does professionalism offer a promising model to counter police deviance?

The police occupation frequently claims to be a profession. If we listen to police administrators, particularly those who speak for the occupation, we hear that policing has already achieved a certain professional status. Police rhetoric makes claims to professionalism, and it is that rhetoric that gives us a rough approximation of where police are in their actual professional development. The rhetoric depicts police interest in "acting like"

* Barbara Raffel Price, "Integrated Professionalism: A Model for Controlling Police Practices," *Journal of Police Science and Administration*, Vol. 7, No. 1, 1979, pp. 93-97. Reprinted by permission.

professionals, and it also provides clues as to how the actual professionalism can work for the occupation. In what follows, the potential of integrated professionalism for preventing police abuses and illegal actions will be described. Integrated professionalism means that professionalism prevails throughout the department at the administrative, management, and line levels.

The Problem: Instilling Self-Control in Police

By law, police are implementors of violent force. They have the potential to wield extraordinary power. Of all criminal justice actors, the police are the most powerful, largely because of the great amount of discretion available to them.[1] They can deprive individuals of freedom, and under certain circumstances, society permits them to injure and, indeed, even kill. Although we give these special powers to the police, we also want to control their use. The American Bar Association has said:

> The continuing failure to devise and implement necessary procedures and sanctions to deal with police abuses is one of the most critical problems now confronting our society.[2]
> [The] courts are ill-equipped to control police conduct.[3]
> The need is for more effective administrative control.[4]

If we are willing to accept the possibility that police, as an occupation, have the ability to control themselves, and if we can imagine them acquiring, or in some cases already possessing, the managerial skills to exert administrative control, then the challenge lies in developing a system of control over improper use of authority and in instilling in police an appetite for participating in that task. The need is for developing voluntary self-control in the police, and that is where professionalism's strength lies. Because professionalism actually promotes a system of beliefs supportive of self-control, it generates self-regulation. Professionalism fosters responsibility (both for the individual and the occupation); it fosters objective standards in decision-making; it puts attention on ends as well as means, and it promotes self-evaluation.

If we look to the professional model and the fundamental traits of professionalism, we see that for an occupation to call itself a profession, it must exhibit a unique and specialized body of knowledge that is written down and can be transmitted abstractly, a dedication to service, self-

1. Lawrence W. Sherman, "The Sociology and the Social Reform of the Police," *J. Police Sci. & Adm.*, 2(3) (1974), p. 259.
2. American Bar Association, *The Urban Police Function* (1972), p. 120.
3. Ibid.
4. Ibid.

regulation, performance neutrality, standards governing internalized decisions, and a code of ethics. In addition to these attributes, a mature profession also pays as much attention to the processes by which ends are achieved as it does to the ends themselves. When the role and importance of process is accepted by the members of an occupation, and when the reward structure of the occupation recognizes the process, then the issues of self-control and structuring constituted authority should become manageable.

Assume for the moment that the professional model is the appropriate system for control of police activity. To be effective it must operate in two fairly distinctive ways. First, the professional model must operate at the administrative level; and, second, it must be present at the line level. Each of the police roles will be considered separately as they affect self-regulation.

The Police Administrator

We know that external remedies to police abuses, such as exist through the courts or through government liability for officer misconduct, provide insufficient deterrence, largely because they react to an event rather than anticipate future events. The more immediate proactive strategies to meet the problem of police abuses have tended to be the responsibility of police administrators. Through leadership, they can (1) articulate clear standards of police conduct, (2) establish the necessary internal rules and procedures, (3) develop appropriate sanctions, and (4) set a climate of respect for the law.

One of the reasons that administrators do not aggressively control officer conduct is because the organizational structure of the criminal justice system works against it. As the system is organized, police must share their own self-regulation responsibility with two other sectors, the courts and political superiors. Where shared authority exists, it generally tends to be abdicated by all parties, but it is most often abdicated by those who view themselves as lower in the status hierarchy. The police consider themselves inferior in status to the judiciary. Their assessment is realistic, based on such differentials as salary, educational level, and public prestige. Until police administrators see themselves as the professional equal of others in government, they are unlikely to fully assume the self-regulation responsibility. The *Task Force Report: The Police* issued in 1967 by the President's Commission on Law Enforcement and Administration of Justice commented as follows on police deference to the courts:

> Unlike internal matters over which the police administrator has complete control, much of what the police do relating to crimes and

criminals is dependent for approval upon the decision of non-police agencies.[5]

As the police increasingly professionalize, they should also be able to increasingly deal on an equal basis with other sectors of the criminal justice system as well as with the political sector. Professionalism enhances one's self-image. As administrators' self-confidence improves, they will be better able to accept their role of controlling their department and will resume some of the responsibility which has by default fallen to other external control units. Thus, one way professionalism can indirectly control police practices is by improving the self-image and self-confidence of the occupation and its incumbents.[6]

Elsewhere this author has argued that a case can be made for progress in police professionalization over the last 100 years by using evidence from police rhetoric.[7] This rhetoric of administrators is especially visible when police defend themselves from a critical public. We hear: "Who are they [the public] to judge us, the professionals?" and "We are true professionals." Data exists that indicate police have become increasingly professionalized as measured by the broadening of professional interests from basic concerns about salary to attention to the technology of policing to, most recently, justifying the occupation's contributions to the social good.[8] Over the years the earlier police concerns remained, and new ones have been added so that the rhetoric has become increasingly rich, diverse, and sophisticated. But by whatever yardstick we care to use, there is no doubt that the professionalizing process is accelerating. In the last decade, there has been a substantial increase in the body of special knowledge; training has become longer and more complex; higher educational standards are being imposed at entrance. Police rhetoric reflects all of these changes, and it is freely used by chiefs.

Professionalism rhetoric plays a positive role for the police as a response to criticism. It helps to protect the occupation. However, it is also the case that the rhetoric had, and still has today, serious dysfunction; it enables

---

5. President's Commission on Law Enforcement and Administration of Justice, *Task Force Report: The Police* (1967), p. 193.

6. The danger of partial professionalization has been demonstrated in the case of the FBI. For years the organization fostered a professional image which the public believed. FBI rhetoric was that of the professional, but it had not adopted the behavior of professionals. Members neither accepted individual responsibility for their actions, nor did they have sufficient independence to act with "right conduct." However, the public acknowledged their professionalism and had confidence in the organization. As a result, the FBI was permitted an enormous amount of autonomy.

7. Barbara R. Price, "The Rhetoric of Professionalism: A Comparative Study of Police in Three Historical Periods" (Ph.D. diss., Pennsylvania State University (1974), and *Police Professionalism: Rhetoric and Action* (1977).

8. R. M. MacIver, "The Social Significance of Professional Ethics," *Annals of the Am. Acad. of Pol. & Soc. Sci.*, p. 297 (1955), p. 118-124.

police leadership to limit reform. By talking in ways that are acceptable to their superiors in the political sector, and by reassuring their own subordinates of their professionalism, police are able to substitute words for action. In effect, in rhetoric, the status of professionalism was assumed by the police administrator long before the reality of professionalism existed. In addition to this negative consequence of the rhetoric, many aspects of professionalism, described in the next section, lead to resistance from administrators.

Ways the Professional Model Can Control Police Practices: The Line Level

Professionalism encourages utilization of discretion by the street officer. It fosters lower-level decisionmaking, because training and education are high priority items in the professional model. Once people have been trained and socialized for a job, they expect to be given the opportunity to use their skills. In law enforcement, operations-level work involves continuous decisionmaking. Citizen calls for service require fresh determination by the officer as each event occurs. The professional model anticipates that substantial discretion and authority will be exercised by the line level and that these professionals will have internalized, through socialization and training, skill in making legal and appropriate responses to citizens.

In conjunction with expanded line-level discretion, professionalism encourages rolemaking by subordinates rather than the more traditional roletaking from the organization. In rolemaking, work expectations are defined more by the officer than the department, which means the burden of responsibility for these activities is on the line level. Team policing enhances this aspect of professionalism in that each team develops special definitions of tasks to be accomplished and objectives to be met. Decentralization, through giving teams authority, requires that a greater degree of accountability be assigned to officers.

Further, professionalism can control police practices because it undermines organizational loyalty of police by encouraging members of the occupation to identify with the larger occupation. As this occurs, incumbents look outside the department for guidance and performance standards. This leads to the emergence of occupationwide standards; and, in turn, these standards reinforce the shifting of identification beyond the department and its own less rigorous standards. As police replace department norms with occupationwide standards, they tend to identify more with the sanctioning of abusive police practices and adherence to high ethical standards.

Another aspect of professionalism breaks down the traditional secrecy of the police organization by encouraging more opening up of communications within the department as well as with the outside. Changes in police practices (such as informing the public about crime problems and police capabilities to respond) can create changed expectations and eventually more realistic demands from the public. In opening up communications, it may become possible to develop interdepartmental review boards and other activities to reassure the public by giving clear evidence that police are, in fact, engaged in self-regulation.

Improved self-image, increased internalized performance accountability, more roletaking and less rolemaking, less loyalty to the department and more to the occupation at large, and decreased secrecy of operations are all ways that the professional model can foster control of police behavior. Administrators are understandably ambivalent about these changes because they undermine direct executive control and require placing greater trust in their subordinates. However, the line level can see the advantages in their own commitment to professionalism (1) as administrators support the changes in the context of providing appropriate training, (2) as chiefs establish sound systems of accountability for checking on performance and establish detailed descriptions of appropriate and inappropriate conduct, and (3) as they create a fair hearing and review structure for alleged officer violations. We know that the "right conduct" (i.e., abiding by legal and organizational rules) of the line level cannot just be mandated by administrative policy. Moreover, use of peer pressure and the setting of an appropriate climate by administration and even direct supervision cannot assure good policing given a dispersed command structure. But the professional model offers a promising approach to police malpractice because under it officers are socialized to conduct themselves within legal constraints. Concurrently, administrators must encourage and reward such behavior.

Only with line level acceptance of their role in controlling police abuse can police malpractice be reduced, and this can happen as the police officer accepts professionalism's demands for internalized standards of behavior, devotion to service, neutrality, and objectivity. The police officer will also have to accept the notion that the process of enforcing the law is as important as the enforcement itself. When officers recognize that how an arrest is made is as critical as the arrest itself, and when they assume the responsibility for the discretion they exercise, policing will be a profession. At the line level there must be as complete a commitment to professionalism as at the administrative level.

If it is the case that the officer is a key factor in creating an internal system for controlling police malpractice, and if that control cannot be assured by direct observation and supervision, then a model of integrated professionalism in which both management and line level are professionally committed may be the most successful control strategy. As the officer professionalizes, independence in decisionmaking will be guided by both a code of ethics and the systematic application of a body of knowledge.[9] This use of law enforcement expertise in conjunction with ethical standards means that police apprehensions will be lawfully executed and the potential of endangering other citizens or the police themselves in the process will be minimized.

Summary

Integrated professionalism implies that professionalism permeates the police occupation at all ranks. Administrators would still retain final responsibility for the conduct of subordinates, but under integrated professionalism, they would not be placed in the impossible position of sole enforcer of police behavior. The proposed model encourages a collaborative effort within police departments for providing community social control and protection through the responsible use of decentralized police authority. When police have a true stake in devising necessary procedures to deal with police abuses, the problems of administrative rulemaking and internal procedures will diminish.

This article began by noting that criticism of police in America has become virtually a chronic state of affairs. Breaking the pattern requires a new model with built-in incentives for reduction of police abuse. The model proposed here has these incentives in that it gives additional autonomy to line-level police while providing for its judicious exercise. For administrators it holds out the prospect of exchanging public dissatisfaction with their organization for public approval of both the department and the administration. Professionalism implies voluntary compliance; it holds promise for both technical proficiency in law enforcement and protection of individual liberties within a system of social order.

---

9. E. Mintz and G. Sandler, "A Service Model for the New York City Police Department" (unpublished, NYPD, 1973).

OVERCOMING OBSTACLES TO PROFESSIONALISM*

Much has been written in recent years concerning the vital need to improve local law enforcement, increase the compensation of police officers, and professionalize the police service. The President's Crime Commission reports have sharpened the focus on the need and have detailed the requirements for meeting it. This article summarizes the needs and the objectives, describes some of the obstacles to meeting the objectives, and suggests practical means whereby the obstacles can be minimized and immediate progress can be made toward major improvements in the police service.

The Changing Police Job

The police service has changed and is changing in its very nature. There is now a nationwide awareness that the police officer is concerned with problems radically different from those which concerned his predecessor.

Increased concern with the civil rights of all citizens, including criminals, has resulted in the need for each police officer to be highly trained in the legal authorities under which he operates and to be highly skilled in scientific detection. In the words of a veteran Manhattan detective, the newly defined rights of suspects "of necessity, make us resort to the sciences."

The requirements and complexities of the police function also increase as our social complex changes—that is, as we become increasingly conscious of poverty, mental illness, unemployment, racial problems, and other social ills. The police department is often the only governmental agency available twenty-four hours a day, seven days a week, to which people can turn for help in family disputes, handling problems with landlords and neighbors, resolving difficulties with youths, and mediating disputes among racial and special interest groups. In many respects and in rapidly increasing numbers of instances, the patrolman of today is assuming a dynamic role that in earlier times was played by the

---

* Carl F. Lutz, "Overcoming Obstacles to Professionalism," *The Police Chief*, Vol. XXXV, September 1968, pp. 42-52. Reprinted by permission.

family patriarch or ward boss. Cast in this role, the police officer is increasingly expected to exercise independent judgment, discretion, sociological and psychological skills in coping with some of the most complex social problems of our times.

TIME magazine has commented that while all this may produce better policemen, it also will require far higher pay than many communities have yet faced up to. The need exists, in this period, for a very high level of skillful performance on the part of law enforcement personnel in an area fraught with social unrest and legal technicalities—for the manner in which many of these problems are ultimately resolved depends in large measure upon the degree of public confidence and respect earned by the individual patrolman in the initial action taken. The demands on every police officer to meet this test are severe.

Nationally recognized law enforcement agencies state that the results of recent self-security by the police service and the implementation of the findings are gaining momentum throughout the country. One of the major results has been the trend toward more diversified police organization in which an increasing number of auxiliary functions are being performed by individuals less well-trained than police officers have to be, and in which the police officer is emerging as a professional law enforcer, equipped with a thorough knowledge of criminal and civil law and its intricate processes, skilled in scientific detection, and trained in human relations.

In the recent past, truly professional law enforcement positions were found only in federal agencies and a few in state and some large city governments. In these times the most serious and wide-spread law enforcement problems exist at local levels. The increase in crime on the streets has made it necessary for all local governments to face up to many more new and serious problems of law enforcement than they have ever before encountered. Local police, even in small suburban and rural towns, have suddenly found themselves confronted with extremely difficult problems in the areas of civil rights, interpretation of constitutional rights of the individual, protest demonstrations, and the growing philosophy of civil disobedience and resistance to law and order.

Recent acts of violence and arson by mobs and individuals have created a national emergency. Hence there is a sudden realization by most local law enforcement agencies that they must now strive for standards of employment and performance at least as high as those in the federal professional law enforcement agencies.

The local police officer is part of the judicial system which includes many professional positions in the courts, the prosecutors' office, the probation departments and in the penal institutions. Almost all of these positions have higher professional requirements than those of law enforcement officers. However, the local police officer has the closest and most sensitive relationship with the community. This includes responsibilities that none of the other people in the judicial system are directly involved with—the *maintenance* of law and order, the *prevention* of crime, and the *courteous* and *helpful* treatment of all the many non-criminal citizens with which there is frequent contact. An increasing consciousness of the role of the police officer in dealing with and protecting the ordinary citizen, and gaining their respect, is a significant element of the changing police job.

What Kind of Person for Police Work?

The changing nature of the police job requires a major swing from "brawn" to "brain." The complexities and the broad scope of law enforcement activities today make it extremely difficult for a person without a high school education to be an effective law enforcement officer. Recent experience has shown that the greater amount of higher education that a police officer has, the greater the possibility that he/she will carry out the duties successfully. In part, this is because the greater educational attainment, the more likely it is that he/she will have the social and other skills necessary to communicate effectively with persons of various cultural, economic and ethnic backgrounds. Following are pertinent excerpts from *Police Compensation*, a research study for the President's Commission on Crime and Criminal Justice by William F. Danielson, Director of Personnel, City of Berkeley, California.

> The educational standard for law enforcement of less than high school will seriously affect the quality of police recruits who will be attracted to the position. There is a kind of "Gresham's Law" which operates in recruitment standards. The recruiting agency tends to attract in greatest quantity the persons who barely meet the minimum standards for the position. Persons whose educational attainment exceeds the minimum standards for a position will not often apply for a position which requires lesser standards of education. If there is no educational requirement to enter the police department such as in the case in a number of eastern cities and states, the attraction of the police job for the high school graduate or the young person with college education is much less than if a high school minimum is required....
>
> The police officer should have the mental capacity to learn a wide variety of subjects quickly and correctly. He/she must continue his/her learning and training throughout his/her active police career. The officer must have the ability and the desire to adapt thinking to technological and sociological changes which affect law enforcement work....

The effectiveness of police officers today more than ever before, because of the changing nature of police work, requires that they be held in high respect by the community. Therefore, integrity must be of the highest order. The acceptance of petty gifts or bribes and special favors, once more or less accepted as part of the compensation of the grossly underpaid policeman of yesteryear, is no longer acceptable in today's society. Even where it may be condoned or not considered a criminal act, whether it be looked at with humor or scorn, it reduces the effectiveness of the police officer by reducing the respect of the community. This adversely affects the cooperative spirit of the citizenry, which is so necessary to effective law enforcement.

What Does It Take to Recruit This Person?

A reasonable starting salary is the most important, but certainly not the only requirement for the effective recruitment of the right kind of individual for the changing police job. The "going rate" for the average high school graduate in the community is the absolute minimum that must be provided. In determining that going rate, it must be taken into account that in a period of relatively full employment the high school graduate has worked for a few years after graduation before achieving the minimum age of eligibility for police service. If a better than average individual is to be obtained, it must be recognized that he/she will have progressed in salary by perhaps as much as 15 percent since first going to work. It also must be taken into account that the young person who has had a year in college would be worth, and might well expect, at least 5 percent more than one who has not. Each additional year of college study that might be desired would require correspondingly higher starting salaries. If, as recommended by Mr. Danielson, applicants with intelligence among the upper 25 percent are desired, the starting rate must be even higher to attract them.

If scientific selection procedures, which are of extreme importance, are effective, sufficient applicants must be obtained to allow for rejections resulting from character reference, criminal record checks and psychiatric examinations, as well as other tests of competence. Mr. Forbes McCann, a recognized specialist in recruitment and selection, suggests a rule he calls the "tenfer" rule—ten applicants for each vacancy you expect to fill with a highly qualified person. In order to have enough applicants, another 5 percent had best be added to the entrance rate as previously determined.

Of course, fringe benefits and working conditions are important, too. However, most police benefit packages are already from 30 to 40 percent of salary, including liberal pension privileges, and the police work week is almost universally down to 40 hours, frequently with premium pay for overtime work.

Of next importance is career opportunity. If the young police applicant is not smart enough to look at his long range opportunity for salary advancement and promotion in a police career, the candidate is not smart enough to be on the force. If this person finds that after a few years of modest salary advancement as a patrolman he/she might have to wait for years more to gain a promotion, primarily on the basis of seniority, and that even if he/she eventually makes chief, the salary structure is so compressed that such high responsibility is inadequately recognized, the candidate is bound to be disinterested in the job. If this individual calculates anticipated career earnings over thirty years of police service and finds there is likelihood that it may be thirty times the annual maximum salary of a patrolman, or at best a sergeant, and compares this to what total earnings might be in other occupations, the candidate will certainly look elsewhere in spite of a good starting salary.

Regardless of the salary in higher ranks, if the applicant feels that there is no program to help one develop and qualify for those ranks, other than by gaining long years of service, he/she will also be disinterested, particularly if he/she is one of the bright young individuals that the police force needs to ultimately fill the commanding officer positions of tomorrow. The customary road to command must be changed.

Lastly, persons of the type needed by our police service today will hardly be attracted by yesterday's typical recruiting method—examination announcements posted on the city hall bulletin board. An energetic, indirect and direct recruiting program will be required.

Indirect recruiting—the general promotion of the police service as a rewarding career, of course, requires that it be made so. The image of the average municipal police department can and must be significantly improved. Corruption, well on the road to elimination in most of our cities, must be completely eradicated, and the people must be convinced that it is. Added emphasis must be given to internal investigation by the establishment of strong intelligence units reporting directly to the chief or deputy chief. The police department must clean its own house. This means not only ferreting out the few bad apples that are found in every barrel, but taking a modern scientific management approach to improvement of its organization, administration, equipment, and enforcement and detection techniques. Much useful help in this regard can be obtained from the International Association of Chiefs of Police, from some of the universities, and from private consulting firms which have specialized in local government operations.

In the direct recruiting effort, recourse must be taken to all modern techniques of positive recruitment with which most public personnel directors are now familiar. In this effort, a new attention should be directed to minority groups, not only because an integrated police force has proven to be a more effective force, particularly in the area of civil disturbances, but because here is a source of well educated and intelligent candidates for the police job that has been overlooked before. There is no need for lowering of standards in the hope that this will increase the employment of persons from underprivileged minority groups. Mr. Danielson, in the paper previously referred to, closes an interesting section on the recruitment of minority group persons for law enforcement positions with the following paragraph:

> The causes of racial justice, equal employment, and law enforcement are not well served by proposals which would lower the necessary standards for entrance into police work. Neither are these causes well served if unnecessary standards are imposed for entrance into police work (such as restrictive residence requirements). If young minority group members are to be recruited into law enforcement, there is no substitute for having a salary and compensation for police which is highly competitive, for requiring unnecessary standards to enter the field of law enforcement, and to use recruiting methods which will reach all sections of the community.

What Does It Take to Keep Them on the Force?

Some of the things already described which will attract good people to the police service will also keep them in it, particularly a good career development program which consciously plans the careers of young policemen with intelligence and high potential. Maintaining and improving a good image of the police department will also help. The provision of a good retirement plan, already available to most police officers, will naturally reduce turnover. However, the most important single element is probably the opportunity for development and promotion. In many police departments, the organization is such that as few as one in four patrolmen has an opportunity for promotion.

The typical police department has a low promotional ratio for one or both of the following reasons. First, there are usually too few ranks in the organization structure—only one broad class of Patrolman, then Sergeant, Lieutenant and/or Captain, and Chief. Within these broad classes or ranks there are substantial differences in individual position values which normally would result in two or more distinct levels of compensation among the positions included in the class. This is particularly true in the typical rank of patrolman.

The other common deficiency is an inadequate number of supervisory positions resulting in spans of control that are too broad. A precinct shift commander, often a lieutenant, or even a sergeant in the smaller cities, may have a large number of individuals scattered over a fairly broad geographical section of the city. Even fifteen or twenty individuals on scattered beats afford a situation where supervision can at best be extremely periodical and limited. In contrast, a fire company, consisting of from three to five officers, always has a fire lieutenant or fire captain directly supervising the company.

These deficiencies in many police organizations reduce the effectiveness of the department through inadequate supervision, minimize incentive, and, of course, result in limited opportunity for promotion from the rank and file.

Last but not least, the intelligent young policeman with potential must be given the guidance and incentive, through the effective execution of a career development program, to develop to his maximum level of competence. This requires that he be afforded opportunity to gain additional education at minimum cost to himself, both in the form of adequate in-service training programs and through the facilities of outside educational institutions. Once having completed his recruit training, a police officer has practically no opportunity for educational development on the job. If he is to be expected to develop to his fullest potential on his own time for the benefit of the department (as well as his own), the minimum incentive that can be supplied must be the payment by the employer of the costs of the training. In addition, there must be tangible reward for educational accomplishment; for example, eligibility for more rapid promotion, extra in-grade salary increments, or cash bonuses.

Obstacles to Progress

To date efforts to significantly improve local law enforcement agencies through the upgrading and professionalization of their personnel have been fraught with frustrations and externally imposed limitations. Only a very few departments can point to any real breakthrough in this effort. There are several obstacles to progress to be discussed here.

There is an inherent rigidity in many civil service laws and regulations which inhibits or even prohibits the exercise of some of the generally accepted practices of modern personnel management. The old concept of equality in treatment of civil service personnel fails to recognize that people are not equal in educational background, intelligence or other personal attributes, and absolutely equal treatment only encourages mediocrity in the public service.

To name a few examples of inflexibility in civil service regulations which are impediments to progress:

(1) The requirement for promotional examinations in any case where there is a higher maximum rate of pay provided for the classification, and requiring slow progress through every successive rank or pay grade.

(2) Provision of heavy weight to seniority on promotional examinations with insufficient or no consideration to past performance or potential.

(3) Rigid and overly restrictive height, weight and residency requirements.

(4) Prevention of rotation of assignments, sometimes even at the same pay level, without reclassification action.

(5) Prohibition of entrance into the police service at any level other than the lowest uniformed rank.

(6) The rule of one on promotional examinations, whereby a promotion might be made on the basis of a written test score highest by one tenth of a percentage point, without regard to other factors.

(7) Stiff tenure and disciplinary requirements which make it almost impossible to remove "dead wood."

Further, there are signs of increasing intervention of state legislatures in local affairs through the passage of certain laws detrimental to progress in the improvement and professionalization of the police service. Although several laws have been passed which assure better working conditions and better starting salaries in the police service they tend to hamstring local authorities or impose costs which the local governments are ill prepared to immediately assume. Most serious are the attempts being made to have legislation which would lock the pay of policemen with the pay of firemen without any regard to the differences in the kind of work involved and particularly to the changing nature of the police job. Although these latter attempts have met with little success to date, there is an ever present danger.

A more indirect blocking of improvement in police pay has been accomplished by some legislatures through the passage of laws which arbitrarily and drastically limit fire service hours without regard to the fact that a fire duty week of fifty-six hours provides a much more advantageous working arrangement than the eight-hour shift, forty-hour week of the typical police department. These laws have burdened municipalities with substantial increases in fire department costs which have naturally left less money available for improvement in police pay....

Again referring to Mr. Danielson's study—because of the disastrous impact on police compensation of the organized campaign of fire-fighters for so-called "parity pay" and for substantially reduced fire duty hours, he has seen fit to document in a remarkably complete and factual way the ramifications and details of this campaign as it has been waged in many parts of the country. An attempt will be made only to summarize the problem here.

The firemen have done much to improve their lot in the last couple of decades, and their lot needed improvement. Traditionally the firefighter has been paid the same as the patrolman, and understandably the average firefighter looks at any increase in patrolmen's pay above his own as indicating a "downgrading" of the fire service with resultant loss of prestige. It doesn't do any good to try to explain to him that an upgrading of an entirely dissimilar service does not represent a downgrading of his service. The unfortunate fact that must be faced is that the organized firefighters are bound to use all of their strength and resources, which are considerable, with the public and the politicians to preserve parity not only to increase their pay but as a matter of pride and prestige. In doing this they will continue to oppose in any way they can any move to improve police pay unless fire pay is concurrently and equally improved.

In commenting on this obstacle to progress in police compensation improvement, Mr. Danielson says in part as follows:

> When salary improvements are proposed for municipal police, however, the demands of firemen's groups are that firemen *must* receive identical salaries.
>
> Acquiescence to demands of firemen's groups undoubtedly has resulted in holding down the salary level of many local law enforcement agencies. To the degree that they caused police salaries to be kept low below the point where qualified men can be recruited and retained as policemen, the demands of firemen's groups have adversely affected the maintenance of law and order in American cities.

The campaign of the firefighters will intensify as the trend towards higher police pay increases. Of course, crusades are important to unionism and this is one in which a great deal of emotionalism is involved. It is highly unlikely that there will be any lessening of this strong opposition to significant improvement of police pay. On the other hand, there is some hope for compromise in the situation—not compromise for compromise's sake but a well justified compromise based on certain facts and conditions.

Representatives of the fire service themselves have often said "stop complaining about the lack of opportunity for promotion in the police department as compared to the fire department and create more opportunities for promotion for police officers." Also, the use of scientific evaluation methods on police assignments indicates that there are some assignments for patrolmen which, if properly isolated, classified and evaluated separately, would not justify higher pay and may not justify pay as high as that of the basic entrance rank of firefighter. This will be discussed further in a later section of this article.

Limitations on funds can also be a formidable obstacle. Obviously, it relates directly to the preceding one in that available funds are seriously depleted if any increase in police salaries has to be duplicated in the fire service. However, there is a natural reluctance on the part of municipal government to grant extraordinary increases to any particular occupational group. All employee organizations and all municipal employees always exert maximum pressure on governmental bodies to cut up the pie on an across-the-board basis as evenly as possible. One cannot expect to convince easily the rank and file employee or his union representatives that a particular occupation has changed so much more than others as to

justify salary adjustments significantly above those provided to other occupations. And yet there are many clear indications that can be brought
to the attention of all employees, and the taxpayer as well, that if better
police services are required, they must be paid for. The simple facts concerning police turnover and unfilled vacancies, as compared to those in
other municipal occupations, present a very convincing picture. It has
been estimated that two-thirds of the police departments in the United
States are below authorized strength. In contrast, most of the cities which
have published turnover figures by department indicate that the department with the lowest rate of turnover is the fire department.

Although the tie-in of fire pay with police pay reduces the availability
of funds where they are most needed, it must be recognized that, to a
lesser extent, across-the-board increases within the police department
without regard to the complexity and difficulty of the respective jobs concerned also represents improper utilization of available funds.

A common problem found in the public service, whenever there is
reason to substantially upgrade and increase the pay of an occupation,
concerns those incumbents who do not meet newly established higher requirements of education and mental ability, but who are present and will
be present until retirement due to the typical provisions for tenure. These
incumbents should be protected because most of them have rendered long
and faithful service, and it is no fault of theirs that qualifications were
lower at the time they entered the force.

Nevertheless, the argument is often used by city councils, city administrators, and taxpayers organizations that you can't raise the pay
grade by a significant amount because you will be overpaying too many
people at the taxpayer's expense. This has encouraged the proponents of
the slow "leap-frogging" approach to police department upgrading—a
small percentage increase in salaries this year, accompanied by a tightening of the selection procedure; another small increase next year, accompanied by a small increase in the educational requirements, etc. Hopefully, by the time salaries get where they should be and are accompanied by
substantially higher entrance requirements, most of the "old hands" will
have been retired. Although this approach makes a lot of good political
and realistic sense, the requirements of the situation regarding law enforcement today makes this snail's pace unacceptable.

It is a well known principle of job classification and compensation that
if a job comprises various tasks at different levels of skill, the pay should
be set in recognition of the highest skill required to be exercised by the incumbent. It is appropriate, for example, to pay a clerk at the going rate
for stenographic skills even though the job may require shorthand only 10
percent of the time, and the rest of the time is spent on simple filing and
other clerical tasks.

In the typical police department there are ranks or classifications that comprise a wide variety of tasks and skills, some of which require high qualifications and others which are more simple and routine. In departments with only a few broad classes or ranks, this situation is found to be extreme. A patrolman classification usually comprises widely different ranks such as directing traffic at a street corner, riding a three-wheel motorcycle to tag illegally parked cars, patrolling in a one-man police car, investigating accidents, and even, in a few departments, performing plainclothes detective work. In many cases certain officers are regularly and permanently assigned to these respective tasks which differ substantially in qualification requirements, complexity, hazard, and the degree of skill required. To make matters worse, these tasks are often assigned on the basis of choice by those with seniority, which frequently results in the most experienced officer performing the lesser tasks.

Yet, in following the principle of paying for the highest skills, all patrolmen must be paid at the level appropriate to the assignment of the highest value. This is expensive and wasteful of funds. It also encourages mediocrity since no incentive is provided for the officer with unusual ability to strive for the more complex and highly skilled assignments. Those who are given such assignments are inclined to resent the fact that others with lesser tasks are paid the same and, therefore, may not perform as well as they otherwise might.

One kind of "lack of room at the top" has been described under the subject of promotional opportunities. Here we are concerned with the unrealistic ceilings imposed on salaries of the commanding officers of most municipal police departments. Even where the patrolman's pay has reached a reasonable level, there is often failure on the part of city councils to adequately recognize the responsibility and heavy burdens that rest with the executive officials. This is a common problem, not only in the police department, but in other departments as well.

Many cities have a history of salary compression brought about by yielding to union pressures at the bottom and retaining an unreasonable ceiling on executive salaries at the top. There is no worse violation of the principles of sound salary administration than that of failing to recognize the unusual burdens and high responsibilities of government executives at the highest levels. Carried to an extreme, this compression can eliminate all incentives for the better people to aspire to the top position.

The incongruity of this obstacle lies in the fact that, with the relatively small number of executive positions involved, the total cost of providing reasonable salaries to executive positions is insignificant compared to the steady succession of periodical across-the-board dollar and the percentage increases granted to the mass of the employees. Often such increases are limited when extended to executive positions.

Unbelievable as it may seem, one state legislature recently adopted pay plan revisions that provided an increase of 20 percent in the rates of the lower half of the pay schedule and 10 percent in the upper half. Another legislature is now considering a bill which would provide 15 percent for the lower third, 10 percent for the middle third and 5 percent for the executive and other higher positions. This bill is being seriously considered because, as one might expect, it was proposed by and introduced for the State Employees' Association, whose membership naturally comprises a high majority of employees in the lower, more populous classifications.

Last, but by no means least, is the obstacle presented by the labor market situation in most of our cities today. The very kind of well educated, young men required in the law enforcement agencies are those being sought after by industrial and commercial employers. Law enforcement agencies are engaged in heavy competition for this kind of manpower. It has been estimated one and a half million young men are of the proper age and have the intelligence, educational background and physical ability for service in local police agencies. About fifty thousand of this one and a half million will be required by local law enforcement agencies this year. The competition for the group comprises far flung industrial and commercial organizations as well as our armed forces. The growth of police departments, now rapidly accelerating due to the increase in population and crime rates, is occurring at a time when the labor market is tightening—and this presents a very difficult obstacle indeed.

In view of certain changes in the organization of police work, however, advantage can be taken of some sectors of the labor market that are not tight as described in the following excerpts from a U.S. Civil Service Commission bulletin:

> In spite of the reduced over-all level of unemployment there remains a number of groups where unemployment is high and where, consequently, prospects for recruitment are quite good. . . .
>
> *Young workers, in the 16 to 21 age group.* This group including many with limited education, has had an unemployment rate nearly three times the average for all workers. While some of the men in this age bracket will now go into the armed services, the group will remain one of the larger pools of available manpower. . . .

In the above reference to the young workers, sixteen to twenty-one years of age, the police cadet program or the establishment of lower level police classifications as discussed later in this article, affords the opportunity to tap this source for the police departments. Before these young men get involved in other careers, the department can skim off some of the cream for ultimate development as professional police officers.

Position Management the Best

The concept of position management, suitably adapted, offers the best hope of overcoming some of the major obstacles to progress in the improvement of local law enforcement and the professionalization of the police service. Before dealing more specifically with solutions that are possible through the application of position management, the principles and techniques involved should be reviewed.

Position management is an important management system that enables the manager to effectively utilize and control the manpower resource. If it were to be described by a single phrase, the best words are "organization analysis to the position level." Position management is the responsibility of the line managers. The technical work involved is best accomplished through the cooperative efforts of the organization or "O & M" analysts and the personnel staff.

The objective of the position management system is: to develop and establish a position structure that provides optimum balance between needs for accomplishing the mission of the organization, economy and efficiency, sound utilization of skills, attraction and retention of competent personnel, motivation of employees, and employee development.

In order to accomplish the objectives of position management, a detailed analysis of the individual positions of the organization is undertaken. In too many organizations, employees in critically short occupations and the more skilled employees (often synonymous) are spending disproportionate amounts of time on tasks that either do not utilize their specialized training and talents at all or do so only to a minimal degree. In order to achieve utilization of such people, position analysis may result in the restructuring or "redesign" of individual jobs as follows:

(1) The "shred-out" of non-professional tasks, so that a smaller number of college trained employees can do the same volume of highly skilled work.

(2) Establishment of new lower level, nonprofessional positions to take over the simpler tasks removed from the professional positions.

(3) Stripping of the simple, unskilled tasks from technical, office, and blue collar jobs so that a smaller number of employees can do the skilled work in these areas.

(4) Establishment of helper, assistant, and junior clerical jobs to take over the tasks removed from the more highly skilled office and blue collar jobs.

In this process of organization analysis at the position level, several considerations must be kept in mind. Briefly enumerated, these are:

(1) The first and fundamental consideration is whether or not the position should be allowed to continue at all. Where duties and tasks can be taken over by others, or no significant contribution to the mission is being made, the position should be abolished.

(2) Workload forecasts must be developed and considered in order to

determine the number and type of positions needed.

(3) Work methods must be understood and consideration given to their improvement in the interest of efficiency.

(4) The relationships among positions must be understood and consideration given to changing them to more effectively accomplish the mission.

(5) The effectiveness of personnel management must be considered and improved if necessary to achieve effective position management.

(6) The characteristics of the labor market will often influence the design of positions; consideration must be given to the shortage or abundance of different kinds of employees needed for alternative position designs.

(7) Pressures from organized employee groups and political pressures must be considered as an obstacle to the design of certain kinds of positions which might otherwise be theoretically advantageous.

(8) The psychological needs of employees should be considered; positions should be designed with thought to the morale and job satisfaction of the incumbents.

Applying the concept of position management to the police department would undoubtedly result in beneficial changes in the structure and the composition of the individual positions themselves. The most revoluntionary result of position redesign would be the "shredding-out" of the simpler, more routine, and less hazardous tasks from the basic ranks or broad classes in the typical police classification structure.

Some of the "shred-out" positions of lesser value will become "civilian" classifications—clerical, technical or blue collar jobs. They would include such classifications as records clerk, armament repairman, storekeeper, precinct desk clerk (assistant to a desk sergeant), automotive maintenance foreman, etc.

After separation of the "civilian" assignments, position redesign at the patrolman level would result in something similar to that proposed by the President's Crime Commission, i.e., a three-way breakout to a *Community Services Officer*, a *Police Officer*, and a *Police Agent*.

The community services officer was suggested as a uniformed but unarmed, young and not necessarily high school trained officer who would be used primarily for improving communications between the people and the police, particularly in slum communities, and in working with underprivileged juveniles. The police officer would be quite like a patrolman in most departments except that he would be relieved of responsibilities which could be performed by community services officers, and he would not have the educational background nor have reached the level of development required of the police agent. The police agent was envisioned as the "professional police officer" of tomorrow, better educated, better trained, highly intelligent, and possessed of scientific and social skills.

Among the tasks normally performed by uniformed personnel, certain assignments certainly can be identified and classified at several levels below that of the new "professional police officer." There are many routine, simple duties and tasks performed by some patrolmen, not those of a "community service" nature, that could be incorporated in lower police classifications. For example, the detective bureau could undoubtedly utilize sub-professionals of lesser qualifications to perform some of the routine digging in libraries, newspaper morgues, and public records that one hears the "Sergeant Fridays" complain about as the bane of the detective's existence. Other simpler police tasks now often performed by a "patrolman" include street intersection traffic control, supervision of school crossing guards, fingerprinting, parking violation and other routine and less hazardous patrol, serving as public building guards, and aides or chauffeurs to commanding officers.

It has already been demonstrated in at least one comprehensive position analysis study of the police assignments normally performed below the lowest supervisory rank of sergeant that as many as five levels of police work may be identified:

(1) A "cadet" or trainee.

(2) A "police services officer" to perform the simplest police tasks.

(3) A Police Officer I to perform the simpler and less hazardous tasks requiring arms and power of arrest.

(4) A Police Officer II, requiring higher intelligence and some college training for the more complex assignments presently included in the typical patrolman rank.

(5) The Police Officer III, requiring substantial college education and in-service training and performing the scientific detection and most complex and sensitive investigation work—a super-detective, if you will.

Among the supervisory and command ranks, the result of position analysis could well be the creation of additional levels or ranks such as *corporal, major,* and *lieutenant colonel,* to augment and improve supervision and decrease the spans of control now often too broad.

The net result of effective position management in the police department should bring about several significant benefits and go a long way toward reduction or elimination of some of the obstacles described earlier in this article.

The "shred-out" of the lesser skilled, simpler, and safer tasks from the broad scope of the typical patrolman classification would result in the establishment of more civilian positions and one or more uniformed police classifications properly evaluated at or below the level of firefighter. This would provide "parity" or "parity plus" for the firefighter classification and should remove the obstacle of militant opposition by the International Association of Firefighters.

The establishment of higher level professional police classifications with higher qualification requirements at both entrance and promotional levels, and additional supervisory positions where appropriate, would at once accomplish the following: (1) provide attractive salaries for college-trained men without overpaying those presently on the force who do not have the higher qualifications and who are not performing the work of highest value; (2) encourage in-service personnel to higher educational and performance achievement in order to qualify for higher pay; (3) provide improved promotional opportunities for all police personnel; (4) hold down the cost of salary improvements by selective establishment of higher salary ranges only for those assignments which justify the same and, incidentally, eliminate the bad economics of paying people at a rate appropriate to the highest skills exercised, while much of their time on the job is spent on simpler and less valuable tasks; and (5) reduce the proportions of higher-educated personnel required by the police department in a tight labor market situation. In regard to the latter, some of the lower police classifications could be filled from the pool of labor that is available in certain categories as described previously in the discussion of the labor market.

The ultimate in professionalization of the police service will require the cooperation of our educational institutions. Some have already established police science programs at the junior college level. A graduate of such study must be afforded opportunity to enter the police service at a level above the lowest patrolman rank. Such a curriculum would ideally be an officer training program similar to the ROTC, which has worked so well in augmenting the officer corps in the armed forces.

Other Efforts for Other Obstacles

Position management alone will not do the whole job. A continuing campaign will be required by public officials and police administrators to fight the passage of bad laws and to liberalize civil service regulations. There is no panacea for success in this area. However, education is the key. City councils, civil service commissioners, legislators, and the public generally must be made fully aware of the facts on the need for improvements and the right ways for bringing about such improvements.

The best position management system will not achieve the improvements of which it is capable unless sound, modern personnel management, including an effective career development program, provides the basis for paying higher salaries to those specific jobs and people that justly deserve higher pay. And it must be part of the educational campaign to convince legislative bodies and the taxpayers that paying executive salaries commensurate with the responsibilities involved represents a small cost, proportionally, and is the only way to provide adequate incentive for executives to shoulder the responsibilities and exert their maximum efforts toward achieving effective service to the public.

Conclusion

In conclusion it appears that a concentrated effort by police administrators, the personnel staff, and the organization analysts, can change the prospect of a long, slow evolution in improving local law enforcement and in the professionalization of the police service into an immediate *administrative revolution*, in spite of the formidable obstacles that appear to be in the way at first glance. The extensive research and new ideas developed by the numerous Crime Commissions, backed up by an imposing body of work by a long list of consultants and advisors and aided by the techniques of position management, provide a large stepping stone for substantive progress.

INDEX